Under the Editorship of
LEONARD CARMICHAEL
PRESIDENT, TUFTS COLLEGE

THE CLINICAL TREATMENT
OF THE PROBLEM CHILD

BY

CARL R. ROGERS, Ph.D.

PROFESSOR OF PSYCHOLOGY, UNIVERSITY OF CHICAGO
FORMERLY DIRECTOR, ROCHESTER GUIDANCE CENTER

HOUGHTON MIFFLIN COMPANY

BOSTON · NEW YORK · CHICAGO · DALLAS
ATLANTA · SAN FRANCISCO

The Riverside Press Cambridge

The Riverside Press
CAMBRIDGE · MASSACHUSETTS
PRINTED IN THE U.S.A.

Editor's Introduction

THIS book is written by a psychologist who has had wide experience in the treatment of the behavior problems of children. In its pages the reader will find no panacea described. The author does not conceal the fact that the problems with which he is dealing are difficult ones and often ones which have as yet only begun to be studied scientifically.

The book is divided into three major sections. In the first of these, the question of the correct diagnosis of behavior problems is discussed. In the second section, those forms of treatment which depend upon a radical alteration in environment, such as the transplantation of the child from his home to an institution, are considered in an illuminating manner. The final section of the book — which will certainly to many readers be its most useful part — is concerned with those methods of treatment which depend not on an almost complete environmental change but upon a constructive modification of the child's own immediate conditions of life.

It will be easy for any academic psychologist to turn aside from the problems with which Dr. Rogers has here dealt, with the statement that psychology is not yet far enough advanced to make possible the profitable consideration of such questions. The result of this negative attitude, which has long been too widespread in psychology, is that those who must deal with the day-to-day problems presented by living children find it difficult, if not impossible, to secure the important advice which scientific psychology is now able to give them. This book, then, is recommended for this purpose. It is a progress report on a difficult subject prepared by a man of extensive practical experience who alertly makes use of every intellectual tool which may help in the hard but socially important work of changing the behavior of living children who are not satisfactorily adjusting themselves to the world in which they are developing.

LEONARD CARMICHAEL

Preface

THIS book has grown out of more than a decade of daily clinical experience with all the varieties of maladjusted children which a modern American community can produce. It was written to fill the real need that exists for information regarding treatment procedures. In regard to every problem youngster the question arises, "What can be done to help this child?" The question is not an easy one to answer. The clinician in the field or the student who is preparing for clinical work may find ample reference to diagnostic procedures, but therapeutic skill is learned primarily through fellow clinical workers or through costly experience. Hence the primary purpose of this volume is to describe and discuss the variety of treatment skills actually used in clinical work. These "ways of practice," which clinicians throughout the country have been evolving over a score of years, are set forth in organized fashion, in the hope that their presentation will lead to a better understanding of treatment techniques and a more critical consideration of their use.

The book is written for the growing number of individuals who are dealing in a professional fashion with the problem children of the community or who are preparing themselves for such work. Psychologists, psychiatrists, social workers, school counselors, visiting teachers, and teachers are included in such a professional group. For these workers, it is hoped that the bibliographies at the end of each chapter, which are selective rather than exhaustive, will be valuable guides to further study in the field. Perhaps the book will also serve to stimulate research by pointing out the serious gaps which exist in our knowledge.

While the author has inevitably drawn upon the experience of the clinic with which he is associated, he has tried to include the experience and practice of others. This purpose could not have been satisfactorily accomplished without the co-operation of a considerable number of authors and publishers, whose generous permission to make use of published material is gratefully acknowledged.

The author is deeply indebted to members of his own staff, whose insight and understanding of children has contributed much to the development of the principles of treatment expressed in this book. To three of these associates, special gratitude is due. Through their own work and experience, through staff discussion, and through critical reading of various parts of the manuscript Mr. Gordon L. Riley, Miss Virginia W. Lewis, and Dr. Chester C. Bennett have each entered into this venture in more ways than could easily be determined or acknowledged.

The book would never have been undertaken had it not been for the generosity of the members of the Board of Directors of the Society for the Prevention of Cruelty to Children, who granted the author a brief leave of absence which made possible the beginning of the work.

Finally, thanks are due to Dr. Leonard Carmichael for his careful editorial reading of the manuscript, and the broad psychological insight which he brings to that task.

CARL R. ROGERS

ROCHESTER, NEW YORK

Contents

PART I. WAYS OF UNDERSTANDING THE CHILD

CHAPTER   PAGE

I. A POINT OF VIEW 3

The Factors that Influence Behavior 4

The Hereditary Factor — The Organic Influences — The Family — Cultural and Social Influences — The Needs of the Organism — The Interaction of Factors.

What is Meant by "Treatment" 12
The Next Step.

Bibliography 15

II. METHODS OF DIAGNOSIS 16

Levels of Diagnosis 16

Personality Tests as a Means of Diagnosis 17

Measures of Traits and Tendencies — Measures of Adjustment — Standardized Stimuli with Individual Response — Use of Personality Tests in Diagnosis.

Diagnosis by the Ego-Libido Method 26
The Weakness of this Method.

Evaluation of Case Histories as Diagnosis 31
Certain Disadvantages.

Bibliography 38

III. THE COMPONENT-FACTOR METHOD OF DIAGNOSIS 40

Basis of the Component-Factor Method 40

Description of the Method — The Hereditary Factor — The Physical Factor — Mentality — The Factor of Family Influence — The Economic, Cultural, and Social Factors — Education and Training — Self-Insight — Descriptive Diagnosis — Reliability of Ratings.

Planning for Treatment 51

An Example of the Method 52

Comments on the Component-Factor Method 56

Why a "Method" of Diagnosis? — Requirements for a Satisfactory Method — What Method to Use?

PART II. CHANGE OF ENVIRONMENT AS TREATMENT

CHAPTER   PAGE

IV. THE FOSTER HOME AS A MEANS OF TREATMENT 63
    The Potentialities of Environmental Change 63
    The Characteristics of the Foster Home 65
      Special Advantages — What kinds of Children May be Placed — Types
      of Foster Homes Available — Essential Qualities in Foster Parents.

    What are the Results of Foster-Home Placement? 77
      Seriousness of the Child's Behavior as Related to Success — "Abnormal
      Mentality and Personality" — Intelligence; How is it Involved? — Age
      as a Factor — Hereditary Defects and Their Influence — The Child's
      Attachment to His Own Family — Social Agency Skill as a Factor in
      Foster-Home Success — The End Results of Foster Care.

    When Shall we Use Foster Homes as Treatment? 97
    Individualized Treatment Through Foster-Home Care . . . 101
      The Selection of the Home — Selection of the Foster Parents — Rela-
      tionship to Other Children.

    Planning the Termination of Placement 106
    Bibliography 107

V. INSTITUTIONAL PLACEMENT AS TREATMENT FOR BEHAVIOR PROB-
   LEMS 109
    Types of Institutional Treatment 111
      Regimented Treatment — Results of Such Treatment for Delinquents
      — Results of Such Treatment in Orphanages.

    An Institutional Program of Individualized Treatment . . . 119
      The Individual Approach — Providing the Proper Task — Group
      Effort — Psychotherapy in the Institution — The Duplication of Home
      and Community Situations — Planned After-Care.

    But" — the Disadvantages of the Institution 131
    Results of Individualized Treatment 133
    Characteristics of the Institutional Child 134
    When Shall Institutional Treatment Be Used? 136
      Institutional Care for the Mentally Retarded Child — The "Spoiled
      Child" — When Family Ties are Strong — The Older Child and the
      Institution — Sex and Institutional Treatment — The Residual Group.

    Conclusion 144
    Bibliography 145

VI. THE ADVISABILITY OF REMOVING A CHILD FROM HOME . . . 147
    Extent to Which Change of Environment is Used as Treatment . . 148

CHAPTER PAGE

Lack of Satisfactory Criteria 150
Earlier discussions of the Problem — Some Attempts at More Definite Formulation.

Elements Requiring Consideration 153
The Child's Behavior — The Family Situation — The Child's Affection — The Degree of Security — Other Family Factors — The Possibility of Change — The Placement Opportunity.

Summarized Criteria for Removal from Home 165
How Might Such Criteria be Tested?

Other Justifications for Removal from Home 170
Criteria that are Unimportant.

Removing a Child from a Foster Home 174
The Place of Environmental Treatment 175
Bibliography 176

PART III. TREATMENT THROUGH MODIFYING THE ENVIRONMENT

VII. FAMILY ATTITUDES AS A FOCUS OF TREATMENT 179
The Importance of Parental Attitudes 179
Attempts to Alleviate Marital Friction — Attempts to Alter Parent-Child Attitudes.

The Means of Changing Parental Attitudes 184
Direct Education — Interpretive Treatment — Relationship Therapy — An Example of Relationship Therapy — Other Approaches to Parents.

The "Treatability" of Parental Attitudes 210
The Motives for Change — The Parent's Own Adjustment — The Parents' Learning Ability — A Fourth Consideration; the Therapist.

Other Aspects of Treatment Within the Family 218
Bibliography 220

VIII. THE SCHOOL'S PART IN CHANGING BEHAVIOR 222
Individual Treatment as It Exists in the School 223
The School's Efficacy in Treatment 226
The School's Resources for Help 229
The Satisfaction of Achievement — Affectional Security — Aids in Social Adjustment — Toward Reality — Toward Independence — The Acceptance of Authority — Personal Counseling.

The Use of Special Resources 245
Teacher's Objections to Individual Treatment 246
Bibliography 247

CHAPTER   PAGE

IX. THE INTELLIGENT USE OF CLUBS, GROUPS, AND CAMPS . . . 249

The Extent to Which Group Membership is Used as Treatment . . 250

Results of Group Experience for Problem Children 252

The Choice of the Group 253
  Initiating the Child into the Group — Following the Child's Adjustment.

The Experimental Use of the Summer Camp as Treatment . . 259
  Matching the Child and the Camp — Organizing the Camp for Individual Treatment — Treatment Techniques in Camp — Camp Experience
  and the Home — Results of Camp Treatment.

The Rearrangement of Companionships 273

Indirect versus Direct Treatment 274

Bibliography 275

        PART IV. DEALING WITH THE INDIVIDUAL

X. TREATMENT INTERVIEW TECHNIQUES: EDUCATION, PERSUASION,
  RELEASE 279

The Qualifications of the Therapist 280
  Objectivity — Respect for the Individual — An Understanding of the
  Self — Psychological Knowledge.

The Basis of Results 284

Children Who are Suitable for Interview Therapy 285
  The Setting of the Treatment Interview.

Educative Techniques 288
  Informational Methods — Informational Methods and Children's Goals
  — Informational Methods and Mental Conflict — Clarification of
  Issues — Facing Consequences — The Usefulness of the Educative
  Techniques.

The Use of Personal Influence 297
  To Use or Not to Use — The Limitations of Personal Influence — Its
  Usefulness.

Expressive Therapies 302
  Catharsis — Ventilation of Conflicts — Expression through Play Tech-
  niques — Informal Use of Play Techniques — Expression through
  Drama — The Values of Expressive Therapy.

XI. TREATMENT INTERVIEWS: DEEPER THERAPIES 322

What is Meant by Deep Therapy? 322

Interpretative Therapy 322
  The Case of John — The Use of Dreams — A Failure of Interpretive
  Therapy — The Causes of Failure — The Effectiveness of Insight.

CHAPTER　　　　　　　　　　　　　　　　　　　　　　　PAGE

Psychoanalysis of Children 332
　The Interpretive Methods of Analysis — Some Distortions — Transfer-
　ence — The Results of Psychoanalytic Treatment.

Therapy Through a Controlled Relationship 340
　The Case of Edward — The Basis of Effective Relationship Therapy —
　Some Other Characteristics — A Comparison with Psychoanalysis —
　The Usefulness of Relationship Therapy.

Other Forms of Deep Therapy 348
Terminating a Treatment Relationship 351
Insight and Re-education 352
The Goals of Therapy 353
Bibliography for Chapters X and XI 357

XII. MAKING TREATMENT EFFECTIVE 359
Variety and Selection of Treatment Measures 359
　What Type of Organization.

The Specialized Clinic 362
　The Results of Specialization.

The Clinic as a Center of Co-operation 365
　Difficulties in the Way — The Case Conference as a Means of Promot-
　ing Co-operation.

The Rôle of Each Professional Group 369
The Results of Planned Treatment 371
　A Fundamental Consideration.

Bibliography 375

APPENDIX 377
INDEX 385

PART I

Ways of Understanding
the Child

CHAPTER I

A Point of View

To WRITE of the treatment of children's behavior problems is a hazardous undertaking. Each year adds to the number of volumes which give us understanding of the causes and bases of behavior, but the knowledge of how to modify and change behavior lies for the most part in the practical experience of clinical psychiatrists and psychologists, social workers, and teachers. Few serious attempts have been made to organize or set down in more than fragmentary form the extent of our knowledge in this area, since practical workers are notoriously backward in giving verbal expression to their techniques. As a consequence we find twenty books dealing with the origin of behavior problems for one which touches upon their treatment. While this makes the need for a comprehensive study of therapeutic methods all the more imperative, it adds greatly to its difficulty. We find large and unexpected gaps in our knowledge, when we endeavor to organize it. We find it necessary in many instances to fall back upon the judgment of the clinician, where our conclusions should be based upon experimental evidence. It is the purpose of this volume to survey the total area of treatment possibilities in a preliminary way, in order to summarize the knowledge which we have regarding the treatment of difficult children, and also to point out with some emphasis those areas where we are in need of further investigation and research.

In this book we shall deal with the child, not with behavior symptoms. One will look in vain for a chapter on stealing, thumb-sucking, or truancy, for such problems do not exist, nor can they be treated. There are children — boys and girls — with very different backgrounds and personalities, and some of these children steal, and some of them run away from school, and others find satisfaction in sucking their thumbs, or in saying obscene words, or in defying their parents; but in each instance it is the child with whom we must deal, not the generalization which we make about his behavior.

THE FACTORS THAT INFLUENCE BEHAVIOR

In order to understand more fully the reason for this point of view, it may be well to review very briefly some of the available data as to how behavior is determined. What decides the form which our conduct, or our children's conduct, shall take? Why is it that some children exhibit, for the most part, a social type of behavior, while others become anti-social? Can we account for all the deviations in behavior which cause children to be described as delinquent, shy, extroverted, or aggressive? Such topics have already been thoroughly covered by others. A brief summary of some of the conclusions is all that can be given here. The reader who is unfamiliar with the field will do well to consult the selected bibliography at the end of this chapter.

The Hereditary Factor. If we are to understand behavior we must begin with those limits of individual capacity, development, and action which are set by the process of inheritance. At the time of conception certain qualities are fixed which have a decided influence upon later behavior and behavior patterns. It is no longer a question whether it is heredity or environment which controls or determines the individual. Indeed it is doubtful if this was ever a question for thoughtful scientists, who have recognized that both the innate equipment of the individual and the conditions of his life experience are of importance, and cannot actually be separately weighed. Of much more interest is the study of specific qualities or attributes in which heredity plays a significantly large part.

One of these attributes is the size and physical constitution of the individual. Ample evidence exists to indicate that the limits of growth and the tendency toward one or another body-type are set by the mechanisms of inheritance. This is not to say, of course, that such qualities for any individual can be predicted by measurements of the parents, since the complex process of combining the genes contributed by the parents insures variability as well as similarity. Nevertheless the essential limits of bodily development are determined at birth, and the modification of these limits through environmental conditions is not great. The influence which these attributes have upon behavior is clear both from scientific study and from everyday observation. The child endowed with a robust physique and a size above the average for his age finds it easier to compete with his fellows, comes more easily into positions of group leadership, and is more likely to stir feelings of pride within his parents. On the other hand, his above-average growth may cause others to expect of him behavior and knowledge beyond that of his fellows. The variety of ways in which this hereditary characteristic may interact with his environment to produce behavior reactions is legion.

Still more important is the intellectual equipment of the child, which is of importance both in creating opportunities and in setting limits for the child. We do not, for our purposes, have to settle the extent to which innate capacity may be modified by education. It is enough to know that intelligence is in large degree limited by hereditary endowment, but that early stimulation and wise training during the infant period can produce changes in the measured intellect. Later the extent to which environment can thus modify intelligence is small. We will not review here the voluminous researches regarding the relationship between intelligence and behavior. The fact that a significant positive correlation is found between intelligence and such qualities as honesty, co-operation, and service to others, suggests the importance of this factor. There is no question but that the child of borderline mentality has much greater difficulty meeting the ordinary societal demands, and hence is much more likely to exhibit "problem" behavior, than the youngster who is better endowed with intelligence.

To the clinical worker the inherited tendencies toward unstable, neurotic, or psychotic behavior are also of significance. To be sure the inheritance of such tendencies has not been so carefully studied nor so positively determined as the inheritance of intelligence. It seems established by Myerson [1] and others that certain psychoses and neurotic states have a tendency to reappear in the descendants. There is also the possibility that the grouping of different types of mental instability in certain family stocks indicates that a predisposition or tendency toward instability may be inherited. Certainly Stockard's [2] work with dogs suggests this possibility in subhuman species. In the light of the available data we are not far afield if we judge that a child whose ancestry boasts of several psychotic individuals and some whose neuroses seem evident is more likely than the average to exhibit erratic, unstable, or neurotic behavior.

As to the inheritance of behavior patterns themselves, the very suggestion would have been derided some years ago. But patient and painstaking investigation, especially of twins, has shown similarities of motor patterns, at least, which are scarcely to be accounted for by environmental influences. Gesell's [3] work, while it lends no support to the popular notion of the child's inheritance of his bad behavior from one of his parents, or from a disreputable uncle or aunt, nevertheless brings to view certain stubborn facts which cannot be dodged. It concedes the possibility that some of the simple elements of behavior, and the ways of adjusting to physical situations, may have a basis in hereditary influences. Thus it is not only the physical and mental equipment of the individual, his size and type and intellectual endowment, which are inherited and which to some extent limit and determine his conduct, but even his behavior patterns themselves which may have some small basis in inheritance.

[1] Myerson, Abraham. *The Inheritance of Mental Diseases.* Baltimore: Williams and Wilkins, 1925. 336 p.

[2] Stockard, C. R. *The Physical Basis of Personality.* New York: W. W. Norton, 1931. 320 p.

[3] Gesell, A. "The Developmental Psychology of Twins," chap. 6 in *The Handbook of Child Psychology*, pp. 158–203. Ed. by Carl Murchison, Worcester, Mass.: Clark University Press, 1931.

The Organic Influences. Scarcely separable from the hereditary determinants of behavior are the organic influences which
operate from birth onward. Subtle glandular imbalances,
often hereditary in their origin, may be at work to cause this
child to be sluggish, listless, and docile, while another child
becomes restless, alert, hyperactive, and consequently annoying and difficult to manage. Much that is untrue has been
written of the influence of the endocrine glands. The most
cautious research, however, finds ample reason to believe that
glandular maladjustment is without doubt a most important
factor in determining certain deviations from normal behavior.
Even the everyday influence of nutrition cannot be disre-
garded. Deficiencies in the quantity of food or in any one of
several vitamins or vital food substances may easily produce
behavior and personality symptoms of a "problem" variety
such as irritability or apathy. The possibility that there may
be a correlation between body-acidity and emotional excitability is also suggested by recent research.[4] In various ways the
subtle aspects of body-chemistry influence personality traits
and behavior.

Of much more significance is the influence of illness. The
direct effects upon behavior of such diseases as epilepsy, encephalitis, and chorea are well known. Likewise the loss of
vitality which accompanies any long illness is recognized. But
it is probable that the indirect effects of illness have an equal
effect upon the child. The increased desire for attention, the
resistance to assuming normal responsibilities, the infantilizing
tendency of bed care, all of these are known to every parent,
as well as to physicians. Where illness or accident results in
a physical deformity, the child's reactions are altered in various ways, primarily compensatory in nature. It is not surprising that in a so-called normal group of young people, the
number of physical defects correlated significantly with feelings
of inadequacy and inferiority.[5]

[4] Rich, Gilbert J. "A Biochemical Approach to the Study of Personality," *Journal
of Abnormal and Social Psychology*, vol. 23 (July, 1928), pp. 158-175.

[5] Paterson, D. G. *Physique and Intellect*, pp. 227-231. New York: Century Company, 1930.

The Family. In any mention of the environmental influences which shape and mold the individual's behavior, the family comes first. The emotional attitude of the parents toward the child's birth and the degree of secure affection which he finds in the family life have long been emphasized by clinical workers as having a profound effect upon behavior reactions. For the most part the behavior resulting from these influences has been studied through case histories alone, an inadequate method. But some of the more recent studies have shown that such attitudes as parental rejection not only can be gauged, but can be proved to be closely associated with the degree of problem behavior and the extent to which it can be treated. This data will be reviewed in a later chapter on the changing of family attitudes. The significance of parental attitudes toward growth and the development of independence also calls for mention. The youngster who has been allowed and encouraged by the parents to continue infantile behavior patterns into the years of childhood and adolescence is a familiar picture in every clinic.

Not only does this direct interplay of affection between parent and child influence behavior, but the other relationships of the home have their effect as well. The relationship between the parents affect the child, and more behavior problems occur in homes where there is deep marital friction than in harmonious homes. Furthermore the home that is broken, whether by death or by marital friction, produces more than its proportion of personality problems in children, with differing family constellations showing different effects. The father-stepmother combination seems to have the most deleterious effect upon behavior, while the children living alone with their mother are the least maladjusted of these broken home groups.[6]

Considerable attention has also been given to the influence of sibling rivalry. Various patterns of jealous behavior and of attention-getting devices have been shown to arise from this

[6] Burgess, E. W. "The Cultural Study of Adolescence," in *Physical and Mental Adolescent Growth; Proceedings of the Conference on the Adolescent.* Cleveland: Brush Foundation, 1930.

source. Attempts to show that the child's ordinal position in the family influences his behavior have not been so successful. No general picture can be drawn of the behavior of the first or second child, or even the only child. In a particular family, however, the child's ordinal position may be a factor of considerable significance.

The ideals and standards of the home affect the child's behavior even more than the ideals of his companionship group, according to the studies conducted by Hartshorne and May.[7] Their evidence, like that cited above in regard to the broken home, points to the primary place of the mother in the home, since the child's standards show a closer association with the mother's ideas than with any other source. Several investigators have shown the close relationship between the wholesomeness of parental discipline and the behavior difficulties of the children. Unwise or unwholesome discipline, even though crudely judged and measured, correlates very significantly with delinquent behavior.

These brief statements suggest rather than describe the steadily accumulating evidence of the vital fashion in which the family group sets and determines patterns of conduct.

Cultural and Social Influences. In any individual, child or adult, much of his behavior is conditioned by the pressure of cultural traditions and beliefs. Anthropological research has clarified for us the way in which our beliefs and actions, from our attitude toward war to our sexual behavior, are molded by the social group. Sociologists have brought this material home to us by studies such as those of Shaw,[8] which indicate that a boy living in the midst of certain disintegrating social influences in one of our large cities has twenty times as much chance of becoming a delinquent as a boy who lives in another part of the city. The cumulative force of low economic status, com-

---

[7] Hartshorne, Hugh, and May, Mark. *Studies in Deceit.* New York: Macmillan, 1928. 720 p.

[8] Shaw, Clifford R. *Delinquency Areas.* Chicago: University of Chicago Press, 929. 214 p.

bined with a crumbling system of social controls and group tradition, is nowhere more forcibly pictured. It is difficult to overemphasize the effects of such forces upon the individual. Even the psychoanalyst, whose interest has been almost entirely centered upon the inner life of the individual, has been forced to a recognition of the strength of these social forces, and the trend of recent years is toward a more careful study of the influence of culture upon personality.

Yet it is not only the broad elements of culture, but narrower and more specific factors which determine behavior. Within the home, the economic level of the family has its effect upon conduct. Levy [9] has shown that problem children coming from the homes of the well-to-do tend to exhibit personality problems and inner tensions and difficulties in personal adjustments, while those from homes of lower economic status tend to develop more outgoing and anti-social behavior and delinquency problems. While these facts are also related to the intelligence level of the home, the economic factor is definitely involved.

The child's behavior is also much influenced by the attitudes and actions of his own companionship group. Both Shaw's work and that of Hartshorne and May give reason to believe that such influence is second only to the family in determining modes of behavior. The child tends to be as honest or as deceitful, as delinquent or non-delinquent, as the group of his companions. Psychologists and others dealing entirely with the individual are prone to overlook or underestimate the strength of such social forces.

The Needs of the Organism. If we could end at this point our description of the elements which give us some understanding of the child, we could avoid confusion and difference of opinion. The conditions which have been described are not, however, the complete story. For the human being, as an organism, has

---

[9] Levy, John. "A Quantitative Study of the Relationship Between Intelligence and Economic Status as Factors in the Etiology of Children's Behavior Problems," *American Journal of Orthopsychiatry*, vol. 1 (1931), pp. 152–162.

certain needs which are vital to the individual. Psychologists differ as to how these fundamental desires are to be classified, but for the purposes of the clinic it may be said that there are two great classes of needs. The first is the need for affectional response from others. This would include the need for recognition, the desire for parental and other affection, the desire in the mature individual for sexual response from a mate. The second great need is the need to achieve, to obtain the satisfaction which comes from accomplishment and from having added to one's sense of self-esteem. Both of these needs the individual must satisfy, at different levels, to be sure, depending on the stage of growth and maturity which has been reached. The way in which it is possible to satisfy them depends on the more basic factors of his life-situation.

The Interaction of Factors. Although very briefly described, these are, in the main, the forces which produce behavior symptoms. It is not however a simple process. The complex interaction and reaction of these forces within the experience of the individual mold and change and shape the patterns of behavior. The sheepish-looking lad who comes into my office and sits beside my desk restlessly fingering everything in sight is not simply a problem of stealing. He is not even the simple total of many facts. He is rather the resultant, if we may borrow a term from physics, of many forces, some of them operating to produce a normal degree of adjustment, others creating maladjustment, still others relatively neutral in their effect. As we endeavor to untangle the web of interaction of these influences some of the major strands stand out significantly. He is endowed with a distinctly subnormal mentality. This fact had little importance during his childhood days in his family, but became decidedly significant as his school life brought him into competition with an average group of his fellows. The consequent academic failure assumes more importance because of a persistent tendency, probably glandular in origin, to be "on the go," over-active, unable to give long periods of concentration. This restless behavior adds to his inability to meet the traditional demands of the school.   His residence in a "delinquency area" brings other cultural forces to bear: the examples of others who have stolen, the lack of constructive community controls.   Thus his desire to achieve, thwarted in other directions, and his need for social response from his fellows, make his stealing almost inevitable.   Were we discussing the situation in full, the many other influences, family and social, physical and hereditary, which round out the picture might be brought into our discussion, each contributing in its own way to produce the present behavior of this boy.

This summary of the bases of behavior may be sufficient to give some notion of the point of view which underlies this book. Behavior problems are not to be attributed to any one cause or group of causes.   Any influence which has a verified effect upon the development of behavior patterns is worthy of consideration.   We have merely mentioned what seem to be the most important general classifications of these influences.   The discussion may also serve to indicate the reason for refusing to deal with behavior symptoms.   It is obvious to anyone who has worked with children's troubles that the only purpose in considering the child's symptomatic behavior is to aid in the process of understanding that behavior.   Once the causes are clear, it is futile to deal with the symptoms.   To enlarge upon this statement it may be well to discuss some of the implications of the term "treatment," as it is used throughout this book.

WHAT IS MEANT BY "TREATMENT"

In reviewing the meager literature on the treatment of misfit children, one is struck by the way in which the writers define the field.   There are those who define treatment in terms of the various professions, and we have discussions of different aspects of psychiatric treatment, or social case-work treatment, psychological treatment, or educational treatment of the individual child.   Usually in such discussions there is little to indicate that the writers are aware of the tremendous degree of over-lapping among the techniques of these various professions when they are dealing with youngsters who come to them. Rather we are given the notion that each profession has its own methods, though the fields of application are never clearly defined. In a second group we might place those writers who approach the problem each from the point of view of his own school of thought. The psychoanalyst, who writes of his thera-peutic methods, tends to make it quite clear that the field of treatment is the field he is describing. Treatment and psycho-analytic methods are for him synonymous. The same is true of those who speak for the school of thought which uses rela-tionship or "passive" therapy, which we will discuss in a later chapter. These writers tacitly assume that passive therapy is treatment and that treatment is passive therapy. Similar statements might be made regarding the less cohesive group of those who stress habit training. This group concerns itself more with the problems of young children, but exhibits the same complacent attitude of assuming that the methods used consti-tute the whole field of treatment.

The present discussion is written from a very different point of view. While readily admitting greater agreement with some schools of thought than with others, while granting the differing contributions of the various professional fields, it seems to the writer that neither of these considerations defines the field of treatment. Rather, if we are to study treatment methods we should consider the steps and the techniques which are actu-ally used by those dealing with children. Regardless of their theoretical viewpoint, regardless of the professional person responsible, what do workers do to change the behavior of problem children? What is the experience and practice, not the theory, of the child-guidance and child-study clinics, the juvenile-court clinics, the departments of individual adjustment in the public schools? What are the means which they have found helpful and effective? It is in a consideration of these actual methods that we may hope to find the type of child, or the type of situation with which each technique is useful. For our purposes we may regard as treatment measures any planned procedures by which professional workers have sought to modify the behavior or the adjustment of the individual child.

With such a viewpoint it will be our intent to survey the various methods used by the many clinics devoted to the study and adjustment of children's problems, as well as techniques used by teachers, counselors, and social workers whose field lies outside of such organizations. In so doing we shall not be concerned to ask what school of thought is represented by any technique we shall be considering, or whether it is a method used by one professional group or another. We shall be concerned instead with the results which the method can achieve with children, and with the sort of situations in which it seems most helpful.

The Next Step. Back of this catholic approach to the causation and treatment of behavior problems lies the belief that the treatment of children's problems may become a science if we are but willing to lay the basis for it by careful examination of the data at hand. At present no such science exists. Yet if the study of methods used brings to light certain general principles whose validity can be tested by further experimentation, we shall have made the first step toward scientific method in this field. If on the other hand we take the viewpoint that human behavior is too complex and intangible ever to be dealt with save as some people possess the art or gift of influencing others, then we admit that we can never deal in any large way with the multitude of ills which we group together as conduct problems, since the talents of the artist can be but little conveyed to his fellows. Only as our treatment of such problems can be placed on a scientific basis can we hope to deal significantly with the social ills which they bring upon society.

This constitutes the challenge to the clinical field. It is widely recognized that the child who today exhibits personality problems and behavior deviations is the delinquent, the criminal, or the neurotic of tomorrow. The damage which these groups inflict upon society, the tragic unhappiness which they bring to themselves and their families, it is impossible to measure. To what extent have we developed rational means of treating the childhood symptoms so as to prevent and avoid the later serious consequences? It will be our purpose, throughout this book, thoroughly to explore this question.

BIBLIOGRAPHY

The Hereditary Factor
Schwesinger, Gladys C. *Heredity and Environment.* New York: Macmillan Company, 1933. 484 p.

Organic Factors
Kanner, Leo. *Child Psychiatry.* Springfield, Ill.: Charles Thomas, 1935. 527 p. Chapter 6 and chapters 19–30 incl.
Louttit, M. C. *Clinical Psychology.* New York: Harper and Brothers, 1936. 695 p. Chapters 14 and 15.

Family Influences
Folsom, J. K. *The Family.* Part V. "Family Problems and Individual Adjustments." New York: John Wiley, 1934. 603 p.

Cultural Factors
Hartshorne, Hugh, and May, Mark A. *Studies in Deceit.* New York: Macmillan Company, 1928. 720 p.
Mead, Margaret. *Coming of Age in Samoa.* New York: Morrow and Company, 1928. 297 p.
Shaw, Clifford R. *Delinquency Areas.* Chicago: University of Chicago Press, 1929. 214 p.

The Process of Adjustment
Shaffer, L. F. *The Psychology of Adjustment.* Boston: Houghton Mifflin Company, 1936. 600 p.

Methods of Diagnosis

IN DEALING with the child who presents behavior difficulties, it is essential that we see below the surface. We must have some knowledge, not only of facts about the child, but of the significance of these facts — their meaning, the way in which they fit together to explain this particular deviation from the normal. This process is termed diagnosis, and aptly so, since the original meaning of the word is closely akin to our own phrase of "seeing through" a complex situation. If we are to devise therapeutic measures which will assist the boy or girl in achieving a normal adjustment, then we must have as clear an understanding as possible of the causal factors responsible for each particular child's misbehavior. It is the purpose of this chapter to discuss some of the methods and techniques which to different workers have seemed helpful in analyzing the child's situation.

LEVELS OF DIAGNOSIS

Because the term diagnosis is used in different ways, it may avoid confusion to indicate some of its varying levels of meaning. In the first place the term may be used as a method of description and classification. This is a favorite use by psychiatrists and physicians. Thus the clinic receives a report from the hospital concluding with the phrase, "Diagnosis; problem child." Now this to be sure indicates that the youngster is not a case of encephalitis or schizophrenia, but it is not particularly helpful. A second level of diagnosis includes some accurate measurement of the condition as well as classification. Thus the psychologist states that this girl is a borderline mental defective, indicating a rather specifically defined condition, based on a scale of measurement. Still another step in the diagnostic process is the determination of what seem to be causal relationships. When the clinician ascribes the child's temper tantrums to the mother's overindulgence rather than to a glandular condition, or to overstimulation at school, or to lack of social companionship, or to any other cause, it is then that the diagnosis approaches the level which we consider important in the treatment of behavior problems. It is this grasp of the relationship between symptoms and causes which has significance. Only when this level of diagnosis is reached do we have any indication of the areas toward which our treatment should be directed. The fact-finding and classifying aspects of diagnosis have their place, but in dealing with the individual child there must be a diagnosis which goes deeper, discovers the meaning of the various elements, and points the way toward treatment.

PERSONALITY TESTS AS A MEANS OF DIAGNOSIS

One means of determining "what's wrong" with a misbehaving or delinquent child is through the use of some of the various personality, character, and attitude tests which have blossomed forth in profusion during the last dozen years. Such tests fall into several groupings, so far as clinical use of them is concerned. Some are measures of the degree to which an individual possesses certain traits, honesty, submissiveness, self-confidence, extroversion, neuroticism, and the like. Others measure the individual's adjustment, the manner and degree of comfort with which he is meeting the demands of family, school, or social group. Such tests do not assume that the attitudes or behavior patterns which the individual exhibits are permanent traits or aspects of his character, but regard these symptoms as resulting from the ease or lack of ease with which he is adjusting to his life situation. Still another group of devices for measurement in this field consists of standard stimulus situations, words, pictures, or ink blots, to which the subject is allowed to make a free response. Here it is the deviation from the usual or normal response which affords the clue to the personality picture of the individual. A fourth means of measurement consists of facing the child with life situations which raise problems of honesty or co-operation or dominance within the group. Here the actual behavior responses are observed and used as means of measurement. This method is of more interest as a means of research than as a practical method of diagnosis, because of the difficulty of arranging such test situations, and will not, therefore, be further discussed here. In regard to the first three types of personality measures, some examples and illustrations may make the methods more clear. No attempt will be made to discuss these tests in detail, since the reader who wishes to make use of such material may consult the already voluminous literature on the subject, referred to in the bibliography.

Measures of Traits and Tendencies. The older tests and questionnaires for measuring and diagnosing personality might be classified as measures of traits. The Downey Will Temperament Test, now largely discredited, was a pioneer of this type. The Woodworth Psychoneurotic Inventory is another early example, effectively used during the war, and, more recently, widely used for children in its revisions by Mathews and Cady.[1] Allport has endeavored to measure traits of dominance and submission. Laird and others have experimented with various ratings and measures of introversion and extroversion. Thurstone has developed perhaps the most complete "Neurotic Inventory" for measuring neurotic tendencies. There are many other tests of this type, though the Thurstone "Neurotic Inventory," above, and the Bernreuter "Personality Inventory," described in the following paragraph, are probably the most widely used.

Bernreuter, by taking the items most significant statistically of the Thurstone, Laird, and Allport tests, and adding some items of his own on "self-sufficiency," has constructed a "Per-

[1] References to the various tests mentioned will be found in the bibliography.

sonality Inventory" which measures these four traits. Because of its convenience, this test is much used. The subject's answers to questions such as the following indicate the degree of neurotic tendency:

Do you consider yourself a rather nervous person?   Yes No ?
Are you touchy on various subjects?   Yes No ?
Are you troubled by shyness?   Yes No ?

For determining the extent to which the individual is independent, "self-sufficient," and unlikely to call on others for help, there are such questions as these:

Do you think you could become so absorbed in cre- Yes No ?
ative work that you would not notice a lack of
intimate friends?

Does it make you uncomfortable to be "different"   Yes No ?
or unconventional?

Introvertive tendencies, e.g. to have few friends, to be sensitive and withdrawn, to care more for one's work than for social ties, are measured by questions like the following, which are closely related to the questions regarding neurotic tendencies.

Do you daydream frequently?   Yes No ?
Do you blush very often?   Yes No ?
Are your feelings easily hurt?   Yes No ?
Do you experience many pleasant or unpleasant   Yes No ?
  moods?

A fourth group of questions measures the subject's tendency to dominate social situations or to submit to the domination of others.

Have you ever solicited funds for a cause in which   Yes No ?
you were interested?

Have you ever organized any clubs, teams, or other   Yes No ?
groups on your own initiative?

Do you ever complain to the waiter when you are   Yes No ?
served inferior or poorly prepared food? [2]

This questionnaire, as may be observed from its vocabulary and the type of experience to which it refers, is primarily constructed for adults. It is, however, usable for boys and girls of high-school age. The Mathews and Cady revisions of the

[2] From *The Personality Inventory*, by Robert G. Bernreuter. Stanford University Press, 1931.

Woodworth Psychoneurotic Inventory may be used with younger children, the lower age limit depending on how formally the test is used and on the child's reading ability. All of these tests present final scores in terms of the traits or tendencies which they purport to measure.

Measures of Adjustment. There is another group of tests of personality which differs in subtle but significant fashion from the foregoing, and endeavors to measure, not traits, but the manner in which the individual is adjusting to various aspects of life. In these tests the methods used, even the questions asked, are similar to those we have already discussed. The purpose of the test, however, as expressed in the scoring, is not to measure some abstract or hypothetical trait, but to measure the individual's degree of adjustment to his family, his school, his social group, or to himself. One of the earlier attempts in this field was Sweet's "Personal Attitudes Test," in which the subject was presented with descriptions of situations as varied as reciting in class and washing dishes. The subject rated his own degree of liking for the experience, but added his rating as to how other boys felt, and also his ideal as to how he "ought to feel." From this the boy's feeling of difference between himself and the group could be measured, also the degree to which he felt critical of himself.

Another test in this group is the writer's "Test of Personality Adjustment," which, like Sweet's, is designed especially for children, in this case for children nine to thirteen years of age. It is constructed from questions used in interviewing children in the clinic, as well as from other sources. Its purpose is to measure the child's adjustment to his own abilities, to his friends, and to his family. The questions are for the most part disguised or indirect, so that in taking the test the youngster is not fully aware of the extent to which he is revealing his attitudes. For example the child's emotional reactions to his own abilities are discovered by his self-rating on a ten-point scale of items such as the following:

Peter is a big strong boy who can beat any of the other boys in a fight.
    Am I just like him?   Yes ————————— No
    Do I wish to be just like him?   Yes ————————— No

Bob is the brightest boy in school.
    Am I just like him?   Yes ————————— No
    Do I wish to be just like him?   Yes ————————— No

Similar questions are arranged with multiple choice answers:

    Are you good-looking?
      ...... I'm not at all good-looking.
      ...... I'm not very good-looking.
      ...... I'm as good-looking as most boys and **girls**.
      ...... People say that I'm very good-looking.[3]

Social adjustment, or the child's ability to get on with his friends, is measured by similar ratings and questions which indicate the child's estimate of his own popularity, the extent to which he possesses social skills, his liking for group as opposed to solitary play. In measuring his adjustment to his family group several different devices are used. For example, the child chooses three wishes from a list of fourteen. Included are such wishes as, "I would like to get along better with my father and mother," and "I would like to have my father and mother love me more." There are also self-ratings and questions in regard to friction with parents, friction with siblings, and the relative degree of affection for different members of the family. The scoring of this test is somewhat cumbersome, but it indicates with a moderate degree of reliability the extent to which a child feels inferior, or maladjusted in his group or at home.

More recent tests of this sort have specialized in one area of adjustment. Smith has developed an inventory for high-school students which measures only their inferiority feelings, their adjustment to their own abilities. Symonds has developed an Adjustment Questionnaire entirely concerned with the child's satisfying or dissatisfying relationship to school. This questionnaire makes use of questions such as the following:

[3] From the *Test of Personality Adjustment*, by Carl R. Rogers. New York: Association Press, 1931.

Are you given a chance to tell or show what you know in your class?

Do your teachers require too much homework?

Do your teachers usually understand your difficulties?

Do any of your teachers mark examinations too severely?[4]

Bell has returned to the notion of measuring several types of adjustment in one instrument. His Adjustment Inventory, though primarily designed for college students, may be used for young people of high-school age as well. It endeavors to measure the individual's adjustment to his home and to his social group. It also includes a section on health adjustment, and one on emotional adjustment which is similar to the neurotic inventories, and measures a quality or trait rather than adjustment to any well-defined group of situations.

Standardized Stimuli with Individual Response. Quite another type of instrument for probing the intricacies of the personality is the technique, scarcely to be described as a test, by which the subject is allowed to make a free response to a standardized stimulus, whether it be a word, a picture, or a meaningless form such as an ink blot. It is through the classification of these responses that the examiner finds clues to the personality of the subject.

The earliest method of this type is the word-association list, in which a word is presented as a stimulus to the subject, who is to respond with the first word which comes to mind. Both the time of reaction and the word given as response are thought to have diagnostic significance. The list most commonly used is that compiled by Kent and Rosanoff. The use of such a technique with children has been studied by Rosanoff, and by Woodrow and Lowell. The purpose of such a list, as it is used with children, is commonly to indicate complexes or areas of the child's experience which for one reason or another have an undue weight of emotional tension. This technique is not widely used today in spite of the volumes which have been written regarding it, because of the difficulty of making anything but a subjective classification of the responses given.

[4] From the *Adjustment Inventory*, by Percival M. Symonds. New York: Teachers College Bureau of Publications, 1935.

Schwartz has devised a set of pictures of social situations to which the individual makes a free response to some standardized questions. Since there is no method of scoring, this device should perhaps be regarded as a technique for interviewing. It is, however, helpful at times as a guide to the child's attitudes toward school, parents, and siblings, and gives some indication of the stage of his sexual interests.

A test of the free response type which has received a great deal of attention in recent years is the Rorschach test. This test makes use of a series of ink blots, some of which are made with colored inks. These are shown to the subject with the simple question, "What do you see?", or "What does this look like to you?" The individual's response is studied from several different points of view. His response is classified as to whether he has perceived the whole blot or part of it, the blot itself or a space enclosed by the blot. It is also studied from the point of view of form, movement, or color, that is whether his response is primarily conditioned by the form or color of the blot, or whether he sees movement in the image that he perceives. The commonness or originality of the response itself is taken into account. Finally, his mode of perception of a blot, as evident in the sequence of his responses, is studied. Has there been some logical progression from whole to individual parts, or vice versa, or are the responses a collection of discrete items? By analyzing the responses in this manner, though the analysis is vastly more complicated than this brief description, the examiner can total the number of color responses, the number of each type of form response, and the like. It is on the basis of the numbers and proportions of these various kinds of responses that the individual may be classified, and the classifications are many — intelligent or unintelligent, schizophrenic, manic, or normal, repressed or uninhibited. As with the word association test, the difficulty in the use of such an instrument lies in the enormous complexity of devising a classification system which is scientific rather than subjective, and then of verifying the fact that the different classifications do correspond with certain personality types, levels of intelligence, or psychotic conditions. Progress is being made in thus establishing satisfactory means of evaluation, but it is necessarily slow, and much of the work with the technique subjective.

Use of Personality Tests in Diagnosis. The foregoing brief description of some of the personality measures which are more widely used in clinical practice [5] may be sufficient to suggest some of the uses as well as some of the limitations of these techniques in diagnosing behavior difficulties. It is plain that the use of such tests tends to objectify and give definite, measured form to facts about the child which otherwise would be more or less vague opinions. If we suspect that a child is unhappy at home, or is unable to get along with other children his own age, and if we find our belief confirmed by scores on certain of these tests, then the tests have served a very useful purpose. The more objective measurement of various aspects of the personality adds new and important facts to the range of information which we accumulate regarding the child.

Another point to be noted is that personality tests have served and continue to serve as a valuable check upon clinical concepts and clinical judgment. The clinician is prone to divide people into groupings, types, and classifications. The

[5] The personality tests which are used by more than two of the eighty-seven psychological clinics surveyed by a committee of the American Psychological Association are listed below. These findings are taken from the "Report of Committee of Clinical Section of American Psychological Association," *The Psychological Clinic*, vol. 23, nos. 1–2 (January–June, 1935), pp. 23–27. The fact should be noted that these eighty-seven clinics are primarily psychological clinics. Clinics primarily psychiatric were not surveyed.

Personality Tests	Number of Clinics Using
Allport Study of Values	6
Bernreuter Personality Schedule	11
Downey Will Temperament	5
Ink blot test (name not given)	2
Kent-Rosanoff Free Association	6
Colgate Personality Inventory (Laird)	4
Pressey X–O Tests	9
Rogers Personality Adjustment	5
Thurstone Personality Schedule	14
Woodworth Psychoneurotic Inventory (including Mathews and Cady revisions)	12

more objective test serves to investigate these groupings in order to determine whether they have any reality when tested by scientific means. Similarly, in trying to understand the individual problem child, the clinician's judgment is to some extent warped by his own experiences and prejudices. The test tends to correct this error brought about by the personal equation.

Furthermore the personality test, no matter what its type, is likely to uncover new and unsuspected areas of tension and maladjustment in the youngster. A response to a question regarding parents, an unusually significant indication of unhappiness in group contacts, may open up for investigation feelings and attitudes which have been festering beneath the surface. This possibility alone justifies the intelligent use of tests of personality and adjustment.

As a means of diagnosis, however, such tests are by no means entirely satisfactory. In the first place, they belong primarily to the fact-finding, descriptive, and classificatory phases of diagnosis, rather than to those which give us the significance and meaning of the facts. It is helpful to know that a young person is of a more dominating type than 90 per cent of the general student population, as measured by a certain test. Whether this is a trait to be modified or left alone, whether it is likely to cause anti-social behavior or not, we have no way of telling from the test. Likewise, to know that a girl of 14 has schizophrenic tendencies as indicated by the Rorschach test or a strong neurotic tendency as measured by one of the inventories is in itself worth knowing, but it contains no clue as to why this condition prevails. Neither the cause nor the significance of the condition is contained in any test finding. This is somewhat less true of the measures of adjustment. In these tests the score alone may indicate no more than a serious maladjustment in school or at home, but a perusal of the individual items of the test may locate with some certainty the cause of the unhappiness.

Another difficulty in using such tests as a means of diagnosis is that their terms do not represent fixed concepts, and consequently are of relatively little help in prediction. In the realm of intelligence, the facts obtained from testing are of value both for diagnosis and prognosis. In the field of personality testing, this is less true. We may measure with considerable accuracy the extent to which an individual feels inferior, but since one of the aims of treatment will be to reduce such inferiority feelings the prognostic significance of the measurement is limited. This applies to nearly all personality and attitude measurements, since the traits or adjustments measured are almost certainly more changeable than is general intelligence.

The matter might be summed up by saying that as aids to diagnosis such tests are extremely helpful; as a means of diagnosis they are scarcely adequate. As aids to diagnosis they rank with all the other fact-gathering facilities with which the clinician surrounds himself, with the tools of social investigation, the tools of medical examination, the tools of intelligence measurement, the techniques of interviewing. The complete diagnosis, however, demands more than the personality test can bring to it. It must have the judgment and ability to see the facts in their significant relationships and to recognize the areas where treatment is indicated. The point is worth dwelling on, since in the enthusiasm for personality tests it has been supposed by some that they were in themselves a sufficient means of diagnosis. We shall not be most helpful in the treatment of children's problems if we regard diagnosis in any such mechanical light.

DIAGNOSIS BY THE EGO-LIBIDO METHOD

A method of diagnosis based on very different assumptions and techniques is the ego-libido method of case analysis developed by Dr. Marian Kenworthy, 1924–26, while she was medical director of the Bureau of Children's Guidance, New York City, and best described and illustrated by Miss Maud Watson.[6] Based primarily on psychoanalytic concepts and devel-

---

[6] Watson, Maud. *Children and Their Parents.* New York: F. S. Crofts Co., 1932.

oped by a psychiatrist, it has none of the experimentally verified or statistically investigated background which is typical of the personality testing field. It does, however, make use of widely accepted psychiatric concepts. Its purpose is to find some way of analyzing or charting the dynamic processes which underlie behavior, in order to place the facts about a given child in meaningful relationship.

In order to understand the method used, it is first necessary to have some understanding of the assumptions and concepts of behavior upon which it is based. In the first place, Dr. Kenworthy sees in each individual two major drives motivating behavior, two spheres of individual development. These correspond roughly to the two classes of individual needs mentioned previously. On the one hand are the ego needs of the individual, the instinct of self-preservation, of domination, the impulses which lead every individual to be "self-maximating." The need for personal achievement, for a sense of accomplishment, for a feeling that "I am someone" belong in this category. On the other hand are libidinal or love needs of the individual, the need for affection from parents, mate, family, or social group. The desire for security, for affectional responses of various kinds, belongs in this area.

Another twofold division of experience is made by this scheme into those experiences which make for maturity as against those which make for immaturity. The former are thought of as constructive, the latter as destructive. Thus the experiences which come to the child, and also the behavior patterns with which he responds, tend toward more grown-up, independent, self-sufficient behavior, or toward infantile dependency, selfishness, and immaturity. Furthermore, each experience is for the child either satisfying or unsatisfying, and the tendency is to repeat those experiences or behavior patterns which bring satisfaction. Thus problem behavior, whether it be enuresis or stealing or running away from home, is satisfying to the child in the circumstances in which he finds himself, although it is also usually destructive and makes for immaturity rather than maturity.

On the basis of these concepts and principles, Dr. Kenworthy established an eight-fold chart, only the headings of which are given in the accompanying table. The experiences of the individual and their behavior responses are then classified as to whether they had an ego or libidinal value, whether they were satisfying or unsatisfying, and whether they tended toward maturity or toward greater infantilism.

HEADINGS FOR THE EGO-LIBIDO CHART

Libido		Ego	
Destructive		Destructive	
Minus (Unsatisfying)	Plus (Satisfying)	Minus	Plus
Of experiences making for immaturity, those that were unsatisfying are to be listed under "Minus," those experiences or behavior patterns which gave satisfaction are to be listed under "Plus."			
Constructive		Constructive	
Minus	Plus	Minus	Plus
Experiences making for maturity are classified similarly in the "constructive" half of the chart.			

The case of Caroline, a twelve-year-old girl who had developed headaches and fainting spells for which there was no organic basis, is cited by Miss Watson as an illustration of the method. In this case the following facts are listed as having minus and destructive value on the libidinal side: the fact that the child was unwanted by the mother during pregnancy, that labor was long and difficult, that her father pushed her away when she tried to kiss him, and that she had few social contacts with other children. Her daydreams of a nice home and friends had a plus libidinal value but were also destructive. Similarly classified were the attention she received from parents when ill and an episode of fainting in a store. (It is of course impossible to do complete justice to the method without citing the case in full.   The selected items are merely suggestive of the use made of the classification.)   A few of the experiences of this child were classified as having satisfying and constructive libidinal value.   Among them were her affection for her small brother and the fact that she helped to care for him, also the intelligent interest taken by a paternal aunt in the girl and her schooling.

On the ego side of the chart for this same child experiences and facts such as these were classed as having an unsatisfying and infantilizing or destructive effect: her small size for her age, her inability to compete in gymnasium, her poor marks in certain subjects such as arithmetic, the lack of adequate family income, and also the fact that she had no room of her own. Constructive but still unsatisfying were listed her fairly good swimming ability and her own superior intelligence.   Both of these are of course potentially pleasant and satisfying, but have not been so in this child's experience.   Classified as having not only constructive but satisfying ego value are her double promotion in fifth grade, and her pride in her own and her mother's sewing.

When the process of grouping the items from a case history is completed, certain elements of diagnostic significance become more clear.   The extent to which there is a weight of conditions or experiences of unsatisfying and destructive value is evident, and this in turn tends to explain behavior which is a compensatory satisfaction, but which is also of an infantile nature. Furthermore, and perhaps most important, is the fact that possibilities of treatment become evident.   Experiences which are constructive but heretofore unsatisfying can be made more satisfying.   In the example cited, knowledge of her superior ability and praise for her swimming achievements might help to make these more satisfying to Caroline.   Furthermore, conditions which have had a destructive and unsatisfying influence may be changed.   Caroline's lack of social contacts with children may be changed by a group membership which would be constructive though perhaps at first unsatisfying.   Or it might be possible to give her a room of her own, which would have considerable constructive ego value. Still another manner in which the balance of these values may be changed is to bring in new influences of a satisfying and positive type. Thus a close relationship with the social worker for a child who lacks affection may greatly add to the constructive libidinal aspect of the situation. If, through treatment measures, it is possible to increase the factors which make for satisfying progress toward maturity, the undesirable behavior of a satisfying but infantile type tends, it is felt, to disappear. This emphasis of the ego-libido method on the direction which treatment should take, and on the specific items which might be altered, is perhaps its greatest contribution.

The Weakness of this Method. While this whole method brings to the process of diagnosis something of the dynamic balance which exists in personality, and avoids some of the pitfalls of the personality tests, its deficiencies are serious. In the first place, the division of all life experiences into ego and libidinal groupings is a step which might easily be challenged, with neither viewpoint able to adduce significant proof. That these concepts are vague and not too satisfactory is indicated by the fact that the same experience must frequently be catalogued under both headings, since the ego and libidinal aspects of it are inextricably mingled. The other divisions of the scheme, between experiences making for more or less maturity, and between pleasurable and unpleasurable experiences, have somewhat more factual backing, though a difference of opinion might well be justified in regard to a particular episode. It is unfortunate that this vagueness of concept tends to make the whole scheme much less useful.

By far its most serious lack, however, is that it endeavors to explain all behavior in terms of emotional reactions to experience. This is a gross distortion of some of the most fundamental knowledge we possess about behavior. The significance of a child's residence in a delinquency area is by no means fully expressed when we determine the emotional value such residence has for him. It may be for him an unhappy experience, with feelings of inadequacy as a member of the gang, or it may be a satisfying and to some extent constructive experience in development of leadership. Neither of these values is sufficient to express the steady educational and cultural influences which press in on the individual in such a neighborhood. The same is true in the case of a child with a hyperthyroid condition. The effect of such a condition upon his behavior is not apprehended by any evaluation of his emotional reactions. This narrowness of structure of the ego-libido method is evident in the manner in which facts and experiences are either omitted from classification, or forced into categories in which they obviously do not fit. Thus, in the case cited, the fact that Caroline had a normal development in infancy, walking with assistance at eight months, combining words at thirteen, and establishing toilet habits at eighteen months, is classified as having unsatisfying, but constructive, libidinal value. The categories are obviously unsuitable to facts of this sort.

While pointing out the shortcomings in such a method of diagnosis, it should be added that it has had rather wide usage among psychiatric social workers, and to a limited extent among psychiatrists dealing with children. It is significant because it has been a genuine attempt to give a framework for thinking about case material which would make the diagnosis evident, clarifying cause-and-effect relationships and pointing out ways in which the treatment processes might grow out of the diagnosis.

EVALUATION OF CASE HISTORIES AS DIAGNOSIS

Approaching the whole problem from a very different point of view, two psychological clinics have recently contributed their devices for diagnosing personality and behavior problems. The basis of their method is the case history of the child, obtained by the social worker, by the clinician, or through the school. Recognizing that in actual clinical work diagnoses are usually made by evaluating and weighing the material brought out in the case history, these clinics have endeavored to short-cut the process by devising an objective case history which contains the most significant items relating to behavior problems. The "Record of Problem Case" devised by the Department of Pupil Adjustment in the Des Moines School contains 55 such items.   The grouping of items are as follows:

Parental and family characteristics   8 items
    These cover parental education, occupational status, marital adjustment, mental abnormality or criminality in the parents.

Material factors in the home environment   8 items
    These include the economic status of the home, degree of crowding, and the type of neighborhood.

Personal factors in home environment   9 items
    Cultural level of family, parents' interest in child, and the standards set and discipline used by both mother and father.

School records and tests   14 items
    Scholarship, attendance, attitudes in school, degree of retardation, deviation between mental age and grade, and child's intelligence.

Developmental and personality history   16 items
    Physical development, appearance and habits, leisure activities, companions, delinquencies, vocational interests.

Each item of this list is rated on a 5-point scale from 0–4, with the ratings rather carefully specified.   Usually the rating is a simple 5-point multiple choice type, but in some instances the two extremes are rated low, the moderate aspect of the trait rated high as in the following:

Mother's Standard of Conduct for Child
  0 Force illegal conduct.
  1 Encourage questionable conduct.
  2 Give little attention to formation or observance of conduct rules — attitude of indulgence.
  3 Lax attitude toward certain types of misconduct.
  4 Expect child to conduct self in intelligently proper manner.
  3 Too critical about trifles, although having good general attitude.
  2 Rather fanatically severe about certain types of conduct.
  1 Too mature standard for age of child.
  0 Expect perfection in conduct — cannot overlook any lapses in conduct from a too-exacting ideal.[7]

[7] From *Record of Problem Case*, by A. S. Hill.   Des Moines, Iowa: 1933.

The total of the different ratings gives the child's total score, a low score indicating a poor total situation, a high score indicating a favorable one.

The Detroit Scale of Behavior Factors is a very similar instrument used by the Psychological Clinic of the Detroit Public Schools. The classifications of this scale are also listed for comparison:

Health and physical factors   13 items
    Illnesses and sensory defects, size, nervous conditions

Personal habits and recreational factors   13 items
    Appearance, self care, eating and sleeping régime, recreational facilities and companions.

Personality and social factors   12 items
    Social and personality type, tendencies toward anger, fear, excitement, pity, etc.

Parental and physical factors of the home   19 items
    Parental intelligence, age, personality, occupation, economic and marital status, child's adjustment to sibling.

The ratings of each item are on a 5-point scale from 1–5, and the total score is obtained in the same manner as the Des Moines Scale.

Certain contrasts between the two lists are at once apparent. The Detroit Scale has 13 items out of 66 covering the area of physical development and illness, with three other items concerning the child's routine of eating and sleeping. The Des Moines Scale has but 4 items out of 55 covering this same area. On the other hand the Detroit Scale regards school experiences as worthy of only 3 items on the scale, while the Des Moines list has 13 items covering every aspect of school life. The Detroit Scale has no rating whatsoever of neighborhood influences, and only one item on companionship, in spite of the fact that this one rating correlates highly with their total results. The Des Moines Scale has one rating for the neighborhood influence, and three in regard to the type and number and age of companions. The Detroit Scale has two items relating to the other children in the family and the child's adjustment to them; Des Moines provides no place for consideration of this fundamental relationship. Further differences might be pointed out, but these are sufficient to indicate that the areas and aspects of experience which are evaluated depend to a considerable degree upon the judgment and bias of those constructing the scale.

In view of these rather pronounced discrepancies it is of interest that the authors of both scales present figures showing that their instruments differentiate successfully between delinquent and non-delinquent or problem and non-problem groups. Dr. Baker states that on the Detroit Scale a group of 181 children selected as being free from behavior problems obtained a median score of 285, whereas two groups of problem children numbering 189 and 50 obtained median scores of 220 and 205 respectively. The difference between the medians is in each case more than 20 times the standard error, indicating that the differences are not due to chance.[8] There is relatively little overlapping between the groups. Only three children from the problem groups exceed the median for the non-problem group, and only two of the non-problem group make scores below the median of the problem groups. Similar findings are reported by Hill for the Des Moines Scale.[9] It is safe to say that such an objectively scored case history is adequate to distinguish reliably between groups of children, and has considerable validity in selecting the individual problem child.

Such scales also place a sound emphasis on causes rather than on symptoms of behavior. The Detroit Scale has but one item out of the 66 for rating the child's general behavior. The remaining items primarily stress those aspects of the child's background, development, and personality which might be responsible for his behavior symptoms. The blank also provides a space for listing those items which receive the rating of "very poor," in order to separate out what seem to be the most extreme causes for special emphasis in treatment.

[8] Baker, Harry J., and Traphagen, Virginia. *The Diagnosis and Treatment of Behavior-Problem Children*, pp. 342–346. New York: Macmillan Company, 1935.

[9] Hill, Arthur S. "The Use of an Objective Type of Case Study in the Analysis and Prognosis of Pupil Maladjustment Problems," *Educational Administration and Supervision*, vol. 21, no. 8 (November, 1935), p. 616.

On the whole it seems plain that scales such as these will do much to assist in the process of making our case-history material more measurable, more relevant. If subjected to much experimentation, progress will also be made in determining what aspects of the case history deserve the greatest weight in our consideration of the child's problems. Likewise, such scales may help to indicate and set apart the group for whom we do not at present have any hope of adjustment within the community. Baker suggests this as one of the uses of the Detroit Scale,[10] and Hill also emphasizes this prognostic aspect. Indeed his preliminary study shows that of those children making scores of 0–99 on the Des Moines instrument, treatment in the community was successful in no instance, while of children making scores of 150–159, treatment was successful in 67 per cent of the cases.[11]

Certain Disadvantages. Like every other method we have discussed, this mode of analyzing and diagnosing behavior has its drawbacks. Perhaps the first to impress the thoughtful student is the pseudo-finality which is implicit in a rigid scoring system. It is perhaps possible to decide that James deserves a rating of 38 out of a possible 65 on his physical development and condition, as compared with a score of 52 for John. But that we are not prepared to decide the weight which this should have in our total evaluation of the problem is amply shown by the fact that on the Des Moines Scale the rating on physical factors has a weight of 7 out of 100, whereas in the Detroit Scale it has a weight of 20 out of 100. If such scales are regarded as experimental only, further amplifications and use, combined with critical re-evaluation both of a statistical and clinical nature, may find them to be very valuable as a means of diagnosis. If because of their rigidity and air of finality they crystallize in their present state, the results may be meager.

Another significant shortcoming of this method is its failure to take adequate account of relationships between facts. As

[10] Baker and Traphagen, *op. cit.*, pp. 35–36.
[11] Hill, *op. cit.*, p. 616.

every clinical worker knows, it is not only the obvious and measurable facts in a case which have importance, but the subtle interrelationships of those facts as well. On the Detroit Scale, for example, a boy would receive a rating of 4 on the item of size if he were only one year undersized for his age. He receives a rating of 5, the highest rating, if he is the older of two children. These ratings may be technically correct, and yet entirely conceal the significant fact that the younger brother is as large as his older brother and possessed of equal mentality. This situation, the primary cause of their intense and bitter rivalry and many other problems growing out of it, would fail to show up on the scale. The inability of scales, such as these we have been considering, to adapt themselves to these interactions of factors and to the interplay of emotional relationships detracts from their usefulness.

The extent to which the Detroit Scale aids in selecting the area of treatment and the type of treatment to be used can best be illustrated by quoting a case illustration, as given by Dr. Baker, of a boy who made a D rating, that is, had a score between 200 and 215 on the scale.

> A. P., fifteen years of age, rated D. He had a score of 201 points and was enrolled in a school for behavior problems. He was transferred to this school on account of the complete failure in his scholastic duties, truancy, and tardiness. . . . The very poor items are as follows: Item 21, time of sleeping — he stayed out until 12 o'clock or later. Item 25, later recreational facilities — he sometimes played on a recreation field, but more often was observing adult sporting events or loafing around beer gardens. Item 26 — his playmates and companions were mostly older boys, some of whom had been in detention homes. Item 27 — he stole coats and other articles of clothing. Item 28, personality type — he wished he were three or four years older to do just as he pleased, and he desired more attention. Item 29 — he had no control over his feelings of anger or revenge and resented any correction which the teachers or parents tried to give. Item 36, vocational interests — he wished to be a big business man or physician, objectives obviously quite beyond his capacities. Item 37, general behavior — he seemed to enjoy stealing and being a leader of other boys. Item 61 — he was brought up

under very strict supervision until a short time previously, when his father had died.   His mother was able to do nothing with him afterward.

The eleven poor items were as follows: No. 18, home duties; No. 19, conditions of eating; No. 22, sleeping conditions; No. 30, fear, dread, anxiety, etc.; No. 33, intelligence; No. 34, interests or hobbies; No. 39, mother's intelligence; No. 40, father's education; No. 41, mother's education; No. 49, economic status; and No. 51, other adults in home.

It is evident that the behavior scale has discovered a large number of factors which are very unfavorable to his best social and personality development.   Upon the basis of these various items and the record of delinquency which he had already established, it seems evident that further trouble must follow unless conditions can be radically changed for the better.[12]

As will be observed, the items which received "poor" and "very poor" ratings are a mixture of behavior and personality descriptions, causative facts about which nothing can be done, such as the father's death or the boy's intelligence, as well as some items which seem definitely detrimental, and toward which treatment might be directed.   It is not easy to know whether it is of more fundamental importance to try to remove the other adults in the home, revamp the eating and sleeping conditions, or aim toward more desirable recreational outlets. It is clear, however, that emphasis on factors such as these is more likely to bring results than treatment of the original symptoms of truancy, tardiness, and school failure.   This fact and the helpful manner in which these scales focus attention on the variety of elements which go into the creation of behavior symptoms are perhaps the greatest assets of this type of diagnostic method.

It would be futile indeed to attempt any comparison of the different procedures surveyed in this chapter.   Each has its significant viewpoint, each makes a helpful approach to this many-sided problem of trying to "see through" the child's behavior.   If a consideration of their variety of methods has

---

[12] Baker and Traphagen, *op. cit.*, pp. 338–339.   Reprinted by permission of The Macmillan Company, publisher.

made us cautious to accept any one approach as being complete or accurate, then we are prepared for the next chapter in which the writer, making use of an author's privilege, presents still another method of analyzing behavior and leaves it for others to criticize and point out its failings.

BIBLIOGRAPHY

Personality Tests

In view of the vast literature on the subject no attempt is made to supply an adequate bibliography. The reader is referred to one of the four following studies which list complete references through June, 1935, and selected references from 1935–1938.

General Surveys of Personality Tests

Baker, Harry J., ed., "Psychological Tests," *Review of Educational Research*, vol. 5, no. 3 (June, 1935). See especially chapters 5 and 6.

Symonds, Percival M. *Diagnosing Personality and Conduct.* New York: Century Company, 1931. 569 p.

Traxler, Arthur E. "The Use of Tests and Rating Devices in the Appraisal of Personality," *Educational Records Bulletin* No. 23, New York: Educational Records Bureau, 1938. 80 p.

Watson, Goodwin B. "Tests of Personality and Character," *Review of Educational Research*, vol. 2 (June, 1932), pp. 185–270.

References to Tests Mentioned in Text

Allport, G. W. "A Test of Ascendance — Submission," *Journal of Abnormal and Social Psychology*, vol. 23 (1938), pp. 118–136.

Beck, Samuel J. *Introduction to the Rorschach Method.* New York: American Orthopsychiatric Association, 1937. 278 p.

Bell, H. M. *The Theory and Practice of Student Counselling.* Stanford University, California: Stanford University Press, 1936.

Bernreuter, Robert G. "The Theory and Construction of the Personality Interview," *Journal of Social Psychology*, vol. 4. (November, 1933). 387–405.

Laird, D. A. "Detecting Abnormal Behavior," *Journal of Abnormal and Social Psychology*, vol. 20 (1925), pp. 128–141.

Mathews, E., "A Study of Emotional Stability of Children," *Journal of Delinquency*, vol. 8 (1923), pp. 1–40.

Rogers, Carl R. *Measuring Personality Adjustment in Children Nine to Thirteen.* New York: Teachers College, Bureau of Publications, 1931.

Rosanoff, I. R., and Rosanoff, A. J. "A Study of Association in Children," *Psychological Review*, vol. 20 (1913), pp. 43–80.

Schwartz, Louis A. "Social-Situation Pictures in the Psychiatric Interview," *American Journal of Orthopsychiatry*, vol. 2 (1932), pp. 124–133.

Smith, Randolph B. *The Development of an Inventory for the Measurement of Inferiority Feelings at the High School Level.* Archives of Psychology, No. 144. New York: Columbia University Press, 1932.

Sweet, Lennig. *The Measurement of Personal Attitudes in Younger Boys.* Young Men's Christian Association Occasional Studies, No. 9. New York: Association Press, 1929.

Symonds, Percival M., and Jackson, Claude E. *Measurement of Personality Adjustments of High School Pupils.* New York: Teachers College, Bureau of Publications, 1935. 110 p.

Thurstone, L. I., and Thurstone, T. G. "A Neurotic Inventory," *Journal of Social Psychology*, vol. 1 (February, 1930), pp. 3–30.

Vernon, P. E. "The Rorschach Ink Blot Test," *British Journal of Medical Psychology*, vol. 13 (1933), pp. 89–118, 179–200, 271–291.

Woodrow, H., and Lowell, F. *Children's Association Frequency Tables.* Psychological Monographs, vol. 22, 5, no. 97 (1916).

The Ego-Libido Method

Watson, Maud. *Children and Their Parents.* New York: F. S. Crofts Co., 1932. 362 p.

Evaluating the Case History

Baker, Harry J., and Traphagen, Virginia. *The Diagnosis and Treatment of Behavior-Problem Children.* New York: Macmillan Co., 1935. 393 p.

Hill, Arthur S. "The Use of an Objective Type of Case Study in the Analysis and Prognosis of Pupil Maladjustment Problems," *Educational Administration and Supervision*, vol. 21, no. 8 (November, 1935), pp. 611–618.

CHAPTER III

The Component-Factor Method of Diagnosis

A METHOD of analysis developed in the clinic with which the author is associated has proven to have some usefulness as a means of diagnosis. It may be termed the component-factor method of analysis. It has been devised in an attempt to avoid certain of the pitfalls of other diagnostic procedures. It is proposed by the author as a practical tool for the worker dealing with children, both as a means of diagnosis and as a helpful way of planning effective treatment. Its aim is not so much to produce a measurement as to be an aid to an objective type of analytic thinking. That it, too, has its own characteristic shortcomings, will be evident from the rather detailed description which follows.

BASIS OF THE COMPONENT-FACTOR METHOD

The basis of the method is as broad as the viewpoint outlined in the first chapter of this book. It recognizes behavior symptoms as being the resultants of many interacting forces and elements both within and without the individual child. Behavior problems are due to the fact that a child of certain hereditary equipment is dealt with in a certain manner by members of his family environment and at the same time affected by certain broader cultural and social influences. If any one of these elements is altered, the behavior picture is also altered. To understand behavior we must view it as the complex result of all these component factors. Thus in the method under consideration, the forces which have operated in the child's experience are grouped under eight factors, defined so far as possible in terms which will have general understanding. Each of these factors, which are described below, are rated in the case of the individual child, on a 7-point scale, ranging from influences which are destructive to the child's welfare, to conditions and forces ideal for the child's adjustment. This rating scale is made more objective by means of sample ratings, with experimentally determined values, set up as guideposts. The statement of the facts and relationships upon which the rating is based is left to description, in the assumption that such conditions are too complex to be forced into narrow categories. So far as treatment is concerned, these ratings, and their descriptive accompaniment, aid in focusing treatment on those elements which are alterable. In the optimism which accompanies such a new field as that of dealing with behavior difficulties, it is easy to lose sight of the fact that some situations cannot be changed, or cannot be sufficiently changed to affect behavior in a helpful way. Consequently, in the analysis of the component factors in the case of a particular child, effort is made to stress the limitations as well as the possibilities of treatment effort. These various aspects of the procedure will be clarified by a more detailed presentation of the method itself.[1]

Description of the Method. The eight factors which are rated are as follows; the hereditary factor, narrowly defined; the physical factor, which includes some hereditary elements as well as later organic conditions; mentality; the influences of the family environment; the economic and cultural factors; the social factor, defined as the influence of the companionship group; the education and training régime outside of the home; and finally the child's own insight into his present situation, a product of past factors, but an influence on future adjustment. No attempt is made to give any mathematical weighting to each of these factors, though their influence is doubtless of

[1] See Appendix A for a copy of the printed blank, with brief instructions, which may be used for making this type of analysis.

unequal weight.   The definitions of these various areas and some discussion of the rating follow.

The Hereditary Factor.   The instructions define this in terms of the inheritance as judged by ancestral qualities.   The child's own abilities, physical and mental, are considered under other categories.   The definition of the area to be rated is as follows:

> Consider the child's strain of inheritance, as evidenced by parents, relatives, siblings; hereditary predisposition to disease; feeblemindedness, epilepsy, or psychoses in the ancestry; evidence of neuroses or physical or emotional instability in the ancestry; marked social inadequacy in the ancestry as shown by chronic alcoholism, repeated jail terms.   On the constructive side consider freedom from disease and taints and marked social adequacy.

In order to give some validity to the ratings of the hereditary influence, nine brief descriptions of varying types of hereditary background were submitted to seven clinical psychologists for rating.   They showed very decided agreement in making the ratings, the standard deviation of the judgments being .38 of a point, on a 7-point scale.   To state the results in another way, 77 per cent of the judgments fell in no more than two categories on the rating scale.   Six of these brief descriptions were chosen as "markers" or guides on the rating scale.   They are given in the table on page 43 with their actual and assigned scale values.   The actual ratings are given in terms of step-intervals from 1 to 7.   The assigned values are on the basis of a −3 to +3 scale, which was the form adopted.   In making actual use of the scale frequent reference should be made to these "markers," since they greatly increase the validity and accuracy of ratings and tend to reduce personal bias.

In some cases, especially of adopted children, or where the case information is meager, there may be inadequate material on which to base a rating.   In such instances the rating may be made upon the best information available, but indicated with a question mark to show its tentative nature.   The significance of a proper rating of heredity in estimating the prospects of treatment is very real, since it is the one factor which we cannot change at all.

Av. rating by clinicians	Assigned scale value	Description
1.0	−3	Both parents feebleminded.
1.9	−2	Mother of borderline mentality, father dull, three uncles have jail records. Maternal aunt in State Hospital, diagnosed dementia praecox.
3.1	−1	Mother has history of chorea, father alcoholic. Both parents average intelligence. Paternal uncles run a hardware store. One sibling regarded as hyperactive.
4.0	0	Parents normal intelligence, sibling dull, no state hospital or institutional care for family or close relatives. Mother shows a few neurotic tendencies.
5.4	$\left.\begin{array}{c} +1 \\ +2 \end{array}\right\}$ [2]	Both parents healthy, high-school graduates, three siblings making average school progress. Grandparents were long-lived farmers.
6.7	+3	Parents college graduates, good health. Grandfather a civic leader, uncles are physicians and business men.

The Physical Factor.   On the rating scale the physical factor is so defined as to include some influences largely hereditary or congenital, such as the type of constitution and the degree of nervous stability, but this factor covers primarily the physical history following birth.   The definition of this area is as follows:

Consider the child's inherited physical and neurological constitution; his physical development, size and weight in relation to the norm; physical defects, inferiorities, or abnormalities; glandular dysfunction; physical instability, nervousness, hyperactivity; disease history, with special attention to long periods of illness, or diseases such as tuberculosis, epilepsy, encephalitis, venereal disease, chorea; defects of the special senses.   On the constructive side consider freedom from illness or defects, superior physique.

[2] The two ratings indicate that the particular description falls on the line between two categories, with clinicians favoring slightly the underscored rating.

Following the procedure described in regard to the hereditary factor, brief case illustrations were rated by the clinic psychologists and used as measured steps upon the rating scale. They will not be given here in full but the two extremes may illustrate the range.

−3   Convulsions in infancy, petit mal seizures, at present time. Frail and underweight. Eye defect requiring glasses.

+2,⎫ Physical condition good. Above average height and weight
+3 ⎭ for age. Few illnesses and those always brief. Seems to resist infection. Physically stable. Athletic type of build.

It has been found in using the scale that little difficulty is generally experienced in rating the extent to which physical factors make for or against adjustment. One type of case, however, causes disagreement among clinicians. One of the case descriptions to be rated cited the case of a well-developed adolescent: "Girl of 15, physically as mature as an 18-year-old, began to menstruate early, has had few illnesses, is robust, considerably over the average height and weight, full of physical vitality." The raters differed more widely in rating this case than in rating the other examples. Whether the girl's physical and sexual precocity was to be rated favorably was questionable. Presumably most wide deviations from the normal are hindrances to successful social adjustment and this fact should be taken into account. The average rating would place this particular example between 0 and +1, though the range was from −1 to +2.

Mentality. In rating the extent to which mental equipment is an element helping or hindering adjustment, these aspects are to be kept in mind:

> Consider the child's mental capacities as shown by his development, intelligence test ratings, school achievement, vocational achievement. Consider special abilities and disabilities which have a bearing on his mental functioning. Consider the quality of his intelligence, alertness, persistence, ability to concentrate.

These qualities are, like the physical aspects, partly or largely hereditary, but have sufficient unity and importance to justify the separate grouping. In making the ratings clinicians agree more closely in their judgments on mentality and heredity than on any of the other factors. This is not surprising in the case of mentality, because it is possible to base the rating largely upon measured qualities. Roughly the ratings correspond to the gradations of intelligence with the defectives rated −3, those of borderline mentality −2, etc. The only exceptions to this type of rating are in the cases of children with special abilities or disabilities, which might alter the rating slightly, or of children with an intelligence quotient above 125 where such extreme deviation from the normal may to some degree hinder as well as aid adjustment, hence lowering slightly the expected +3 rating.

The Factor of Family Influence. Under this heading attention is given to the emotional atmosphere of the home, the attitude patterns which have to such an important degree shaped and influenced the child's behavior. The area which the scale includes under this heading is so defined as to eliminate the hereditary, cultural, or economic influences which might be thought of as an integral part of family life. These are rated as a part of other factors.

> Consider the family circle within which the child has developed — the attitudes which have surrounded him. Consider the emotional atmosphere within the home — marital discord or harmony, sibling rivalries, attitudes of domination, oversolicitude, rejection, or normal parental love. Take account of frictions or conflict in regard to illegitimacy or other family irregularity. The child's reaction to the home is also to be considered — reactions toward parents and siblings, toward family standards and discipline. Consider the degree of community of interest with other members of the family.

It seems especially true, in regard to this factor of family environment, that while a general judgment is possible in regard to the wholesomeness of the family influence, we must recognize that this judgment is made up of many counterbalancing items which cannot possibly be crammed into a limited number of categories. It is for this reason that the brief but accurate description of the constructive or problem-creating relationships within the family is as important as the general rating itself. Because of the complexity of the situation to be considered, it was found, clinicians were in slightly less agreement in making ratings of this factor than of factors in other areas. The standard deviation of their judgments for items in this area was .59. The illustrative ratings which serve as steps on the rating scale are here given in full.

-3   Mother quite openly immoral, father a weak individual who plays little part at home except when drunk, when there are terrific quarrels. Mother controls children by beatings. They are at least partially aware of her immorality.

-2   Parents not congenial; whole home dominated by father who is rigid, puritanical and uses excessive discipline. He favors daughter and rejects this boy. Home atmosphere very tense. Mother furtively takes the boy's side.

-1   Father died when child in infancy. Mother centers all her attention and affection on this only child. Mother is extremely oversolicitous and over-indulgent, and has few outside interests.

 0   This boy is somewhat his father's favorite, and being the oldest child, tends to dominate his younger sibs. Parents are both interested in the home, seem happy together and have a great deal of affection for their children.

+3   Parents are very congenial. Family atmosphere harmonious and pleasant. Many special interests and activities fostered by parents. Children encouraged to develop independence. This child feels very secure in the parental affection.

The Economic, Cultural, and Social Factors.   The influence which cultural patterns have upon behavior, and the controlling effect of the attitudes of the companionship group, have been the subject of some very enlightening recent sociological researches. The combination of these two factors with the economic in such a way as to produce delinquency has been thoroughly reported by Shaw.[3] In arranging for their inclusion in a scale for rating the individual child, it seemed best to combine the economic and cultural influences under one heading,

[3] Shaw, Clifford R. *Delinquency Areas.* Chicago: University of Chicago Press, 1929.

reserving for separate consideration the interplay of experience between the child and his companions. The definitions of the areas to be considered under these two factors follow:

> *Rating on Economic and Cultural Influences.* Consider family income, status of father's occupation, social standing in the community, degree of comfort and educative influences within the home; consider the community type — whether delinquency area, residential area, rural area; consider the community standards of behavior and culture; the schools, libraries, and recreational resources available.
>
> *Rating on Social Factor.* Consider range and extent of child's social experience; isolation or group contacts; the type of companions available; the social skills the child has achieved considered in relation to his age; experience in group membership and leadership; organizing ability and social initiative; status in the schoolroom group; friendships, with own and opposite sex, considered in relation to age; social relationships with adults; general social maturity or lack of it.

For each of these factors sample ratings have been measured and placed on the scale for guidance, with values from −3 to +3, as in the case of the previous categories.

In making the ratings of these factors it was found that clinicians showed a satisfactory degree of agreement, with a standard deviation of approximately .5 of a step-interval. The statistical expectation would therefore be that two-thirds of the ratings on a particular case would fall within one step on the 7-point scale.

In spite of this generally satisfactory agreement, it was found in rating the social factor that there was one type of case which proved puzzling. This was best exemplified by a boy who had become a successful leader of a delinquent gang. Here his social experience had been such as to bring out qualities of leadership and to develop social skills. He was well liked by his group but generally defiant and unable to adjust with adults. His leadership was often exerted in anti-social directions. Here it was difficult to make any general evaluation of the social factor. Obviously he was satisfactorily adjusted to the smaller group and quite unadjusted to the larger community group. The general rating necessarily expresses a compromise between these two aspects and the average rating was at the o point of the scale, though individual ratings ranged from −1 to +2.

Education and Training. There is some question whether this factor belongs in the scale. It refers not to the education in academic subjects but to the training in personality and character which has gone on through institutions other than the home, primarily, of course, the school, though church school, camp, or other influences for training should also be taken into account. Much of the research regarding behavior, such as Hartshorne and May's, indicates that institutions such as the school or church school have little influence on behavior apart from the influence of the social group itself, yet there seems some reason for including this factor. Certainly the type of school atmosphere results in definite goals of behavior, whether negative or positive, which influence the patterns of conduct. The area as it is defined is as follows:

> Consider the education, training, and supervision which the child has had outside the home. Ordinarily this will mean primarily his school experience. Consider such things as the type of school which the child has attended; the changes of school; the continuity and consistency of school experience, consistency of discipline, both in school and between home and school; the degree of healthy stimulation, the extent to which tasks have been adapted to ability; the insight shown by teachers and school authorities; the behavior ideals actually inculcated; the co-operation and similarity of viewpoint between home and school.

This factor, like the others, is rated on the scale from −3 to +3.

Self-Insight. The seven factors which have been described would seem to be the basic elements which, coming together in complex fashion, determine the behavior of the individual. For the young child an evaluation of these factors should be sufficient to gain an understanding of the child's reactions. With the older child, however, the attitudes which he holds toward himself and his behavior are decidedly significant and worthy of evaluation. That these attitudes are formed by the interaction of the other factors in the child's experience is undoubtedly true, but they also operate as an important influence to shape his future behavior. Consequently one further item has been added: the rating of the individual's insight, planfulness and ability to take responsibility for himself. In the very young child this rating has less value and less meaning, and should probably be rated near the average unless there is some adequate factual basis for rating it otherwise. In the older child its meaning is much more clear, but it is not easy to obtain the facts upon which a rating can be made with assurance. For the most part such a rating must be based on a knowledge of the child's attitudes as judged through contacts where rapport has been good. To some extent, however, it can be based upon observation of the child's behavior. The area as it is defined is as follows:

> Consider in relation to the norm for his age, the degree to which the child has or lacks understanding of his own situation and problems; consider such things as defensiveness, inability to admit faults, or tendency to depreciate self and exaggerate faults. Consider not only intellectual understanding of problem, but emotional acceptance of the reality situation. Consider child's planfulness and willingness to take responsibility for self; ability to be objectively self-critical. Consider stability of attitudes — whether erratic and changeable or cautious and settled.

In rating items for placement on this scale, it was found that clinicians showed about the same variability as in rating family influences, with a standard deviation of .56 in their judgments. The items placed upon the rating scale as typical examples are these:

−3 This girl blames everyone else for her troubles and readily excuses herself. She will not face the fact that her situation is serious, and has a breezy optimism entirely unrelated to reality.

−2,⎱ This boy's sex behavior indicates real mental conflict. He
−1 ⎰ can give a fair verbal account of the cause of his behavior, but his actions are little influenced.

0 This boy has a rather inadequate knowledge of his own assets and liabilities; he has thought only a little about his

own future; he realizes to some extent the fact that his parents tend to keep him childish. He shows no serious behavior problems.

+ 2,⎫ Living in a most unhappy home situation, this boy makes
+ 3 ⎬ calm judgments as to the degree to which he and stepfather
      ⎭ are to blame, and helps make plans for his own future, away from home, on a carefully reasoned basis.

Descriptive Diagnosis. Recognizing that even this method of rating analysis misses some of the inter-relationships which have significance in causing behavior symptoms, it is wise to add to the ratings a brief descriptive diagnosis, which pays particular attention to the interplay of these eight larger groupings of influences. The fact that certain physical factors as well as family influences both combined at the same period to make the child feel inadequate may not be entirely clear from the ratings. Or the cumulative effect of rejection at home coupled with rejection by teachers at school may need emphasis. Such facts, which have a tendency to escape any schematic way of representation, should be included in this descriptive statement. Here also there is the opportunity to link up the causative factors with the behavior symptoms, for which, as will be noted, there is no place on this scale.

Reliability of Ratings. Since the purpose of the scale is not to obtain a score value, no exhaustive study of reliability has been made. As an indication of its reliability, however, it might be stated that six raters, all clinical psychologists, rated each of five cases on each of seven factors (the category on education and training had not at that time been added to the scale); and of the total of 210 ratings thus made, 138, or 66 per cent, were in agreement within two categories on a 7-point scale. In the remaining 34 per cent judgments were scattered over three, or even four, places on the scale. Agreement in rating these cases was highest in rating mentality, with hereditary and family influences next highest in agreement. The rating of the child's self-insight was lowest, indicating that this factor is probably more intangible, less clearly defined than the others.

PLANNING FOR TREATMENT

When the factual basis for the ratings has been briefly described and the ratings themselves completed, the scale serves as a useful aid in planning treatment. The total picture of the child's situation is before the clinician, not only in general terms as to whether each factor has been largely destructive or constructive, but also in specific terms of the conditions, attitudes, and relationships which are responsible for that summarized judgment. If the ratings on all the factors are low, it indicates not only the gravity of the situation, but also the fact that a low level of adjustment is probably all that can be hoped for. If the ratings are "spotty" with some factors very constructive and others tending strongly to destroy a satisfactory adjustment, attention can be given to those factors rated low.

Furthermore, the limitations of change are kept plainly before the worker, as has been mentioned earlier. The hereditary factor can never be changed, mentality but rarely. If the low ratings are largely in these categories, we know at once that the opportunities for more than palliative treatment are very few. We shall discover also, as we go on to discuss the various types of treatment, that certain other conditions are stubbornly resistant to change. These too we may recognize as limitations of our effort. An analysis of this type also brings to light the points in the picture where changes may be easily and effectively made in the family attitudes, or in the realm of social adjustment or self-insight, or in some other area, which may make it possible definitely to change the influence of that factor. These changes in the constructive direction either strike directly at the causes of misbehavior, or so improve the comfort of the child's general adjustment that misbehavior is no longer necessary. In thus planning treatment it is of great advantage to have the conditions described specifically rather than in general terms. Thus the chart reveals that it is overindulgence on the part of the mother or a jealousy of his younger sister which is a part of the child's problem, and not merely poor "discipline" or poor "adjustment to siblings."

Once the steps are outlined which may change the constituent elements of the child's behavior, this treatment plan may be indicated on the same diagram on which the original ratings have been made. If the treatment program is carried out, how much change can be expected within a year's time in the family influence, or in the social factor, or in the economic and cultural situation? A careful re-rating of every factor on this basis, with arrows indicating the direction and probable extent of treatment influences, is a helpful step. Again it affords a realistic basis for judging how much can be expected in this child's situation.

AN EXAMPLE OF THE METHOD

Without giving the full case history upon which the ratings were based, an example may be cited of the use of the component-factor method in the analysis of a typical case. The child in question is similar to many youngsters referred to a clinic in that his behavior deviations are sufficiently serious to give concern not only to the parents but to the school as well.

Paul is a boy of 8, brought to the clinic by his father because of an accumulation of problems. He has stolen money and small articles from children at school, from stores, and from home. Twice he has gone into other homes to steal. He is destructive of his own and others' belongings. He is often cruel and mean to other children. He does not respond to the parental discipline.

Following a thorough investigation of the situation, the following analysis was made. Both the diagrammatic ratings and the items upon which they are based are given to illustrate the procedure. Reference to the definitions of areas to be rated, and to the sample ratings, will be helpful in understanding the chart.

Hereditary. In mother's family borderline mentality, sexual promiscuity, criminal records. Many evidences of instability, including enuresis among adults. Mother herself erratic, dull. Father not above average ability, comes of simple working family. One cousin psychotic, diagnosis unknown. Rating −2.

CASE OF PAUL

COMPONENT FACTOR ANALYSIS

Factor	−3	−2	−1	0	+1	+2	+3
Hereditary		x					
Physical			x				
Mentality		x					
Family		x					
Economic-Cultural				x			
Social		x					
Education-Training			x				
Self-Insight		x					

Physical. Slow in infant development, always "nervous," restless, jumpy. Few serious illnesses. Head injury six months ago from twenty-foot fall. Present physical examination largely negative. Rating −1.

Mentality. Low dull normal intelligence with no special abilities noted. Some bizarre responses. Inability to concentrate interferes with educational achievement. Rating −2.

Family. Much marital discord. Mother 10 years younger than father, interested in another man, takes little interest in her two children. Shows marked favoritism to the youngest, rejects Paul. Father still fond of mother, hopes to win her back. Very strict with Paul and uses poor methods but tries to understand him. Wants help. Paul jealous of younger brother. Aunt and grandmother live in home, former fond of Paul, latter not. Rating −2.

Economic-cultural. Father an auto mechanic, self-supporting most of his married life. He is proud of home, keeps it up. Home in fair urban neighborhood, with few recreational facilities. Parents both native born, but father retains much of old-world tradition. Rating 0.

Social. Normal opportunity for social contacts, but antagonizes group with his bossiness, meanness. Has achieved few social skills for his age. Shows some initiative and daring in group, generally in pranks or destructive activities. Has no close friends. Disliked by adults in community. Rating −2.

Education-training. Second year in parochial school. Large

classes, little individual attention, tasks assigned are too difficult.   Discipline is strict, consistent with home discipline.
Rating —1.

Self-insight.   Little insight, even for an eight-year-old.   Cannot admit his misbehavior, tells of others who are worse than he.
Cannot verbalize his dislike for his brother, but indicates it by
complaining of brother's behavior.   Has little understanding of
parental attitudes.   Takes little responsibility for self.   Rating —2.

A descriptive diagnosis of Paul's problems sums up the ratings.   "Paul's physical instability, probably inherited, is increased by the rejecting attitudes and marital friction he meets
in the home.   The desire to win affectional satisfaction accounts
for his jealousy of his brother and possibly for his meanness to
other children.   His low mentality, coupled with his restless-
ness, makes school achievement poor.   He is finding very few
healthy satisfactions at the present time.   There is the possibility that organic brain injury may be a causative factor."

After examination of the case analysis, certain steps seem
possible which would be directed toward the basic elements of
Paul's maladjustment.   First is the necessity of trying to
lessen the various strains of the family situation.   Work with
the parents to determine whether their marital life can be
rebuilt, or whether separation is necessary, is one aspect.
Efforts to lessen the mother's favoritism are also indicated, as
well as education for the father in methods of management and
discipline.   The available techniques for dealing with parental
attitudes will be discussed later.   For the boy a short period
of observation away from home seems advisable, since this
might be of help in determining whether his behavior is in
large part caused by organic or environmental factors.   The
treatment, in other words, includes still further steps in diagnosis.   In regard to his hyperactivity the physician's recommendation is for a better régime of sleeping and rest.   Paul's
educational placement is another source of maladjustment
which can be altered by a change to a smaller class or to a
"slow-moving" grade.   He seems too young to attack the
social maladjustment directly.   Group membership is scarcely

feasible, though improvement in the home situation or in his adjustment to his school group should reflect itself in the social situation. How to aid Paul to gain more understanding of himself is a question. Whether to attempt this through interviews with the child is a matter which we shall discuss later. It is sufficient to note here that because of his age, mentality, and defensiveness it was not felt advisable, though some clinics would undoubtedly have included such an attempt as one aspect of treatment.

In the light of the suggestions noted above, the diagram was rated once more, with arrows to indicate the clinician's judgment as to the approximate amount of change which might be expected in one year. The reasons for these estimates follow:

CASE OF PAUL
TREATMENT POSSIBILITIES

Factor	-3	-2	-1	0	1	2	3
Hereditary		x					
Physical			x→				
Mentality		x					
Family		x——————→?					
Economic-Cultural				x			
Social		x——→					
Education-Training			x——→				
Self-Insight		x——→					

Physical. The better physical régime may have a calming effect, but no great change may be expected in this area.

Family. Any clarification of the family situation seems likely to be an improvement over the present tangle. Whether the family unity is restored or the parents separate and Paul goes with his father, some improvement seems likely. The co-operative attitude of the father is some guarantee that his methods of managing Paul are alterable. The whole situation contains too many unknowns to rate with any assurance.

Social. Improvement here would be due primarily to a more

comfortable adjustment at home and school, and would be small.

Education and training.   To have work fitted to his ability in a class where he could have more attention from the teacher would definitely improve this aspect.

Self-insight.   With less pressure from his father and from the school for impossible achievement, Paul can be more free to recognize his own shortcomings.   With better parental management his ability to take responsibility for himself can be improved.

This analysis both of the situation and its treatment give reason to expect that Paul's behavior may be guided into more normal and more constructive channels.   Yet the low ratings of heredity and mentality keep us from too optimistic judgments.   We cannot expect a thoroughly normal adjustment, and our prognosis should be moderate and cautious.

An illustration such as this should suffice to make it plain that the method here proposed is not a mechanical device which sums up the individual in a score, but is a tool to aid in analysis of case material.   The situation of the individual child is too complex to grasp in toto.   To think helpfully about the child and his possibilities, tools are needed which will objectify the material, clarify the analysis of it, and encourage breadth of thinking and absence of bias in planning treatment measures. The extent to which this break-down of the case into its component factors accomplishes these ends is the measure of its merit.

COMMENTS ON THE COMPONENT-FACTOR METHOD

Certain aspects of the component-factor method should perhaps be mentioned before we leave the topic.   Unlike the ego-libido method or the evaluation of case histories, the component-factor method places all its stress on causative factors, none on the behavior symptoms.   Whether this is sound or not depends to some extent on the point of view.   At least it operates to correct the usual point of view which places most of the emphasis on the behavior problems and on direct methods of attacking them.   The writer's experience leads him to place full weight on the elements which go to make up conduct patterns, since in these elements, if they can be so readjusted that normal reactions are possible between the given individual and his environment, lie the clues to successful treatment.

The categorical divisions which are made in the rating scale are kept, so far as possible, on a common-sense, realistic basis. Any person with technical training, who deals with children, recognizes and already thinks in terms of the child's mentality, the family influences, the social factors, and the like. The categories which are used, while they may be faulty, are not at least likely to be misunderstood.

The method contributes to the field of treatment the concept of limitations, which is conspicuously lacking in other modes of analyzing or diagnosing behavior. It helps to divide more clearly those aspects which cannot be changed from those which we may be able to alter, and thus promotes a healthy realism which has not always been an accompaniment to clinical endeavor. It also assists in overcoming individual bias in regard to treatment. One worker may see for every child the virtue of group activity, another the need for sex education or the possibilities of therapy based on a deep relationship to the worker. The method here described tends to reduce such individual predilections by drawing attention to the variety of individual needs and of possible points of attack.

Why a "Method" of Diagnosis? The question may well be raised, "Why use any schematic or objective system of diagnosis? Why not merely think intelligently about the child in order to determine the causative elements in the situation?" Relatively few practicing workers in the clinical field use an objective diagnostic procedure in the majority of cases. Why, then, devote time to the topic?

The primary answer is that one cannot think about the cause-and-effect relationships which have brought about problem behavior in a child without basing such thinking upon some framework. It may be based upon a Freudian ideology or a narrowly behavioristic approach, or upon a completely sociological and cultural view of behavior, or upon some other basis or combination of bases. There is great advantage, however, in making explicit and definite the framework within which the diagnosis is built. This every objective method of diagnosis endeavors to do. Thus, if all causative influences are thought of as lying within the sphere of feelings and emotions, this is made plain, as in the ego-libido method. If a variety of forces are thought of as causative, this too will be evident, as in the case-history evaluation, and component-factor methods.

Diagnosis can never be mechanical, nor will diagnostic thinking ever be replaced by a device of any sort. Nevertheless, diagnostic procedures such as we have described bring our thinking into a conscious framework which can be criticized, checked, and improved. They avoid the smugness of an "intuitive" diagnosis which cannot be confirmed or denied by another observer. They help to correct for personal bias. Improvement in diagnostic thinking can only come about as we objectify our methods and thus allow for continual study and correction of our basic procedures.

Requirements for a Satisfactory Method. From the discussion in this and the previous chapter of four different ways of making a diagnostic analysis of personality and behavior problems, it should be possible to glean some of the required elements for a more satisfactory method. It is probable that none of the methods described is fully satisfactory, but a consideration of the strengths and weaknesses of each approach — personality tests, the ego-libido method, case-history evaluation, and the component-factor method — suggests the desirable elements which would obtain in an ideal diagnostic procedure. Some of these elements might be listed as follows:

1. A method of diagnosis should take into account all the aspects of the life situation which might influence behavior. It should not be limited to narrow areas of the total picture.

2. It should rest on well-defined concepts or bases, so that

everyone using the procedure will understand it so far as possible in the same way.   If it is grounded on concepts of a theoretical nature, or concepts which belong only to one school of thought, or bases which cannot be accurately defined or measured, its usefulness will be greatly limited.

3. The ideal method of diagnosis should be able to picture not only meaningful facts from the individual's experience, but significant cause-and-effect relationships between these facts.

4. It should be able to indicate the areas of the child's maladjustment where treatment effort can most effectively be aimed.   This does not of course necessarily mean that treatment efforts will be made in areas where maladjustment is greatest, but that therapy should be undertaken in ways which give the greatest promise of success.

5. The method should be as scientific and objective as the data and our present means of measurement permit. It should avoid a pseudo-objectivity which may inhibit the improvement of method and plan.

A consideration of each of the proposed diagnostic tools will show it to be lacking in some respect when judged in this way. The future will most assuredly bring to us more refined and satisfactory methods.

What Method to Use?   The survey which we have made of these differing techniques of diagnosis should serve better than any abstract statement to illustrate the confusion and at the same time the vitality of the field we are studying, the causation and treatment of behavior problems.   If we look for accepted dogmas or a solid body of long-established scientific fact, we shall look in vain.   Instead we see a science in the making, full of crude half-truths, bristling with questions to be answered, hypotheses to be proved or disproved, and calling for the utmost in balanced judgment.

This applies both to the methods of diagnosis which we have been considering and to the broader field of treatment effort which is to be presented in the following portions of the book.

Certainly, so far as diagnostic techniques are concerned, there is no best method; there are only methods which need testing and experiment and revision. It is for this reason that four approaches rather than one have been described. It should be quite evident that, in the circumstances, whatever method is used will need to be based on a thorough investigation of all the facts, and the best insight and understanding which the clinician can bring to the situation.

PART II

Change of Environment as Treatment

The Foster Home as a Means of Treatment

ONE OF the most common methods of changing behavior is to transplant the individual completely from one environment to another. The wealthy citizen who is concerned over the escapades of his wayward son begins to consider the possibilities of a boarding school three hundred miles away, where his offspring will have new friends, new surroundings, a new school, and separation from father, mother, and home. The family welfare agency, dealing with a very difficult boy, envisions the glowing opportunities of a foster home and what it could do for the child. Even the psychiatrist, who more than most is apt to depend on processes that are internal rather than external, falls back with surprising frequency on gross changes of environment to accomplish his purpose. Placement in a sanitarium, or camp, or in a selected boarding school, forms a large part of the treatment suggested in the psychiatrist's private practice, where presumably he is able to choose the most effective methods without being too much bound by considerations of time and expense. It seems that such commonplace adoption of this mode of altering behavior is worth careful scrutiny. We shall investigate the data and experience available in order to discover the types of situations in which a complete change of environment is desirable and effective in changing conduct.

THE POTENTIALITIES OF ENVIRONMENTAL CHANGE

Considered from the point of view of causation of behavior, it is relatively easy to understand why environmental treatment should be a very powerful method. In the first place the child is lifted bodily from any emotional tensions in the home which may be at the root of his unsatisfactory behavior. He is not, to be sure, freed from them, since he already carries with him the profound effects of such influences; yet to be released from the daily sarcasms which spring from a parental rejection, or to be out of hearing of family quarrels which divide his loyalties, is a real gain. We cannot deny the lasting harm done by destructive parental attitudes during early childhood, but we should be equally unrealistic if we failed to admit that such forces become assimilated by the child in less harmful ways when these destructive attitudes are replaced by a more normal parental environment. Hence in treating a child through a complete change of environment, we have the opportunity of altering, at one stroke, all the aspects of family life which are so apt to create misbehavior, whether it be parental rejection or overindulgence, jealousy of brother or sister, conflict in the adjustment of the parents to one another, or any other factor or complex of factors which is awry in the family picture.

Scarcely less important is the complete alteration of the social milieu. This is especially noteworthy when we take a youngster from the "delinquency area" type of neighborhood and place him in a new setting. He leaves behind the traditions of gang depredations, of lack of community control, of hero-worship of older delinquents, and enters a new cultural group, which, if wisely chosen, brings to bear the powerful but stimulating force of socialized community standards. Even the friendships the child has had are left behind and new ones substituted. This change may be constructive or destructive, depending on the particular child's situation, but it is one of the elements which makes this mode of treatment so revolutionary in its effects.

If we fit our consideration of change of environment into the framework suggested in Chapter III, we readily see that the placement of a child away from his own home and neighborhood leaves untouched only the factors of hereditary influences, innate mentality, and physical constitution. The other factors which seem closely associated with the formation of behavior tendencies — family influences, the cultural and economic factor, social and group influences, educational influences — all these are changed.   Even the child's insight into his own problems is likely to be changed, since removal from the situation brings with it a greater chance of objectivity.   In short, if our suggestions for the understanding of behavior are correct, a change of environment should be capable of bringing about extreme changes in behavior, depending of course on the degree to which the behavior was caused by factors other than heredity or mental capacity, and on the degree of difference between the original and the new environment.   In this and the following chapter an attempt will be made to examine the truth of this hypothesis.

THE CHARACTERISTICS OF THE FOSTER HOME

There are a number of possibilities of placement for the child for whom a change of environment is desired.   A children's institution, a boys' or girls' camp, a boarding school, a wage home, or a farm job, would all involve the complete change of scene which we have been describing.   All of these will be discussed to some extent in subsequent chapters, but for the present we will confine our discussion to the foster home, which has a number of specific advantages as a means of treatment.

In 1930 well over 100,000 children were being given foster-home care by some four hundred child-placing agencies.[1]   In the vast majority of cases board was being paid to the foster parents for the care of these children, and the agency had ceased to regard this financial bond as an embarrassing or disturbing fact.   Instead it had become one of the best assurances that the agency could demand skilled and patient help from the foster parent as a paid assistant in the process of developing normal children.   How many of these 100,000 children are to

[1] White House Conference on Child Health and Protection.   Committee on Socially Handicapped.   *Dependent and Neglected Children*, Sec. IV, C-1, p. 26.   New York: Appleton-Century, 1933.

be regarded as behavior problems is a question, but the proportion is large. A relatively small proportion of children receive care purely because of dependency.

Special Advantages. The foster home has achieved this place in the realm of child care and treatment primarily because it offers the child a chance to make a normal adjustment to a normal community life. From what we know of the psychological transfer of training, this is ideal. There is a maximum of identical elements between the foster-home situation and the community situation which the child must later face. This is not true of institutional placement, particularly in institutions of the older style, where the child may learn to make an excellent adjustment within the institution and still be quite at a loss to meet the very different aspects of life as he finds it outside.

Another advantage of the foster home, particularly to the small child, is that he may find there the emotional security and anchorage which seem so necessary to the development of the personality and which we are unlikely to find in any other place outside of the child's home.

The objective of foster-home care, especially in treating the child who is a behavior problem, is to give him the environmental elements which make toward normal growth and development, and to prepare him so far as possible for a normal place in family and community life. Eventually he is either to return to his own home, which in the interim of his placement has been helped to achieve attitudes and standards suitable for a growing boy or girl, or failing such rehabilitation of his own home, he is to be established as an independent, self-supporting member of the community. This latter is by no means an easy goal to attain, and the initial aim is usually to re-establish the child with his own parents or relatives.

What Kinds of Children May be Placed? When is the foster home used as a treatment measure? What sorts of children, with what types of behavior difficulties, have been placed? What foster homes are most satisfactory? Is foster-home care successful in altering behavior?   These are some of the questions which naturally come to mind in the consideration of this problem.   Fortunately, several studies have been made of groups of children placed for therapeutic reasons in foster homes, and we shall examine with some care this record of accumulated experience before discussing the problem in more general terms.

What are the characteristics of problem children placed in foster homes as a part of treatment?   In our own clinic we have examined the records of 152 children who came to us from their own homes, in order to determine what types of children were chosen for institutional care, for foster-home care, and for treatment in their own homes.[2]   There were several outstanding differences between the foster-home group and the other groups. They were younger, the median age being 10 years, 10 months, while the median of the group treated in their own home, was 13 years, 1 month, and the median for the institution group was 15 years, 1 month.   It should be pointed out that while the median age of the foster-home group differs from that of the others, yet the range of age in this group is from 2 to 17, and the interquartile range (containing 50 per cent of the group) is approximately 8 to 14 years.   As to sex, it was found that the clinic was more likely to allow boys to remain at home, while girls were treated by placement either in foster homes or in institutions.   Thus of the whole group of girls, 31 per cent remained at home, 47 per cent were placed in foster homes, and 22 per cent were placed in institutions.   Of the boys 55 per cent remained at home, 34 per cent were placed in foster homes, and 11 per cent were institutionalized.

The accompanying table points out certain other differences between the three groups.   The foster-home group is more predominantly of native-born parentage, while the other groups contain a larger percentage of foreign-born parentage.   The foster-home group tends to be brighter, with the majority of

[2] For a brief account of this study see "Three Surveys of Treatment Measures Used with Children," by Carl R. Rogers, *American Journal of Orthopsychiatry*, vol. 7 (January, 1937), pp. 48–57.

children in the average and dull normal groups, with 10 per cent of borderline mentality, and with no defectives. These children tend to come from broken homes. They are not the most serious group from a behavior point of view, if we may judge from the number of behavior problems which they present as checked on the research sheet used. While a wide range of problems is presented in this foster-home group, including stealing, ungovernable conduct, difficulties in social adjustment, and the like, there is one way in which the group differs significantly from the clinic cases as a whole. Fewer problems of sex misconduct, particularly among girls, are dealt with in foster homes than in the children's own homes or in institutions. As will be seen from the table, children with sex problems are usually recommended for institution care, while stealing problems are dealt with primarily in the child's own home, with foster-home placement as a secondary possibility, and institutional placement as the last resort. Children who are technically delinquent are usually dealt with either in their own homes or in institutions. Twenty-six per cent of the group as a whole were court delinquents, but only 10 per cent of the foster-home group are so classified.

CHARACTERISTICS OF CHILDREN REMAINING AT HOME, GOING TO FOSTER HOMES, GOING TO INSTITUTIONS

	Own Home Group	Foster-Home Group	Institutional Group
Number in group..................	68	60	24
Median Age	13–1	10–10	15–1
Mentality.........................	Largely dull normal	Dull normal and average. (No defectives)	Defective and borderline
Nationality			
American....................	46%	71%	41%
Italian	24%	3%	21%
Other.......................	30%	26%	38%
From "normal" two parent homes...	56%	33%	67%
Average number of "problems"......	2.2	1.8	3.8
Sex problems distributed	37%	14%	49%
Stealing problems distributed	58%	30%	12%

In a study of 100 children selected for foster-home care at the Institute for Juvenile Research, Chicago, the findings in regard to the type of child placed are very similar.[3]   The median age was slightly over ten years, with the girls slightly older than the boys, which was also the finding in our study.   The mental level of the children was below the average for the general population but probably not below the average for the social and economic background described.   The median intelligence would fall between the dull normal and average group as in our own study, though seven of their group were mental defectives.   The Chicago group included a larger proportion of children of foreign-born parents, only half the group being of native-born parentage.   Seventy-eight per cent of the children came from broken or irregular homes.   All of these children were serious behavior or personality problems.   The basis of the decision regarding their removal from home will be discussed later.

A third study of foster-home children, made by Dr. Healy and his associates [4] indicates that foster-home placement may be used for a much more difficult group of children than is ordinarily thought possible.   Backed by a special grant of funds, and with the purpose of experimenting with the possibilities of foster placement, Dr. Healy and his associates had 501 children placed in foster homes.   A careful study of the results was made.   Of these children 51 per cent were court delinquents (contrasted with 10 per cent in our study).   Of 386 delinquents for which the facts are given 25 per cent were problems of sex misconduct (the corresponding figure for our group would be 9 per cent).   Unfortunately, there are no figures in regard to age and no satisfactory figures in regard to mentality.   The median age at first referral to the Judge Baker Foundation was approximately twelve years, but the range was from 5 to 18 years.   In regard to mentality 10 per cent of the group is de-

[3] Hopkins, Cornelia D., and Haines, Alice R.   "A Study of One Hundred Problem Children for whom Foster Care was Advised," *American Journal of Orthopsychiatry*, vol. 1 (January, 1931), pp. 107–129.

[4] Healy, William, Bronner, Augusta, Baylor, Edith M., and Murphy, J. Prentice. *Reconstructing Behavior in Youth*.   New York: A. A. Knopf, 1929.

fective, but the remainder of the group is classed under psychiatric, rather than psychological, terms as "normal," "abnormal and peculiar," and "psychotic." As to nationality only 41 per cent are children of native-born parents.

These three studies indicate that in three rather widely separated cities there is a certain consistency as regards the type of child treated through foster-home placement, though in each instance the variations are important. In general the children come from broken homes, only one-fifth to one-third of the group living with both of their own parents. Stepparent situations and homes broken by desertion or divorce are extremely common in this group. In age the children range from infancy to older adolescence, with ten to eleven years as the typical age. There is a large proportion of children of foreign-born parents, ranging from 29 per cent in our study to 59 per cent in the Boston group. The group is most consistent in intelligence level, with an average mentality between the dull normal and average group, or, expressed in numerical terms, with a median I.Q. of about 90. In degree of behavior problems there is a wide range, from children with minor personality disturbances to "repeaters" in juvenile courts. In general, however, they are a group with less serious problems than the group which receives institutional care.

With this generalized picture in mind of the group of problem children who are treated through foster placement, we may turn our consideration to the homes to which they go.

Types of Foster Homes Available. While there is great variety in the foster homes in which children are placed, it is the experience of most child-placing agencies, backed by some research data, that certain generalizations can be made. The majority of foster homes are rural or suburban, partly, no doubt, because housing conditions make it easier for the rural or suburban homes to accept and find room for another individual in the family.[5] The economic status of the foster home

[5] In the study by Healy *et al.* (*op. cit.*, p. 122), of the 1222 homes used 19 per cent were urban, 41 per cent suburban, 40 per cent rural.

is likely to be moderate, neither of the level requiring public assistance not so comfortable economically that the item of board is negligible. There has undoubtedly been in recent years a trend toward a higher type of family giving foster care, due in large measure to the fact that clinics and agencies have increasingly regarded the task of foster parentage as one demanding skill and insight to an unusual degree.

In age, foster parents are definitely older than we would expect to find were we studying a group of children in relation to their own parents. In the case of 910 children placed by the State Charities Aid Association [6] the median age of the children was approximately nine, and the median age of the foster mother approximately forty, at the time of placement. Although this study dealt with placement made nearly a generation ago, proof that the situation has not materially changed is contained in a recent study made by Miss Dudley.[7] In 22 foster homes, all moderately successful, the median age of the foster mothers was 40 to 50, and the median age of the foster fathers approximately 50, at the time the children were placed. In general the typical foster mother has had some experience with children, usually her own, who are now sufficiently grown up that she is free to take others. This accounts for the fact that foster parents are usually older than "own parents" with children of comparable age.

It is significant that in most foster homes the foster mother is the outstanding individual. The frankest and most satisfactory explanation of this fact is given by Miss Dudley:

> In nearly all of the families it seemed that the woman was the dominant figure in the household, often being aggressive, and, usually, more responsible than her husband. Social workers who place children usually recognize this tendency and attempt to explain it. In the first place, unless a woman is somewhat aggressive she does not have the initiative to go outside of her home to get children to board, unless under the direct suggestion of her

[6] Theis, Sophie Van S. *How Foster Children Turn Out.* State Charities Aid Association Publication no. 165. New York: 1924.

[7] Dudley, Virginia. "Foster Mothers Successful and Unsuccessful," *Smith College Studies in Social Work*, vol. 3, no. 2 (December, 1932), pp. 151–182.

husband. Then, too, if a woman who is ordinarily dominated by her husband does take children, obstacles in the relationship between the social worker and the mother frequently arise. The mother may experience conflict between loyalty to the husband and loyalty to the social worker; or she may feel guilty about making decisions without her husband's consent; or she may be sensitive to all of her husband's feelings about the foster child and decide to give up the child when the first difficulty arises. In short it is usually hard to do family case work unless the social worker is in good rapport with the person who is dominant in the household.[8]

A study of 35 foster homes in Cleveland, made by Dr. Markey and Miss Noble, confirms this picture.[9] Using possibly superficial definitions of masculinity and femininity, they found that in none of the homes was the man distinctly the dominant parent. In a majority of these foster homes the foster mother was definitely the more "masculine" parent, being more aggressive and dominating. The effect of this situation upon the foster child is worthy of attention. For some personalities it might be helpful, for others harmful.

It is important to stress the fact that while the above generalizations in regard to the average foster home are important, the variety of possibilities in foster-home placement is a vital element in their successful use. Every child-placing agency of good standards has not only homes which fit in with the general picture described, but also homes which run directly contrary to these facts. It is possible to place a problem child in a city home, with young foster parents, where the foster father is the dominant figure. There are successful homes where unmarried women or widows give excellent care, particularly, very often, to older girls. In the agency with which the author is most familiar there are several homes which might be classed almost as specialized small institutions. One, for example, is a home which gives excellent care to young mentally defective children; another is a home where the foster parents have given

[8] Dudley, *op. cit.*, pp. 159–160.

[9] Markey, O. B., and Noble, Helen. "An Evaluation of the Masculinity Factor in Boarding Home Situations," *American Journal of Orthopsychiatry*, vol. 6 (April, 1936), pp. 258–267.

excellent care to difficult small boys, but find it much less possible to deal with the greater need for freedom in adolescence.

Essential Qualities in Foster Parents.   While there is this variety in the foster homes available, there seem to be certain qualities necessary in foster parents for successful work with problem children.   It is of interest to note the similarity of phrases with which different workers attempt to describe the subtle emotional qualities of the foster parents which tend to make them successful or unsuccessful in dealing with children. Miss Theis stresses the point that foster parents who gave excellent care "showed a sympathetic understanding of the child's nature and encouraged to the utmost the development of his aptitudes and possibilities." [10]   Miss Helen Witmer, summarizing Miss Dudley's material, pointed out, of the successful foster mothers, that "their discipline might be stern or easy-going but it was always consistent and the children knew what to expect; and whether the women were warm-natured or rather reserved, the children felt secure in their fundamental interest and affection." [11]   Strikingly similar is the analysis which the present author wrote, at almost this same time, of the success of a particular foster home: [12] "the outstanding success of this home is in meeting the boys' needs for security."   This, it was felt, was due to settled, consistent attitudes on the part of the foster parents, and to their "patient, sympathetic interest in the child."   A second reason for the success of the home was the foster parents' ability to give each child sufficient recognition and praise for achievement, adjusted to the child's own abilities.

Dr. Healy and his associates stress more the affectional atmosphere of the home.   They describe the "kindly, generous, warm-hearted foster mother who possesses a sense of humor," and the "geniality, frankness, and warmth" of the foster home

[10] Theis, *op. cit.*, p. 200.

[11] Dudley, *op. cit.*, p. 171.

[12] Rogers, Carl R., "A Good Foster Home — Its Achievements and Limitations," *Mental Hygiene*, vol. 15, no. 1 (January, 1933), p. 39.

which gives "a sense of freedom and a common sharing of everything in the home." [13]

There is admittedly at the present time no adequate way of validating these statements, yet it seems clear that the suitability of a foster home for the care of problem children depends more upon certain types of attitudes than on any external factor. These attitudes might be summarized as follows:

1. An attitude of intelligent understanding. This involves ability to look at the child's behavior as a natural result of his makeup and experience, rather than as an infraction of moral rules, or a deviation from adult convention. It also requires the creative imagination to understand the way the child feels and the motives for his acts.

2. A consistency of viewpoint and discipline. This element of stability in management gives the child the comforting feeling of knowing where he stands with reference to some standard. The consistency of viewpoint seems more important than the actual type of discipline itself, since every clinic or child-placing agency can point to successful homes with very diverse views on discipline.

3. An attitude of interested affection. It is the moderate type of affection which seems most helpful, not the glowing enthusiasm of the emotionally starved parent. "Fundamental interest and affection" is perhaps the best descriptive phrase. It is a primary factor in the child's security.

4. Satisfaction in the child's developing abilities. Only if the foster parent finds this satisfaction will he wisely reward the youngster for achievement, and permit the child more and more freedom to grow in independence.

When one analyzes present-day methods of home-finding, it is evident that more attention is being given to qualities of the kind listed than was formerly done. Previously, the emphasis was largely upon physical and moral standards of the home. Much more progress can still be made, however. An attitudes test, of the sort increasingly used by psychologists for

---

[13] Healy *et. al.*, *op. cit.*, pp. 127, 129.

a variety of purposes, could be devised to measure, at least to some extent, just such qualities. Given to prospective foster parents, it would probably have much more value than the sheaf of references ordinarily obtained from the clergyman, the school principal, and from neighbors.

A typical foster home of the very successful sort is described in Miss Dudley's report.

> Mrs. C. has for four years been one of the most admired foster mothers. She is a fine, sensitive person in her early fifties, tolerant, with a broad vision and an intelligent approach to people. Mr. C. is a little older than she — a good natured, friendly, fatherly man, intelligent and companionable. He is a mechanic by trade, but has been out of work for a year. Their four daughters are all over twenty; one of them is married and the others are at home. The home is a small farm, fifteen miles from Boston, from which the girls commute to work in town. During the last year they have been using up their savings, because Mr. C. has been out of work. The whole family has active interests in the community life and a strong family feeling. They entertain friends most of the time, informally, and have as a family a much wider horizon of intellectual and social interests than most people in their economic position.[14]

Another example showing the usual characteristics of a foster home, suburban location, moderate economic status, foster parents forty or over, and foster mother dominant, is taken from the previously mentioned study by the author. Both this and the preceding illustration exemplify the emotional qualities which make for a successful foster home.

> The home is located on the outskirts of the city of Rochester. The house is spacious and light, and the yard is large, though none too large for several active boys. The foster mother is without question the key factor in the home. Short, stout, and efficient, or "little but nice" as one of the boys described her, she manages the home and the boys with equal success. She has had no direct preparation of any kind for her task, although her training as a nurse has been a helpful background for the work, and her reading of books and pamphlets on child care has increased her theoretical grasp of the problem. It is primarily her personality

[14] Dudley, *op. cit.*, p. 164.

which has made her successful. She herself is a childless middle-aged woman, yet she has never shown the ultra-emotional affection toward the boys which so often serves as a compensation for childless wives. She does have a liking for the boys. As one of the youngsters put it, "No matter how bad a boy is, or what he does, she likes him just the same." She also has a creative imagination, shown in her resourceful handling of difficult situations and her gifted use of meager equipment. Simple toys, shovels to dig with, hammers and nails become, under her suggestions, interesting projects which occupy her boys for days at a time. Birthdays, trips to the movies, picnics, and holidays are topics that the boys speak of for months afterwards because "mother" has the knack of investing such occasions with the festive touch. Her imagination and innate insight are equally well shown in her handling of the boys. William, having "tried out" previous foster mothers so successfully that it had been necessary to move him several times, renewed his tactics in this home within the first few days of placement. "I'm tough!" he said, slapping his chest. "Are you?" answered mother, "I'm tough, too." William looked decidedly surprised and in a somewhat lower tone of voice asked, "How tough are you?" "I'm tough like you," confided the foster mother. "Well" said William in a subdued voice, after a thoughtful pause, "I'm not so tough."

The foster father, Mr. Thompson, is a quiet, unobtrusive man who plays a much less prominent part in the home, but a constructive part, nevertheless. He is a painter who has been employed less than half of the time during the past four years. As a consequence he is at home a great deal and has given much of his time to the boys. He has some knack with tools, and has constructed swings and a make-shift jungle-gym in the back yard, while in the basement he has built two stout work benches of the right height for small boys. He enjoys their company, and they like to flock about him if he is working at home. So far as the actual care of the group is concerned, he supervises baths, dispenses cod liver oil, administers very rare spankings when they are thoroughly deserved, and makes himself indispensable in other ways.

From an economic point of view, the money paid for board by the children's agency has undoubtedly been a considerable factor in the family life. Although the rates are low, it has been the source of a cash income, and has been appreciated as such. It would seem fair to say that the financial motive for keeping the children has operated largely as a stimulus toward doing a satisfactory job of child-caring.   It has never been the dominant motive, but goes along with a wholesome interest in children.[15]

WHAT ARE THE RESULTS OF FOSTER-HOME PLACEMENT?

What degree of success may we hope for when problem children are placed in foster homes?   Several studies have been made which give us partially satisfying answers.   As is usual in research which deals with such complex human situations, the answers are not always clear-cut and many angles are left untouched, yet a careful consideration of this material throws much light on the use of foster homes in treatment.

A brief description of the research studies which have been made will perhaps be helpful in orienting our thinking.   The earliest study is one made by the State Charities Aid Association of New York, under the direction of Miss Sophie Theis.[16] Although strictly speaking this is a study of 910 dependent rather than problem children, actually we find that this term is somewhat misleading and that it deals to a considerable extent with children who were conduct problems.   These children were placed in the years following 1898, and the criterion for their inclusion in the study was that they should have reached the age of 18 by January, 1922, when the survey was begun.   The median age at the time of placement was 9 years. Of the whole group of children 35 per cent were under 5, 21 per cent between 5 and 10, 38 per cent between 10 and 15, and 6 per cent over 15 at time of placement.   The purpose of the study was not to follow their adjustment during the time of placement, but to see how they turned out as adults.   Although the children are spoken of as "adopted" children, they are for the most part foster-home placements, less than one-third of them being legally adopted.

By far the most complete research into outcomes of foster placement was the one conducted in Boston by Dr. Healy and his associates, to which reference has already been made.[17] They made and followed 501 placements of difficult and delin-

[15] Rogers, *op. cit.*, pp. 23–24.   [16] Theis, *op. cit.*   [17] Healy, *op. cit.*

quent children and analyzed the results in detail. It is a pioneering study in the field of treatment evaluation and supplies much of our most valuable knowledge in regard to the efficacy of foster-home treatment.

Another landmark of scientific evaluation is the study of the treatment of delinquency made by the Gluecks.[18] The controversy aroused by its discouraging findings has not often been equaled in the clinical and social work field. While few of the delinquents were treated in foster homes, there is some data which has a bearing on our interest.

A particularly satisfying study because of its investigation of several new angles of the problem is the one made by Miss Hopkins and Miss Haines of one hundred children selected for placement in 1927 by the Institute for Juvenile Research. They give a number of facts about the homes from which the children came, the results of placement, and the results with a group of children for whom placement was recommended but not carried out.

Special aspects of foster placement are dealt with in other studies. Professor Frank N. Freeman and his associates, in an extremely careful study conducted in Illinois which might well be a model for research methods, have investigated the influences of foster-home care upon intelligence. While their primary interest was to separate the influence of heredity from that of environment, their results interest us because they indicate from another angle the effects of foster-home treatment.[19] In the Child Study Department, Rochester S.P.C.C., Miss Barker and Mr. Rappaport studied the outcome of two years of foster-home care for 46 girls who were sexual delinquents.[20] They compared this group with a group of 45 girls who were

[18] Glueck, S., and Glueck E. T. *One Thousand Juvenile Delinquents.* Cambridge, Mass.: Harvard University Press, 1934.

[19] Freeman, Frank N., Holzinger, Karl J., and Mitchell, B. C. *The Influence of Environment on the Intelligence School Achievement and Conduct of Foster Children.* Twenty-Seventh Yearbook of the National Society for the Study of Education, part 1, pp. 103–217. Bloomington, Ill.: Public School Publishing Company, 1928.

[20] Barker, Margaret, and Rappaport, Mitchell. "Community Placement as a Treatment Policy for Sex-Delinquent Girls," *Mental Hygiene,* vol. 18 (April, 1934), pp. 218–232.

sent to institutions.   Other studies of the results of child-placing work have been made by students of the Smith College School of Social Work, under the direction of Miss Helen Witmer.

In general we may say that the results of these studies indicate that foster-home placement is successful in bringing about a normal adjustment in a majority of cases.   There are only a few special groups in which less than half of the children do well, and in some groups success is achieved in all but 5 per cent of the cases.   Our main interest, however, is not in learning the general success or failure of foster care, but in knowing what factors make success or failure likely.   Consequently we shall examine a number of items which seem to have a significant relationship to the outcome of foster-home placement.

Seriousness of the Child's Behavior as Related to Success.   If we accumulate the data from the studies mentioned we find that treatment in a foster home is definitely less successful as the child's behavior tends toward confirmed antisocial acts. There is a rather interesting progression in which we find that children who present only personality or habit problems make a better adjustment than children who have been apprehended in a first delinquency or whose delinquent behavior has not yet taken them to court.   In turn we find that this group shows a higher rate of success than confirmed delinquents who have been in court for repeated offenses.   Some of the data on which these statements are based appears in the accompanying table. As will be seen from the last three items of the table, the total group of problem and delinquent girls in Healy's study makes a better adjustment than one sub-group for which figures are given, the group of girls who are sex delinquents.   This bears out the statement that the more confirmed or serious the misbehavior, the less the chance of success.   The group studied by Barker and Rappaport, though defined as an almost identical group in problem, makes a somewhat better showing.   This may be due to differences in other factors as will be brought out later.

DEGREE OF BEHAVIOR DIFFICULTY AND ITS RELATIONSHIP TO
SUCCESS IN FOSTER HOME

Author		No.	Success (per cent)	Failure (per cent)	Comments
Levine [21]	Children who exhibited no behavior or personality problems	19	100	0	Jewish Home Finding Society
Healy [22]	Non-delinquent children, personality and habit problems......	87	90	10	Placed by private agencies
Hopkins & Haines [23]	Behavior and personality problems......	58	79	21	Institute for Juvenile Research. Six additional cases indeterminate outcome
Gundlach & Phillips [24]	Behavior and personality problems......	40	73	27	New England Home for Little Wanderers
Healy	Delinquents — first offenders..........	61	82	18	Placed by private agencies
Healy	Delinquents — not taken to court......	120	75	25	Placed by private agencies
Healy	Delinquents — repeated offenders....	191	64	36	Placed by private agencies
Healy	All problem and delinquent girls.......	167	75	25	Placed by private agencies
Healy	Girls who are sex delinquents..........	46	61	39	Placed by private agencies
Barker & Rappaport [25]	Girls who are sex delinquents..........	46	80	20	Rochester S.P.C.C.

[21] Levine, Rae. "Foster Children: The Jewish Home Finding Society and the Institute for Juvenile Research," *Smith College Studies in Social Work*, vol. 6, no. 1 (September, 1935), p. 58. (This group is too small for serious consideration, but its total success is in line with expectations.)

[22] The figures cited in this table from Healy's study are based on material from Tables 11 and 19, Appendix C, *Reconstructing Behavior in Youth*.

[23] Hopkins and Haines, *op. cit.*, p. 123.

[24] Gundlach and Phillips. "Problem Children in the New England Home for Little Wanderers," *Smith College Studies in Social Work*, vol. 6, no. 1 (September, 1935), p. 53.

[25] Barker and Rappaport, *op. cit.*, p. 223.

It should be noted that while more extreme or confirmed conduct problems militate against success, there is a surprising degree of favorable outcome in all these groups.   Even seriously delinquent boys show a high rate of success in such placements, and girls who are sexually delinquent, the group which the average agency and community are most ready to "send away," show a ratio of 60–80 per cent success.   All of these studies prove clearly that there is no type of behavior which cannot be treated in the foster-home environment.   This fact has become a commonplace of clinical knowledge, yet it is still true that agency conservatism, as well as community attitudes and tradition, keep us from utilizing foster care in many instances.   The fear that the girl who has had sex experience will continue her behavior and become pregnant and that the boy who is steeped in sex interests will be a teacher of other youngsters is still likely, in many instances, to keep such children from the opportunities of foster care.

"*Abnormal Mentality and Personality.*"   Dr. Healy in his study makes much of the fact that children diagnosed by the psychiatrist as of abnormal mentality or peculiar personality have much less chance of success in foster homes.   In fact, of the whole group of 102 children so classified and placed by private child-placing agencies, only 46 per cent are successful, whereas of children of "normal" mentality 87 per cent are successful.   When we attempt to analyze this abnormal group further we find that it is a conglomeration of very diverse elements.

Nearly half of the group are so-called peculiar personalities: "cases of excessive stubbornness, bad temper, sullenness, grudgefulness, moodiness, etc." [26]   It seems obvious that the decision as to what is "excessive" must be a very subjective one.   Especially is this evident when we discover that the following descriptions apply to "problems of personality" which are not abnormal and which in 97 per cent of the cases are solved by placement: "stubborn, unmanageable, very disobedi-

[26] Healy *et al., op. cit.,* p. 70.

ent," "excessive temper," "moody spells," and "excessive interest in sex." [27]

The next largest proportion of this "abnormal" group is composed of psychopathic personalities in which are grouped various instabilities, never defined, and "possibly inherited." [28] Still another grouping is the constitutionally inferior personality, children who, though possessing normal mental capacity, "are characterized by lack of stamina to meet difficulties; they evade or run away from unpleasant situations." Still another small sub-group shows temporary instabilities during adolescence. The five psychotic children in the group are also classified here.

In addition to these rather vaguely defined instabilities, Healy includes in his abnormal group three types of difficulty more specifically organic, post-encephalitics, epileptics, and children of "traumatic constitution" who show various unstable traits associated with severe head injuries. This group is a very small one, and on the whole prognosis is poor.

We cannot, of course, compare these children which Dr. Healy and his associates classify as of abnormal mentality and personality with any other group, because the bulk of the classification is based on subjective criteria. It seems fair, however, to draw two conclusions from the study of these hundred children who were by and large so unsuccessful under foster care. In the first place the earlier conclusion seems reinforced, that the more confirmed or excessive the patterns of misbehavior, the less likely is success. In the second place children who exhibit personality instabilities and conduct disorders which are in part due to hereditary or constitutional defect are not hopeful subjects for foster-home treatment. Thus epileptic traits or psychotic tendencies, or even psychopathic trends, all of which are likely to be associated with similar tendencies in the ancestry, make foster-home prognosis poor. Also the brain injury cases, whether due to disease or accident, are unlikely to be successful. All of this is quite natural, if we think in terms of the fundamental factors which foster-home placement

[27] Healy et al., op. cit., p. 73.   [28] Healy et al., op. cit., p. 70.

changes. It alters the family environment and the social and cultural and educational surroundings, but it can change but little the constitution with which the child is endowed by heredity, and can have small influence on deep-seated organic defects due to injury or disease. Consequently behavior which arises from hereditary or organic sources is much less likely to be helped by foster care. It is of interest, however, that even as high a proportion as 46 per cent were aided in this way.

Intelligence — How is it Involved? There are two questions in regard to the relationship between intelligence and outcome of foster care. The first is, to what extent is intelligence correlated with successful placement? The second is almost the reverse, to what extent does satisfactory foster-home placement improve intelligence? An answer to the second question can be much more definite. Freeman's study approached this problem in several ways, though mention of one will suffice here, since his results were consistent throughout. One group of 74 children was located who had been tested before placement while living in inadequate home environments, and retested after some years in adoption or foster homes.[29] It was found that of this group the half which had gone into foster homes above the median in economic and cultural standards made significant gains in intelligence ratings. This amounted to an average increase of 5.3 points in I.Q. Since during the years which elapsed between the two tests some decrease in I.Q. would be expected (due to the faulty standardization of the Stanford-Binet test), Freeman calculates a suitable correction, and concludes that the real increase in I.Q. amounts to 5.3 plus 5.1 or a total of over 10 points in I.Q. The children who went to foster homes below the median in culture made a much smaller gain in intelligence, or, an average increase of .1 in I.Q., to which should be added the correction of 5.1. Freeman's study also shows that, when the whole group is redivided on an age basis, those who were in the foster homes during the earlier period of their lives, approximately during

[29] Freeman *et al., op. cit.,* pp. 116–120.

the period from 6 to 10, made an increased rating of 10.3 points in I.Q., while those whose period in the foster home was roughly from 10 to 14 achieved an increase of only 4.7 points in I.Q., both of these results being corrected figures.

There are other studies which support Freeman's conclusion and still others in progress which are endeavoring to measure how much a satisfactory foster-home environment from infancy on can improve the intelligence level. In the case of children placed in foster homes because of behavior problems, where placement is usually made after the age of 6, the following statement sums up our present knowledge. The child who is removed from an inadequate, culturally limited home and placed in a home of better cultural and intellectual standards is likely to show a slight but significant increase in intelligence, this change being greater the younger the child. Rather rarely, however, will this change be sufficient to change a child from one category of mentality to another, i.e. from borderline to dull normal, or from dull normal to average.

As regards the other question, the extent to which intelligence is associated with placement success, our information is meager. In the first place a strongly selective factor enters in, since few children of defective or borderline mentality are placed in foster homes. In our own clinic the figures on a group of 292 problem children show that of the mentally defective children only 7 per cent were recommended for foster-home care, while 21 per cent of the borderline group, 39 per cent of the dull normal group, 42 per cent of the average group, and 63 per cent of the mentally superior children were so recommended.[30] Obviously only the more stable and promising children of the very low intelligence levels are given the opportunity of foster-home placement, so that the level of success should be rather high with this selected group.

That this seems to be true is indicated by Healy's figures, where 14 (70 per cent) of the 20 mental defectives placed by private agencies were successful.[31] The 29 defectives placed

[30] Rogers, Carl R. "Three Surveys of Treatment Measures Used with Children," *American Journal of Orthopsychiatry* (January, 1937), p. 51.

[31] Healy *et al.*, *op. cit.*, Table 16, p. 309.

by public agencies were much less successful, as will be mentioned later. Healy does not give a complete mentality classification, but mentions that of those with superior mentality 80 per cent were successful.[32]

Barker and Rappaport found that in their group of girls with problems of sexual delinquency there was a slight tendency for success to be associated with lower intelligence, a fact which they attributed to the selective influence already mentioned. Gundlach and Phillips endeavored to investigate the question, but their groups of dull and bright children differed in age and sex as well as in mentality, so that various factors may have influenced their inconclusive results, which showed approximately the same degree of failure in both groups.

The most suggestive data comes from the study by Hopkins and Haines. They find, as shown in the accompanying table, a definite tendency for the average group to be more successful than either the bright or dull groups. Numbers are negligible, however, in the superior group, and the study needs much more verification.

INTELLIGENCE AS ASSOCIATED WITH FOSTER-HOME SUCCESS [33]

	Success		Failure	
	No.	Per cent	No.	Per cent
Children with I.Q.'s under 80.....................	12	26	7	58
I.Q.'s 80–110	33	71	3	25
I.Q.'s 110 and over	1	3	2	17
	46	100	12	100

Clinical experience would suggest that, as in school behavior and in other similar areas, success in foster-home placement is most closely associated with average intellectual endowment, while difficulties multiply for the child who is seriously subnormal or for the very superior child. There are plenty of instances, of course, of very dull boys, even mental defectives,

[32] Healy *et al., op. cit.,* p. 65.   [33] Hopkins and Haines, *op. cit.,* pp. 125–126.

who have made a moderate and harmless adjustment in simple rural foster homes, but for the most part the demands of the home and the community are too much for the child of defective or borderline mentality, and misbehavior is almost sure to result.   To a lesser degree the superior child is apt to chafe under restrictions imposed by foster parents who may not be as intellectually gifted and who, in addition, are "not my own folks."   There is need for much more research in this field to discover accurately the relationship which exists between intelligence level and foster-home success.

Age as a Factor.   We may tabulate the data from the two studies which have investigated the extent to which age is associated with the results of care in a foster home.   The steadily rising rate of failure as the placement is made at an older age is obvious.   It is quite evident that if we are to deal with difficult tendencies through foster care, the earlier the child is placed the more hopeful the outcome.

RELATIONSHIP OF AGE TO SUCCESS IN FOSTER HOME

Author		No.	Success %	Failure %	Comments
Theis [34]	Dependent and problem children placed under the age of five..............	271	86	14	90 per cent of this group had satisfactory relationship with foster parents
Healy [35]	Delinquent children placed at ages 5 to 8............	38	82	18	Placed by private agencies
Theis	Dependent and problem children placed at ages 5 to 18...................	526	73	27	About 40 per cent had satisfactory relationships with foster parents
Healy	Delinquent children placed at ages 13 to 18	124	60	40	Placed by private agencies

It would be a mistake, however, to assume that the better results of earlier placing are due entirely to the fact that in the younger child conduct patterns are not so deeply fixed.   This

[34] Theis, *op. cit.*, Table 57, p. 227.
[35] Healy *et al.*, *op. cit.*, Appendix C; Table 14, p. 308.

may be a part of the explanation, but clinical experience suggests another reason. The young child, transplanted into a foster home, finds it relatively easy to take over the foster parents as his own. To these people he forms genuine emotional attachments, responds to them with the same ambivalent reactions of dependence and desire for freedom which he would normally show to his own parents. The foster home forms for him a true family environment. In the case of the older child, this is rarely true. He is not emotionally free to regard these people as his parents. He is, through some combination of circumstances, living with them or, as it is more accurately described, "boarding" with them, but they are not his parents, and he does not consistently regard them as such. This situation is indicated by the figures given by Miss Theis [36] that, of the children who were placed at ages under five, 90 per cent were rated as having formed thoroughly satisfactory relationships with their foster parents, while of the group placed after the age of twelve, only 30 per cent were so rated. Of these older children the relationship was entirely unsatisfactory in 25 per cent of the cases, and temporarily satisfactory in 45 per cent. This latter group was reasonably contented in the foster home, but never formed any lasting or deep emotional tie with the foster parents.

With the older child, in other words, the foster home changes his social environment, but only partially changes his family environment. He is living in a new dwelling, but his emotional ties, positive or negative, are to his own family, and only rarely to the new pair of adults with whom he is living. Frequently among children's agencies, we find a laudable desire to aid an older boy or girl who has never known any degree of emotional security in his own home. While the child's need is for affection, it does not mean that he will necessarily find the security or affection which he needs in a foster home. The chance is indeed rather slim. As will be pointed out in the following chapter, the security which such children crave can probably never be satisfied by a parent-person, but must be partially

[36] Theis, *op. cit.*, Table 57, p. 227.

satisfied by security in group approval, and in other situations where they can gain some substitute emotional response or recognition.

Hereditary Defects and their Influence.   Entirely aside from the continuing interest in the problem of hereditary versus environmental influences, it is important to know, in planning treatment for the individual child, whether a poor heredity reduces the chance of success.   The very inadequate data which we have indicates that there is less chance of successful adjustment in the case of children who come from poor hereditary stock, though the difference in results is not especially striking.   Theis studied a group of children whose parents were considered, by community standards, to be of poor or inferior mental ability.   Of this group 68 per cent proved capable of making a good adjustment following foster-home placement, although their ability to absorb education was poor, two-thirds of them failing to complete the eighth grade.   On the other hand, of children whose parents were known to have "good mental ability," 80 per cent were successful in foster homes.   As in all such studies, this is not purely a study of heredity since the children of the inferior parents had in a majority of the cases lived with these parents for five years or more and hence were subjected to an unsuitable environment. The authors of the Boston study tend to make light of the hereditary factor, commenting as follows: "What is ordinarily called poor heredity plays little part, then, compared to other factors in the situation." [37]   Their figures, as will be observed in the table, scarcely justify such optimism.   For purposes of making a more accurate comparison, these figures refer only to children whose family or relatives show diagnosed instances of mental disease, mental defect, or epilepsy.   The figures regarding alcoholism and crime in the family are omitted, because they would be regarded as doubtfully hereditary.   The cases cited are those placed by private agencies only, in order to rule out extraneous factors relating to skill of placement, as will be explained later.

[37] Healy *et al.*, *op. cit.*, p. 250.

RELATIONSHIP OF HEREDITARY DEFECT TO FOSTER–HOME SUCCESS

Author		No.	Success (per cent)	Failure (per cent)	Comments
Theis [38]	Children of mentally inferior parents..........	143	68	32	
Theis	Children of parents with good mental ability.....	74	80	20	
Healy [39]	Children whose parents, grandparents, uncles, aunts of siblings show diagnosed cases of mental disease or defect, or epilepsy.................	146	67	33	Private-agency placement
Healy	Children whose heredity was without known defect...................	74	82	18	Private-agency placement

In connection with these figures it is well to recall the discussion relating to the various types of abnormality of personality, some of which are undoubtedly due to hereditary influences. All in all it is safe to conclude that a defective heredity, while by no means a bar to successful placement, is likely to reduce the chance of success.

A brief picture of a child whose instability, probably inherited, has stood in the way of foster-home success is Donald, whose history was first reported by the author in 1933.

"UNSTABLE"

When Donald was three years old, his mother was committed to the State Hospital with the diagnosis of dementia praecox, and he was placed in a foster home. He did not remain long in this home, although his second placement lasted for more than two years. Then followed a rapid succession of homes, seven in all, before Donald was seven years old. In every case he was removed primarily because of his persistent enuresis, which had been a problem ever since infancy. He was also mischievous, moody, and sulky. Masturbation was reported as a problem in several homes, particularly in one where Donald seemed to prefer to sit

[38] Theis, *op. cit.*, p. 140 and Table 63, p. 232.
[39] Healy *et al.*, *op. cit.*, material from Appendix C; Table 22, pp. 311–312.

by himself for long periods. He never made friends, and was disliked and teased by other children because of his pompous behavior.

It was at the age of seven that Donald was seen in the clinic. A psychological examination indicated average mentality, ruling out lack of intelligence as a factor. Donald's outstanding need, it was felt, was his need of security, so necessary for every child but especially important in a youngster of his instability. It was this which led to his placement in the Thompson home, in the hopes that he might find there something of the stability which his other homes had lacked.

It has been four years since Donald entered this home. At first he sulked when he could not have his own way, and never retaliated when imposed upon. Gradually he acquired more "spunk," and soon really enjoyed playing with the other boys. He took part in the routine of housework, although he was never thorough or quick. In school his work was a failure at first, and is still very poor, largely because of Donald's extreme slowness. He does three problems while the rest of the class do twenty.

In other respects his behavior has not greatly improved. In playing games, he is still insistent on having his own way, or he "won't play." The boys at home tolerate this somewhat, but at school he is not well liked. He responds well to praise, but becomes sullen and "shut in" when scolded. Mrs. Thompson, like previous foster mothers, feels that Donald is a "peculiar" child. He bears an air of injury and always feels that he is slighted and discriminated against. When all the boys are given a piece of candy, Donald feels sure the other boys have the larger pieces. He always feels someone is picking on him or blaming him in spite of the fact that he recognizes the security of this home. Indeed the choicest description of the quality of the Thompson home we have from his lips. Said another boy scornfully to Donald, "You might think you belonged here." Don replied, "I do."

He is the one boy in the group who has failed to catch the cheerful frankness of the home atmosphere and make it his own attitude. At a recent clinic contact he still showed the same defensiveness which has always characterized him. He was unwilling to admit any failings on his own part, and showed great concern over very trivial things. He claimed his birthdate was "all mixed up," although this confusion proved to be a discrepancy of ten days.

It is his enuresis, however, which is the outstanding failure. While not as persistent as when Donald first went to the home, it is far from cured. Charts, rewards, surprises, washing of bed clothing, have all been tried for periods of months at a time. The medical clinic has found no organic cause for the enuresis and has tried pills, and diets, and restriction of fluids. They even experimented by injecting sterile water into Donald's arms, accompanied by much powerful suggestion to the effect that this was a new medicine which would surely cure his bed-wetting. None of these methods have helped any more than the spankings and whippings which were the "treatment" for enuresis in some of Don's earlier homes.[40]

Five more years have gone by since this report was written. Two foster-home changes have been necessary. Donald is nearing eighteen, a boy of sour disposition and poor social adjustment. He is not vocationally planful, though handicapped in his work efforts by developing gastric ulcer. After fifteen years of foster-home experience, we still have an apathetic, peculiar child, who is making only a passive and fundamentally unsuccessful adjustment.

The Child's Attachment to His Own Family. Although it is not a factor which has been studied statistically, the emotional bond between the child and his own family is a most significant element in determining whether or not his adjustment will be aided through foster placement. In the rush of enthusiasm for foster care which was evident several years ago, children were frequently removed from obviously unsuitable homes, in order that their incipient delinquent trends might be overcome through the wholesome environment of normal family life in a foster home. In an important group of these cases, the children not only failed to adjust, but gave evidence of an extremely strong tendency to return to their own homes, thus setting up new problems of defiance and runaway behavior with which the agency had to deal. A succession of such experiences has led to a much more careful evaluation of the factor at present under discussion, the child's attachment to his own family.

Our experience would indicate that, where a child is free to

[40] Rogers, Carl R. "A Good Foster Home — Its Achievements and Limitations," *Mental Hygiene* (January, 1933), pp. 31–32.

form new parental attachments, likelihood of foster-home adjustment is greatly increased.   If he is unhappy or rejected at home, or the victim of fierce competition with his siblings, he may settle contentedly into a new foster home in which these irritating situations do not exist.   If his parents are removed by death or imprisonment or illness, so that the need of foster care is an obvious part of reality, then too the child can emotionally accept such care and respond to it.

On the other hand, where there exists in the child a strong emotional tie to parents who are willing to keep him, there is a barrier against successful placement which many good social workers have endeavored in vain to break down.   This applies to children who are removed from home as delinquents and placed in foster homes.   If they look upon placement as punishment, which they are likely to do in spite of a careful interpretation on the part of court and agency as to its therapeutic function, and if their sole desire is to return home as soon as possible, foster placement has little effect.   The author recalls several instances of delinquent boys who, after a period of foster-home placement, have endeavored to prove to the social worker and the clinician that they have "a good record" and consequently should be allowed to go home.   In such cases the grave question is whether they should ever have been placed at all.

This point is particularly clear in dealing with children who are not themselves behavior problems, but whose families are so far below the community norms of morality or cleanliness or child care that removal has been made by the court.   In such instances, where the child is strongly bound to his inadequate parents, placement is fraught with risks.   The child can admit no fault in his parents and wishes to be with them.   Attempts to persuade him to the contrary only make him more defensive as regards his parents, and more antagonistic to the agency and community which has brought about the separation.   Most child-placing agencies could name children whose problems have been increased and intensified by this type of situation.

It should also be noted that the child's attachment to his parents is not influenced to any appreciable degree by community norms of behavior. The mother may keep a disorderly house, or the father be a confirmed drunkard or criminal, and still hold the child's affection to an extreme degree. This raises many questions regarding the removal of a child from his own parents, questions which will be discussed in a later chapter.

Certainly this whole question of emotional attachments has much to do with the failure or success of foster placement, and is probably of as much importance as the factor of age at time of placement. Where the child feels a strong affection for his own parents, it is difficult for him genuinely to accept new foster parents. This difficulty may be increased by frequent visits with his parents or frequent letters from them, or by any circumstance which confirms his feeling that the agency is holding him against his will. If, for example, he runs away and goes to his own home, only to be removed a second time from parents who wish to keep him, real foster placement becomes almost an impossibility. On the other hand, even where there is a strong bond of affection, the child may accept foster placement if his own parents recognize the need for it, co-operate in making the plan, and give their approval to the placement. This observation holds many clues for the case worker.

Social Agency Skill as a Factor in Foster-Home Success. To anyone who has ever dealt at firsthand with children's problems, it is obvious that such treatment as placement in a foster home depends for its success not only on factors within the child, but on the skill and ability and resources of the case worker, who must select the proper home, interpret the placement to the child and to the parents and the foster parents, and guide and assist in the continuing process of adjustment. Fortunately we have data bearing on the importance of this point from the Boston study. The several private child-placing agencies which co-operated in the research had at their disposal more adequate funds, better trained workers, better home-finding facilities, than the two public agencies, the State Division of Child Guardianship and the Juvenile Court. Figures showing the degree of success in the total number of cases placed by the two groups, public and private, have little meaning, because the public agencies had a larger proportion of delinquents and a smaller proportion of seriously unstable children than the private agencies had, thus confusing the issue.   If, however, we take specific and comparable groups, the difference in results is striking, as is evident in the accompanying table.

RELATIONSHIP OF AGENCY SKILL TO SUCCESS [41]

Group	Placing Agency	No.	Success (per cent)	Failure (per cent)	Comments
Court delinquents....	Private	132	63	37	The private-agency group contained a larger proportion of children of abnormal mentality and personality
Court delinquents....	Public	118	52	48	
Delinquents of normal mentality..........	Private	154	85	15	This would seem to be the fairest available comparison
Delinquents of normal mentality	Public	91	53	47	
Mental defectives, delinquent and non-delinquent............	Private	20	70	30	
Mental defectives, delinquent.............	Public	29	52	48	

While these figures can only be suggestive, the indication is clear that with the same group of children a better agency may be 10 to 30 per cent more successful than a more poorly equipped agency.   The difference between the worst type of child-placing agency and the best would certainly be greater.

[41] The figures for this table are from Healy *et al.*, *op. cit.*, Table 19, p. 310; Table 27, p. 316; and the figures regarding mental defectives from a comparison of Table II, p. 307, with Table 26, p. 315.

Undoubtedly it is not only the professional equipment of the agency which causes such discrepant results, but also the personality and effectiveness of the individual worker. This conclusion is suggested by the findings of the Gluecks, who point out the decided difference in results obtained by different probation officers with their juvenile charges, although the groups of probationers were quite comparable.[42] Clinical experience with various workers in children's agencies leaves no doubt that the same results would obtain in the field of foster care.

The End Results of Foster Care. What of the final outcomes of foster-home placement? What becomes of the children if and when they return to their own homes? Questions such as these are of vital importance but with our present information are relatively unanswerable. The study conducted by Miss Theis was, to be sure, a study of final outcomes, made when the children were adult. It is not typical of present placement methods, however, since the great majority of children never returned to their own homes, but remained in foster homes or launched out independently. It does indicate that a satisfactory life adjustment is made in three-fourths of the cases. The Boston research also has some data to add, since 159 of their cases were discharged from foster care for a long enough period to make a follow-up study.[43] (The length of time following discharge is not specified.) Of these 71 per cent were doing well in the community, 29 per cent failing. Division of the group shows that of 94 children who were successful during placement, 88 per cent are doing well; of 65 children who were failures during placement, 48 per cent are doing well. This last figure is of interest. The authors suggest that it may represent a group of children who learned something during placement, despite their failure, or a group which has become more stable as they matured. It is also possible of course that this 48 per cent represents in part those children who should

---

[42] Glueck and Glueck, *op. cit.*, p. 177.

[43] Healy *et al.*, *op. cit.*, Tables 37, 38, pp. 323-324.

not have been treated in foster homes, and who make a better adjustment in their own homes.

In general the findings of these two studies, while inadequate as final answers to the question, seem to warrant some assurance that the favorable results of placement carry over into later community life. Directly contrary to them are some of the facts collected by the Gluecks in their investigation of juvenile delinquency. Of the thousand delinquent boys studied, 41 were placed in foster homes or with relatives.[44] Of these only 6, or 15 per cent, remained non-delinquent during a five-year period following the close of treatment. The other 35 were arrested one or more times during this period. While this foster-home group shows less recidivism than the group as a whole (85 per cent compared with 88.2 per cent for the total), it is a very sharp contrast to the comfortable conclusions of the other two research studies.

The only explanations which would seem in any way to account for this sharp discrepancy are the following. The court delinquents were one of the less successful groups in the Boston study, 57 per cent of them making good adjustments in foster homes. The period of placement for the boys studied by Glueck was very short, in a number of instances less than six months. The measure of success for the Glueck cases, freedom from arrest, is a strict one, since some of these boys may have been making a generally satisfactory adjustment in spite of one arrest. Finally, the delinquents, if returned to their own homes, would be returned to the very areas of the city where every social influence would tend to draw them again into delinquency.

Whether these speculations are the real explanation or not cannot be determined until we have further and more conclusive studies on which to base our judgment. In any event the facts which we have reinforce clinical opinion by indicating that the true and lasting success of foster care is determined not only by the various factors we have already described, but by the degree of intelligent skill shown in transplanting the

[44] Glueck and Glueck, *op. cit.*, p. 173.

child back into his own family, or into the community on a self-supporting basis. Ordinarily this means a skilled rehabilitation of the child's family or relatives to a point where they can again take care of him.

WHEN SHALL WE USE FOSTER HOMES AS TREATMENT?

Having completed our review of the elements involved in foster-home care, and of the experience of various clinics and agencies in its use, it may be helpful to turn our information about so as to focus it on the individual child in need of help. When is it advisable, in cases of behavior difficulty, to use care in a foster home as the most likely means of assistance? The very first step in such a decision is to determine whether or not it is wise to remove the child from his own home. This is a matter of such vital importance that the following chapter is devoted to its discussion. If, however, the decision has been made that the child's problems can be better cared for away from home, a foster home should be our first choice, providing the child can succeed there. The reason for such a positive statement is the point raised early in this consideration of placement, that the foster home offers a type of experience most similar to the community experience of later life. Consequently, if we may look for success in placement, we will do well to choose a foster home in preference to other types of care.

We may say that for some types of children, success in foster-home placement is almost a 100 per cent certainty. For other types of children, less skillfully handled, the chance of success may be as low as one in five, a 20 per cent prospect of success. In judging the chances of success for the particular child, we may make use of the factors previously outlined, which are briefly summarized in the accompanying table and somewhat arbitrarily classified as to conditions favorable to successful placement. In regard to any given child, if all the conditions are those classed as favorable, success may almost be guaranteed. Where as many as three of these factors are definitely unfavorable, successful placement is very dubious.

Summarized Criteria for Prognosis in Foster-Home Care

	Favorable	Intermediate	Unfavorable
1. Behavior Patterns	Personality or habit problems only. First antisocial behavior [45]	Early antisocial behavior	Confirmed delinquent behavior. Many confirmed behavior difficulties
2. Age	Under nine years at time of placement	Nine to twelve years inclusive	Placed at thirteen years or over
3. Heredity	Ancestry relatively free of defects mentioned in opposite column	Few or slight hereditary defects as noted in next column	Ancestry in which there are two or more instances of serious and probably hereditary mental disease, epilepsy, extreme neurotic behavior or other severe instabilities in ancestry
4. Stability	Relatively stable disposition, ability to maintain a given course of action	Moderate degree of emotional instability or neurotic tendencies; moderate degree of hyperactivity	Organic instabilities; — epilepsy, post-encephalitic reactions, brain injury reactions. Other instabilities; — psychotic or psychopathic tendencies; highly neurotic behavior; "peculiar" traits; highly erratic and impulsive disposition; extreme physical hyperactivity. Especially unfavorable if coupled with unfavorable hereditary factors

[45] Note that the sort of behavior problem makes little or no difference. Individuals toward whom the community may feel an abhorrence, because of dramatic first delinquencies, may nevertheless be very satisfactory foster-home material.

SUMMARIZED CRITERIA FOR PROGNOSIS IN FOSTER-HOME CARE (*continued*)

Favorable	Intermediate	Unfavorable
5. Attachment to Own Family		
Lacking in emotional security with own parents; rejected or unhappy with own parents; dislike for own family situation	Moderate attachment to own family, coupled with other emotional satisfactions; strong attachment to own family coupled with parental co-operation in placement plan	Strong and devoted affection for own parents and strong bonds of family unity, even though it be a unity against the community. Especially unfavorable if coupled with parental antagonism to foster-home care
6. Intelligence		
Average, dull normal, or superior intelligence	Very superior intelligence; borderline mentality	Defective mentality
7. Skill of Available Placing Agency		
Agency with trained workers, some with psychiatric training, case loads under 60, experienced supervisors. Agency doing selective home-finding and placing, carrying on education of foster parents, paying adequate board rate, carrying on intensive supervision in foster homes, visiting once a month or more as needed. Psychological and psychiatric service available both for diagnosis and treatment	Agencies falling between the two extreme descriptions	Agency with untrained workers and supervisors, case loads over 75, making superficial investigations of foster homes, placing children without careful matching of child and home, paying inadequate board, leaving foster parents to own devices, making infrequent supervisory visits. No psychological or psychiatric service

If, as stated above, as many as three of the factors listed in this table are definitely unfavorable there is probably not much more than one chance in three of success. This does not necessarily mean that foster placement should not be tried, but there should be careful consideration of other means of dealing with the problem, and some plan should be made for dealing with the child if foster-home care, after a reasonable trial, proves to be a failure.

There is no intent that the above classification should be used as a rigid or inflexible means of determining the advisability of placement. It should, however, prove useful in analyzing the facts regarding a particular child, and in basing the decision on the essential rather than on the non-essential considerations. Use of it as a definite scale of judgment would help to determine the weighting which should be given to the various factors, but this has not as yet been done. Its essential accuracy can be partially borne out, however, by noting from the Boston study the results of placement of groups of children who combined three of the unfavorable factors.

DEGREE OF SUCCESS IN PLACEMENT WHEN THREE FACTORS ARE UNFAVORABLE [46]

Group	Unfavorable Factors	No.	Success (per cent)	Failure (per cent)	Comment
Delinquents, of abnormal mentality and personality, placed by public agency...	1, 4, 7	42	21	79	There are probably a few first offenders in this group
Delinquents, over 13, of abnormal mentality and personality.................	1, 2, 4	55	35	65	May contain some first offenders
Repeated offenders, mentally defective, placed by public agency............	1, 6, 7	19	42	58	
Delinquents, over 13, placed by public agency.........	1 (?), 2, 7	60	52	48	There may be some non-delinquents, and certainly some first offenders in this group

[46] Calculated from Healy, *et al.*, *op. cit.*, Table 25, pp. 313–314; Table 14, p. 308; Table 27, p. 316; Table 13, p. 308.

The figures in this table confirm the experience of the author in suggesting that, of the seven factors mentioned, those which deserve the most consideration are the degree of behavior difficulty, the degree of instability in the child, and the skill of the placing agency. Such speculations as these, however, must wait for further proof.

INDIVIDUALIZED TREATMENT THROUGH FOSTER-HOME CARE

It is not the intent of a volume such as this to discuss the methods of carrying out foster-home placement. There are other writings, to which reference is made in the bibliography, which take up in detail the various techniques of the task which the agency and the case worker assume when they accept a difficult child for placement. There are, however, certain features of this work which are of such importance from a treatment point of view that they must be mentioned briefly here.

The Selection of the Home. When the first two steps in placement have been taken, namely the decision to remove the child from his home and the decision that he will respond to foster-home care, the next choice is in regard to the foster home. Many poor choices of foster home are made by conscientious workers because they have not clearly defined the important elements which they wish to find. It is a helpful scheme to outline rather definitely the ideal foster home for the child in question, matching it with the homes available or using it as a guide in the investigation of new homes. The ideal home is rarely found, to be sure, but we are apt to approach it more nearly if our goal is clearly in mind.

Especially in regard to the child who is a behavior problem, it should be born in mind that what is being sought is not merely an adequate environment for physical care, but a total life situation which has within it therapeutic possibilities for this child. The foster home, to be successful, must be not merely a negative experience, keeping the child out of an unwholesome home and away from undesirable social influences.

It must be a positive experience, in which a particular environment, chosen for this particular child, carries within it the elements which will create in the child healthy attitudes toward the foster parents, the social group, and toward himself.

The selection of such an environment begins with such simple choices as the location of the home. Shall it be a farm home, with its greater freedom of activity, more generous outlets for energy, better training in simple manual vocations, and small school group? Shall it be a village or small-town home where the change from urban life is not so extreme, where there are more social opportunities, but little likelihood of gang activity, and where there are school classes of moderate size providing an average degree of competition? Or shall it be an urban home, close to special educational facilities, where more community and health resources are available, and where the child will perhaps be in closer touch with his own family? There are of course no answers to these questions save in terms of the individual child, but they need to be carefully considered.

Due regard should also be given to the cultural level of the home. Some of the most tragic failures in placement result when children of average or less than average ability are placed in homes where superior foster parents endeavor to hold them up to superior standards of behavior and achievement.

Arthur, an attractive twelve year old, was adopted at the age of 3½ into a home where the parents were college graduates, the father engaged in engineering work. The foster parents are people of high ideals, very strictly religious, and anxious for what they regard as "average" achievement. In their endeavor to bring this about they have used more and more pressure, until at the time they came in desperation to the clinic, regarding Arthur as a very "bad" boy, they were insisting that he bring all his books home from school each night in order that they might tutor him in his seventh-grade work, and in addition were keeping him from all movies, most athletics, and refusing to let him associate with the "vulgar" boys whom he tended to choose as friends. They were quite unable to understand why he was lying about his school marks and behavior, stealing from them, and becoming more and more disobedient. The fact that he had only dull normal ability, (an I.Q. of 88) was ample explanation of his difficulty in adjusting to this home.

While this child happens to be an adopted youngster, rather than a boarding placement, the picture could be duplicated in less extreme form in foster-home situations. Over-placement, in which too much is demanded of the child, is perhaps most apt to result in overt-behavior symptoms, but under-placement, in which an able child is not sufficiently stimulated to develop his capacities, is equally poor from a long-time social point of view. The child's own home, and the prospect of his returning to it, should also be an influence in selecting the foster home. If the boy or girl is from a home of strongly foreign culture, and is likely to return home after two or three years, there is a real risk of so Americanizing him that he cannot fit again into his own home or nationality group.

Selection of the Foster Parents. We have already mentioned the type of qualities which, in general, insure the success of foster parents in dealing with children. For the individual child, however, our questions must be more specific. Is he likely to respond better to young parents, who will perhaps be more understanding of adolescent rebelliousness, or will he adjust best to the older individual, of a "motherly" or "fatherly" type? Is this child most likely, judging by past experiences, to form deeper contacts with a father-person or a mother-person? Our decision in this regard will make decided differences in our choice of foster parents. Is this child the emotionally starved individual who needs much demonstration of interest and affection, or is he the type who is socially well adjusted and consequently will find his satisfactions outside the home, making relatively little emotional demand on the foster parents? Does this child need freedom to act and make decisions for himself, or is he the overindulged youngster who primarily needs foster parents who can be consistently firm so that he may learn that there are limits to self-expression?

It goes without saying that to answer such questions intelligently a thorough clinical study of the child's personality and his emotional needs is necessary. It is only on the basis of such a thoroughgoing diagnostic process that an intelligent and effective treatment plan can be made.

Relationship to Other Children.   In planning placement it is particularly important not to reproduce in the foster home the counterpart of irritating sibling situations in the child's own home.   If this is a child who has been extremely jealous of a younger sister, it is folly to place him in a home with a younger foster child. Frequently insecure, affection-starved children need to be placed alone, where they may for a time feel themselves the center of parental attention.   They may begin to learn the give and take processes of social adjustment outside the foster home, rather than in the foster family.   With any youngster whose problems are primarily in the realm of child-parent relationships, we should be cautious about having other children of what might be called a "competing" age in the foster home. Children who are widely different in age may, however, be an asset to the placement situation.   The insecure older girl may be helped by being in a home where there is an infant, or the young boy rejected by his parents may profit by being placed with a 17-year-old.   Let the differences in age be reduced, however, and difficulties are apt to be created.

With the child whose misbehavior has been brought about largely through neighborhood influences, the typical young "gang" delinquent, for example, placement with other lads his own age may be an essential to success, since loneliness and lack of social outlets may cause him to run away if he finds himself the only young person in the home.   Sometimes the theory of "the one rotten apple spoiling the barrel" causes a worker to be fearsome about placing such a delinquent in contact with other children.   While the problem should be given consideration, particularly with sex delinquents, it is easy to exaggerate the risk of "corruption" of other problem children by a delinquent placed in their midst.

In all these decisions we should not be guided too strongly by a goal of all-round adjustment, but rather by the goal of immediate comfortable adjustment.   Occasionally, a worker dealing with a solitary type of child places him in a foster home with several others of his own age, with the aim of molding him into her pattern of well-rounded adjustment.   While this is at times successful it would seem to be a much sounder approach to aim first toward making the child emotionally comfortable in his foster home without competitors. It is as the child acquires confidence in his ability to cope with this easy adjustment that he reaches out independently for wider experiences.

One aspect of the foster-home situation on which many placements come to grief is the presence of the foster parents' own children in the home. It is very rare indeed that placements are successful if the "own" child and the foster child are near enough in age to compete with each other for parental affection. This is not necessarily due to favoritism on the part of the parent for his own child, though of course this occurs. It is often due to the fact that the situation is an impossible one from the point of view of the foster child. No matter how impartial the foster parents may be the child is sure to feel that he is less liked than the "own" child. Each reprimand or criticism is looked upon as proof of this fact, and almost never does the foster child feel genuinely secure in such a home. It is not surprising that in the group of successful foster mothers studied by Miss Dudley, there were almost no "own" children of an age to compete with the foster children.[47]

The foregoing sections illustrate the ways in which the case worker and the clinician, working together, can define the optimum foster-home situation for any particular child. It is also possible to decide in advance which are the most important elements of the picture. With one child a farm home, far removed from his own family, is the absolutely necessary requirement. Other desirable aspects may be waived if the ideal home cannot be found. With another youngster an understanding, strongly masculine foster father with some interest in mechanical contrivances is the prime need, and a home with such a foster father would be desirable whatever its geographical location.

The experience of the agency with which the author has been connected indicates that foster-home replacements, costly both in money and emotional disturbances, can be greatly reduced if this type of carefully planned placement is carried out.

[47] Dudley, *op. cit.*, p. 147.

PLANNING THE TERMINATION OF PLACEMENT

In a great many instances, as records show, placement is carried out on a hand-to-mouth basis, meeting the child's urgent needs as they arise. The agency is then suddenly confronted after some years with the fact that the child is too old for foster-home care and some other plan must be made. The subsequent hasty return of the child to the very situation from which he came leads to the numerous failures in community adjustment which have been previously cited. It should be recognized from the moment that the child is accepted for placement that planning for the termination of care is as necessary as planful selection of the foster-home environment.

In some instances, it will be evident from the first that the child can never return to his own home. If the family unit is completely broken, or parents entirely inadequate or defective, there may be no possible chance of return. In instances of this sort steps may be taken to build up bonds between the child and other relatives, even though at the time there is no possibility of care being given by such relatives. Also the foster-home situation may be so chosen that the child will have a maximum opportunity of staying on through adolescence and obtaining employment in the vicinity.

In the majority of cases, where there is a possibility of return to his own family, this should constitute a goal of treatment work. It is necessary that the agency think in realistic terms in regard to the child's own family. In most cases it is futile to suppose that they can sufficiently solve their problems to reach the same standards as would be set for a foster home. Yet many workers seem to have this in mind as a measuring rod. It is also well to bear in mind that in thinking of the readiness of the family again to care for their child, physical care is probably less important than the degree of normal family life that is possible. Formerly the return home was approved if there was assurance of good physical care and if the family met the conventional moral requirements. It would seem much more important that the emotional qualifications of the home be sound. If the parent-persons give indications of a fairly stable union, or if one parent, living alone, is reasonably well adjusted, or if there is assurance that the child is wanted, and will not be seriously damaged by parental mishandling, then the home may be regarded as ready for the child's return. Consideration must of course be given to the social environment, and to the physical standards of the home, but the emotional atmosphere is the primary point in this issue of rehabilitation.

There are many natural reasons why the agency and the clinic have tended to overlook this important task. In the first place, their interest centers in the child rather than in the family, though there are many indications that the pendulum is swinging away from this child-centered type of work. It is also likely to seem, especially with the child under fourteen or fifteen, that his attachment to his own home is not particularly strong and that consequently we can leave the home out of our area of concentrated effort. It is only as adolescence develops that the boy or girl feels a keener need for linking himself in some human chain which extends from the past to the future. He begins to show interest in relatives, in his ancestry, in knowing something about his birth or paternity, in case these are under a cloud. It is then that we begin to realize, sometimes too late, the supporting social strength that exists in family ties, for which anything else is a poor substitute.

BIBLIOGRAPHY

General Discussion of Foster Care:

Murphy, J. Prentice. "Foster Care for Children," in *Social Work Yearbook 1935*. New York: Russell Sage Foundation, 1935.

Sayles, Mary B. *Substitute Parents*. New York Commonwealth Fund, 1936. 309 p.

Thomas, Dorothy Swaine, and Thomas, William I. *The Child in America*. New York: A. A. Knopf, 1928. 538 p.

Thurston, Henry. *The Dependent Child*. New York: Columbia University Press, 1930. 337 p.

White House Conference on Child Health and Protection. Committee on Socially Handicapped. *Dependent and Neglected Children*, Sec. IV, C-1. New York: D. Appleton-Century Company, 1933. 439 p.

Techniques of Child Placing:

Healy, William, Bronner, Augusta, Baylor, Edith M., and Murphy, J. Prentice. *Reconstructing Behavior in Youth*. New York: A. A. Knopf, 1929. 325 p.

Hewins, Katherine P., and Webster, L. J. *The Work of Child Placing Agencies*. U.S. Children's Bureau Publication no. 171. Washington, D.C.: Government Printing Office, 1927.

U.S. Children's Bureau. *The A.B.C. of Foster Family Care for Children*. Children's Bureau Publication no. 216. Washington, D.C.: Government Printing Office, 1933.

U.S. Children's Bureau. *Foster Home Care for Dependent Children*, Children's Bureau Publication no. 136. Washington, D.C.: Government Printing Office, 1929.

Williamson, Margaretta. *Social Worker in Child Care and Protection*. New York: Harpers, 1931. 485 p.

Research Bearing on Foster Home Placement:

Barker, Margaret, and Rappaport, Mitchell. "Community Placement as a Treatment Policy for Sex-Delinquent Girls," *Mental Hygiene*, vol. 18 (April, 1934), pp. 218–232.

Dudley, Virginia. "Foster Mothers Successful and Unsuccessful," *Smith College Studies in Social Work*, vol. 3, no. 2 (December, 1932), pp. 151–182.

Freeman, Frank N., Holzinger, Karl J., and Mitchell, B. C. "The Influence of Environment on the Intelligence School Achievement and Conduct of Foster Children," *Twenty-seventh Yearbook of the National Society for the Study of Education*, part 1, pp. 103–217. Bloomington, Ill.: Public School Publishing Company, 1928.

Gundlach, Carol, and Phillips, Arlene. "Problem Children in the New England Home for Little Wanderers," *Smith College Studies in Social Work*, vol. 6, no. 1 (September, 1935), pp. 51–54.

Healy, William, Bronner, Augusta, Baylor, Edith M., and Murphy, J. Prentice. *Reconstructing Behavior in Youth*. New York: A. A. Knopf, 1929. 325 p.

Hopkins, Cornelia D., and Haines, Alice R. "A Study of One Hundred Problem Children for whom Foster Care was Advised," *American Journal of Orthopsychiatry*, vol. 1 (January, 1931), pp. 107–128.

Jones, M. E. St. Edward. "Foster Home Care of Delinquent Children," *Social Service Review*, vol. 10, no. 3 (September, 1936), pp. 450–463.

Levine, Rae. "Foster Children: The Jewish Home Finding Society and the Institute for Juvenile Research," *Smith College Studies in Social Work*, vol. 6, no. 1 (September, 1935), pp. 55–60.

Markey, Oscar. "An Evaluation of the Masculinity Factor in Boarding Home Situations," *American Journal of Orthopsychiatry*, vol. 6 (April, 1936), pp. 258–267.

Rogers, Carl R. "A Good Foster Home — Its Achievements and Limitations," *Mental Hygiene*, vol. 15, no. 1 (January, 1933), pp. 21–40.

Theis, Sophie Van S. *How Foster Children Turn Out*. State Charities Aid Association, Publication no. 165. New York, 1924.

Institutional Placement as Treatment for Behavior Problems

As a mode of dealing with problem children and juvenile delinquents, institutional placement has a much longer history than foster-home care. Individual orphanages, whose function has been primarily to care for dependent children, and only incidentally to alter their behavior, can trace their history through more than a century of American life. One of them has attempted an interesting account of its changes during that period.[1] Reformatories and correctional schools for young delinquents in this country originated with the establishment by the "Society for the Reformation of Juvenile Delinquents" of the "House of Refuge" on Randall's Island, New York City, in 1825. This institution, a significant advance in the treatment of child offenders, was torn down as outmoded in 1935, a symbol of the slow rate of change in institutional methods of dealing with children and adolescents.

Partly because these early attempts at reformation were modifications of a penal system, the goal of such institutions has been and in many cases still is a confused one. Punishment is looked upon as almost inevitably a part of the goal, treatment of the child's behavior being in many cases a secondary aim. All too often the two aims are mingled so that moralistic punishments are meted out with the thought that they will in some miraculous fashion improve the behavior of the child, in utter disregard of everything that we have come to know regarding the causation and treatment of behavior. Thus in one institu-

[1] Solenberger, W. E. *One Hundred Years of Child Care in New Haven.* Children's Community Center, New Haven, 1933.

tion, a boy who is found practicing sodomy is required to stay an extra period of six months in the institution, an interestingly medieval approach to the problem. In institutions for the dependent, such as orphanages, this conflict between punitive and treatment goals is not so apparent, though frequently an earlier moralistic approach has been carried over, dominating the more scientific notions of treatment effort which have been permeating the institutional field.

On account of the older historical roots of institutional care, and also because its methods tend to become fixed in the brick and mortar of its institutional plants, there is an enormous range and variety in the institutional treatment given to children. There is no doubt that the difference between the "best" and "worst" children's institution is far greater than between the "best" and "worst" foster home or child-placing agency. There are also, of course, the differences that exist between different types of institutions, the school for the mentally defective, the orphanage, the private school for delinquents with its freedom of policy, and the state or county school for delinquents. Each of these groups might also be further divided into subgroups, a bewildering variety of functions.

In considering some of the elements of this complex situation, we should keep clearly in mind the purpose of this chapter. We should like to determine what the different varieties of institutional care offer to the child with behavior difficulties, and when institutional placement is advisable as a means of treatment. We shall not be concerned with the methods of institutional management and care, except as they affect the child, since several excellent monographs already exist on this topic.[2] Neither shall we concern ourselves with the technical differences between orphanage and industrial school, or between school for defectives and school for delinquents. No attempt will be made to discuss the various detention homes and "study" homes whose functions are primarily diagnostic. It is institutional care as a means of changing juvenile behavior that is our sole interest.

[2] See the list of books in the bibliography on institution management and program.

TYPES OF INSTITUTIONAL TREATMENT

Anyone who is familiar with children's institutions recognizes that treatment policies vary widely, not according to the label of the institution, but according to its viewpoint. At one extreme of this scale of variability we find the institution where children are dealt with *en masse*, where punitive and "moralistic" measures prevail, where enforced discipline and regimentation are evident. At the other end of the scale we find the institution where the primary emphasis is on individualized treatment, and where self-discipline and the development of individual initiative is the goal. Differences of this sort between institutions are sharp and often clearly marked. They are far more important than the minor differences which exist between schools for the dependent, the delinquent, and the defective. Thus the staff of an orphanage with the individualized approach to treatment would find much in common with the staff, of similar viewpoint, of a state school for delinquents; but they could scarcely find a common ground of discussion with staff members of the mass-approach type of institution, even though it were another orphanage. This contrast will be made more plain by picturing in greater detail the kinds of treatment typical of these two main types of institution.

Regimented Treatment. There are a number of graphic accounts of how the disciplinary institution appears to the young delinquent.[3] These are no doubt colored to some extent by emotion, prejudice, or even outright falsehood. To see mass treatment in its average form, as it exists in most of the juvenile correctional institutions and many of the orphanages in this country, one need only turn to the objective, moderately worded description of a state school for boys, as described by research workers of the United States Children's Bureau.[4] Of the five

[3] See for example the account by a young criminal in Shaw, Clifford R., *The Jack Roller*, pp. 47 ff. Chicago: University of Chicago Press, 1930.

[4] Bowler, Alida C., and Bloodgood, R. S. *Institutional Treatment of Delinquent Boys, Part I. Treatment Programs of Five State Institutions.* U.S. Children's Bureau Publication no. 228, pp. 176–211. Washington, D.C.; Government Printing Office, 1935.

institutions they describe, this one makes the fewest gestures toward individualized treatment, but it is probably no better and no worse than most such schools.

The boy who is brought to this school immediately after court hearing, by a sheriff or probation officer, first is asked a few questions by the clerk, then is taken to the quartermaster to receive the uniform which will make him undistinguishable from the other 990 boys in the school, and then has his hair clipped off. It would be difficult to imagine more effective means of submerging the individual boy, with his individual problems, his fear, his rebellion, and his worries, into the mass.

Following two weeks in the receiving cottage the boy is assigned, on the basis of age and size and with no regard to his problems or attitudes, to a "cottage" composed of 70 to 90 boys with a married couple in charge. From this point on almost every aspect of life is routinized and regimented. The groups are up at 6 A.M. Setting-up exercises are followed by breakfast, which according to observers the boys "entered in military line, going to their places and taking their seats on signal in complete silence. They then said grace in unison before the signal to begin eating was given." [5] This is the regular procedure for all meals. In addition to seven hours per day of school and shop training under poorly qualified instructors, there is a period of military drill each day. Everywhere the boys go they march, "long, silent shuffling lines of boys marching two by two about the grounds." In the evening the boys are permitted to read or play games, but there is no talking observed above a whisper. Usually a goodly proportion of the boys are "on line," simply standing on the side of the room as punishment, unable to talk or take part in any activities. For more serious offenses the time is lengthened that the boy must "serve," or corporal punishment may be administered.

As month after month of this automaton existence goes on, minor irritations add themselves to the major ones. Much of the discipline is carried on by boy officers, monitors, who are

<hr>

[5] Bowler and Bloodgood, *op. cit.*, p. 191.

often poorly chosen, and who in any event are very likely to use their position as a means of bullying and intimidating the others.   In one such institution they are known as "P.C.'s," "privileged characters."   Added to their authoritative demands, which are often unfair, is the fact that the boy has nothing which he can feel is his own.   He sleeps in a large dormitory.   His clothes are institution clothes.   His mail, both incoming and outgoing, is read by institution clerks.   He does not even have a locker in which to keep personal possessions. Only in the too-brief periods for sports and athletics is there the slightest possibility of genuine freedom of expression.   It is not surprising that the observers remark that "little or no spontaneous conversation and laughter were observed at any time about the grounds."   Neither is it surprising that they noted "something about the expression on the faces of the boys, sullenness and sometimes fear or hate," which indicated the tensions they were under.

After nine to eighteen months of such regimentation the boy is ready for parole.   No home visit is made, though a perfunctory inquiry is made about the home.   No arrangements are made for returning to school or entering a job.   The chaplain talks to groups of boys who are leaving and urges them to affiliate with a church.   The superintendent also talks to the group and urges them to maintain good records.   The boy is released on parole, going back to the very environment from which he came.   He is now one of 300 boys, scattered over a large section of the state, who report to one parole officer, an individual with no preparation for this type of work.   If, during the year following his release, the boy maintains occasional contacts with the parole officer and if he remains undetected in any delinquency, he is discharged.   He has completed a period of institutional treatment.

There is little need to comment on this whole procedure of "reformation."   Indeed there is little point in describing it save to say that it is common in this country, and that remnants of the viewpoint may be found in almost every institution, no matter how progressive.   Considered from the point of view of the causation of behavior, its influence is entirely bad. No real attempt is made to determine the cause of the boy's delinquency or the ways in which the institution could alter those basic causes. Nothing is done to deal with the boy as a distinctive and individual problem. On the contrary, powerful repressive influences are brought to bear to annihilate every outward sign of difference, no matter what attitudes may be inwardly growing as a result of such treatment. Although the purpose of the institutional period is so to change the boy that he will be capable of making wiser social choices later, every possibility of choice or of personal initiative is minimized or removed, only suddenly to be returned to the boy as he walks out the gate of the institution. The extent to which all individual choice is removed sometimes reaches ludicrous proportions. The author was being shown through an orphanage essentially of this type, and the new plumbing was being exhibited with pride. All the boys lined up to wash before a long trough, while the attendant turned on one central valve which allowed the properly warmed water to run from the spout in front of each boy. Thus even the ritual of washing was standardized, and the simple choices of hot or cold water, or of allowing the water to run for a longer or shorter period, were removed from the child's control.

Successful outcomes in such an institution may arise from several sources. If the boy is a fairly healthy individual from a personality point of view, he may suffer through such an experience and after release throw off to as large an extent as possible its ill effects. He should of course never have entered this or any other institution in the first place. If the boy is mentally low grade, or of a very suggestible and docile sort, he may respond with a moderate degree of comfort to this complete ordering of his life, and may adjust following the institutional period, providing he falls into the hands of individuals who direct him in a social, rather than an anti-social, direction. Finally there may be the occasional boy who is sufficiently terrorized by his experience at the institution that fear keeps him to some extent from anti-social activities. As we shall see, however, there is good evidence that fear is an exceedingly poor long-time motive for behavior.

Results of Such Treatment for Delinquents. We have some knowledge of the outcomes of this type of institutional care, primarily from the records of institutions for delinquents. Healy and Bronner studied a group of Chicago delinquents in 1909–14 and followed their later careers by reinvestigation in 1921–23. Of 420 boys and young men studied by them 311 were committed to institutions and 109 were not. The institutions were roughly comparable to the institution described. Discipline was strict, parole methods almost non-existent. It was discovered that of the boys committed to institutions 70 per cent were failures in later adjustment, while of the group not committed only 34 per cent were failures.[6] As Healy points out, we must recall that the more difficult offenders would be committed, hence we might expect a lower rate of success in this group. The extreme difference lends some weight, however, to the hypothesis that the institution actually intensified the boys' problems rather than reduced them. This is further borne out by the fact that the institutional group tends to "graduate" into further institutional placement. Of Healy's group of 311 institutional boys, 55 per cent appeared in adult court once or more, and 43 per cent were committed to adult correctional institutions one or more times. The group of boys not committed contributed a much smaller proportion, only 21 per cent of them being committed to adult institutions. The full extent of this finding is reinforced when we know that the 157 adults in institutions have been committed 364 times to juvenile institutions and 272 times to institutions for adults, an average of four commitments apiece. It seems quite plain that, for a certain group, institutional treatment has merely fitted and trained them for further institutional care.

[6] Healy, William, and Bronner, Augusta F. *Delinquents and Criminals, Their Making and Unmaking*, p. 73. New York: Macmillan, 1926. The corresponding figures for girls are not as outstanding, but indicate the same trend. Of 169 girls committed to institutions 54 per cent were failures, while of the 86 not committed, only 29 per cent were failures.

The study made by the Gluecks of inmates of the Massachusetts Reformatory bears out Healy's findings, although it deals
with somewhat older youths, who averaged 20 years in age at
time of commitment.   Of this group of 422 whose post-institutional record was traceable, 73 per cent had been rearrested
during the five-year period, and 6 per cent more were known
to have committed crimes for which they had not been apprehended.   Only 21 per cent had remained free, so far as known,
from criminal activities.

Probably the best and most recent study of the results of such
institutional care is the follow-up study of 751 boys made by
the United States Children's Bureau.[7]   These boys were under
care in five state institutions for varying lengths of time during
the period extending roughly from 1918 to 1924.   The follow-up
investigation was made in the years 1930–32, after the boys had
been discharged from all institutional supervision for a period
of at least five years.   Of the total group of 623 boys whom it
was possible to locate, 32 per cent were rated as making a generally successful adjustment in their employment, their social
adjustment, and their conduct.   A second group representing
33 per cent of the total were making a doubtful adjustment,
giving the investigators some uncertainty as to whether society
might have further trouble with them.   Slightly more than
one-third of the group, or 35 per cent, were definitely failures
in adjustment, having come into further conflict with the law
and adjusting poorly in other ways.[8]   Expressing the results
in terms of recidivism rather than in ratings of adjustment, we
find that 66 per cent of the group had been arrested one or more
times following their discharge, 58 per cent had been convicted
of some crime, and 42 per cent had been committed to penal
institutions because of their post-parole delinquencies.[9]   From
either of these modes of expressing results it is clear that there
is only about one-third of the group who have succeeded in

---

[7] Bowler, Alida C., and Bloodgood, R. S.   *Institutional Treatment of Delinquent Boys,
Part II.   A Study of 751 Cases.*   U.S. Children's Bureau Publication no. 230.   Washington, D.C.: Government Printing Office, 1936.

[8] *Ibid.*, p. 98.   [9] *Ibid.*, p. 82.

making a reasonably normal adjustment without again becoming involved in delinquent activities. This is a much lower ratio of success than was found in foster-home placement. It must of course be borne in mind that the institutional delinquent is a much more difficult child than the average foster-home youngster, so that we are unable to say whether it is the type of child or the type of treatment available in institutions which accounts for the lower rate of success.

It is quite unfair to judge the present status of any of these five institutions by the results which they were achieving fifteen or more years ago. Consequently they are not here mentioned by name. Also we have insufficient information to indicate the degree to which they dealt with their boys on a regimented mass basis. Nevertheless it is of interest that the institution which has been described above as having a repressive program in 1932, and which we shall call institution E, makes a definitely poorer showing than the other four schools, though the differences are not great. For example, the boys from this institution in general adjustment were found to be 28 per cent successful, 32 per cent doubtful, and 40 per cent unsuccessful, while the boys from institution D, which made the best showing, were 36 per cent successful, 30 per cent doubtful, and 34 per cent unsuccessful. Or, if we consider the results in terms of arrests and convictions, institution E may be compared with the average of the other four institutions as follows; of the boys from institution E, 71 per cent were arrested, 60 per cent convicted, and 50 per cent committed to other penal institutions; of the boys from the other four institutions, 65 per cent were arrested, 58 per cent convicted, and 40 per cent committed.[10]

These differences are not particularly impressive, but they are in the direction which we might expect. We might summarize the situation in this way. Five state institutions dealing with delinquent boys in the period around 1930 undoubtedly had differences in the degree to which they used an individualized approach, though none of them had anything like an

[10] Bowler and Bloodgood, *op. cit.*, Tables 42, 44, 47, 54.

adequate parole system for establishing the boy in the community. It is of interest that the institution which seems to have used the highest degree of routinized and regimented treatment, and which still follows such policies, has definitely the poorest results with its boys. There does not seem to be any other factor which would account for this difference in results.

Results of Such Treatment in Orphanages. It may be noted that all of the above studies deal with delinquents, rather than with orphanages or institutions for behavior problems. Unfortunately we have no real study of outcomes of the regimented type of orphanage care. There are two studies which are of interest, though by no means conclusive. Slawson, in his excellent study of delinquents in New York State made in 1921–24, found that the orphanages contributed far more than their proportionate share to the delinquent group. Thus 13.3 per cent of the delinquent boys in correctional schools had at one time been in an orphan asylum, whereas only 1.8 per cent of unselected New York City children had ever been in an orphanage. The proportion was 7.4 times as large as would be expected.[11] As Slawson points out, the orphanage group is a group in which family relationships are abnormal, and abnormal family status is definitely associated with delinquency. Hence it is not clear whether these boys became delinquent because of unfortunate family situations or because of orphanage treatment. At least orphanage placement had not prevented delinquency.

The study made by Miss Theis, to which reference was made in the previous chapter, also gives some additional information as to the results of orphanage care. We are safe in assuming that this care was of the routinized sort, since it dates back a full generation, when all institution care was largely mass treatment. She compared a group of 84 children who had never been in an orphanage, but who had lived for five years in their own very undesirable families, with a group of 96 children who

[11] Slawson, John. *The Delinquent Boy*, p. 379. Boston: Badger, 1926.

had had five years or more of institutional care before place-ment. As far as her study showed, the two groups were com-parable as to family background, and were placed in compar-able foster-home environments at about the same average age. The orphanage group made a "capable" adjustment to the community in 66 per cent of the cases, proved "incapable" in 34 per cent. The other group which had never had the "advan-tages" of institution care, but had lived in families of the most unpromising sort, proved to be "capable" in 82 per cent of the cases, failed in 18 per cent. It would seem that the net effect of orphanage care of this type, so far as we can judge, is detri-mental rather than helpful.[12]

AN INSTITUTIONAL PROGRAM OF INDIVIDUALIZED TREATMENT

If this relatively gloomy picture presents the type of care and the results obtained in the majority of orphan asylums and juvenile institutions, what is the program in those institutions which give more than lip service to the ideal of treating the individual? As mentioned earlier, the older notions of institu-tion care have a tendency to cling, yet there are many examples of institutions organized to treat effectively the individual child. In the field of care of delinquents at least five in New York State come within that class: the Berkshire Farms School, Canaan, New York, the Children's Village at Dobbs Ferry; the State Agricultural and Industrial School, Industry, New York; the Training School for Girls, Hudson, New York; and the Warwick State School, Warwick, New York. In other states other schools have acquired outstanding reputations for their progressive programs. Among these are the Whittier State School, Whittier, California, which is most effectively described in a volume by Fenton;[13] El Retiro School for Girls in Cali-

---

[12] Theis, Sophie Van S. *How Foster Children Turn Out*, pp. 150–152. New York State Charities Aid, 1924.

[13] Fenton, Norman, with collaboration of Fenton, J. C., Murray, M. E., and Tyson, D. K. *The Delinquent Boy and the Correctional School*. Claremont, California: Clare-mont College Guidance Center.

fornia, an excellent school whose career was closed by politics; [14] The Sleighton Farm School for Girls, Darlington, Pennsylvania; the State Home for Boys, Jamesburg, New Jersey; and no doubt others, less well known to the author. In the realm of institutional care of dependent children it has been the author's privilege to see something of the metamorphosis which Hillside Home, in Rochester, has undergone, and to know something of the changes and policies in the New England Home for Little Wanderers, Boston, and in the Children's Community Center, New Haven. It is significant that in each instance the determination to meet and deal with individual needs has meant that the "orphanage" has branched out to include facilities for foster-home care as well, and is thus taken out of the purely institutional category.

The programs of many of these schools are recorded rather fully in special studies to which reference has been made and in annual reports. Without attempting to describe them individually, an account will be given of the type of treatment available to the difficult child who enters this sort of institution.

The Individual Approach. From the moment that the child enters the institution, and increasingly during his first few weeks' stay, he cannot help but be impressed by the number of people who have a genuine and friendly interest in him as an individual. The first friendly chat with the social worker or superintendent, the careful, unhurried physical examination, the hours spent with the psychologist, testing his fitness for various types of academic and vocational work, his long confidential talks with the psychologist or psychiatrist, all bring home to him the fact that he, as an individual, counts. He begins to lose his preconceived fears of institutional life; he finds himself thinking about his own abilities and goals; he has, for the first time, perhaps, an opportunity to present his own side of his life story and to talk frankly about his own problems and behavior. Few young people can maintain throughout

[14] See the article in *The Survey*, October 15, 1927, pp. 83–84, "Begun in Idealism — Ended in Politics."

this reception period the attitudes of hostility, resentment, defiance, or fear which they may have brought to the institution.

The genuineness of this interest in the child himself is given greater weight as a planned program of treatment within the institution is developed for the individual. In most of the larger institutions the final shaping of such a plan takes place in a case conference in which superintendent, psychologist, psychiatrist, school principal, cottage parents, recreational supervisor, and social worker take part.[15] In this conference the general aspects of treatment, based on a discussion of the child's needs, are mapped out. Suitable cottage placement, suitable school placement, and shop or trade training based on the child's aptitudes are planned. His special interests in the recreational or activity field are discussed. Finally, there is an initial attempt to plan for his rehabilitation in the community, even before the treatment program has commenced within the institution.

In many of these schools the child is called in at the end of the case conference, and the plan is discussed with him in friendly fashion, minor modifications being made at his suggestion. At Whittier School the additional opportunity is given for the boy to select, from among the staff members whom he has met, one person who shall act as his counselor, an individual to whom he may go at any time with his problems. It would seem that this choice of a special counselor should give the child, more than anything that has gone before, the belief that his individuality is fully respected.

The therapeutic effect of procedures such as these during the first few weeks of institution care is considerable. Away from the influences which have brought about much of his problem behavior, the child has the opportunity to think about his situation, to discuss it with others who can give him added factual data about himself, and thus to gain a considerable degree of fresh insight into his own behavior. It is not surprising that several of the homes for dependent problem children, recog-

[15] For a vivid picture of such a case conference, see Fenton, *op. cit.*, chap. 3.

nizing that this initial period is the most valuable period of institution care, have ended it there, making their plans for further treatment in a foster home or some other living arrangement. The same plan might well be tried by institutions for delinquents with the less difficult children who come to them.

Providing the Proper Task. It has become one of the axioms of mental hygiene that a feeling of achievement is a basic necessity to personal development and mental health. Nowhere is there a better opportunity to meet this need than in the children's institution. The academic school system, the vocational training, the maintenance work of the cottage and institution are all under one direction and may be managed flexibly so as to fit the child into tasks in which he can achieve and find satisfaction.

School work is the first element of this task. Many studies have pointed out the typical school retardation of institutional children. Slawson's study points out that the average delinquent boy in an institution is decidedly below the norm in abstract intelligence but up to the general population in ability to work with his hands, that he is, in short, the type of child most likely to be a misfit in our academically minded public schools.[16] For these children the institution has the opportunity of fitting the "book work" to the level of their mentality and achievement, and of giving them ample work in the manual and mechanical trades for which they are fitted. In many institutions the elementary school work is on some type of individual "contract" basis, so that the child may begin at his own level in school work and go forward at any rate of speed of which he is capable. In such a plan it is important that remedial instruction in basic subjects be available in order to overcome disabilities, especially in reading and arithmetic. This has assumed additional importance as more and more children from institutions return to public schools rather than go directly into jobs.

It is the vocational or shop program of these schools which

[16] Slawson, *op. cit.*, chaps. 2 and 3.

offers the greatest variety of outlets to the child and in many instances points the way for public-school curricula. In modern boys' institutions, the boy may select carpentry, electrical work, drafting, farm work, printing, shoe repair, laundry, tailoring, painting, masonry, tinsmithing, or some other type of work. In better girls' schools all phases of domestic science, gardening and farming, child care, commercial courses, beauty-parlor work, and the like are offered to the newcomer. While the child, with guidance, chooses one or two of these types of work, this choice may be reconsidered later if it proves to be unsatisfactory. In some institutions there is a "try-out" shop, where the boy or girl can get a taste of several varieties of occupations in order to make a more intelligent choice.

In addition to these more formal types of instruction the maintenance work of the institution, that is, the care of the cottages, the preparation of meals, the raising of foodstuffs, and the repairs to buildings and plumbing and electrical systems, may be used constructively in the development of the individual. While there is always the risk that such maintenance work will be overdone, it also offers many real educational advantages. The boy of low ability may find in simple maintenance work the best training for his future occupation. Such work also carries with it the implication of being real work, necessary to the community, which it is often difficult to achieve in shop instruction.

It is perhaps clear from the foregoing paragraphs that even for the child who represents the most extreme deviation from the normal in intelligence and abilities, some suitable task can be found in the institution. It is of course true that few institutions utilize with sufficient flexibility all the educational possibilities along this line, but in most progressive institutions a child's educational and vocational tasks are much better suited to his individual needs than in the community which he has left behind. It is perhaps in this realm of fitting the individual to his task that the institution has its greatest opportunity of carrying on treatment which is basic and which strikes at fundamental causes of misbehavior.

Group Effort.   Another feature of treatment within the institution is the training in group life and socialized participation
in group projects.   Athletics is an important part in the program of any such school.   Here, in reasonably graded groups,
the boy or girl can learn the lessons of physical competition,
team play, and need for leadership.   There are, however, many
other outlets.   Music groups for band, orchestral, or chorus
work meet the needs of some of the group.   A robed church
choir has proven very popular in one institution.   Libraries,
supervised by the children, open the doors to wider reading.
Radio clubs, handicraft groups, model airplane clubs, all provide places for enthusiasts.   Dramatic programs offer possibilities for personal development.   Boy and Girl Scout work
has been highly developed in a number of the better schools,
and both boys' and girls' institutions have organized summer
camps.   The Boy Scouts may no longer be able to boast that
their members rarely come before juvenile courts, but they have
the much greater satisfaction of knowing that the organization
is working where it is needed.

The therapeutic possibilities of these group projects lie not
only in the activity itself, and in the learning of a social give-
and-take, but in the necessity for organization and leadership
of these interest groups.   This gives an opportunity for self-
government and self-direction of the most valuable sort.
Furthermore this degree of self-government is natural and
functional, similar to the best opportunities the child might
have in the community.   It stops short of the too great degree
of control which is given the children in institutions of the "junior
republic" sort.   Almost invariably any attempt at complete self-
government on the part of young people leads to drastic and
unwise discipline being dealt out to non-conforming individuals.
Our best expert knowledge is insufficient to treat these children
suitably.   It is too much to suppose that children who are themselves difficult or delinquent individuals will do a better job.

Psychotherapy in the Institution.   Although most of the institutions with a program of individualized treatment have psy-

chiatric and psychological service of some type, the amount of psychotherapy that is carried on in institutions is very small indeed. For the most part the work of clinical psychiatrists and psychologists has been to plan and organize the child's environment and program in the institution so that it will have the maximum therapeutic effect. Occasionally there are regular "follow-up" contacts with the child at stated intervals. In some schools the atmosphere is such that the boy feels free to come in and talk over his problems with the psychologist, and some casual but important therapy takes place in this way. There has, however, been little continuing therapy based on the relationship between clinician and child and little attempt to deal with unconscious motivations and conflicts. It is not surprising that even such a moderate student of the situation as Professor Glueck comments, in discussing a particular delinquent:

> He [the psychiatrist] is concerned rather with the routine of examining and classifying inmates on their admission than with the much more important therapeutic possibilities of the individual prisoner. Psychiatry, or any other art purporting to deal with the stresses and strains of the human mind, will get nowhere unless and until a serious effort is made to experiment with various forms of personality analysis of criminals and with different methods of psychotherapy and character reorientation. To call this man a psychopath and stop there is not the beginning, but the end of wisdom.[17]

There are two significant experiments in the field of psychotherapy within the institution. The first was an attempt by Aichhorn, head of a children's institution in Vienna, to deal with a group of twelve extremely unstable delinquent boys.[18] These boys were literally outcasts within the institution. They were not tolerated by the other cottage groups, which had settled rather contentedly into the freedom of the régime Aich-

---

[17] Glueck, S., and Glueck, E. T. *Five Hundred Criminal Careers*, pp. 60–61. New York: Knopf, 1930.

[18] See Aichhorn, August, *Wayward Youth* (New York: Viking Press, 1935), pp. 167–185, for a fuller account of this project. This work was carried on in the early 1920's, the published account in German appearing in 1925, and the English translation in 1935.

horn had instituted.   The only point of similarity among the
twelve was their tendency toward aggression.   They were quar-
relsome, full of uncontrolled rages, and had no feeling of group
unity.   In their own homes and in previous institutional life
severe disciplinary measures had had little or no effect.   After
holding personal interviews with them, Aichhorn came to the
conclusion that they needed a program of affection and kindness
rather than restraint.   Since the remainder of the institution
staff disagreed with him, he and two women helpers assumed
the responsibility themselves.   His thinking in regard to the
children he summarized thus:

> It was evident that we were dealing with human beings who
> had been deprived of the affection necessary for their normal
> development.
> This fact indicated the path our work must take.   First we
> had to compensate for this great lack of love and then gradually
> and with great caution begin to make demands upon the children.
> Severity would have failed completely.   Our treatment of this
> group could be characterized thus: a consistently friendly atti-
> tude, wholesome occupation, plenty of play to prevent aggres-
> sion, and repeated talks with the individual members.[19]

Under this plan, the children were treated with patience and
kindness, no matter what their behavior, and no attempt was
made to curb them by force.   Under these circumstances the
aggressive behavior of the group increased by leaps and bounds
until furniture was broken and windows smashed; fighting was
extreme, and the boys even refused to eat together at table,
each instead taking his food away to his own corner.   This
period of aggression culminated for each boy, according to
Aichhorn, in a series of very violent explosions which had the
obvious intent of provoking violent restraint on the part of
those in charge.   When this was not forthcoming, the boy generally collapsed into a fit of weeping.   Following this high point
of aggression the group, while it fluctuated in its behavior, became much more manageable and began to build up a close
emotional bond to the workers in charge.   At the end of three

[19] From *Wayward Youth*, p. 172, by August Aichhorn. Copyright 1935. Published
by The Viking Press, Inc., New York.

months, improvement in behavior and group unity was very noticeable. At this time a Christmas festival served as a means of heightening the pleasurable emotional bonds of the group. Following this, Aichhorn gave up the direct leadership of this group, which was placed in the hands of one of his associates, a psychologist, and had them transferred to a new cottage. The group was now regarded as no more difficult than any other group, though they had to learn to accept increased demands placed upon them by the leaders, as they would have to accept community demands later.

While Aichhorn explains his results by means of Freudian theory, this is probably not essential. The major point is that he followed through a planned mode of educational treatment and psychotherapy designed to reduce aggressive tendencies, and to some extent critically observed the results. To what degree his own personality was significant in the results can scarcely be determined until someone else tries a similar procedure.

A second significant experiment, this time based on purely psychotherapeutic measures, is reported by Dr. Healy and Dr. Alexander.[20] Both as a research into the etiology of crime, and as an experiment in psychotherapy, psychoanalytic treatment was given to eleven criminals over a maximum period of ten months in 1931-32. Ten were boys or young men from 15 to 28 years of age. The eleventh was a young woman, a persistent shoplifter. Five of the eleven were serving sentences in institutions during the period of analysis. They were without exception very difficult cases in which courts and clinics, probation officers and institutions, had failed to help their fundamental problems. In each instance there was good evidence that the delinquencies were based on some type of mental conflict.

The methods used in this research will be discussed further in connection with other psychotherapeutic techniques. It should be pointed out here, however, that the analyses were

[20] Alexander, Franz, and Healy, William. *Roots of Crime, Psychoanalytical Studies.* New York: Knopf, 1935.

much more striking in illuminating the "roots of crime" than in their favorable effect on the social behavior of the individual. Of the five in institutions only three proceeded for any length of time with the analysis, and of these one ceased to come when his problems as he revealed them became more than he could face, penned up in the institution for several years to come. Another was released from prison but was soon returned for another holdup. The third had been out of prison only two months when the account was written. The results were not much more favorable with the six who were outside of the institutions during their analyses. On the whole the findings of the book, so far as therapy is concerned, point to the immense weight of social factors in the causation of delinquency, and indicate that even though improved insight may be brought about within the institution, it may not be enough to alter behavior.

While neither of these experiments has been more than partially successful, both of them are honest and reasonably scientific attempts to see to what extent psychotherapy can be used in institutional life. Much more experimentation of this sort is needed.

The Duplication of Home and Community Situations. In the progressive institution, every effort is made to provide the child with a situation which is comparable to normal community life. In the cottage, where not more than twenty to twenty-five boys or girls live in a group, there is some semblance of family life, with cottage parents knowing each child intimately and supplying to some degree real parent-substitutes. The extent to which the cottage parents can conduct themselves as foster parents is a test of the quality of care given at the institution. Fenton [21] stresses the part which cottage parents play in teaching the boy the essentials of social etiquette and standards of social behavior. Such teaching is an important part of the child's preparation for community living.

An institution which has endeavored to teach children in

[21] Fenton, *op. cit.*, pp. 128–130.

regard to earning and spending is Hillside Home, Rochester. Here each older child, boy or girl, is assigned a particular chore or task, these jobs being rotated at intervals. The child is paid a certain amount per month for his work. The amount paid is on a sliding scale and depends on whether the child's supervisor regards the work as well or poorly done. This money is credited to his account, and it is understood that it is his only source of clothing but that it may be used for other purposes as well. In buying their clothing, the children may purchase economically from the Commissary at the Home, or they may indulge in flashier tastes by shopping in the city stores. They may, with few restrictions, draw out their money for any purpose which they desire. The educational results of such a scheme are outstanding. It restores to the individual much of that freedom of choice which is so essential to more mature living. Other institutions have similar plans, of value in proportion as they give a child a genuine incentive for earning and a freedom to make mistakes in the spending of money.

Another way in which institutions strive to keep the child close to normal life is through allowing trips and visits. In more and more schools and orphanages, the child is permitted to go home alone for holidays, to leave the institution to attend a church or "movie" of his choice, or to go with a group on hikes and trips. These experiences are therapeutically valuable. They tend to break down the walls, whether visible or invisible, which surround every institution. They also tend to develop initiative. Those dealing with children are apt to forget that to go for one or two or five years without ever boarding a street car alone, or buying one's clothing, or paying one's way into a movie, or calling on a friend at his home, is negative social training of the most virulent sort. It puts a premium on passive docility which the institution must be at pains to remove.

Planned After-Care. As with foster-home care, the most crucial portion of institutional treatment deals with the effective transplantation of the boy or girl into his functioning place in the community. In the modern institution the planning for this process begins with the child's entrance into the institution. Later comes the decision as to whether or not the child is ready for placement in the community. This decision is not based, in the best schools, on the length of time within the institution, or even on the child's completion of some system of credits or merits, but on the basis of the individual's ability to make a normal and healthy social adjustment. Steps have been made to bring this decision down to a more rational and scientific basis in institutions for delinquents by devising prognostic measures to determine the chance of community success. Fenton [22] gives one such table for delinquent boys. Glueck has worked out predictive tables for inmates of reformatories for young women [23] and young men.[24] He points out particularly that the usual criteria which are apt to determine the question of parole, namely, the type of delinquency and the seriousness of the offense, have practically no relationship to parole success. In general these predictive tables are based on facts concerning the individual's early history and his adjustment within the institution.

Following the decision that the boy or girl is ready for community life, there are a number of steps which need to be taken before final release. The child needs to be prepared for his community freedom by being given more freedom within and outside of the institution, while still under supervision. All the devices mentioned above for encouraging initiative and choice need to be developed and emphasized. In addition to this, careful consideration must be given to the place where the child will live. Case work with the family, to prepare them for the child's return, is carried on if it is not already under way. Foster-home or wage-home placement will be made available by the best institutions to those children who should never return to their own homes. Some institutions, particularly training schools for girls, have been successful in developing

[22] Fenton, *op. cit.*, p. 158.

[23] Glueck, S., and Glueck, E. T. *Five Hundred Delinquent Women*, chap. 17. New York: Knopf, 1934.

[24] Glueck, S., and Glueck, E. T. *Five Hundred Criminal Careers*, chaps. 16–18.

colonies or clubs in which the girls can live in the community, as any other employed girls might do. Certain adjustments will need to be made in regard to the neighborhood and the school or job to which the child will return. The co-ordinating councils which have been established in a number of cities as neighborhood organizations to aid in the prevention and treatment of delinquency may be of assistance here in developing an attitude on the part of schools, employers, police, and others, which will be friendly and helpful to the delinquent child, rather than hostile and suspicious.

All of these preparations, both of the child and of the proposed environment in which he will live, make the release from the institution a much less dramatic, a much more helpful affair. Instead of being a complete shift from repression to freedom, from dependence to attempted independence, the release from the institution is, as it should be, one step in a whole series of educational steps toward normal self-support and independence. The child embarks on this new step with the supervision and help of friendly workers whom he has already come to know within the school. While the steps as described have had particular reference to the delinquent child the process is much the same, though the terms may be different, for the child who has been placed in an institution for dependents because of his or her behavior difficulties.

"BUT" — THE DISADVANTAGES OF THE INSTITUTION

While the foregoing sketch of treatment processes in the progressive institution is not overdrawn (except in the sense that few institutions carry out all the measures indicated), there are certain other aspects of the situation which should not be omitted from consideration.

No matter how ingeniously the program may attempt to overcome it, the fact remains that the institution represents an artificial and unreal environment for the child. Even in the better schools the opportunity to face real problems and make real choices of the sort which will be demanded later is limited. Experience with excellent institutions for dependents indicates that no child can spend several years in such an environment without losing something of his initiative and his spontaneity.

It also seems to be true that the institution, in spite of its excellent means for meeting the child's need for achievement, has much less opportunity of meeting the need of the boy or girl for emotional security. It is often difficult for foster parents to make one or two children feel secure. It is much more rare to find cottage parents who have any success in helping fifteen to fifty boys or girls feel that they "belong" and are liked and wanted.

Nowhere do the artificialities of institution life show up more clearly than in relation to the problem of smoking. Smoking is completely taboo at almost all institutions, in spite of the fact that many of the boys or girls have smoked persistently over long periods before their arrival. In some schools the attempt is made to base the prohibition on the ground of fire hazard rather than on moral grounds, but the total effect is little changed. The complete prohibition raises the whole issue, which ought at best to be a matter settled by education, good taste, and judgment, into a position of central prominence in the child's daily life. Boys from most institutions speak as though it were the one ever-present disciplinary problem. It is, in addition, in every institution responsible for boys' spying and "snitching" on one another. It leads to various minor "rackets." It inevitably produces deceit and cunning of all kinds. Fenton finds that it ranks second as a reason for assignment to the "Lost Privilege Cottage" at Whittier, exceeded only by the problem of runaways.[25] The situation is very similar in other institutions. In brief, this question of smoking, which has little or no community importance, which is not a delinquent or immoral act, which has no relation to successful after-adjustment, is raised to a problem of prime importance simply by the artificialities of institutional life.

[25] Fenton, *op. cit.,* p. 30.

RESULTS OF INDIVIDUALIZED TREATMENT

It is most unfortunate that we have no study which would reveal what institution care at its best might accomplish with difficult or delinquent children. As has been mentioned before, the only comparative study available is that made by the Children's Bureau, and during the period of institution care evaluated (1918–23), none of the institutions had a thoroughgoing program of individualized treatment. Whittier State School in California had adopted such a program as a very definite goal and was making changes in that direction, but many aspects of its work were in a pioneering stage. Consequently we do not know how much the slightly better results achieved by the more progressive institutions at that time would be increased if they were studied now. Our hopes should not be too sanguine, however. There is strong reason to believe that for a considerable group of those sent to institutions for delinquents we do not yet have adequate knowledge to bring about changes in their behavior. This group is composed of those children whose hereditary and physical and cultural background contains so many factors making for maladjustment that we cannot cope satisfactorily with their problems, or at best can bring them only to a comfortable adjustment in the institution, rather than to a normal adjustment in the community.

The only study which has been reported of outcomes in a progressive institution is that being made by Fenton and his associates.[26] This is an investigation of 400 boys who entered Whittier School during the years 1928–30 and are reported as of October, 1933. Fenton is justifiably cautious in drawing any conclusions after so short a period of post-institutional experience and almost the only general statement which can be made is that, of the 400 boys, 28 per cent have made a definitely satisfactory record which they will very likely maintain, and 18 per cent have very definitely failed, having been committed to correctional institutions. For the majority of the

[26] Fenton, *op. cit.*, pp. 148–158.

group, however, it is either still too soon to pass definite judgment, or their adjustment is only fair, or their record is unknown. We can only hope that this and similar surveys will be completed in order to throw more light on the potentialities of the best institutional treatment.

One profound practical difficulty in comparing institutional results is that the poorer institution usually has a more hopeful group of children with which to work. There is good reason for this paradox. The community or state with sufficient social vision to establish and support a progressive institution also maintains other services for problem children. As a consequence, more children are dealt with in the community, a smaller proportion are sent to institutions, and this smaller group contains a higher ratio of the very unstable and more difficult children. Hence it is a common experience of institutions to receive their most hopeless youngsters from the communities with the best educational and child-welfare facilities. This tendency is indicated in the study made by the Children's Bureau where the most regimented and probably least adequate institution, institution E, received a much larger proportion of first offenders than the other four institutions. Of the commitments to institution E, 30 per cent were first offenders, a relatively hopeful group, as compared with an average of 21 per cent for the other four institutions. This factor would of course influence final results and must be borne in mind in making any institutional comparisons.

CHARACTERISTICS OF THE INSTITUTIONAL CHILD

The type of child found in institutions varies decidedly according to the institution policies. Consequently we shall limit our observations here to those findings which apply generally to almost all institutions. Unfortunately most of the studies have been made of children in institutions for delinquents rather than of children in institutions for dependents.

In the first place the institutional child comes in general from a very inadequate socio-economic background. Many studies

have pointed out the high incidence of poverty and assistance from relief agencies in the families of institutional children. Along with this goes, as might be expected, a correspondingly low level of occupational status on the part of the parents. Perhaps the most striking finding regarding the home is the degree to which institutional children come from broken homes where father or mother is dead, parents separated or divorced, or where there is a step-parent situation. Slawson found that only 55 per cent of the boys in four institutions for delinquents came from homes where they were living with both parents, while 81 per cent of public-school children resided in such homes.[27] This finding is corroborated by Fenton, who found that only 41 per cent of the Whittier boys resided with both parents.[28] Other researches give similar results. It should be noted, however, that children placed in foster homes are even more likely to come from broken homes.

In age, too, the institutional children differ somewhat from foster-home children. Institutions for delinquents or pre-delinquents have a definitely older group of children than we find under foster-home care. They are of course a more homogeneous group in age. The average age in the four institutions studied by Slawson ranged from 13 years 9 months to 17 years. Less than 5 per cent of the 1664 children were under 12 years of age, while of foster-home children 50 per cent or more are under 12. In homes for dependents the age would vary according to the function of the institution, but since few such organizations continue to accept young children for care, the average age would probably be higher than in the foster-home group.

In regard to intelligence, there is a decided variation between institutions, depending on their policy of admission and on the facilities for diagnosis and care of mental defectives. The situation is well exemplified by the fact that at Whittier School in 1919, 30 per cent of the boys were feebleminded. In 1926 there were but 4 per cent in this group, since defectives were then being diagnosed and sent elsewhere. Consequently we find a variety of average intelligence quotients in different studies:

---

[27] Slawson, *op. cit.*, pp. 353 ff.   [28] Fenton, *op. cit.*, p. 117.

an average I.Q. of 78 at the House of Refuge, on Randall's Island, New York, for a group of older delinquent boys in the early 1920's; an average I.Q. of 81 for 198 dependent children in county homes; [29] an average I.Q. of 91.7 at Whittier in 1932,[30] when practically all mental defectives were being transferred to other institutions. It is conservative to say, however, that, in abstract intelligence, institutional groups either for dependent or delinquent children are decidedly below the average in intelligence, and that ordinarily not more than 15 to 25 per cent will be above the norm for unselected children (though the statistical expectation would be 50 per cent).

It is significant that as a group delinquent boys in institutions show much better ability in non-verbal and mechanical tests than they do in tests of abstract intelligence. Slawson found that nearly 50 per cent exceeded the norms for unselected children in mechanical tests and 33 per cent exceeded the norms on a variety of non-verbal performance tests [31] (again the expectation would be 50 per cent). Clinical experience would indicate that this "manual-mindedness" is typical not only of children in all institutions, but also of all problem children coming to our behavior clinics.

In physique Slawson found his group to be of nearly average height, above the average in weight, showing more cases of visual and auditory defect than is found among unselected school children. Whether these findings would apply to other institutional groups besides delinquent boys we do not know.

WHEN SHALL INSTITUTIONAL TREATMENT BE USED?

With these facts in mind as to the type of child in institutions, the type of program offered, and the degree of successful social treatment, we are ready to raise the question, "When is institutional treatment indicated?" It does not seem possible, at the present state of our knowledge, to do more than discuss

---

[29] Cobb, Margaret E., "The Mentality of Dependent Children," *Journal of Delinquency*, vol. 7 (1922), pp. 132–140.

[30] Fenton, *op. cit.*, p. 64.   [31] Slawson, *op. cit.*, pp. 192, 212.

in a general way the considerations which should determine this decision. Certainly no such definite criteria can be laid down as were proposed in regard to foster-home treatment. It should be recognized that the first part of any decision for institutional care is the decision to remove the child from his own home, which we will shortly consider. Having made this decision, the next step is the consideration of foster-home care. It is only the child who cannot be dealt with in his own home, and who has a poor prospect of foster-home success, that we should consider for institutional care. If this seems to be defining institutional treatment entirely in negative terms, let us look at some of the positive aspects of the situation.

Institutional Care for the Mentally Retarded Child. For children of defective or borderline mentality, institution care is often advisable. For individuals of this group, when adjustment in their own home is out of the question, foster-home placement is frequently very dubious. They are, in general, apt to respond and to be docile under the degree of regimentation which every institution demands. Furthermore, since they are always likely to be dependent on others for management and direction, the loss of initiative and the development of dependence in an institution are not so unfortunate. Indeed it may prove to be a helpful factor in their later adjustment.

An analysis of our own clinic recommendations for 292 problem and delinquent children studied in the department illustrates sharply the extent to which recommendations for institutional care are associated with mentality. The accompanying table shows that for children above the borderline level institutional treatment is rarely recommended. While there is no data from other clinics with which to compare our findings, it is probable that this tendency is typical. It is only the poorly organized community, with poor diagnostic service and few social resources for treatment, that sends many children of average or above average mentality to institutions.

There are other types of children who may profit from institutional treatment, particularly in those communities where

RECOMMENDATIONS FOR INSTITUTIONAL AND OTHER CARE AS
RELATED TO MENTALITY [32]

(Child Study Department, Rochester S.P.C.C.)

	Defective	Border-line	Dull Normal	Average	Superior
Number in group..................	29	48	94	102	19
Institution for defectives recommended.......................	66%	10%	0%	0%	0%
Institution for delinquents recommended.......................	0%	8%	4%	4%	0%
Orphanage care recommended.....	0%	0%	2%	2%	0%
Total institutional care recommended.	66%	18%	6%	6%	0%
Care in foster home recommended....	7%	21%	39%	42%	63%
Continue in own home or present foster home.......................	24%	48%	43%	44%	26%
Other residence recommended........	3%	13%	12%	8%	11%
Total.......................	100%	100%	100%	100%	100%

institutions are available which have programs of the individualized type described. It is doubtful that placement in the institution offering a regimented program is ever advisable as treatment, save possibly for mentally low-grade children. Such placement may be justified as a necessary protection to the community in certain cases, but this scarcely constitutes treatment of the individual. The more modern training school or institutional home can, however, be of particular help with certain rather specific types of children or configurations of social situations.

The "Spoiled Child." There is, for example, the child who has been consistently overindulged over a long period of time with no adequate home control, the "spoiled child" who has grown into early adolescence with no training in adjusting to the demands of others. Frequently this type of child, because of age and the confirmed pattern of his behavior, is unsuitable for foster-home placement, especially when he wishes to remain in his own home and continue his control of the situation.

[32] This material is quoted in part from the article by the author, "Three Surveys of Treatment Measures Used with Children," *American Journal of Orthopsychiatry*, vol. 7 (January, 1937), p. 51.

Such a child, we find, may profit from a period of wise institutional treatment, where reasonable demands are made upon him, demands which he cannot escape. Dr. R. R. Williams, out of his experience as psychiatrist at Children's Village, also stresses the value of the institutional régime for this type of youngster, and states his viewpoint thus:

Let us consider in detail some of the effects which we have briefly outlined. First, that of bringing conformance to group standards. This very effect of which we disapprove in such an extreme degree ... is the effect desired with some children, but to a lesser degree. We want the individual to gain an insight into the rights of others, into his own assets and actual achievements in relation to those of the group. Certain individuals can secure this only through rigid regulations or controls. All of us have seen children, adolescents, and adults who are thinking in terms of themselves only; egotistic, selfish individuals, giving little or no thought to the rights and needs of others. Long have they been the center of the stage, pampered by relatives and friends to the point where they are well nigh unbearable, not only when with relatives and friends, but outside of the home as well. When a boy has developed this in childhood and carries it over into adolescence, what is to be done?

What would you do with Larry, a boy of sixteen, man grown, rather good-looking, with an income and an inheritance; spoiled from infancy by his father, an older sister, a grandmother, even by his stepmother (his mother having died when he was three). He had been the center of attention during infancy and childhood. At the age of thirteen he was getting beyond family control, he was shuttling from school to school, private and public, manifesting a dissatisfaction with all phases of his life, school, home, income; a boaster, a show-off, a fabricator regarding his achievements, but with no real achievements except that of cheer leader, which offered him an opportunity to occupy the center of the stage. When he added to this an entire disregard of advice of relatives and guardian, when he ran away from the private school, stole money from home to continue his travels, what would you do with him? Here is a type which needs the levelling influence of institutional controls; it is the effect desired.[33]

[33] Williams, R. R. "The Effects on Personality and Social Attitudes of Institutional Placement," *Proceedings of National Conference of Social Work, 1928*, pp. 231–238. Chicago, Ill.: University of Chicago Press.

When Family Ties are Strong.   When the emotional bond between child and parent is very strong, yet separation seems imperative, institutional care may offer more constructive possibilities than a foster home.   Placement in an institution offers less threat to this emotional bond, both for parent and child, than the substitute affection offered by a foster parent. Institutional placement allows the child to keep his emotional security anchored in the home situation, while he profits by the well-adapted program and the normal group life of the institution.

> Franklin was a ten-year-old whose very neurotic and unstable mother realized her inability to cope with the boy's growing deceit, his stealing and his very poor adjustment to the group at school.   She also felt that for Franklin to live in the home where she quarreled continuously with her brutal, drinking husband, was unwise.   As a consequence she twice made her own arrangements with a child-placing agency to put Franklin in a foster home.   Each time he was in several different homes.   Sometimes the home proved unsuitable, the boy was given poor care, and the agency moved him.   In other instances, where the foster home was satisfactory, the mother herself removed the child when she saw that he was becoming indifferent to her, and bestowing his real affection on the foster parent.   Although intellectually willing to face this problem she was quite unable emotionally to allow her boy to take root in a foster home.   However, when she took him home, all his behavior problems reappeared.
>
> It was at about this time that she came to the clinic, where it was suggested, after analysis of the previous experience, that she place him in a small children's institution, where the boy could have considerable freedom, wholesome activities, and where through her visits he could continue to feel himself primarily attached to her.   This plan has worked very satisfactorily for several years.   Franklin and his mother have built up a much more satisfying emotional relationship than existed in the strife of his own home, and on the other hand he has had the advantages of stable and reasonable control by cottage parents, a much greater help toward maturity than his mother's erratic measures.

The Older Child and the Institution.   In the weighing of the various possibilities of placement away from home for children over twelve, the institutional home shows certain advantages which should be considered. The fact that these children often fail to form any deep emotional attachment to foster parents has already been discussed. With those older children who seem unlikely to form such a bond, and whose annoying behavior, in addition, makes several changes of foster home likely, the children's institution may offer the better possibility. If it is a progressive institution, the program will probably be a richer, more stimulating one than can be offered in the foster home. There will be no changes of residence, hence a greater feeling of stability. In those institutions where there are "alumni" groups, the child may, even after leaving the institution for a job, feel more of a natural attachment to it than he would have felt for a home where he had "boarded" rather than lived.

Sex and Institutional Treatment. There is some evidence that institutional treatment works out more satisfactorily for girls than for boys. Whether this may be due to a greater docility and acceptance of institutional régime on the part of girls is a matter of speculation. It may also be connected in some way with the fact that girls are primarily institutionalized for sex misconduct. Possibly the time spent in the institution allows sufficient development of judgment and emotional control so that sex delinquency and misconduct automatically tend to decrease. Whatever the explanation, the Gluecks found important differences in their study of 500 reformatory men as compared with 500 reformatory women, as the accompanying table indicates. Fewer women than men were arrested for further delinquencies in the post-parole

BEHAVIOR FOLLOWING RELEASE FROM PAROLE [34]

	Women (per cent)	Men (per cent)
Arrested for delinquency following parole.........	38	73
Delinquencies, but no arrest made...............	38	6
No further delinquencies following parole.........	24	21

[34] For the figures regarding young men see Glueck and Glueck, *500 Criminal Careers*, p. 184. For the corresponding figures regarding young women delinquents see *500 Delinquent Women*, by the same authors, pp. 233, 236.

period, and a slightly larger proportion of women made a successful adjustment without further delinquencies. It is difficult, however, to interpret the findings in view of the large number of women who continued to some extent their delinquencies, mostly sex offenses and drinking, without being sufficiently flagrant in their behavior to come to official notice. Consequently we can draw no conclusion from the available data, but simply suggest the possibility that problem girls may profit more from institutional treatment than boys with a similar degree of behavior difficulties.

The Residual Group. While with the groups mentioned above special consideration should be given to the possibilities of institutional care, the fact remains that in large measure the institution should be used for the misfit group whom we cannot hope, with any degree of success, to treat in the community. This will be particularly true of the institution for delinquents, less true of the orphanage which accepts problem cases, in many instances of the special types mentioned above. The children whom we recommend for treatment in institutions for delinquents will be made up to a considerable degree of the children who combine various traits of poor prognostic significance. There will be children of unstable organic and emotional make-up, whose instability has led them into more and more conduct problems and delinquencies. There will be children with serious hereditary evidences of mental disease or defect, who are themselves showing mental abnormalities as well as behavior difficulties. There will be other boys and girls who constitute the failing percentage of other types of care. Although they may have traits which would make foster-home care or treatment in their own home the logical plan, yet if repeated skilled attempts along these lines produce no improvement, and misbehavior and delinquency continue, the institution becomes the measure of last resort.

Many of the boys and girls in this residual group cannot be restored to a normal social adjustment by any methods which we now know. For such, an extended period of care, possibly over many years, must be planned. Often a modified institutional scheme, a colony group, either on the farm or in the city, would provide a supervised environment in which these individuals could achieve some type of reasonably contented though not independent sort of existence. It would save them from a "release" to community life which only results in further delinquency and further institutionalization. With others of this residual group, a hospital type of care may be needed. Fenton suggests such a plan as follows:

> A small proportion of the boys are unchanged or even worse after their stay at the juvenile correctional schools. These include those emotionally unstable children, for whom present medical and psychological science can do little — at least in the ordinary state school. This group of children needs hospital-school care and should neither remain at the state school indefinitely nor be "tried out" in the community. [35]

We need to face the fact that if institutions continue to make evaluations of the results of their treatment, we shall soon have tools of prediction comparable to those which have been devised for adult prisoners. We shall know, with some assurance, that a particular child with a combination of traits tending toward poor prognosis has eight chances out of ten of failing to become a self-supporting, law-abiding citizen. For such a child continued institutional care of one of these specialized types may well be the best plan. Both the Gluecks [36] and Fenton [37] have made a start toward devising such a prognostic scale, though only Fenton's applies strictly to the institution. Once we have such instruments we shall see even more clearly than we do now that for some children we shall need very long periods of control, which means segregated care of the institution type.

It will seem to some that such a viewpoint lays stress on the custodial aspect of institutional care. Rather it emphasizes

---

[35] Fenton, *op. cit.*, p. 140.

[36] Glueck, S., and Glueck, E. T. *One Thousand Juvenile Delinquents*, chap. 11, Cambridge, Mass.: Harvard University Press, 1934.

[37] Fenton, *op. cit.*, chap. 10.

the laboratory possibilities. If we carefully diagnose our child problems, treating most of them through community measures, it means that we shall turn over to the institution, except for certain special groups, only the most difficult boys and girls. We shall have no right to expect of them a high percentage of success with this group, but we shall properly demand that they become laboratories for research into behavior difficulties and their treatment. As in many other fields, the knowledge gained from this difficult and none too hopeful group may give us many helpful techniques for use with more normal children.

CONCLUSION

In summary it may be pointed out that the institution which relies on mass treatment, whose work ends as the child is released, has little if any place in the realm of treatment techniques. For the institution which individualizes its program to meet the child's needs and regards his replacement in the community as one of its main goals there are various situations in which it may be the most effective means of treatment. It has advantages in dealing with the mentally retarded, which no other plan has. It is often helpful in exercising a healthy degree of restraint and control over the child who has for too many years been the egotistical center of his universe. It has the opportunity of dealing with the child who is emotionally attached to his parents, without breaking down the constructive values of that tie. It frequently can be of assistance to the older child who needs placement but cannot accept foster parents. It is possibly to be considered more favorably for girls than for boys, though this is an open question. Finally it is to serve as the placement for those children whose life has been formed by such a weight of unchangeable and destructive factors that successful adjustment in the community can scarcely be expected. For these children it is to be a pioneer in the treatment field, devising and experimenting with any mode of therapy which gives promise.

BIBLIOGRAPHY

General

Mayo, Leonard W. "Juvenile Training Schools," *Social Work Year Book 1935*. New York: Russell Sage Foundation, 1935.

Reckless, W. C., and Smith, M. *Juvenile Delinquency*. New York: McGraw-Hill, 1932. 412 p.

Shaw, Clifford R. *The Jack Roller*. Chicago: University of Chicago Press, 1930. 205 p.

Slawson, John. *The Delinquent Boy*. Boston, Mass.: Badger, 1926. 477 p.

State of New York, Department of Social Welfare. *The Delinquent Child and the Institution*. 1935. Compilation of papers by various authors.

Van Waters, Miriam. *Youth in Conflict*, chap. 9, "The Value of Correctional Education." New York: Republic Publishing Co., 1925. White House Conference on Child Health and Protection. Committee on Socially Handicapped. *The Delinquent Child*. New York: Century, 1932. 499 p.

Williams, R. R. "The Effects on Personality and Social Attitudes of Institutional Placement," pp. 231–238. *Proceedings of National Conference of Social Work, 1928*. Chicago: University of Chicago Press, 1928.

Concerning Institutional Management and Program

Bowler, Alida C., and Bloodgood, R. S. *Institutional Treatment of Delinquent Boys, Part I. Treatment Programs of Five State Institutions.* U.S. Children's Bureau Publication no. 228. Washington, D.C.: Government Printing Office, 1935. 324 p.

Cooper, J. M. *Children's Institutions*. Philadelphia: Dolphin Press, 1931. 696 p.

Fenton, Norman, with collaboration of Fenton, J. C., Murray, M. E., and Tyson, D. K. *The Delinquent Boy and the Correctional School.* Claremont, California: Claremont College Guidance Center, 1935. 182 p. *Handbook for the Use of Board of Directors, Superintendents and Staffs of Institutions for Dependent Children.* U.S. Children's Bureau Publication no. 170. Washington, D.C.; Government Printing Office, 1927.

Preventing Crime — A Symposium. Ed. by Sheldon and Eleanor Glueck. New York: McGraw-Hill, 1936. 509 p. Part IV, "Intramural Guidance Programs," deals with programs of Longview Farm, Children's Village, George Junior Republic.

Reeves, Margaret. *Training Schools for Delinquent Girls*. New York: Russell Sage Foundation, 1929. 455 p.

Solenberger, W. E. *One Hundred Years of Child Care in New Haven.* Children's Community Center, New Haven, 1933. 96 p.

Studies of Results

Bowler, Alida C., and Bloodgood, R. S. *Institutional Treatment of De-*

linquent Boys, Part II. A Study of 751 Cases. U.S. Children's Bureau Publication no. 230. Washington, D.C.: Government Printing Office, 1936. 149 p.

Craig, Elizabeth. "Types of Boys Amenable to Treatment in a Junior Republic," *Smith College Studies in Social Work*, vol. 5 (December, 1934), pp. 129–159.

Elliott, Mabel A. *Correctional Education and the Delinquent Girl.* Harrisburg, Pa.: Pennsylvania Department of Welfare, 1928.

Fenton, Norman, with collaboration of Fenton, J. C., Murray, M. E., and Tyson, D. K. *The Delinquent Boy and the Correctional School.* Claremont, California: Claremont College Guidance Center, 1935. 182 p.

Glueck S., and Glueck, E. T. *One Thousand Juvenile Delinquents.* Cambridge, Mass.: Harvard University Press, 1934. 341 p.

Glueck S., and Glueck, E. T. *Five Hundred Criminal Careers.* New York: Knopf, 1930. 365 p.

Glueck S., and Glueck, E. T. *Five Hundred Delinquent Women.* New York: Knopf, 1934. 539 p.

Healy, William, and Bronner, Augusta F. *Delinquents and Criminals, Their Making and Unmaking.* New York: Macmillan, 1926. 317 p.

Psychotherapy and the Institution

Aichhorn, August. *Wayward Youth.* New York: Viking Press, 1935. 236 p.

Alexander, Franz, and Healy, William. *Roots of Crime, Psychoanalytical Studies.* New York: Knopf, 1935. 305 p.

The Advisability of Removing a Child from Home

WE HAVE discussed the various types of care outside of the child's own home without once taking up the basic consideration of the conditions which justify such drastic treatment. This may seem to be putting the cart before the horse, but there are good reasons for this order of approach. All too often children's agencies, behavior clinics, and juvenile courts, in making the decision concerning a child's removal from home, take into account only the home situation itself or the child's behavior in this situation. This oversimplifies the problem. It is not only a question of the situation in which the child is living, but also of the alternatives which are ahead if he is removed from this home. Consequently we approach this problem, of vital interest to social workers, teachers, and parents, as well as to courts and clinics, from a much more practical and realistic point of view, if we have clearly in mind at the outset the possibilities and limitations of foster-home and institutional care. We shall not so readily fall into the error, common to lay people, teachers, or those not closely associated with the problems of child care, of thinking that the removal of a child from an unhappy or distressing home situation is the solution of all ills. We shall realize that it is not merely a question of determining whether the child's behavior or the home situation is "bad," but of determining the essential elements of such a total situation, and whether there is a possibility of improving them through the available alternatives of care outside the home.

EXTENT TO WHICH CHANGE OF ENVIRONMENT
IS USED AS TREATMENT

This whole question of arranging a complete change of the child's environment as a part of therapy is by no means an academic one. Every child-guidance clinic, every children's agency, every juvenile court, makes use of such a method in a surprisingly large proportion of cases. It is only recently that we have begun to have any notion of the extent to which such methods are used in dealing with children who present behavior problems. It may be of interest to review briefly some of this evidence.

In their study at the Institute for Juvenile Research, previously mentioned, Hopkins and Haines found that of 996 problem children referred to the Institute for help, removal from an unsatisfactory home environment was recommended for 171, or 17 per cent. Of these, institution care was suggested for 52, foster-home care for the remaining 119.[1]

Hartwell's study of *Fifty-Five Bad Boys* is an account of the types of psychotherapy used with a clinic sampling of difficult and delinquent boys. The whole attention of the writer is focused on the psychiatric aspects of treatment. It is therefore all the more surprising to note that in 20 cases (36 per cent) of the 55, a change of environment is a part of the treatment scheme.[2] For the most part this represents a change from home to a foster home, though in a few instances a change to a private boarding school or an institution is involved.

If we choose to analyze from this point of view some of the material brought out in Glueck's study of 1000 delinquent boys, we find that change of residence is a frequent recommendation for this group. The Judge Baker Foundation

[1] Hopkins, Cornelia D., and Haines, Alice R. "A Study of One Hundred Problem Children for whom Foster Care was Advised," *American Journal of Orthopsychiatry*, vol. 1 (January, 1931), p. 107.

[2] Hartwell, Samuel W. *Fifty-Five Bad Boys.* New York: Knopf, 1931. The cases in which such changes are made are as follows: nos. 2, 9, 11, 12, 14, 15, 18, 24, 26, 31, 34, 36, 39, 41, 47, 48, 49, 53, 54. In addition case no. 46 should perhaps be added. The information is not clear, though foster homes were used earlier by the clinic in treatment of this boy, before Dr. Hartwell undertook therapy.

clinic, after studying these delinquent youths, recommended a change of environment for 53 per cent of them.   Care in a foster home or with relatives was advised for 32 per cent, institutional care for 18 per cent, and the army, navy, or placement for 3 per cent.[3]   Careful examination of the facts indicates that these recommendations regarding place of living are not only the most frequent type of recommendation, but also probably the most significant.

Another careful study of delinquent boys and girls treated in three child-guidance clinics is reported by Dr. Healy and Dr. Bronner.   A total of 143 children was dealt with.   Of those treated by the New Haven clinic 36 per cent were removed from their own homes and placed either in foster homes or institutions as a part of treatment.   In the Boston group 40 per cent were removed.   In Detroit 54 per cent were placed.   Healy's material indicates that the proportion removed from home is larger where resources are better.   Thus New Haven had few agency resources for making foster-home placements, so that only 6 per cent of their children were so placed, and 30 per cent went to institutions.   In Detroit, 42 per cent were placed in foster homes and only 12 per cent in institutions.[4]

Two of the studies made in the Child Study Department, both of which have been mentioned, indicate that change of environment is a very important part of our own clinical treatment.   It was found that of 163 problem children who came to the clinic from their own homes, a change of environment was recommended for 58 per cent.   Not only does it apply to children who are living in their own homes, but also to those whose problems develop while they are residing in foster homes.   Of the latter group of 91 a change of environment was recommended for 52 per cent.   It was also found that such changes were advised much more frequently for girls than for boys.   For 135 problem and delinquent boys, treatment involving removal

[3] Glueck, S. and Glueck, E. T.   *One Thousand Juvenile Delinquents*, pp. 114–115. Cambridge, Mass.: Harvard University Press, 1934.

[4] Healy, William, and Bronner, A. F.   *New Light on Delinquency and its Treatment*, p. 154.   New Haven, Conn.: Yale University Press, 1936.

from their present residence was advised in 42 per cent of the cases. For the group of 96 girls, such treatment was advised in 65 per cent of the cases.[5] The surprising part which such treatment may play in dealing with a seriously delinquent group is shown by Barker and Rappaport's study of sexually delinquent girls. Of this group of 96, removal from home was recommended in 94 per cent of the cases.[6] This is an astonishing proportion in a clinic which felt that it favored maintaining the child in his own home whenever such a plan was feasible.

It should not be expected that these various studies show any consistency as to the proportion of children who, as a part of the treatment process, are removed from their own homes. Obviously the groups of children are not comparable. It is plain, however, that such removal plays a very important part in several different child-guidance clinics, a much more important part than one would gather from a perusal of the literature. In anywhere from one-fifth to three-fifths of the cases coming to such clinics, a major portion of treatment consists of supplying a new environment for the child, usually with the thought that this new environment will continue for from one to several years.

LACK OF SATISFACTORY CRITERIA

In view of the widespread practical use of environmental therapy it might be supposed that the matter had already been widely studied and valid principles established to guide clinicians and others in the choice of such a method. Curiously enough, this is not the case. Perhaps because of its complexity, possibly because the question has been regarded as a simple one, there is no research study worthy of the name which investigates the conditions under which it is advisable to remove a child from his home. Consequently we shall confine our-

---

[5] These figures are taken from the author's study, "Three Surveys of Treatment Measures," *American Journal of Orthopsychiatry*, vol. 7 (January, 1937), p. 50.

[6] Barker, Margaret, and Rappaport, Mitchell. "Community Placement as a Treatment Policy for Sex-Delinquent Girls," *Mental Hygiene*, vol. 18 (April, 1934), pp. 222 ff.

selves in this chapter to statements based on clinical experience, both our own and that of others.   It scarcely needs to be added that such tentative judgments are a poor substitute for suitable scientific studies.

Earlier Discussions of the Problem.   Previous to 1930, there seems to have been no attempt whatsoever to formulate in any definite way the conditions under which it may have been advisable to remove from home a child who was a behavior problem.   Even in discussions regarding the dependent child, who so often presents a picture of behavior difficulties as well, criteria were couched in such vague terms as "unfit home," "exposed to cruelty or abuse," "physical, mental, or moral welfare endangered," and the like.   There is frequently an emphasis on the advisability of keeping the child's own home together whenever possible.   Perhaps a typical statement of this earlier period is the conclusion reached by the White House Conference on Child Welfare in 1919, under the heading "Removal of Children from their Homes":

> Unless unusual conditions exist, the child's welfare is best promoted by keeping him in his own home.   No child should be permanently removed from his home unless it is impossible so to reconstruct family conditions or build and supplement family resources as to make the home safe for the child, or so to supervise the child as to make his continuance in the home safe for the community.   In case of removal, separation should not continue beyond the period of reconstruction.[7]

While the spirit of this and similar statements seems in line with our thinking today their content is so vague as to be of doubtful help in any attempt to apply them to the situation of a particular child.

Some Attempts at More Definite Formulation.   The later White House Conference of 1930 makes the first definite state-

[7] From "Resolutions on Standards Relating to Children in Need of Special Care adopted by Washington and Regional Conferences, 1919."   These resolutions are quoted in full in report of 1930 White House Conference entitled *Dependent and Neglected Children, Report of Committee on Socially Handicapped*, pp. 66–71 (Homer Folks, Chairman).   New York: D. Appleton-Century Company, 1933.

ment of conditions which justify removal.   This statement stresses the emotional relationships of family life as being more of a determining factor than outward conditions, but is vague as to what behavior tendencies constitute reason for removal. This statement is far superior to the earlier pronouncements and is here quoted in full.

> Removal from the family home is warranted when the child presents deviation from normal standards of physical or mental health, or deviations in behavior beyond the capacity of the family to deal with.   Here may be included extreme crippled conditions, feeble-mindedness, and delinquent behavior, but none of these deviations themselves constitute adequate reasons for removal, unless evaluated in relation to the family setting in which they are found.
>
> Removal of children from the family home may also be warranted when relations between parent and child, or between one child and the others in the family group show stubborn resistance to case-work treatment in the given setting, and when temporary removal to foster care may make possible a re-education of the members of the group for life together, or for more wholesome relations even in separation.
>
> There are also rare situations where the form of the family group affords an impossible setting for child development. As already pointed out, incomplete families are not necessarily unsuitable settings for child development, and social work is learning new ways of filling gaps in the motherless, as well as the fatherless home, but foster care is still necessarily resorted to when these plans fail or when complete orphanhood exists.[8]

Still another formulation of the policy of one clinic in determining this question is given by Hopkins and Haines.   They state that the staff policy of the Institute for Juvenile Research in regard to the removal of children from their homes is as follows:

> 1. Children should remain in their own homes unless there is very well-defined and well-authenticated evidence that the home is having a deleterious effect on the child.
> 2. A child should remain until it is clear that intensive social treatment makes no fundamental change in the family patterns.

---

[8] *Dependent and Neglected Children, Report of Committee on Socially Handicapped,* pp. 139-140.

3. In a recommendation for removal of a child from his own home, foster-home care should be first considered and if possible tried.

4. Large-scale institutional placement should be used only for children with special defects or anomalies of a serious nature or, admitting failure to understand the problem, as a protection to society.[9]

Although this brief statement of policy could be elaborated further, especially as to what degree of "deleterious effect" is sufficient to warrant removal, it, like the previous statement, throws a sound burden of proof upon those who would remove the child from home. It may be helpful to take up in greater detail a consideration of the factors involved.

ELEMENTS REQUIRING CONSIDERATION

Anyone who has participated in case conferences where separation of the child from his home is a possible course of action will readily recognize that at the present time any well-validated criteria of judgment are out of the question. The problem has so many subtleties, it is so bound up with the deepest and least ascertainable individual attitudes, that even the wisdom of a Solomon, fortified with facts obtained by researches we now only dream of, might find the solution difficult. Yet we must also face the fact that such decisions are being made every day and that if removal from home is to continue to be an important aspect of our therapy we should at least attempt some analysis of the important features of the situation. Only as our methods of diagnosis become more thorough and accurate can we hope to improve our ability to choose constructively, in the case of a particular child, between the advantages of therapy in his own home, and treatment in a foster home or institution. With this attitude in mind, and thinking necessarily more in terms of individual cases than in terms of generalized facts, we will consider several topics which have a bearing on the decision as to separation of child and family.

[9] Hopkins and Haines, *op. cit.*, p. 110.

The Child's Behavior. In regard to the child's conduct disorders, there would seem to be one crucial question which would assist in deciding whether he could be dealt with more satisfactorily at home or in some other environment. Is there a close association, probably of a cause-and-effect variety, between the parental attitudes or family situation and the child's misbehavior? Is there evidence, in other words, that the stealing or runaway behavior or sex misconduct is due, wholly or in large part, to the family environment? This takes us back at once to the adequacy of the facts upon which we are basing our diagnosis. If we have made a thorough investigation of the social and cultural situation, the school history, the health factor, as well as of the family adjustments, we shall be better able to determine the effect of each of these upon behavior. In the case of Elwyn, for example, even a brief summary indicates plainly that his own misbehavior developed in large measure because of the rejecting attitudes on the part of the parents.

Elwyn's mother Flora is a girl who "reformed" after a period of institutional care. In her youth she was poorly supervised by a subnormal mother and at the age of 13 was causing concern because she was entertaining boys in her room in her mother's absence. There was continuous report of delinquencies until the age of 17, when she became pregnant, and tried unsuccessfully to bring about an abortion. She was committed to an out-of-town institution, where Elwyn was born. He remained there with his mother for nearly five years. Following her release, her adjustment improved, and at the age of 23 she married an earnest, steady young mechanic, a somewhat righteous and severe young man, who has tried hard to accept Elwyn, but in times of annoyance regards the boy as the mother's burden. The parents have been congenial, but Elwyn's behavior has been troublesome, due in part to his decided hyperactivity. Flora has felt that Elwyn is the one source of real friction between herself and her husband.

In the past eight months, since the birth of a new baby brother, matters have become much worse. Elwyn torments the baby, runs away from home, teases, and is unkind to other children. In spite of his average intelligence, his school work is poor.

The psychologist in summarizing the situation, mentions the

mother's struggle to make a good social adjustment, adding this comment on the mother-child situation. "Elwyn is an illegitimate child, born when the mother was only seventeen. She rejected him from the first, making futile attempts at abortion. Her pregnancy with him led to her commitment to the institution. Now she is married to a decent, industrious man, is a good home-maker, and has an attractive baby, to whom she is devoted. In this peaceful home Elwyn's very presence strikes a jarring note, since he is a constant reminder of the mother's delinquent girlhood, and when he behaves badly the result is that much worse. . . . Looking at it from his point of view one realizes that after his first 4½ years at the institution where he was much indulged by everyone and where he was his mother's sole interest, he had suddenly to share his mother with her new husband, and then lost even the greater part of his remaining hold upon her when the new baby came. It is not surprising that home became so unsatisfactory that he would prefer to spend his time elsewhere, nor that having lost his sense of importance, he would resort to various unacceptable ways of gaining attention."

In other instances we find parental attitudes of overindulgence largely responsible for misconduct on the part of the child. Such a youngster was George, whose response to his mother's indulgent solicitude grew into a delinquency pattern of a very serious nature.

George D., an attractive 14-year-old of average mentality, was brought to the Child Study Department when the police of another city picked him up on a runaway trip. It was found that he had failed in a Junior High School, had been dismissed or had run away from three private boarding schools, and had been doing some serious stealing from stores and parked cars. He frequently bullied his mother into giving him money, and had forced her to give him $20 when he ran away. He paid no attention to his mother's wishes or commands, but did entirely as he pleased.

George had been adopted by Mr. and Mrs. D. as a very small infant. The D's were a childless couple, in their early forties at this time. They were extremely devoted to the baby. When George was two his adoptive father died, and from that time on Mrs. D., a college graduate, interested in parental education, dedicated her time and thought and money to George. The case worker reports "she has exhausted her means in trying to please him and win his affections." She bought horses for him to ride, expensive toys to amuse him, tried to fulfill his every wish and whim. George became more and more difficult at home and at school. About the age of ten he learned of his adoption, and after this showed even less affection for his mother. At the time of the clinic study he frequently told his mother he did not like her, never showed any appreciation for the things she did for him, and never apologized or felt sorry for his behavior. It was, of course, quite impossible for the mother to see that her own attitude was almost entirely responsible for the boy's behavior.

In many cases the causes of misconduct do not lie in the family situation. For example, there is Albert, a boy of better than average ability, whose behavior was not unlike that of George. The neighbors complained rather frequently of the mother's lack of control over the boy. Careful study over a considerable period of time led the clinic and the psychiatrist to feel that in all probability the primary cause of his behavior was organic, due either to possible encephalitis at the age of two, when he had a high fever and was unconscious for some days during an attack of influenza, or to an inherited psychopathic tendency, his ancestry having several examples of extreme instability, and the mother herself being regarded as erratic and unstable. In this instance, though the mother's personality may have intensified Albert's problems to some degree, his behavior seemed to be primarily determined by organic or hereditary factors. Other instances might be cited of mentally subnormal children whose misbehavior, truancy and the like, grows out of too great demands which the school places upon them. In still other instances it is the social milieu, the neighborhood influences, and the gang on the corner which are the essential determinants of the child's behavior. In all these situations the child's misconduct develops primarily out of factors other than the family environment. Hence we would do well to consider a program of treatment to be carried on within the child's home, rather than separate the child from his family.

The Family Situation. Clinical experience with difficult children continually forces upon us the fact that externals of family life are relatively unimportant.   It is the tissue of emotional relationships which has significance.   This is especially true when we are considering the matter of placement away from home.   All too often, as we look back over clinic and agency records, we find instances where problem children have been taken from their homes because of gross moral lapses on the part of their parents, or because of conditions of shocking neglect, only to return to these same homes after one or two or five years of care away from their families.   Our treatment would have been much sounder had we recognized the strength of these family bonds, and worked through rather than against them.   And even when we feel we have learned this lesson, the next instance of shocking parental immorality is likely to bring from the case worker or teacher the thought, "This is too much. The child *must* be removed from such influences."   We are slow to learn, when learning runs contrary to our deep-seated prejudices.

This is not to say that children should always remain in their own homes.   There are conditions under which they should surely be removed.   But these conditions have little or nothing to do with the moral standards in the home, or even with the physical neglect of the child.   The basic consideration is the affectional situation which exists.   Thus we find Dr. Hartwell returning an eleven-year-old boy to a home where outward conditions were utterly deplorable (the parents were selling liquor and drugs and conducting a house of ill fame), because the boy's attachment to his mother was the most vital aspect of his experience.   The outcome in this case was successful, though not without its difficulties.   Had the boy been kept away from home the outcome would almost certainly have been poor.[10]   In our own experience we have not infrequently returned to their own inadequate and socially undesirable homes children who forced us to recognize that their family ties were one reality the clinic had to face.

In this whole question it is the child's affectional bond to

---

[10] Hartwell, *op. cit.*, case of Roy Waldock, pp. 215–220.

the parent which is important. As Miss Maud Morlock says,

> We have learned that the child's reaction to the family situation is the greatest single factor to be considered at every stage. While we as social workers have in mind a certain norm of family life, we are realizing, too, that separation of child and parent is in reality a major operation socially, and as such, presents unusual hazards. The most perfect institution or foster home, even equipped with individual towels and toothbrushes and spotless linen closets, may not mean that conditions are conducive to the full development of a particular child. We are thinking less and less of these material things and more and more in terms of the child's emotional needs.[11]

The Child's Affection. Our own experience would indicate that the parent's degree of affection for the child is rather less important as a consideration than the child's affection for the parent. Where the child loves his parents with a strong, wholesome love, it is nearly always unwise to consider removal from home. Certainly where this normal affection is reciprocated by the parent, removal should never, it seems safe to say, be recommended as treatment for the child's misconduct. Where a child is relatively indifferent to the parents, the situation may justify placement. This indifference may be due to simple neglect on the part of the parents, allowing the child to shift for himself. It may be due to the development through parental overindulgence of strong egocentric interest in the youngster which makes him demanding of others, but unable to extend any deep affection to anyone. Whatever its origin, this lack of a strong bond makes the home situation less of a therapeutic possibility and enhances the chance of treatment away from home.

The child who is unwanted or fundamentally disliked by the parent presents many special problems in regard to separation from home. Such children are of course relatively frequent among "problem" cases. Sometimes the child recognizes his

---

[11] Morlock, Maud A. "Recent Gains in Family Protection as Measures of Child Welfare," *Annals of the American Academy of Political and Social Science*, vol. 151 (September, 1930), p. 55.

rejection and tends to give up the parent, looking for affection elsewhere. This type of youngster it may be possible to treat satisfactorily away from home. He may, in fact, rejoice in the opportunity to get away from home and to find parent-substitutes. But there is also the occasional child who has never fully accepted his rejection by the parent and who continues to be bound by the strongest bonds of affection to a parent who shows little affection in return. One of the most intriguing girls followed by our clinic has been of this type. Removed from a mother who showed no affection for her and who had nothing but unfavorable comments to make regarding her, Alma has been unable to accept her foster parents as substitutes or to build up a basis of reciprocal affection with her mother. Consequently she continues over a period of years to worship her mother, yet is always disappointed in the mother's failure to visit her, to write her, or to show any reasonable response. Whether she has been helped by removal from her mother is a question. Within the last month she has decided to enter a convent, and it may be that this identification with her mother church is a first real recognition that she cannot rely on her own mother for affection, but must turn elsewhere for substitute satisfactions.

The Degree of Security. Interwoven with this question of child-parent affection is the whole matter of the child's security in the home. Often this term is loosely used, yet clinically it seems to represent a very real and fundamental entity. The child who has a sense of "belonging," who feels that he fits in with the family group and has a place there, is secure. Several items may help to form this attitude. Dependability and stability of family life, a sense that life is going on in a familiar recognized fashion, has its part. A feeling that he is accepted by the members of the group also contributes to this attitude. This sense of security exists at different levels of maturity, ranging from the dependent type of security which the infant feels in his mother's love and dependable care to the self-security of the mature individual who finds that his acceptance by the larger group, and his feeling of fitting into a niche in the functioning community, give him his sense of "belonging." For children, however, the basic elements of security lie in the family circle, and are closely tied up with the degree of parental affection on the one hand, and the consistency and stability of family life on the other.

The child who is already secure in his own home should rarely be removed from home in order to clear up behavior difficulties.   The situations in which this might be advisable are usually with children like George (described above), where there is considerable security for the child but where there is, on the other hand, an overindulging parent-person.   It is scarcely necessary to add that if there is a wholesome love relationship between child and parent, in addition to a sense of security, removal is never justified.   If these two conditions prevail, we have the most important bases for a healthy psychic life.   We cannot improve on this by placing the child elsewhere. The question is largely academic, however, because serious behavior difficulties based on unfortunate parental attitudes could scarcely arise in a home where the child found both normal affection and security.

Other Family Factors.   Another aspect of the family relationship which deserves discussion is the degree of mental conflict which is aroused in the child by the behavior or attitudes of his parents.   Marital friction and quarreling, or the infidelity or immorality of one parent, may produce a terrific strain of conflict and confused loyalties in the boy or girl. Where such mental conflict is intense, the treatment of the child's problems may often be more satisfactorily carried on away from home, where the continual recurrence of conflicting situations may be avoided.   Whether or not such conflict exists can be determined only through close contact with the child, with a sufficient degree of rapport so that his own feelings can be expressed.   It is futile to judge it from the superficial elements of the family picture, since some children, particularly those who obtain some satisfactions outside the home, may live in atmospheres of immorality and parental discord without ever feeling deeply conflicted in regard to it. On the other hand, the child whose life is lived largely within himself may be tremendously upset by family frictions.

This discussion applies primarily to those sources of mental conflict in which the pull of conflicting desires is continually aggravated by present situations. The child may be aware of a mother's promiscuous relations or may be asked by one parent to spy on the infidelities of the other. Such situations force themselves into the child's life, continually upsetting the balance of his emotional attachments. Where the child is conflicted over some fact of past importance, such as his own adoption, or possible illegitimacy, the situation is usually better handled within the family circle if parental attitudes are at all constructive. We will discuss later the methods of psychotherapy which may be utilized in such circumstances.

One final feature of the family situation which is of importance in determining the advisability of removal is the matter of family loyalties. While this is often somewhat synonymous with the degree of affection between parents and children, it is not necessarily so. There may be strong cultural traditions of family unity which have great force, even though the family life is a bundle of minor frictions. Where this spirit of "one for all, and all for one" exists in great measure, the likelihood of constructive separation of child from family is much reduced. This same spirit of loyalty to one another may however open up new possibilities of treatment — there is the possibility of resources among relatives, the chance of making the family an emotional as well as a cultural unit, and the use of pride in the family group as a motivation. The futility of struggling against such powerful loyalties could well be illustrated by examining placement failures where running away from the foster home or institution has been a part of the failure. Rather frequently in this group we find children whose stubborn loyalty to family groups in which they seem somewhat unhappy has brought to nought all the well-intentioned efforts at treatment through placement.

Before leaving this topic it might be pointed out that there are two qualifying factors which modify certain of the statements which have been made. The age of the child is significant, since attachment to the parent or a feeling of family loyalty is not such an outstanding barrier to placement in the younger child as in the older. Hence in some cases treatment away from home may work out satisfactorily for a young child, where it would have proven unsuccessful in an older child with similar attitudes toward his family. A further modifying factor is the degree of family co-operation, which was mentioned in discussing foster-home care. If the parents are willing to have the child live away from home for a period of treatment, this may offset certain family loyalties which would otherwise make success doubtful. The placement itself becomes then a part of, not an opposition to, the bonds of family affection. Both of these qualifications should be borne in mind in making decisions regarding placement.

The Possibility of Change. Before removing any child from home it is not only the situation as it exists which must be thoroughly understood and evaluated, but the extent to which that situation may be changed. As previously mentioned, the basic causes of misbehavior may be quite outside the area of family relationships, that is, social factors, physical conditions, hereditary tendencies. In such instances, methods of treatment will need to be devised to alter such causative factors, but removal from home will scarcely need to be one of these methods. If, however, the child's problems are closely related to the family situation then the crucial question narrows down to this extent: Is it possible to alter the attitudes of parent and child so that misbehavior is no longer likely to result? While this is still a difficult question to answer, it at least rules out extraneous and non-essential considerations.

How can we know whether Mrs. Bolton will ever be able to show any real affection for Jimmy? Can Arthur's parents modify their ambition for him and expect C's and D's on the report card instead of A's? Could George's mother change her overindulgent ways and give the boy a healthy degree of discipline? These questions are not as completely unanswerable as they may seem. In the following chapter, when we take up in greater detail the means of changing parental attitudes, we shall also discuss the limits of changeability. It is sufficient for our present purpose to note that where the parent's attitude has persisted over a long period of time and where it meets a deep emotional need, the possibility of change is not to be regarded optimistically. In the case of George, briefly described on page 155, it will be seen that the unsatisfied longing for children created in Mrs. D. the first great need for finding an emotional outlet in a child. The husband's death still further deprived her of normally satisfying emotional ties and necessarily caused the concentration of affection on George which was responsible for his difficulties. This pattern of behavior has continued for fifteen years. It is then highly unlikely that we shall be able to change this attitude, both because it is a long-established one and because it meets deep and fundamental needs.

It is of course true that in our present state of knowledge we shall in many instances be unable to determine whether the attitude patterns of parents or children are amenable to change. In such instances we shall be forced to rely upon trial and error. If the best available case work and psychotherapy is unable to affect these attitudes, then we shall have to consider them for practical purposes as unchangeable. It is especially important that all available methods be employed in instances where attitude changes seem possible. Sometimes the destructive parental attitude is a recent one, as in the case of a girl who has adjusted rather satisfactorily at home up to the time of adolescence, but where the continuing rigidity of her father's management brings on a rebellious phase as she seeks more freedom for herself. Frequently, in parents of small children, destructive attitudes are the product of direct education. They are overstern, overlenient, or oversolicitous, primarily because of direct education by friends, relatives or parent-education groups. They are under the impression that they are doing the correct thing and hold to it for that reason. This attitude is usually easy to change because it is only superficially held and is not necessarily essential to the emotional life of the parent.

Although in most instances it is the parent's attitude which is causative and therefore needs to be changed, there are instances in which it is the child's attitude which stands in the way. Kurt is an example of such a situation.

> Kurt had been very fond of both parents, and was somewhat babied by his mother. His life was happy because he never realized the deep rift between his parents, caused by his mother's affairs with other men, the father keeping this situation hidden. After the mother's death, the father remarried in less than a year. His second wife was much older than he, and had been his housekeeper since the death of his first wife. Though very congenial with her as long as she was the housekeeper, Kurt turned against her completely when she usurped his mother's place. His bitterness against her was carried to a degree where she was afraid this 14-year-old boy might murder her. He would not touch food she cooked, nor speak to her. Careful investigation revealed no objective basis for his hatred. Weeks of clinic contacts made no observable impression. He was then placed in a good children's institution, with the suggestion that contact between Kurt and his father and stepmother be gradually encouraged. It was more than a year before he was again friendly with his stepmother.

The Placement Opportunity. Even though everything in the child's situation seems imperatively to demand his removal, there is still one further consideration, that of the chance of success through placement. Is there for this youngster a likelihood that foster-home or institutional placement will result in success, that behavior difficulties will cease, and that the child will develop into a useful citizen? Unless there is a strong possibility of such success the drastic step of removal from home seems unwise. The situation is similar to that of the surgeon who is contemplating a drastic operation. Unless the chance of success is fairly great, he will not expose the patient to the risk of undergoing the knife. We should have the same reluctance to expose the child to all the subtle risks and unexpected elements involved in a complete change of environment, unless a successful outcome seems reasonably sure.

Thus where a child has but borderline mental ability, symptoms of deep-seated instability, and is already past the more plastic childhood years, removal from home is difficult to justify as a treatment measure, even though misbehavior has arisen through unwise parental management and though family ties are unsatisfactory. We are forced to realize that the outlook is poor, whether the child is kept at home or removed from home. Consequently the better plan may involve such palliation of the home situation as we are able to achieve, and is to be preferred to running the risks of placement when success is so doubtful.

On the other hand if the youngster in question is likely to succeed in placement, as far as can be judged by the criteria outlined in the two preceding chapters, then placement may reasonably be used.

> Such a youngster is red-headed little Floyd, seven years old, possessed of all sorts of scandalous information which he uses with other small youths to show his superiority of knowledge. He has very superior intelligence, though his school work has been poor. He has little deep affection for his mother so far as can be determined from a diagnostic study, but time alone can verify this judgment. His mother is a coarse, promiscuous woman, who has never tried to keep Floyd from knowing or witnessing her casual sex alliances. His knowledge of sex affairs comes from this source. It is quite evident that Floyd's youth, his good mentality, the fact that his behavior patterns are not deeply set, the slight attachment for his mother, all make the chances of successful placement very good indeed.

SUMMARIZED CRITERIA FOR REMOVAL FROM HOME

The subjective nature of the discussion thus far makes it sufficiently plain that no such definite criteria can be stated for the removal from home as were given in regard to choice of a foster home. Rather with the hope of provoking satisfactory study and research than as a statement of verified fact, the attempt is made in the following paragraphs tentatively to set up the conditions under which it is wise to remove a child from home in order more adequately to deal with conduct disorders.

The material below is so tabulated that removal from home is advisable as treatment when the statements most accurately describing the child's situation are found in the left-hand column. If, under even one category, his situation is accurately described by the statements in the right-hand column, then placement, in the opinion of the writer, is a doubtful plan of treatment.

CRITERIA FOR REMOVAL FROM HOME

Conditions Making Placement Advisable	Conditions Making Continuance in Own Home Advisable
Behavior	
Behavior difficulties of more than average seriousness, definitely associated with, and probably caused by, parental attitudes, management, or behavior.	Behavior difficulties definitely associated with some other cause or causes — hereditary, physical, or social — rather than with parental attitudes.
Family Atmosphere	
Child has little affection for parents.	Child has normal degree of affection for both parents.
Child feels emotionally insecure at home.	Child feels emotionally secure with his parents.
Child is rejected by one or both parents.	Child has strong family loyalties.
Parents' affection for child is of unwholesome type, causing too great dependence or infantile attachment.	
Parents' behavior and attitudes are such that they have caused great emotional conflict in the child.	(The above conditions lose some of their force if the child is young, or if the parents are desirous of treatment through placement.)
Child has little loyalty to family group.	
Possibility of Change	
The parental attitudes which seem to cause misbehavior are fixed, deep-seated, and of long standing.	Parental attitudes which are associated with misbehavior are recent, or superficially held, or conditioned by factors which may be changed.
Skilled efforts to change essential attitudes of parent and child have failed.	
Placement Opportunity	
The child possesses the characteristics as to age, intelligence, stability, type of behavior, etc., which indicate better than 50 per cent chance of success away from home.	The child possesses characteristics which make him a poor risk for placement.

The limitations of this outline are obvious. The terms are some of them vague, and would doubtless be differently defined

by different people.   The judgments that must be made are to
a considerable degree subtle and subjective.   Also we have no
suitable techniques for determining some of the facts called for
in the outline.   We must fall back on various empirical methods.   How, for example, are we to determine the degree of
affection which 9-year-old Marie has for her parents?   She
says she is unhappy at home, yet this may be the expression of
a mood.   On a personality test she indicates that she wishes
that her parents showed her more affection and gives other evidence of insecure feeling.   Several skillful interviews may be
sufficient to clarify the matter.   If Marie proves to be inhibited, finding it difficult to express herself, it may be necessary
to arrange for a temporary period of placement away from home
in order to obtain a true estimate of her attitudes.

In the clinic with which the writer is associated we have been
able to accomplish this through the temporary foster homes
maintained by the Society for the Prevention of Cruelty to
Children.   If placement seems advisable, yet the child's fundamental attitudes are still in doubt, a period of one to three
weeks in a temporary home is, if possible, arranged.   Here the
observations of the foster mother and the interviews of the clinician both aid in determining the genuineness and depth of the
child's attachment for the family.

We must often employ similarly empirical methods in deciding the extent to which parental and family attitudes are alterable.   If we are in doubt on this score a few months of effort
to change attitudes is wise before taking any final step in regard
to the child's removal.   The techniques to be used in altering
family attitudes will be discussed later.

With all their limitations, however, the criteria stated above
seem somewhat more definite, somewhat more applicable to the
individual child, than the formulae previously suggested.   The
degree to which they are a reliable and valid aid to decision is
unknown, since they lay no claim to a basis in research.   They
are based only on clinical judgment.   In the writer's experience, few children are treated with great success by placement
whose situation is accurately rated by any statement from the

right-hand column.   If behavior is due to some other cause than the family milieu, if family ties are normal and wholesome, or if there is good chance of changing destructive family attitudes, then the outcome of placement is not likely to be all that we desire.   Certainly, too, little is gained by removal if the child is the type who is likely to fail either in foster-home or institutional care.   If this formulation of criteria is regarded as a crude rule-of-thumb, to be tested by judgment as well as by further study and research, its use may be helpful.

How Might Such Criteria be Tested?   The opportunity for testing decisions regarding removal from home is not difficult to find.   This opportunity lies in the fact that in some cases it is not possible to carry through a separation from home, even though this is clinically regarded as the best basis of a plan of treatment.   This failure to adopt such a plan offers one of the few clear-cut possibilities for experimentation which exist in the clinical field.   We have then two groups for which removal from home seems the most desirable treatment.   With one group this treatment is carried out; with the other, through circumstances over which the clinic has no control, the treatment is withheld.   A comparison of outcomes might well be crucial.

There are two such studies which may be cited, both unsatisfactory because of very small numbers, but both of interest as indicating the possibilities if this type of research were carried further.   Hopkins and Haines in their study of cases in Chicago found that in the group of 100 children for whom removal from home was recommended as a part of treatment 64 were actually so removed; in 6 cases the outcome was unknown; and in 30 instances the placement was not made by the agency which had asked advice, and the child was either allowed to remain at home against the clinic recommendation or placed in an institution.   When these cases were investigated 24 to 32 months later, it was found that of the 64 children placed in foster homes 19 per cent were failures, but of the 30 children who had been treated contrary to clinic advice 91 per cent were failures, 14 of them having been in institutions.[12]   Allowance should be made for the fact that some of the 14 may have been placed in institutions because the agency felt they were too difficult for foster homes, and hence might have swelled the ranks of foster-home failures had they been so placed.   Also the authors do not state how they gauged the adjustment of the children who were in institutions at the time of the follow-up study, as some of them must have been.   Nevertheless, with all allowances, the fact seems to stand out that the clinic had good grounds for recommending a removal from home, and their recommendations were justified by results.

The second study is an unpublished research made in the Child Study Department, Rochester S.P.C.C.   In 1932 the department studied 114 delinquent boys and girls before their appearance in Children's Court and on the basis of a conference among the interested agencies and workers mapped out a treatment plan for each child.   This suggested plan was sent to the court previous to the hearing.   In 89 cases the action taken by the court was in line with the treatment suggested.   In 6 cases the court made minor but possibly significant changes, such as placing a boy on unofficial probation where a suspended sentence and intensive probation had been suggested, or sending a child to one institution when another had been recommended.   In 19 cases the court adopted some entirely different treatment plan than that suggested, usually allowing the child to remain at home when foster-home or institution care had been suggested.   (Incidentally this should be of interest to those who suppose that clinics operate to urge judicial "leniency."   The clinic is not more lenient, but merely has different criteria for selecting the cases requiring drastic treatment.)

Fifteen months later these cases were reviewed and divided into two groups, the first containing those who were making a sufficiently good adjustment so that there had been no further delinquency, no reappearance in court, and no gross evidences of failure.   This we called, for lack of a better term, the "adjusting" group, since it was too soon to determine whether they

[12] Hopkins and Haines, *op. cit.*, p. 127.

were successful and a considerable number were in institutions where our only knowledge was that they were adjusting to the program there.   The second group, 13 in number, was made up of those who were gross failures within the fifteen months. Eleven of them had reappeared in court, one had been killed on the last of several runaways, and one girl after failing to adjust had run away and disappeared.   The allocation of this failure group is of crucial interest.   Of the 89 cases where the court had followed the treatment plan mapped out by the clinic conference, one was a failure and was transferred from the recommended institution to another.   Of the 6 cases where minor changes had been made in the plan, one was a failure.   Of the 19 cases where the court had adopted some totally different residence plan than that suggested, 12, or 63 per cent, were failures within the fifteen months.   The accompanying table gives in somewhat more detail the facts upon which these statements are based.

FOLLOWING OF CLINIC RECOMMENDATIONS REGARDING
RESIDENCE AS RELATED TO OUTCOME OF CASE
(Child-Study Department, Rochester S.P.C.C.)

Type of Residence Plan Recommended	No.	Recommendations followed		Recommendations not followed	
		"Adjusting"	Failed	"Adjusting"	Failed
Remain home under supervision....	30	30	0	0	0
Foster home......................	23	17	0	3	3
Institution for delinquents.........	33	19	1	4	9
Institution for defectives..........	22	22	0	0	0
Totals.......................	108	88	1	7	12
Percentage of failure..........		1%		63%	

OTHER JUSTIFICATIONS FOR REMOVAL FROM HOME

It may be mentioned in passing that separation of the child from his family may at times be necessary for other than treatment purposes.   These other reasons for removal fall outside our range of interest and need be mentioned only to make clear the limitations of our discussion.

It is often necessary, of course, to remove a child from home simply because the home is no longer able to provide physical care. If both parents are ill, or a father is left with a motherless family of children, placement in homes or institutions may be the most feasible plan of care. There may or may not be behavior problems which need attention. Obviously the criteria we have been discussing do not directly apply here, although the stress on the importance of family attachments has merit in the consideration of any family problem.

Still another cause which occasionally operates to force the removal of delinquent children from their homes is the need for protection of the community. Dealing with serious behavior problems, one frequently runs into the neat dilemma of choosing between what is best for the individual and what is best for the larger group. A 17-year-old boy is found to have been tampering sexually with small girls. Careful study reveals early experiences in which an older boy taught him to handle infant girls, which conditioned much of his sex drive toward this goal. Considering only the individual, psychotherapy seems to be indicated to get at the root of the problem. But from the community point of view protection for other little girls is demanded. The two goals are only partially compatible. Similarly in the case of a boy who is stealing persistently and burglarizing houses. If during a period of treatment stealing persists, how long before society's demands for protection become paramount to our interest in the individual welfare? Without attempting to answer the unanswerable, we see that cases arise, particularly among the delinquent group, where removal from home and placement, usually in an institution, seems imperative to protect the community welfare. Naturally the criteria given above do not aid in making such a decision.

The important point for the clinician in such circumstances is to see clearly the purpose of such institutional commitments. If the protection required by the community runs contrary to the treatment needs of the individual, let us view the placement in that light, as a necessity, and not as a treatment measure. There will also be the instances where the two goals may be reconciled, where the protection needed by the community and the preferred treatment for the individual both point to institutional care.

A word of caution might be added as to the need of a long-time point of view in considering this question. Concern for the immediate welfare of the community causes police and judges, teachers and laymen, to demand institutional care for many offenders. If such care is not the best treatment for the problems of the individual, then we may be only guaranteeing later dangers to the community. Considerable present risk is justified, if a plan of treatment within the community has some chance of restoring the individual to normal adjustment.

Criteria that are Unimportant. It is quite possible that the significance of the criteria which have been suggested lies as much in what has been omitted as in what has been included. Most of the bases upon which such a decision is commonly made have been omitted from the list. Comment on some of these might be in order.

1. *The seriousness of the behavior problem.* Removal from home is perhaps most often based on the degree of annoyance which the child's behavior is causing. This is quite unsound. While children should not be separated from their families for trivial reasons, if all four suggested criteria are favorable to treatment by placement, this should be carried out even though the behavior symptoms are only moderately disturbing. As this chapter is being written efforts are being made to bring about the removal from home of an 8-year-old boy, whose behavior includes bullying and tormenting other children, some petty stealing in school, and several episodes of exposing himself to little girls. There are no major delinquencies of any sort. Yet this boy's behavior arises from the parental misman-agement of a vacillating indulgent mother and of a severe erratic father. The parental attitudes have kept Raymond infantile and selfish. We have tested the changeability of the parental attitudes through several years of effort in dealing with the problems of an older brother, and were so unsuccessful

that this brother became delinquent. Furthermore Raymond is intelligent, young, physically stable, and should respond well to foster-home care. Consequently it seems the height of folly to wait for problems to become more serious before bringing about a separation. Often years of valuable time are lost through failure to see the situation in its potential aspects. If serious misbehavior is inevitable, and home environment such that removal is advisable, we should recognize placement as the immediate goal, rather than wait for the behavior patterns to set into less plastic form.

2. *The degree of moral laxity in the home.* The whole system of dealing with behavior difficulties on a "moralistic," punitive basis has much older cultural roots than any of the more recent and more scientific approaches. One expression of the older system, frequently evident, is that children whose behavior has come to the attention of school, agency, or court are removed from their parents if deviations from accepted moral standards exist in the home. Illegal alliances between the parent-persons, extra-marital relations on the part of one parent, questionable associations of a separated parent with members of the opposite sex, promiscuous sex behavior, these have all been the basis for removal from the home. As has been pointed out, it is not the externals of the home nor the conventionality of family life that determine whether it is suitable for the child. Extreme immorality on the part of the parent is, to be sure, often associated with lack of affection for the child, and frequently may destroy the child's security or build up emotional conflicts. It is these latter aspects which have significance, however, rather than presence or absence of a marriage certificate, or the reputation concerning conventionality of behavior.

3. *Neglect of the children.* This is a favorite legal basis of removal. Unless it is coupled with emotional neglect and rejection, physical neglect has less importance than is often given to it. If the emotional relationships within the family are sound, education of the parents, making available adequate financial resources, and aiding family management by intelligent supervision will be much better modes of treatment than

the removal of the child.   Certainly removal from home because of poverty has no excuse in a modern world.

REMOVING *A CHILD FROM A FOSTER HOME*

If a child is failing to adjust in a foster home and behavior problems are increasing rather than diminishing, a whole group of questions arise to perplex the conscientious worker.   Shall the child be removed from his foster home?   Would another home, more adequately chosen to meet his needs, be advisable? Or will such a move be upsetting to the child and unproductive of a better adjustment?   Is the solution to change the attitudes of foster parent and child in the present setting?   All of these questions are of course very similar to the problems we have been considering in the removal of the child from his home. Shall we use the same criteria in making our decision regarding change of foster homes?

The Boston study, already frequently referred to, lists nine conditions which justify the child's removal from one foster home to another.   Undoubtedly such a list might be elaborated still further.   In the writer's opinion, however, such listing of specific conditions may confuse rather than clarify the issue. It would seem that the same criteria already suggested as applying to the home may be used in determining the advisability of a foster-home change.   If the child's behavior is directly traceable to the foster parents or the foster-family situation, if the child lacks affection and security in the foster home, if the prospect of changing the damaging foster-parent attitudes is poor, then the change is justified.   Otherwise, particularly if the affectional relationships are good, treatment should be continued in the foster home.

One other consideration which assumes greater importance in the foster-home than in the own-home situation is the matter of over- or under-placement.   If a youngster is placed in a home of a cultural level in which he cannot continue, and which will estrange him from the cultural habits of his family and relatives, then in case behavior problems arise a change in placement might be justified on what would otherwise be regarded as inadequate grounds.

For the most part, of course, if the foster home is well selected in the first place, a change will seldom need to be made in order to treat the behavior difficulties. Much more often a change in placement is forced upon the worker by the foster parent who finds the task too great, or the behavior difficulties too annoying, or has not the patience to wait for the improvement which is likely to come as fundamental causes are corrected. Certainly no one who has known the patience and ingenuity and persistence shown by the great majority of foster parents caring for children can criticize their unwillingness, in some instances, to continue with the burden.

THE PLACE OF ENVIRONMENTAL TREATMENT

Three chapters have been given over to a consideration of the question, "Where shall the child live?" Although on the face of it this seems to be a simple question, the facts brought out indicate clearly that the selection of the child's total environment has tremendous importance in dealing with delinquent and problem behavior. This importance arises both from the fact that it is a very widely used form of treatment measure, and from the fact that both foster-home and institutional placement have a decided effect in altering children's behavior. It is a means of treatment much more feasible with children than with adults, the latter being more firmly rooted in every way in their environment, the obstacles to change often insuperable.

As a mode of treatment the selection of a place of residence which will have a therapeutic effect does not necessarily appeal to the imagination. Such a choice has about it none of the mysterious elements or technical verbiage which make some types of therapy so alluring. It is nevertheless the only sound foundation for all the more subtle or more refined sorts of treatment which we shall proceed to consider in the following chapters. Too often we find agencies and schools wasting precious remedial and therapeutic effort on children who cannot possibly make a normal adjustment in their present home setting.   It would have been far better if the effort had been expended in getting the child into a home or institutional setting where more refined methods had a chance of success.

It is because of the great importance of the choice of a place of residence as a means of treatment that the attempt has been made to set forth criteria which may be of practical help in deciding when a child should be removed from his own home, when care in a foster home is advisable, and when the institution should be called upon to care for the child.   The fact is freely acknowledged that for the first and last set of criteria the scientific backing is very meager, but they are nevertheless stated with the hope that serious students of children's problems will find some stimulus toward filling these gaps in our knowledge and toward modifying, disproving, or reinforcing the criteria which have been tentatively advanced.

BIBLIOGRAPHY

Hopkins, Cornelia D., and Haines, Alice R.   "A Study of One Hundred Problem Children for whom Foster Care was Advised," *American Journal of Orthopsychiatry*, vol. 1 (January, 1931), pp. 107–128.

Morlock, Maud A.   "Recent Gains in Family Protection as Measures of Child Welfare," *Annals of the American Academy of Political and Social Science*, vol. 151 (September, 1930), pp. 46–56.

Rogers, Carl R.   "Three Surveys of Treatment Measures Used with Children," *American Journal of Orthopsychiatry*, vol. 7 (January, 1937), pp. 48–57.

White House Conference on Child Health and Protection.   Report of Committee on Socially Handicapped, sec. IV, C–1, pp. 99–141.   New York: D. Appleton-Century Company.

PART III

Treatment Through Modifying the Environment

Family Attitudes as a Focus of Treatment

THE IMPORTANCE of the family as a factor in the causation of behavior difficulties is equaled by its potentialities in the field of treatment. The child-guidance clinics have led the way in pointing to the need of changing family attitudes and methods of child care, if problem children are to be helped. It is not surprising that studies have shown that for children who are being dealt with in their own homes the most numerous and most important treatment measures are those designed to effect some change in the family atmosphere. Consequently, in considering all the modifications of the child's emotional, social, and physical environment which are useful techniques of individual therapy, we shall first survey the resources for help and the obstacles to help which lie within the home.

THE IMPORTANCE OF PARENTAL ATTITUDES

In a notable group of studies to which we shall have occasion to refer again, Miss Helen Witmer and various graduate students at Smith College have brought to light facts which are of basic importance. In these studies a group of 197 children's cases from the Institute for Child Guidance, New York City, was examined to determine the factors associated with the success or failure of the child's adjustment at the time the case was closed. A further study of each case was made several years after the clinic contact in order to determine the later degree of failure or success and the factors associated with this final result. The greatest part of their findings was negative.

Such items as the child's age at the time of clinic study, the sex, school placement, ordinal position in the family, even the child's symptomatic behavior, showed no relationship to the outcome of treatment, as judged by the Institute staff at the time the case was closed. Intelligence showed but a slight relationship with outcome. The nationality or religion of the child, the economic status of the home, the size of the family — these too were of no help in predicting the outcome. But when ratings were made of the marital adjustment of the parents, of the "emotional tone" of the home, or of the behavior and attitudes of the parents toward the child, it was discovered that these less tangible factors bore a striking relationship to the clinic's success in dealing with the child. In the home where the parents were finding satisfaction in their married life, where the home atmosphere was free from strife and friction, and where parents had a normal degree of affection for the child, it was possible to overcome the child's difficulties in the overwhelming majority of instances. But where the reverse of these conditions prevailed the results were consistently poorer, in some instances the majority of the cases being failures. This was so in spite of the fact that the Institute workers had been aiming to improve these very conditions, seemingly without success. With justification Miss Witmer concludes her study with the remark that "the findings of this paper thus lend weight to the mental hygiene hypothesis that parent-child relationships are of fundamental importance in determining personality development, and at the same time they suggest that the methods of therapy generally employed are not very successful in remedying the more serious difficulties that arise out of family maladjustment." [1]

Such challenging conclusions force us to examine with critical care those techniques which clinics and clinic workers have been using in attempting to change family situations. They offer a sharp contrast to the earlier policy of child-guidance clinics where the task of altering parental attitudes was often

[1] Witmer, Helen L. and students. "The Outcome of Treatment in a Child Guidance Clinic," *Smith College Studies in Social Work*, vol. 3 (June, 1933), p. 399.

turned over rather casually to the social worker as a secondary measure, while the psychiatrist applied his superior skill to what seemed to be the nub of the situation, the child himself.

Attempts to Alleviate Marital Friction. Often enough, in analyzing the basic influences in a child's adjustment, deep-seated friction between the parents is found to be a part of the problem, as in the case of Paul (discussed in Chapter III). Where this is true, if the child is to remain in the home, some means must be found to help in the solution of the marital problems. Otherwise complete alteration of the child's behavior is unlikely. Miss Witmer found that distinctly better results were obtained in working with children whose parents were living together in a satisfactory relationship than with those children whose parents were definitely dissatisfied with their marital life. Intermediate results were obtained in homes where the parents were divorced or separated, or where the parents had a resigned or neutral attitude toward the frictions of their married existence. While the facts are hardly conclusive they seem to indicate that the tenseness of a home where parents are deeply dissatisfied is worse so far as the children's behavior is concerned than is the home which has broken.

As to the possibilities of aiding marital tangles, we find widely discrepant results. The Mowrers, in a study of domestic discord in Chicago, reported that family-welfare agencies had been able to adjust only 4 per cent of the 1573 families they had attempted to help, but also found that the methods they used were largely of the "ordering and forbidding" type, which have long proven inadequate for most purposes of case work. A more favorable report is given by Miss Hixenbaugh of 101 serious cases of marital maladjustment coming to the social work department of the Dayton (Ohio) Court of Domestic Relations.[2] Of this group 47 were "reconciled" and a better adjustment reached, 20 were "adjusted" in the sense that separation or support was arranged for, or the situation cared for

---

[2] Hixenbaugh, Elinor R. "Reconciliation of Marital Maladjustment — An Analysis of 101 Cases," *Social Forces* (December, 1931), p. 235.

in some other manner short of divorce, 10 were divorced, and 24 were still current at the time the report was made.

The most recent study, and without doubt the one of greatest interest, is that made by Mrs. Harriet Mowrer of the methods of dealing with 120 situations of marital maladjustment. These were families of all economic and social levels, for the most part Jewish, all of adequate intelligence, and were referred to Mrs. Mowrer in her capacity as Domestic Discord Consultant of the Jewish Social Service Bureau of Chicago, or came to her as private clients. The treatment of these couples extended over periods of two to four years. Of the 120 pairs, 66 were separated at the time of the first contact, but at the close of treatment there were but 12 couples separated or divorced. Mrs. Mowrer regards 70 of the 120 as having made a complete adjustment, 32 more a partial adjustment, and only 18 couples as having failed to reach any adjustment.[3] There is of course no more than casual reference to the children in these homes, since the author's primary interest is in the marital situation itself. The contrast with the figures given by Mrs. Mowrer and her husband in the earlier study indicates the difference which better understanding and improved techniques can make. A scrutiny of these methods will repay our attention. Before making such a study, however, we shall consider the attitudes of the parent toward the child, which have even more significance than the attitudes of the parents toward each other.

Attempts to Alter Parent-Child Attitudes. If we were to gamble on the outcome of treatment in the case of a problem or delinquent child and had to base our gamble on one item alone, we would do best to disregard the child entirely and investigate simply the way in which the parents behave toward the youngster and the attitudes which they hold toward him. This is the somewhat startling conclusion to which one is forced by the studies of Miss Witmer and her students. They found that among clinic cases where there was an extreme lack of

[3] Mowrer, Harriet R. *Personality Adjustment and Domestic Discord*, p. 273. New York: American Book Company, 1935.

affection for the child on the part of the parents there was no improvement in 64 per cent of the cases. At the other extreme, when a normal affectional relationship existed between the child and his parents, and where the faults were those of inadequate handling of the child, only 3 per cent of the cases were unimproved, and 97 per cent were either satisfactorily or partially adjusted. Between these two extremes were varying degrees and combinations of parental attitudes, with treatment results also showing variation. Aside from complete rejection, the most disastrous situations seemed to be those in which the mother rejected the child and the father was indulgent, 53 per cent of failures being found in this group; and the situations in which the mother was highly protective, finding in the child an outlet for her emotions. In this group 43 per cent were failures. While the numbers in these sub-groups are small, ranging from 17 to 54, the consistency of the trend lends weight to the findings.[4]

A still later study conducted by several Smith College students,[5] of 125 cases of severe maternal rejection from five different child-guidance clinics, corroborates some of these findings. Of the 125 children 51 per cent were still failures in adjustment at the time treatment ended. In regard to the parental attitudes themselves the finding was even more striking. In 18 instances the parents' attitude was greatly modified. In 24 cases there was some improvement. With 83 parents (66 per cent) no change at all was achieved.

From still another source similar findings are reported.[6] In a very intensive program of treatment of delinquents sponsored by Dr. Healy there were 123 cases in three clinics where the attitude of the parent was clearly an important factor in the child's problem and where treatment was attempted. Of this group it was found in 58 cases (47 per cent) that the parent was not essentially modified even though first responses to

---

[4] Witmer, *op. cit.*, p. 370.

[5] See *Smith College Studies in Social Work*, vol. 7 (December, 1936), pp. 164–165, for abstracts of these theses.

[6] Healy, William, and Bronner, A. F. *New Light on Delinquency and its Treatment*, p. 156. New Haven, Conn.: Yale University Press, 1936.

treatment were favorable. In 28 cases some modification of the parent's attitude and behavior toward the child was achieved. In 37 instances the parental attitude and behavior were much modified. This study is not directly comparable to the previous one, since it covers all types of destructive parental attitudes rather than deals specifically with attitudes of rejection. Nevertheless it is significant that in both studies failure is reported in half or more than half of these attempts to alter parents' attitudes toward their children.

It cannot be sufficiently stressed that these results obtain in spite of the clinic's efforts to change the destructive attitudes described. The studies reported cover groups of cases selected from nine child-guidance clinics, including those with the most highly trained personnel and the most intensive programs of therapy. The parental attitudes were recognized as an important focus of therapy. Throughout varying periods of treatment it was the purpose of clinic workers to alter these attitudes. Against this background of intensive effort by skilled workers, parental ways of behaving toward children show a stubborn resistance to change which we should fully face and recognize. The discovery of adequate methods of dealing with parental attitudes is a goal toward which our best research efforts should be bent.

THE MEANS OF CHANGING PARENTAL ATTITUDES

In a mood of critical skepticism inspired by the sort of factual data we have been considering, we turn to a consideration of the available methods of changing the attitudes of parents toward each other and toward their children. We shall recognize that important as parental attitudes have been proven to be the task of altering them is difficult, and such studies as have been made indicate that with our present knowledge success is possible only in a moderate proportion of cases. If we can define more clearly the sorts of parental situations where successful treatment is most likely, we shall be able to avoid certain blunders in therapy.

Although the problems of friction between husband and wife and between parent and child are as old as the race, there are very few careful studies which have investigated the techniques used in changing these attitudes. As is true of other topics we have considered, much more research has been done in regard to the classification and measurement of parental attitudes, than in regard to the changing of these attitudes. We shall here limit our discussion to three of the treatment methods most widely used in clinical and case-work practice; direct education of parents, interpretation of the individual to himself, and the establishment for treatment purposes of a close relationship between parent and therapist.

Direct Education. To the beginner in clinical work, education of the parent seems the answer to a great many of the problems which children present. Sometimes this is thought of as education of the parent in a group where he may learn modes of marital adjustment or methods of child care. More often it is thought of as a process of individual education, in which the clinician, who has come to understand the basic elements in the problem, conveys to the parent this understanding and the facts upon which it is based, so that the next steps in treatment become as obvious to the parent as they are to the clinician. It is not until this educational approach has been tried on numerous occasions that the clinician realizes its extreme limitations in dealing with this type of situation.

An example of the simplest sort may make this plain. A mother requests help with her child, a girl of 11, who is difficult to manage and has never been allowed to attend school. It needs little more than a glance at the child to recognize that she is the type of mental defective known as Mongolian, and a brief examination establishes her mental development as approximately that of a three-year-old. The obvious step for the clinician seems to be to educate the mother as to the nature of mongolism, to point out to her that there is no known cure or remedy for the condition, that she must face the tragic fact that her child can never develop much beyond this point, and that institutional care is the only sensible and kind procedure for the welfare of both child and parent. Recognizing that this information may be upsetting and disappointing to the parent, there would seem to be no difficulty in at least conveying the simple facts regarding the condition and the experiences of others with similar children. We find, however, that this mother, of at least average intelligence, is quite unable to digest this information. She insists that the child can read and write at the very moment that the youngster is making unintelligible sounds to indicate its wants, unable to formulate a complete sentence. She is sure that the child has shown great improvement in the past, then shifts to the notion that she will show great improvement in the future. In spite of the explanation of the nature of mongolism, she states that the child's condition is due to the refusal of the educational authorities to let her attend school. Finally she reveals that four other competent physicians and psychologists have examined the child in the last five years and have given her substantially the same diagnosis and suggestions as are being given to her now. Although she reports this, she seizes upon some minor circumstance or statement of each examination to fortify her own viewpoint. She leaves, having gained nothing from this attempt to "educate" her, nor, it would seem, from any of the four previous attempts.

While perhaps this illustration is more simple than are most attempts to change parental attitudes, the results are no different than in countless other endeavors to alter parental behavior or attitudes by direct education. The fact that parents may be able easily to absorb training for a job, or to educate themselves in regard to current events, or to learn a new system of contract bridge, does not mean that they can learn even simple factual data when this goes contrary to their emotional needs. Unfortunately educational psychology is much richer in techniques for imparting "neutral" information than in techniques for teaching in emotionally charged situations.

There are, however, many instances where direct education of parents on an intellectual level has been productive of good therapeutic results. Frequently, for example, situations of marital friction may be definitely aided by instruction of one parent or both in certain areas where their lack of information has created difficulty. A course in cooking or home economics for the wife may so help to reduce the daily annoyances and disappointments of housekeeping as to improve decidedly the home atmosphere. Counsel in regard to a program of budgeting or the techniques of family management of money may smooth out many of the difficulties between husband and wife. In other instances where extravagance or miserliness is more strongly motivated, or has a greater emotional value to the individual, educative efforts fall on stony soil. Frequently in marital situations where there has been sexual maladjustment, instruction in the techniques of sexual intercourse may be of very great assistance in adjusting these difficulties. Perhaps the most striking illustrations of factual information altering marital situations come from the experiences of the birth-control clinics, where instruction in means of contraception may remove much of the fear and insecurity of a marriage relationship, and make possible a more normal and satisfying family life. In such situations the change in the attitudes of the parents toward each other may be very marked.

Cases might be cited in which parent-child relationships have been helped and adjustment made more easy through direct education. Young mothers with small children are often able to assimilate and use simple instructions in the proper régimes of sleeping, diet, and physical care for their children. Such instruction may lessen the tension of doubt which the mother has been under and may lessen also the irritability of the child. Instruction in the matter of suitable toys or help in the development of a constructive program of activity is also useful in many situations. Parents may respond to information of a general nature, such as a description of the common traits and difficulties to be anticipated in adolescence, or to very specific instruction, such as the suggestion of a specific method of giving an allowance. Frequently suggestions in regard to home responsibilities for the child are well received. A parent with a child of a certain age may be helped by a description of the normal degree of independent behavior achieved by the average child of that age. Parents may also absorb education as to the poor results of making comparisons among their children, or to the need of separate activities for rival siblings. Attempts may also be made to extend educational efforts into more interpretive fields. Not only the facts about the child's mentality, but the implications these have for his adjustment to the family and to other life situations, may be explained to the parents. Their ability to accept such explanations will depend both upon the facts and upon their own reactions. When we go still further, and endeavor to interpret to the parents the effects which their attitudes or methods of discipline are having upon the child, the result is even more dubious. In such areas they are much more likely to hold already certain opinions and attitudes with a strongly emotional tinge. Consequently they are able to assimilate only such information or instruction as does not run contrary to their own emotional needs.

No better indication of this could be found than in the usual difficulty in treating feeding problems in young children. In almost every case of this sort, the recipe for treatment may be very briefly stated in some such words as these: "Place a wholesome meal before the child three times a day. Pay no attention as to whether he eats or not. Remove the remaining food in 20 or 30 minutes, or when the family is through with its meal." Simple enough instructions, and almost invariably effective when tried, there is probably not one parent in ten, with a child presenting feeding difficulties, who can fully accept this simple bit of education and can cease being overattentive to the child's eating.

We shall discuss in the following pages some of the differences in the parents themselves which account for the great differences in their accessibility to treatment. It may be well at this point to make some observations in regard to the situations where a direct educational approach is particularly applicable. It may have been noted in the preceding paragraphs that when the information to be conveyed is genuinely new to the parent, in a field where he has no already established opinions, it is more likely of acceptance. Where the new information is of a sort which the parent has been trying to obtain, the outcome is even better, as with young parents seeking information regarding child care, or with parents desiring information regarding contraceptive methods.   In these instances, there is a readiness for change which makes the results gratifying, and the degree of alteration in parental behavior and attitudes is noteworthy.   Miss Ruth Gartland found in a study of parents coming to a Chicago clinic that 40 per cent were sufficiently free from serious emotional involvement in the problems of their children to use educational suggestions of the sort which have been mentioned.[7]   This percentage would doubtless differ with various groups of parents.   To the writer, the figure seems high for parents of children studied in the clinic, perhaps normal for average parents.   A study of treatment techniques suggested in our clinic cases showed that direct educational techniques had been recommended much more frequently with foster parents than with own parents of problem children.   This tendency had no doubt been due to a feeling that foster parents, being less emotionally involved, could absorb and use specific suggestions and factual data more often than the own parents.

In general, though a direct educational approach may often be unsuccessful, the clinician, teacher, or case worker is justified in its frequent use even where success is somewhat doubtful.   It is by all odds the simplest and most direct form of psychotherapy, and wherever there exist blind spots of ignorance or inadequate information which are hampering a family relationship, an educational approach should be considered.   It is most likely to be effective where the parent is already motivated to desire such information, or where the facts to be given have a neutral emotional tone so far as the parent is concerned and may be learned like any other factual data.   There would seem to be only one real risk to be considered in the use of such technique.   If a parent is given information which runs strongly counter to his own emotionally determined attitudes he will not only reject the information but may reject the worker as well.   To this extent a direct educational approach may block

[7] Gartland, Ruth.   *Psychiatric Service in a Children's Hospital.*   Chicago: University of Chicago Press, 1936.

further therapeutic effort, and this must be borne in mind in deciding upon treatment.

Examples of this type of treatment approach could be gathered by the dozen from the files of any clinic or agency dealing with children and their parents. The one given below from our own clinic records is selected because it is not only quite specific and detailed, but also indicates the strongly advisory attitude which, for better or for worse, usually accompanies such education. In this particular instance the parents were able to accept most of the suggestions, with the result that for several years Arthur's problems were much reduced.

> Arthur is an unstable ten-year-old youngster who feels rather rejected at home and has been a problem because of his petty thefts from the parents, his aimless running away and consequent failure to come home for meals.
>
> In conference it was thought that the best plan for treatment was to continue to make practical suggestions to the mother as to how to deal with the boy. These suggestions are outlined below and it was understood that the visiting teacher and psychologist would interpret them to the mother. This was first done by the psychologist. Later on the visiting teacher also talked to the mother. The suggestions are as follows:
>
> "*a.* It was suggested that the mother keep money out of his hands, except for his own spending money. It seems inadvisable to have him run errands where the carrying of money is involved. Until the running away is definitely cleared up, it is probably best to remove this temptation from the boy.
>
> "*b.* The mother should make supper time as attractive a period as possible. Both the meal and the activities immediately before and after supper should be interesting, so that Arthur will feel that he is missing a good time if he remains away from home. The father's co-operation in this should be gained. There might be stories or games immediately after supper in which the father and the boy would participate. A work shop in the basement, no matter how crude or simple, might be of help in binding Arthur to his home.
>
> "*c.* The mother should be urged to revise her methods of punishment. If Arthur knows that every time he stays out late he will get a licking as soon as he gets home, the natural reaction is to stay out even later. It was suggested that little be done at the time he comes home, but that the next morning he should

have to wash the dishes or do some mildly unpleasant type of work. If he stays away from home during the day, it might be sufficient punishment to have him go to bed immediately after supper, missing the games and good times."

While this educational approach made no attempt to alter the mildly rejecting attitudes which the parents held toward the boy, it proved to be sufficient to cope with the problem for some time.

Interpretive Treatment. It has long been realized that if a person understands fully why he reacts and behaves as he does it is much simpler to control or alter these reactions. A technique for accomplishing this goal is the process of interpretation, in which an effort is made to help the individual see his own behavior as it has developed, to understand the cause of his reactions, and to see the rôle which he plays and the satisfactions he is obtaining. If successful, this process results in a higher degree of insight and in the individual's more complete understanding of himself. If Mr. L., a strict, repressive father, can come to see that he is trying to stamp out in his boy his own unruly impulses, he has some chance of being able to alter his methods. If Mrs. S., who complains about the unhappiness of her married life, can understand the extent to which her own overindulged childhood has made her a childish, dependent wife, looking for attention rather than a chance to share responsibility, she may have a basis for developing greater maturity.

We are indebted to Mrs. Mowrer in the volume previously noted for one of the clearest expositions of this technique as related to the treatment of marital friction. Indeed Mrs. Mowrer regards this as her primary mode of therapy in treating discord between husband and wife. She stresses the point that even in the first interview, once the client's history has been fully told and the analysis of the situation made by the interviewer, "the problem of the social therapist becomes that of giving this interpretation to the patient. This process is crucial in treatment because it involves not only interpreting the behavior of the patient on the part of the social therapist, but getting him to accept this interpretation.   His acceptance depends to a large degree upon the extent to which the analyst is able to identify the patient with the analysis or interpretation. In other words, it is necessary that the analysis of factors come out of the facts as presented by the patient himself and that he see that this is true." [8]

Mrs. Mowrer further gives an almost verbatim account of the interpretation which was given to one patient, a woman who had developed many neurotic illnesses to escape from the unpleasantness of family situations.   After reviewing with Mrs. A. her early sheltered childhood, her early attempts to escape difficult problems (her marriage was one of these escapes), and the painful shock of her first marital sex experiences, she goes on with interpretation in these terms.

> Then as you have explained, four days after marriage you got sick and went to the hospital.   You don't remember that there was anything wrong with you except that you felt pains all over. But anyway you were glad to get away from everything.   Things seemed unbearable.   So you really met the first problem of marriage by going to the hospital.   And as you have told me, you have been meeting new problems ever since by going to the hospital.   You say you have been in the hospital thirteen times; each time for a different ailment.
> You didn't want a baby.   You hated your first baby and at first you wouldn't take care of it.   You felt that you were no more than a baby yourself and that you should be in the baby's place, receiving the attention and petting.   You missed all the petting that you had as a child.   You felt jealous of the baby. Of course, you felt that it was rather wrong for you to feel that way; jealous of your own baby.   Then you realized that you could get attention, also — much as the baby was getting — by being sick.   I don't know, of course, I am not sure that was the case.   You probably know whether or not that is what happened. It is true that most people do get more attention when they complain of being sick, don't they?   We are all somewhat like that. Were you any different from that?   From all that you have told me about your feelings — quite frankly, you know — we would say that was what happened, wouldn't we?
> You never got any satisfaction out of staying with your hus-

band.   At first it was painful; then when you got over that, you really wanted to, but never enjoyed it.   It is hard for you to think of yourself as actually wanting to stay with your husband as you still hold to those old ideas that it is shameful for a woman to admit that she wants sexual relations.   Of course, it is natural for you to have those ideas.   Many women have had them in the past, but now we are taught to believe differently.   It does us harm to want something and always feel that we shouldn't. Wanting sex relations is no different from wanting anything else; food, for example.   It seemed to you that your husband was always in a hurry to stay with you and get it over with.   You never got any satisfaction, but you never talked to him because you thought it was no use.   You got more and more disgusted and resentful because you blamed him.   Then you told him you were sick and that you couldn't stay with him.   Again it seems you used sickness as a way of getting out of something that was unpleasant to you.

Of course, all of us are inclined to develop excuses for not doing things which are unpleasant.   If we have an appointment with someone we don't like, we sometimes "develop" a headache. We "kid" ourselves a lot sometimes, or at least try to do so.   So it isn't so unusual — this thing of using sickness as a way of escaping unpleasant things — but sometimes a person does it so often that he just reacts that way mechanically.   He actually believes he is sick.   Perhaps that is true in your situation.   Do you think you have used sickness as an excuse all through your marriage?   (At this point Mrs. A. A. showed her acceptance of this part of the analysis by saying: "It is true that I know if I get sick enough, someone else will do things for me.   I hate housework; it gets under my skin to do it.   If I get 'sick,' I don't have to do it.   I know when I go out with my husband in the car and I don't want to go, but I feel that I should go, that I come back always feeling all kinds of pain although I felt real good when I started.   Maybe it is because I didn't want to go in the first place.") [9]

This is an excellent example of the process of interpreting the individual to himself.   It is the type of technique which is often described, but rarely given in such specific terms.   It would seem to this author that the technique of interpreting Mrs. A's behavior patterns is satisfactory except that it is made with rather breath-taking speed and abruptness.   This

[9] Mowrer, *op. cit.*, pp. 244–245.

woman has thought of herself in rationalized terms as being too ill to take up her normal family responsibilities. To get her to accept a very different view of herself as an individual endeavoring to escape responsibilities involves more than a presentation of her pattern of escapes, even though this presentation is plausibly and logically made and clothed in facts related by the client herself. The closing sentences, which indicate that Mrs. A. can give partial agreement to this interpretation and can even add to it in minor ways, do not necessarily prove that she has made the interpretation her own and can act upon it. Without presuming to criticize Mrs. Mowrer's technique, since she has found it highly successful, it is only fair to add that most therapists would probably have used many interviews to cover the same degree of interpretation which is here given in a portion of one interview. Thus if on one occasion Mrs. A. had come to recognize her first hospitalization as an escape from her first unsatisfactory experience of intercourse, and in subsequent interviews had been helped to see her methods of escape from the responsibilities of child-caring, and her continued and conflicted escapes from sex relations, the process would have been more gradual, but very possibly more lasting. This more usual type of procedure would have enabled her to make more of the interpretation herself, thinking it through, phrasing it in her own terms, rather than listening to the analysis in the therapist's words. The fact that Mrs. Mowrer kept up contact, often for two years or more, with these cases of marital difficulty makes it seem likely that she found ways of making the process more gradual than would appear from this quotation.

There seem to be certain conditions which govern the effectiveness of this therapeutic process of aiding the individual to understand himself. In the first place, as Mrs. Mowrer points out, the interpretation must be based on the facts and statements given by the parent, and must be in terms of his own experiences. It is worse than useless to indulge in the generalized, "you-are-suffering-from-an-inferiority-complex" type of interpretation. The parent needs to see, not in technical terms, but in terms of his own past, how he has balked at mature responsibilities, or how he has come to reject or over-indulge his child, or how he has been seeking to dominate his children and his spouse. These patterns must be in terms of events of last week or last year, not in easily misunderstood psychological terms.

A second condition of success with this type of treatment is that the therapist should never go beyond the parent's capacity for acceptance. It must continually be borne in mind that the goal is that the parent should see himself in a different light. This new viewpoint he must genuinely feel. It is not achieving this purpose to argue with the parent, or to try to impose certain views upon him. Thus, in the type of interview quoted from Mrs. Mowrer, the parent frequently can accept and feel only a part of the interpretation, but not all. Mrs. A. might well have responded, "It is true that I sometimes feel sick to put off my husband, but I love my baby. I do not get sick because of my baby." It is in this type of situation that the therapist needs to avoid any coercive or overpersuasive attitude. If the parent's modification of the statement is accepted for the present, without criticism or argument, the possibility of fuller insight at a later stage is much greater. The diagnosis of the situation and the interpretation of the parent's reactions must be a genuinely mutual process, both parent and therapist sharing in the effort. Some parents may be able to understand and accept a thoroughgoing analysis and interpretation of their own behavior. Others may be able to accept only a very fragmentary interpretation. Some of these differences are due to differences in the parents and to the extent to which their attitudes are alterable, a topic which will be discussed subsequently. No doubt some of the differences in results are due to the techniques and attitudes of the therapist. If he (or she) adopts an understanding rather than a critical attitude, accepting the parent for what he is; if he makes no attempt to browbeat or argue with the parent; if he builds up a relationship of confidence and trust; and if he has considerable prestige with the parent, then we may expect a higher degree of capacity on the part of the parent to accept and absorb the interpretation which is given to him.

A third condition of the effectiveness of such interpretive therapy which has already been suggested is that for effective learning the parent must discover the interpretation for himself, or it must be frequently restated to him in a variety of forms, or both these methods must be utilized. It is not, in other words, a process which takes place once and for all time. It must be gradually and increasingly apprehended and learned. Frequently the beginner in treatment, whether in the clinic or the social agency, feels that the end has been achieved when the parent first gains some notion of the rôle which he has been playing in regard to the child. This rôle will need to be reinterpreted as new episodes arise, and will need rephrasing and re-explanation on many occasions before any real insight has been gained. Frequently there will be "relapses" in this learning process if the emotional acceptance has been only partial. Thus Flora, the young mother of Elwyn (see Chapter VI, p. 154) who had so many profound reasons for rejecting the boy because of his illegitimacy and the strain which he put on her relationship with her respectable husband and her much-wanted new baby, came to accept to some degree the fact that Elwyn's problems were due to her rejection. She was able to help in planning and carrying through a foster-home placement for the child, even though this meant an implied confidence that other parents could give the child affection which she had been unable to give. She confided to the new social worker some of her feelings of rejection as reasons for placement. A year and a half later, when she wished to try Elwyn again in her own home, after a successful period in two foster homes, she gave various reasons for his early misbehavior, none related to the true picture. When it was suggested that his conduct might have grown out of a feeling of being unwanted at home, she expressed surprise and stated, "I remember Miss W. talked with me about that before. I don't see how it could be true, because I've always treated the children alike." Her acceptance of the previous interpretation had not been complete, and had quite dropped out during an interval of casual rather than therapeutic contacts.

Relationship Therapy.   In recent years the terms "relationship therapy" or "passive therapy" have come to be applied to another method of dealing with parents whose attitudes create problems in their children.   Rooted in many respects in the psychoanalytic concepts of Otto Rank, its development has come almost entirely from the field of social case work, where it has aroused a great deal of interest.

It would be difficult clearly to define the process, but certain of its characteristics may be noted, with the initial qualification that many of those holding the viewpoint feel that it is a non-intellectual process which can be but poorly grasped intellectually, but must be felt or experienced to be grasped. With the understanding that this mode of therapy is primarily emotional rather than intellectual, these brief comments will picture certain major elements of it.

1. It applies only to those parents who have a desire to be helped.   This, naturally, is not always easy to judge or determine, but unless the individual feels a considerable desire to change himself in constructive fashion, he is not material for this type of therapy.   Often enough the parent who comes to the worker with no other thought than to have someone change this "bad" child, feels, underneath this superficial aloofness from the situation, a considerable burden of responsibility and guilt for the child's development, and fundamentally would like help.   This type of attitude is most likely to be discovered in the sort of relationship which is built up.

2. The relationship between the worker and the parent is the essential feature.   This bond is one in which the parent feels confidence in the worker and freedom to express thoughts and feelings often inhibited.   The worker endeavors to provide an atmosphere in which the parent can come freely to experience and realize his own attitudes.   The worker creates this atmosphere by her acceptance of the parent, by her failure to criticize, by her refusal to impose on the parent any program or

recommendations, and by her refusal to answer questions except when the parent genuinely desires an answer and is unable to answer for himself.   The relationship is, for the worker, a relatively impersonal and objective one.   Miss Heath, for example, explains to one mother that it is inadvisable to take luncheon together, thus limiting their contacts to office interviews.   On the other hand those interested in passive therapy have shown a healthy appreciation of the interactions of such a relationship, recognizing that the therapist, as a particular individual, makes a distinctive impress upon the parent, just as the parent to some extent influences the therapist.

3. The effect of this relationship upon the parent may be characterized by the terms "clarification of feelings" and "acceptance of self."   Thus, in the free and non-critical atmosphere which exists, the parent through expressing his real feelings without defensiveness or rationalizations comes to clarify his thinking and feeling and thus to understand himself more clearly.   The type of insight which is gained differs markedly from the imposed interpretation quoted from Mrs. Mowrer's book, and differs in lesser degree from the more gradual process of self-discovery and guided interpretation which was suggested in the discussion of Mrs. Mowrer's methods.   It is typical of relationship therapy that it does not aim toward such clarification and insight primarily as a means to the end that the individual will change his attitudes or personality.   Their stress is very frankly upon the individual's full realization and acceptance of himself.   Any changes will come from normal growth in personality once the parent can accept himself and his limitations.

The attitudes and aims governing this whole relationship are well summarized by Dr. Frederick Allen in the following description of the work of the Philadelphia Child-Guidance Clinic.

> We are prepared to take people as we find them — willing, resistive, skeptical — and create a situation which from the beginning gives both parent and child the feeling that here is a place which imposes nothing beyond helping them to clarify what

they are ready to do in their relation to us — where they can feel the interest is in them as people, not as problems, and where if they continue they are doing so because there is some desire and not because of our decision. They become participants — not recipients of help from the very beginning.

From the beginning, our relation to parent and child is based on a respect for the integrity and capacity of that person — limited though at times it may be — and disguised as it frequently is by a sense of defeat and failure. We do not bring into our relation with them, except where our own human limitations prevent it, a preconceived conception of what they should be or how they should manage their relationships. We are anxious that this relation shall provide an opportunity for both parent and child to get a clearer understanding and acceptance of what they are, at that time, and what they are able to do, with the strengths they have, to deal more responsibly with a reality which is theirs and which no one, however well equipped, can assume for them.[10]

4. As is suggested by a portion of the above quotation, another characteristic of this viewpoint is its reliance on the parent himself to determine independently the manner of dealing with the child. There is no attempt to lay down a course of action for the parent, nor to influence his decisions, though the aim is to help the parent clarify his thinking and take into account the meaning and significance of his choices. Even where the parent decides upon some treatment of the child which the worker thinks inadvisable, no objection is interposed, since there is the feeling that even mistaken decisions, independently made, make for growth. The viewpoint is well stated by Miss Heath as follows:

In the type of treatment just described the worker takes a more or less passive rôle. She seeks to give insight by impersonal and objective comments, such as, "One wonders if you may be doing this." If resistance is encountered, the worker feels no need to force her conception on her patient. She may wait a while, later interpreting some of the reasons for turmoil if the experience proves destructive. If the patient tends to be dependent, desiring an expression of the worker's opinion or sanction, she throws the decision back to the patient. Even though the

---

[10] From talk given by Dr. Allen at the tenth anniversary of the Philadelphia Child-Guidance Clinic, April 16, 1935. Published in pamphlet form by the Clinic.

patient chooses what appears to be a destructive course of action, the worker will not dominate the situation by making the decision for the patient. She may, however, help him to see the various advantages and disadvantages of several courses of action. And not infrequently the worker is surprised that what she considered a destructive choice may provide valuable experience for that individual's growth. What may be destructive experience to an individual in one stage of growth may prove constructive in another stage.[11]

The aim of such a passive approach is to bring about a higher degree of integration and self-realization in the parent, to the end that whatever his manner of dealing with the child it will be less confused, less conflicted, and consequently more constructive for the child. There is the added assumption (which might be difficult to prove) that the parent's fuller understanding of himself in relation to the worker carries over into other relationships.

It will be difficult, under any circumstances, to determine the effectiveness of this method of dealing with parental attitudes. Enthusiasts claim much for it, and since their criteria are largely intangible measures such as the freedom from inner tensions and the greater degree of personal comfort achieved, any measurement of success is difficult indeed. From those who are most interested in relationship therapy we find no mention of the degree or proportion of success, and it is probably unlikely that such a study will be made. The final judgment of the efficacy of such treatment will be only very slowly and gradually made by any scientific means. Indeed it seems likely that its major value may be, not in the percentage of cases assisted, but in the fresh viewpoint of non-interference and reliance upon the individual's own tendency toward growth which it has emphasized. It has real significance in that it attempts to give some answer to the question of how education and growth may be brought about in parents whose destructive attitudes are emotionally charged. Such parents are, as we have seen, quite unapproachable through the technique of direct education.

[11] Heath, Esther. *The Approach to the Parent*, Introduction, p. xv. New York: Commonwealth Fund, 1933.

An Example of Relationship Therapy.   Because the process is a slow one, and subtle emotional changes are more significant than the intellectual techniques used, suitable examples are difficult to give.   Excerpts from the case record of a family situation treated in our own department may give some hint of the progress of such treatment.

Mr. and Mrs. Perri were a young couple, 32 and 28, respectively, with a family of three attractive children, 9, 7, and 3, who were beginning to exhibit various behavior problems.   The parents had been known to the protective agency intermittently over a 6-year period, because of bitter quarreling, temporary separations, and reconciliations which did not reconcile.   There had been disagreements over the mother's working, the father's drinking and unwillingness to work, over the management of family funds and over the handling of the children.   The protective agent had on one occasion persuaded them both to make certain concessions, and reach a definite agreement upon which they could make a fresh start.   Within twenty-four hours there was a terrific battle and the mother left home for a time.   Shortly before our treatment contacts began, the father had been arrested for assaulting the mother with a knife, and the interested agencies, the psychiatrist who saw the father, and the parents were all agreed on separation.   Within a few days the father had promised to reform and the parents were living together again.   Within a month there was much quarreling, particularly over management of the children, and an appointment was made for the mother to see the worker at the Child Study Department.   Throughout this whole earlier period the attempts to educate, supervise, control or advise the parents had all met with complete failure.   Seemingly they could not be happy together — nor could they be happy apart.

Over a seven months' period the worker had frequent interviews with the parents and the brief quotations from the record have been chosen rather to indicate the worker's approach than to represent a complete record of the family situation.   The mother came in for the first contact, again looking for someone to manage the situation.   The worker's attitude is clearly shown in an excerpt from the interview.

"Mrs. Perri said that the agent [from the protective agency] had told her that this worker would be able to tell them how to treat their children and how to handle their problems.   Mrs. Perri said that she was very anxious for suggestions and if she is not doing what she should she would certainly want this pointed out to her. Worker then said that sometimes a person on the outside could see reasons for difficulties more readily than those who are in the situation all the time. That did not mean that one could give specific directions for handling children under all circumstances at all times. Worker felt that sometimes by discussing little problems and finding out with the parent what seemed to be taking place with the child, better understanding could be gained and therefore the parent or any one working with the youngster would have a basis for meeting situations under varied circumstances. Worker did not feel that she could say to either parent that any particular method is either right or wrong, or that either parent's attitude is better for the youngster. Perhaps worker could help them think through together what their objectives are for their youngsters and what kind of parents they wish to be for their particular children."

Following this first contact the mother wished to return and did so, talking over much more fully her difficulties with her husband and her children. Arrangements were made for the children to have psychological examinations, to which the father violently objected. The protective agent told him he must bring the children, which he did, leaving them outside the building while he came in to talk with the worker. The situation was explained to him, and the decision left in his own hands. He decided to leave the children for their appointment. Later he phoned for an appointment, and when he arrived, wanted to know "what plans worker had for his children." Worker replied that she had no plans for the children, and then, "explained to Mr. Perri what had been explained to his wife as to the type of service which could be given. Worker emphasized the fact that the care of the children was the parents' responsibility and that she could only make suggestions and explanations which might help them work out solutions to their problems. Mr. Perri said that he thought this was a good idea. He could prove that he was a good father and that he was interested in his children. He had cared for them when his wife was sick last summer, he could prove this by the neighbors. He washed their clothes, got their meals for them, and played games with them. While he was busy around the house he always knew just what they were doing for he watched out the window. He had no difficulty with them at all. He then said that he didn't want to criticize but if he did say so himself he got along better with the children than his wife did. When he told them to do something they did it, but they had no respect for their mother. She fusses with them all

the time and they get around her.   After Mr. Perri repeated this
type of thing in different ways, worker suggested that some people
do seem to have better results with children than others.   Some
are too easy and the children learn that they can get away without carrying out requests.   On the other hand, sometimes children react quickly to some people because they are afraid.
Furthermore it was pointed that just as people are different so
are their methods of doing things different.   Perhaps it was
important for parents to work together on what they want to
give their children from a long time or general point of view,
that is, as a preparation for life.   Possibly with both parents
working toward the same objectives for the children it was not so
necessary that they use exactly the same methods as it was for
each to understand the other and discuss differences, to try to
work out big differences rather than worry and disagree about
insignificant details.   It is important to be consistent but for
parents to disagree makes children unhappy.   Perhaps, by discussing differences with some one outside and doing some reading
if they wished, it might help them to understand each other's
ways better.   If Mr. Perri wished to come in to discuss problems
as they arise worker would be glad to try to help.   He asked if he
could come in the next week."

As will be observed, the father was under considerable pressure
to prove his rightness and superiority, and no check was placed
upon this, nor was he in any way contradicted.   The worker
merely tried to help clarify the fundamental situation, leaving
the burden with the parents.   No attempt is made to give information unless it is really desired, and the worker immediately
stops when she realizes that the father does not wish material on
the psychological examination.

"He asked how the children had done on the tests.   Worker
started to give a general discussion of each child.   He did not
seem especially interested except to tell what he thought.   He
thinks that they are very bright and there is nothing wrong with
them.   He is glad little Bobby goes to nursery school so that he
can be away from his mother part of the time.   He is no problem
at school at all and just loves it.   Then abruptly Mr. Perri decided that he had to go back to work."

During this contact and following ones with the father the
worker maintains this same attitude, though occasionally more
direct suggestions and interpretation creep in, as in the following
interview, when the father has been talking at length about all the
minor differences over the children which "drive him crazy."

"Worker asked if she might suggest that first he try to control himself before talking about any of these things at home.   Perhaps controlling himself once will help the next time.   If he is angry, wait until he is less upset and then tell his wife how he feels. Possibly if this is done he will find that he can help her understand his point of view better but when it ends in both becoming angry and quarreling they cannot expect to get anywhere.   More than the fact that they do not help each other if they get upset about everything, parents' arguments make children very unhappy. Children often try to find things to do outside the home if they realize that everything starts quarreling at home.   Thus, they may get into trouble.   It makes children feel that they are different from others if their parents quarrel — they feel inferior and unhappy and then other problems begin.

"Although worker can point out some of these factors they will have to work them out together.   It is not enough to observe the differences.   It will be necessary to discuss, compromise with each other and overcome them.   He listened intently and said that that did seem reasonable.   He would try to do this; if he saw things at home which he disagreed with he wouldn't say anything until he had discussed it with worker.   He left the office after thanking worker and saying that he would come at the same time next week."

Meanwhile the mother in her contacts with the worker has been going through a more fruitful process of clarification in her thinking.   In her second interview she definitely states she is going to part from her husband, and is only helped to think through the various aspects of her problem.

"Mrs. Perri isn't going to talk about her difficulties any more. She will go ahead with the separation.   Then when she and the children are settled alone she would like to feel that she could come to worker for help.   Worker wondered if there would be opposition on the part of her husband if she were to take the children.   She supposed there would be but she certainly would never consider letting them go with him or his family.   Worker also wondered if the children were prepared for this.   Mrs. Perri guessed that she had not thought about this but felt even though it would be hard for the youngsters it would be better in the long run."

It was nearly a month later that the mother was seen again, several contacts with the father intervening.   The mother never again during the whole period mentioned separation as a possibility.   Without advice to confuse her, but with some clarification of the issues, she decided the problem herself.   The fact that the father's attitudes had improved following his contacts with the worker was no doubt another factor.   The mother now in her contact brings up new problems and shows considerably more ability to think them through and cope with them.   School problems of all the children and the persistent enuresis of Mary, the 7-year-old, are thus discussed.   She also shows somewhat more understanding of her husband, and of the part she plays in the marital friction.

"The mother went on to say that she had resolved on New Year's Day to be pleasant and to keep her temper regardless of what her husband did."   She recognizes her husband's need for her affection and plans to try to "kiss him every evening even if he does try to push me away."   Worker "pointed out that making an adjustment now will mean a series of compromises and maybe she will have to give in more than she feels is her share, but perhaps it would be worth trying.   She said that anything is worth trying and that she knows she is to blame part of the time.   She will do anything to make the children happy and they do love their father, too."

The father, who has made somewhat less progress than the mother in his degree of insight, continues in his interviews to make complaints about his wife, to try to get the worker to pass judgment on her and on himself.   On one occasion after complaints about new frictions, he suggests that the mother go away for a time to visit.   The worker again takes a somewhat more active and interpretive rôle than when she is dealing with the wife and discusses the plan in these terms.

"Worker wondered if this was not an unsatisfactory way out for such an arrangement would only be for a limited time.   It was remarked that if he really thought his wife needed a rest it was very thoughtful of him to accept the responsibility for the children.   However, if this were not necessary did he suppose that he preferred not to have her around?   Perhaps he wanted her out of the home so he could have his own way.   As he denied that this might be an escape, worker wondered how it would be if he talked over the plan with his wife, persuaded her to have another examination at the hospital, and then if it was felt that she was not gaining properly they might find the plan a good one."

A few days later the mother returned with a new and crucial question.   She had been offered a very satisfactory position. She described the job and then "wanted to know what worker thought about it.   Worker asked her if she wanted to work outside the home.   Mrs. Perri said she had thought it all through very carefully and this was her opinion at this point.   She felt that if there is any possible way for a family to support itself, it should be done. It didn't look as if her husband would get a job, therefore from the point of view of the taxpayers she thought they as citizens owed it to the city to get off relief. On the other hand Mrs. Perri feels that conditions at home with Mr. Perri are better than they have ever been. There are still difficulties but she feels better able to meet them and feels more encouraged that they can get along if they work hard enough. She wouldn't think of doing anything to upset this. That is the most important thing. If she goes to work she fears that everything will be undone. It was her going out to work before which started all of the difficulty. Her husband is jealous and suspicious when she is away. More than that this kind of job is better than any her husband can possibly get, that makes him feel badly and he takes it out on her by being mean. All of this would spoil everything. She didn't know what to do."

It is of interest to contrast the mother's thoughtful weighing of emotional values at this time with her handling of the situation several years earlier when she had accepted a job and brought on a storm of family troubles, until she lost the position on account of illness. Although she did not again discuss the matter with the worker, she did not accept the job.

In further contacts there are fluctuations in treatment progress. Both of the parents, at different times, bring in questions about their sex relationships which have been a part of the problem though probably their unsatisfactory adjustment in this realm is an effect, rather than a cause of difficulty. The worker tried having both parents in to talk over the family situation together. This was not particularly successful. The father seemed more defensive, and less mature than the mother, though the discussion was peaceful and brought some agreement on matters of sleeping routine, the children's responsibilities at home, and the like. The basis of agreement was in each case worked out by the parents, the worker merely clarifying the points of view.

Later the mother came in at different times for help on the problem of sex education for the children, the advisability of a school transfer for the children, and the question of her own religious faith, which she felt she was losing. There was in these later interviews, much less notion of asking the worker to decide, and much more self-reliance evident. In no case did she seem to decide the issue during the discussion, but in each instance she appeared to be able to gradually make her own choice.

There were of course relapses in this picture of improved family relationships. On one occasion Mr. Perri arrived home early and finding no dinner ready he became, according to his wife, "very angry and started a fuss. Mrs. Perri said that she spoke up quickly which was a mistake. At that point he hit her across the face with a towel. Jean saw the whole thing and started to cry. Mrs. Perri said nothing to him but tried to comfort Jean. He continued by throwing his watch across the room. Afterward he tried to make up for it and every once in a while since had asked if she had been down to see worker. She was sorry it had happened for everything had been so much better. Also, instead of buying snow suits for the children as he has promised for so long he went downtown and bought himself two new suits. He said that his mother paid for them. Mrs. Perri said that she would try not to get upset by it and guessed that there were bound to be some hard times. However, she hoped that he would come in again. She was beginning to have more confidence in herself though and felt with a little help from time to time she could meet the situation in spite of her husband."

On another occasion, she reported as follows: "On the whole, conditions at home had been going smoothly. About two weeks ago Mr. Perri came home with two men, all three having been drinking. They were very loud and disgusting, and each was carrying a bottle. Mrs. Perri's first reaction was to become angry and disagreeable. She wanted to order them out as the children were still awake and she did not want them to see such goings on. She said that she was very glad she realized what the effect would have been if she had shown her feelings. She was as pleasant as she could be under the circumstances. She waited for two days until she was sure that she was calm about it before talking with Joseph. She told him that this could not happen again. She refused to have the children see this sort of thing. The husband became angry immediately but his attitude since then has been very good. He has said from time to time 'You were afraid of me once, now I am afraid of you.' Mrs. Perri seemed to have a good deal of confidence in her ability to cope with the situation. She is deriving a good deal of satisfaction from her attempts at adjustment."

Throughout these later contacts the mother's increasing sureness is matched by her increasing insight both into her own situation and that of her husband. Some of this is revealed in these comments about her family and her husband's new job. On one occasion she remarked "Miss G, everything is going beautifully at home. Joseph took the job in a beer parlor which I talked to you about and which I did not want him to take. I feel that I have misjudged him for he has worked very hard and has never even shown signs of having had anything to drink when he comes home.   The old man in charge of the place has taken a fatherly interest in him and has made Joseph feel he wants to make good." In regard to the management of the children she has subtly taken the leadership.   "Every time I mention the subject of changing schools, Joseph objects and says I'm not going to.   I have not pushed very hard but I am sure that I will try something else. Bobby is developing nicely too.   I like to go to the nursery school and watch the children.   The other day a little boy said, 'Hello, Bobby,' and then gave him a poke.   Bobby said, 'Hello, Jerry,' and returned the poke.   Bobby is going to be a real boy.   How he does love his father!   Goes to the corner and waits for him very often.   Of course Joseph thinks this is wonderful.   Bobby believes that his father can do almost anything.   When it was raining the other day, Bobby said, 'Why doesn't Daddy put the rain back up in the sky?'"

An excerpt from a later contact illustrates her changed feeling toward her husband.   "Mrs. Perri again said that things were going nicely and just wanted the worker to know that; she would go now.   As she rose to leave she said, 'Well I really do feel that Joseph is happy and that even though he is not earning very much money it is a good experience for him.   He just loves this kind of work and if he sticks at it maybe it will mean something to him.'"

As the mother achieved more ability to handle the family situation herself she asked less frequently for interviews, and at the end of seven months ceased coming, expressing her appreciation and her intention of renewing the contact in case new problems arose on which she needed help.

In evaluating the case treatment so briefly described above, it is evident at once that we must judge it by different standards from those we have applied to other techniques of treatment. The goal was not to solve the family friction, nor to do away with the behavior problems of the children.   It was to provide an atmosphere in which the parents could develop more mature ability to handle their own problems themselves.   With the mother the relationship was effective in accomplishing this. With the father, it was much less effective.   This may have been because he was more immature at the outset, or because the worker used a more direct and interpretive approach which he was unable to accept.   It may have been due to the fact that the worker was seeing both parents, and that a difference in the relationship was inevitable.

In any event the argument for this type of therapy is that its gains are real, even though slow. The Perri family may in the future break up under some new stress. They may again quarrel about the children. It seems almost certain, however, that whatever the reality situation, Mrs. Perri at least will be better able to cope with it, will understand it more deeply, and will to some extent make wiser choices as to her own course of action.

We shall still further discuss the use of relationship therapy in the chapter concerned with direct treatment of children through interviews. It is sufficient at this point merely to point out that it rests upon the attitude and feeling of the worker, rather than upon any specific techniques employed. Relationship therapy represents the art of dealing with parents, rather than any science of human relationships, yet it has importance as an attempt to bring about education of feelings and attitudes, rather than education of the intellect. It also represents, if successful, a more practical method than psychoanalysis, with its more ambitious but similar aim.

Other Approaches to Parents. It is not to be supposed that under the three headings which have been used all modes of changing attitudes have been classified, nor that the discussion is complete. We have, indeed, omitted some of the methods most commonly used in such situations. Many of the older records in the protective department of our own agency close with the words, "Parents warned and advised." This naïve faith in the "ordering and forbidding" technique has long since passed, and few would suggest that it is effective in controlling the deeper attitudes which our whole experience indicates are so influential in creating children's problems. Similar remarks might be made as to the process of arguing with parents to change their viewpoint. Even the use of strong advice, backed by prestige or personal influence, is a dangerous and ineffective technique.

At the other end of the scale we have said nothing of the more intricate processes of psychoanalysis, feeling that from a treatment point of view they are not practical except in the rarest of instances, and that psychoanalysis of the parents as an indirect method of dealing with the child's problems is too costly and too uncertain of results to be more than experimental. Miss Annette Garrett reports on some 25 cases of "attitude therapy" [12] in which the social worker carried on what amounted to a psychoanalysis of the parent (in each case the mother), seeing the parent two or three times per week for a period of two years, with a psychiatrist supervising the analysis. Outcome is reported in 8 families. One marital situation improved greatly, 6 others improved to some extent. One mother was referred to an analyst, because her problems were too difficult. For the 8 children, there was marked improvement in 3 cases, a lesser degree of improvement in 4 cases, no improvement in 1 case.[13] While it is to be hoped that such experimentation will continue, it is obviously too elaborate a procedure to be of wide use.

In a subsequent chapter on treatment interviews with children, more detailed techniques will be analyzed, many of them applicable to work with parents as well as with children.

THE "TREATABILITY" OF PARENTAL ATTITUDES

It was pointed out before beginning the discussion of these techniques for altering parental attitudes that, at best, our success in using them is limited. Whether we pin our hopes to an educational approach, to an interpretive process, or to the changes arising out of a deep and controlled relationship, or to the intelligent and selective use of all three, we shall find many parental situations which our best efforts are unable to change. In facing this fact it seems prudent to consider the

[12] See Moore, K., "A Specialized Method in the Treatment of Parents in a Child Guidance Clinic," *Psychoanalytic Review* (October, 1934), for a very clear account of this type of treatment.

[13] Garrett, Annette. "Attitude Therapy," in *Readings in Mental Hygiene*, p. 40. Ed. by Groves, E. R., and Blanchard, Phyllis, New York: Henry Holt and Company, 1936.

conditions which make for success or failure in such treatment.

There have been very few efforts to face frankly this question of the elements in a family or parental situation which determine its "treatability." Miss Fern Lowry, thinking in terms of the difficult parent situations met by the family welfare worker, suggests that items such as the following seem to determine the extent to which behavior and attitudes may be modified.

> "(1) the duration of the symptom behavior, (2) the extent of the area of life experience affected by it, (3) the rigidity of the related attitudes, (4) the use the individual makes of it — the emotional value the behavior has for him, (5) the alternative sources of satisfaction, (6) the mobility of the environment, (7) the quality of the relationship it is possible for the therapist to establish with the client...." [14]

While this is a helpful beginning, the writer would like to suggest a somewhat different outline, perhaps of more practical use, to determine the kind of parental attitudes which are amenable to change and those which are not. Faced with a particular parent how shall we know whether therapy should be directed toward the destructive attitudes of this parent, or toward some less resistant aspect of the case? Mrs. Wright has all her life indulged her only son, from the time she walked the floor with him as an infant to her present predicament of allowing him, illegally, to use the family car, buying inordinate amounts of clothing for him, and paying high fees for gymnasium training which he rarely uses. Shall we endeavor to make over her attitudes? Or Mr. Nye, whose young son is his despair, and who shows such extreme favoritism toward his still younger daughter. Is he treatable, or shall we look to other ways of helping the boy? Or in a situation such as that of Mr. and Mrs. Perri, how shall we determine whether or not it is wise even to attempt an alteration of attitudes? It would seem that the decision might be based on a consideration of three factors, the strength of the parent's motive for change,

[14] Lowry, Fern. "Problems of Therapy in Family Case Work," *Social Service Review*, vol. 10 (June, 1936), p. 201.

the degree of personal need which the attitude fills, and to some extent upon the learning ability of the parent.

The Motives for Change.   In considering the parent's motive for change we find a wide range of differences.   There is, for example, the smugly self-satisfied parent who has succeeded in making some type of stable and moderately satisfying adjustment to his total life situation, but who retains repressive or rejecting or overindulgent attitudes toward his child which are destructive of the child's adjustment.   Such a parent is unlikely to want help and has, indeed, very little motive for changing.   He regards his child as "bad" and usually makes evident his desire for changes in the child.   Any thought of changes in his own attitudes are intolerable, primarily because they would fundamentally upset the balance of his own life adjustment.   A number of instances from our own clinic experience immediately come to mind.   One father, whose repressive and rejecting attitudes have helped to make his fifteen-year-old son a serious behavior and delinquency problem, brought the boy to the clinic himself.   During several years of contact with this situation, with the boy both in his own home and, for a period, in a foster home, we have been forced to recognize how little it is possible for the father to alter his attitudes.   If our efforts had been to any degree successful in changing his rigid, punishing, dictatorial attitude toward his son, it would necessarily have changed his similar attitude toward his wife.   It would have undermined his position as complete master of his household.   And this in turn would have made his humdrum work intolerable, since his only compensation for working in a routine job much below his real ability is his mastery at home.   In a word, any significant change in his own attitude toward the boy would have necessitated a readjustment of his whole life balance.   And to what end?   Merely to improve his boy's behavior, while very possibly lessening his own sources of emotional satisfaction.   There is, in the situation, no motive or drive of sufficient strength to create a desire for such a change.

Toward the other end of the scale one thinks of young families such as the Perris, where marital friction and disagreement is the major difficulty and is a source of behavior symptoms in the child.   Here, while the quarrels may be somewhat satisfying to the ego of each partner, and to some extent as a partial release from the tension set up by sexual maladjustment, yet there are the strongest biological as well as cultural drives toward achieving a more harmonious unity.   Consequently there is a much more fundamental desire for change than in the previous type of situation.

It has not, to the writer's knowledge, been pointed out that parental attitudes in situations of marital maladjustment should in general be easier to change than parental attitudes in situations of a destructive parent-child relationship.   In the case of parental discords a better adjustment means, almost inevitably, a more satisfying sexual adjustment, more satisfying personal relationships, a more normal social status, and the like.   Consequently there is real motive for change.   In the parent-child situation the child may have strong desires to alter himself, but for the maladjusted parent there is often no greater emotional satisfaction in a normally independent child than in one who is a satisfying object of repression or indulgence or oversolicitous care.   The only increased satisfaction to the parent may be in fewer annoyances from the child's behavior.   While this difference is stated as a hypothesis only, it is interesting to note that Mrs. Mowrer had a much higher degree of success with her group of quarreling and separated parents than Miss Witmer reports for the Institute cases of parental attitudes toward children.   While we cannot be sure that the two groups are comparable, both at least were being dealt with by highly trained workers, exercising the best techniques available.   Possibly the clinics on marital counseling may look forward to somewhat greater success in dealing with discordant parental attitudes than the child-guidance clinics have had in dealing with destructive parental attitudes.

The Parent's Own Adjustment. The second factor worthy of consideration is the degree of emotional need which is filled by the attitudes in question. Thus the parent who is comfortably adjusted to his work, who has a normal group of friends and recreational outlets, and a satisfying relationship to his mate is comparatively free to change his attitudes toward his child. If a father or mother of this type is getting considerable satisfaction out of keeping a child very dependent, a change in attitude is quite possible. The parent will be losing a certain degree of satisfaction by freeing the youngster, but he has, in Miss Lowry's words, "alternative sources of satisfaction."

There are on the other hand parents whose whole source of emotional satisfaction is their relationship with their children. Mrs. Wright is such a woman. Her marriage was a marriage of convenience, without love on either side, entered into because she was a lonely and unhappy girl. Her life with her temperamental husband was consistently unhappy. Family finances were meager and she tried at various times to help support the family, but her work was not congenial, nor was she successful in it. Their only child, a handsome, well-formed boy, was the very center of her life. She slaved for him, she indulged him without limit, she shielded him from any paternal discipline, she excused his failures, and helped him out of his escapades. She can never understand why, as he grew older, he developed such unruly and delinquent behavior as to bring him into court, nor why his contempt for her has mounted as he has grown increasingly selfish and self-centered. Here any hope of changing the mother's indulgent attitude is almost futile. It is her one outlet for affection. To her the boy represents husband, and child, and social life. Her need for this type of satisfaction is shown by its persistence over a fifteen-year period. To alter her attitude would involve such a complete reorganization of her whole life as to be quite impractical from a therapeutic point of view.

Confirmation of this point of view is to some extent contained in a recent study by Miss Bronner, another of the Smith College students whose researches have thrown much light on this whole field. Studying 103 child-guidance clinic cases in which alteration of the parental attitudes was attempted, Miss Bronner finds that 19 per cent of the parents improved greatly in their attitudes, and another 36 per cent showed some improvement. On the other hand 45 per cent showed no change whatever, or withdrew from the clinic. When an attempt was made to relate these facts to the personal adjustment of the parents an interesting degree of association was discovered, the maladjusted parents showing much less tendency to respond to treatment than the small group of well-adjusted parents. The data is shown in the following table.

RELATION BETWEEN DEGREE OF PERSONAL MALADJUSTMENT AND DEGREE OF CHANGE IN PARENT'S ATTITUDES [15]

Change in Attitude	Extent of Maladjustment			
	Little	Moderate	Marked	Total
Marked improvement..............	5	12	2	19
Some improvement...............	7	25	6	38
No change — little treatment.......	..	12	1	13
No change — some treatment.......	..	18	15	33
Total......................	12	67	24	103

Since the above was written Miss Pearl Lodgen has published a study of the treatability of parental attitudes.[16] She examines the cases of 30 mothers and their children who were treated by the Judge Baker Guidance Center. In 15 instances considerable alteration was made in the mother's attitudes, and in the other 15 no significant change was achieved. Treatment of the children was successful in every case where the parental attitude was altered; but, where the mother was resistant to change, treatment was successful only when a

[15] Bronner, Eva B. "Can Parents' Attitudes Toward Their Problem Children be Modified by Child Guidance Treatment?" *Smith College Studies in Social Work*, vol. 7 (September, 1936), p. 10.

[16] Lodgen, Pearl. "Some Criteria for the Treatability of Mothers and Children by a Child Guidance Clinic," *Smith College Studies in Social Work*, vol. 7 (June, 1937), pp. 302–324.

mother substitute was provided through placement in a foster home, or a close tie built with a motherly relative, or a similar step taken.

In comparing the treatable with the untreatable mothers Miss Lodgen finds certain differences in personality, attitudes toward children, and general adjustment. Those mothers with whom treatment failed were inclined to be dominating and aggressive, with some tendency to be irritable, excitable, and self-centered. They tended to show rejecting attitudes toward their children, and to be unhappy and maladjusted in their marital relationships. Miss Lodgen regards this last item as being a more important differential factor than their attitudes toward their children.

Those mothers who responded favorably to treatment showed quite different characteristics. They "consisted largely of women who had a strong feeling of insecurity and inferiority, who were strongly conscientious and took their duties very seriously." [17] Their attitudes toward their children tended to be of the overprotective and overindulgent variety. They were very decidedly better adjusted in their marital relationships than the previous group.

This valuable and suggestive study, while needing confirmation through the study of larger numbers, helps to define with some precision the personality type of the mother who is amenable to treatment. It also gives added emphasis to the general point we have been considering, that the satisfactions of a generally normal adjustment, especially in the marital relationship, are essential if we are to expect significant changes in parent-child attitudes.

The Parents' Learning Ability. In determining the accessibility of a parent to treatment measures, his readiness to learn must also be taken into account. This is not merely a question of his intellectual capacity to learn, though intelligence is a factor. It seems probable that less intelligent parents can less readily absorb direct education, though whether the

[17] Lodgen, Pearl, *op. cit,* p. 319.

intelligent individual is more capable of achieving emotional insight than the less intelligent is an unsettled question. Experience would indicate some correlation between mental ability and capacity for insight. In addition to the question of intelligence itself, age is somewhat of a factor in this respect. The older individual is probably somewhat less adaptable and hence less capable of learning. Also the parent of more than two score years is apt to have a degree of confidence in his present status quo which makes him less ready to learn. The stability of the parent is still another item to consider, since the erratic, impulsive, and unstable individual is less likely to be capable of consistent and constructive learning than the parent of steadier disposition.

A Fourth Consideration; the Therapist. In this discussion of the techniques of changing parental attitudes, and of the factors which make such treatment feasible, it has been quite impossible to lay down any definite criteria as to the type of technique to adopt for a particular situation. We are discussing a realm which is still largely an art, though by no means incapable of being studied by scientific means. Three items have been mentioned as significant in deciding whether a change of attitudes is feasible. First is the depth and strength of the biological and cultural motives which create in the parent the desire for change. Second is the satisfaction which the parent is obtaining from his attitude, to be judged by the importance which it has in his total emotional organization, and the alternative satisfactions which might be substituted. Finally, the parent's capacity for learning, as indicated by intelligence and age and emotional steadiness, has some importance, though probably less than the first two. To these three it is necessary to add a fourth which often determines the outcome, namely the emotional adjustment and maturity of the case worker, clinician, visiting teacher, or marriage counselor who is endeavoring to bring about the changes. Just as foster-home placement is less successful when practiced by poorly trained workers, so are differing results with parents obtained by workers of different personal qualifications, even though they may attempt to use the same techniques. Because the available treatment methods are tools of an artist rather than mechanical devices, the worker's emotional maturity is important in making the balanced judgment as to choice of techniques. Likewise a quick sensitivity to change in mood is necessary. When giving direct educational suggestions, the worker must be quick to sense the sudden resistance which means that the parent is no longer accepting or able to absorb, and that repetition is a little worse than futile. In the subtleties of interpretive therapy also, there must be a quick appreciation of the parent's limit of acceptance, and an ability to understand the parent's viewpoint, without emotional identification either with the parent or with the child. And in the use of relationship therapy, the very nature of it restricts its use to those individuals who have a capacity for an almost intuitive sensitivity to feelings and attitudes, as well as a profound respect for the integrity of the individual. The worker will thus need to evaluate himself in relation to the task, as well as evaluate the parent and the practicable modes of treatment.

OTHER ASPECTS OF TREATMENT WITHIN THE FAMILY

Although the methods of management which parents use, and the atmosphere which they create by their attitudes, constitute by far the most important area of treatment effort within the home, there are certain other treatment possibilities which deserve some comment.

Frequently the presence in the home of grandparents, other relatives, boarders, or servants may prove to be serious irritants or definitely destructive elements in the child's adjustment. This may come about in various ways. The increased tension on the part of the parents may make them less able to deal with the child, or they may impose restrictions in regard to noise, play activity, and the like which would not be a part of the home routine if the family were alone. Not infrequently, too, the outsiders may have definitely harmful attitudes toward the child, either overindulging and pampering him, or taking a profound dislike to him. Situations of sibling jealousy can be greatly increased when the favoritism of a relative coincides with favoritism on the part of the parent. The means of dealing with such situations can scarcely be generalized. Sometimes the only solution is to work toward ridding the family group of outsiders and to this end help the parents to face the problem. At other times the goal will be to change in a constructive direction, through the techniques we have been describing, the attitudes of these outside members of the family group.

There are also occasions in which some definite physical change within the home is an aspect of treatment. Situations of sibling jealousy are likely to be handled largely through changing the parents' attitudes, or in some instances through direct therapy with the child, but it also involves occasionally such changes as a separate room for the child, a work bench for special projects and the like. Such suggestions are usually, of course, a part of the direct educational treatment attempted with the parent. In a few cases it may seem advisable to discuss with the family the possibility of moving, either to provide more normal recreational and activity outlets, or to separate the child from unwholesome neighborhood situations which may be having a bad effect.

The worker should be alert to every type of opportunity for improving the family situation, and consequently should not overlook these less usual possibilities. On the other hand the major treatment possibilities in the home lie in the education of the parents, whether that education be on a direct teaching basis, inculcating better methods of child management and training, or whether it be of a subtler type involving a re-education of emotional attitudes which effect behavior.

BIBLIOGRAPHY

General References

Folsom, J. K. *The Family*, chap. 17, "Individualized Treatment." John Wiley & Sons, 1934. 604 p.

Healy, William, and Bronner, A. F. *New Light on Delinquency and Its Treatment*. New York: New Haven, Conn.: Yale University Press, 1936, 226 p.

Lowry, Fern. "Problems of Therapy in Family Case Work," *Social Service Review*, vol. 10 (June, 1936), pp. 195–205.

Rank, Otto. *Will Therapy*. New York: Alfred A. Knopf, 1936. 291 p.

Robinson, Virginia. *A Changing Psychology in Social Case Work*. Chapel Hill, N.C.: University of North Carolina Press, 193c 204 p.

Reynolds, Bertha C. "The Role of the Psychiatric Social Worker in Therapy," pp. 46–69. Published in the *Institute for Child Guidance Studies*, ed. by Lawson Lowrey. New York: Commonwealth Fund, 1931.

Witmer, Helen L. and Students. "The Outcome of Treatment in Child Guidance Clinic," *Smith College Studies in Social Work*, vol. 3 une, 1933), pp. 341–399.

The Techniques of Treating Marital Discord

Hixenbaugh, Elinor R. "Reconciliation of Marital Maladjustme t — An Analysis of 101 cases," *Social Forces* (December, 1931), pp 230 36.

Mowrer, Ernest R. "A Sociological Analysis of the Contents of oo Case Records with Specific Reference to the Treatment of Fa ly Discord," *Social Forces*, vol. 7 (June, 1929), pp. 503–509.

Mowrer, Harriet R. *Personality Adjustment and Domestic Disc d.* New York: American Book Company, 1935. 220 p.

Nimkoff, Meyer F. "A Family Guidance Clinic," *Sociology and Soc l Research*, vol. 18 (January-February, 1934), pp. 229–240.

Techniques of Treating Parent Child Relationships

Allen, Frederick H. "Evolution of our Treatment Philosophy in Child Guidance," *Mental Hygiene*, vol. 14 (January, 1930), pp. 1–11.

Beard, Belle B. *Juvenile Probation*, chap. 3. New York: American Book Company, 1934. 219 p.

Bronner, Eva B. "Can Parents' Attitudes Toward Their Problem Children be Modified by Child Guidance Treatment?" *Smith College Studies in Social Work*, vol. 7 (September, 1936), pp. 1–16.

Garrett, Annette. "Attitude Therapy," in *Readings in Mental Hygiene*, pp. 36–40. Ed. by Groves, E. R., and Blanchard, Phyllis. New York: Henry Holt and Company, 1936.

Heath, Esther. *The Approach to the Parent*. New York: Commonwealth Fund, 1933. 163 p.

Irgens, Effie M. "Must Parents' Attitudes Become Modified in Order to Bring about Adjustment in Problem Children?" *Smith College Studies in Social Work*, vol. 7 (September, 1936), pp. 17–45.

Lee, Porter, and Kenworthy, Marian. *Mental Hygiene and Social Work*, chaps. 3 and 4. New York: Commonwealth Fund, 1931. 320 p.

Levy, David M. "Attitude Therapy," *American Journal of Orthopsychiatry*, vol. 7 (January, 1937), pp. 103–113.

Lodgen, Pearl. "Some Criteria for the Treatability of Mothers and Children by a Child Guidance Clinic," *Smith College Studies in Social Work*, vol. 7 (June, 1937), pp. 302–324.

Moore, Katherine. "A Specialized Method in the Treatment of Parents in a Child Guidance Clinic," *Psychoanalytic Review*, vol. 21 (October, 1934), pp. 415–424.

Moore, Madeline V. "The Treatment of Maternal Attitudes in Problems of Guidance," *American Journal of Orthopsychiatry*, vol. 3 (1933), pp. 113–127.

Murphy, G., and Jensen, F. *Approaches to Personality*. New York: Coward McCann, 1933. 427 p. Chapter 7, by Dr. John Levy, deals with "The Child Guidance Approach."

Watson, Maud. *Children and Their Parents*, pp. 77–118. New York: F. S. Crofts Company, 1732.

CHAPTER VIII

The School's Part in Changing Behavior

THERE IS a wealth of literature in regard to the adjustment of the individual child in school. Over a period of years the leaders in education have become more and more conscious of this as one of their major tasks. There have been reports and counter-reports as to the best type of classroom groupings. Reams have been written on the diagnostic use of tests, both of intelligence and achievement, in bettering the child's placement. The literature in regard to the special class, the opportunity type of class, and vocational training in the school, has grown apace, much of it motivated by the increased interest in fitting the curriculum to the child. "Educational diagnosis," "remedial teaching," "boys and girls advisors," are only samples of the areas of educational activity which have become commonplace because of this interest in the individual, an emphasis almost entirely lacking a generation ago.

It is not at all the purpose of this chapter to review these various educational advances, nor even to discuss them. We shall rather take for granted the fact that the school which is without the various modern aids for the adjustment of the individual pupil is at least conscious of these lacks and is aiming to fill them. Our purpose is to view the situation from the standpoint of dealing with the child whose conduct difficulties persist in spite of the up-to-date organization of the school. We shall consider the flexible use, as treatment techniques, of all the various opportunities and resources of the present-day school. It is in this same way that we have studied the use of foster homes as treatment resources, without discussing the techniques of placement procedures, and have examined the treatment resources within the family without discussing specific techniques of child care and training.   The worker who is dealing with the problems of the child needs not only to have some acquaintance with these detailed technical studies in each field, but also needs to understand all these fields in a new "frame of reference," namely their specific use as therapeutic resources for the individual child.   It is in this light that we shall regard the school.

INDIVIDUAL TREATMENT AS IT EXISTS IN THE SCHOOL

Although most school officials and educators give assent, at least in theory, to the processes of individual educational diagnosis, and to treatment of the causes of misbehavior rather than of the symptoms, observation would indicate that the theories are not always put into practice.   Indeed many school teachers and principals would seem to be much more in accord with the school official, himself a teacher of teachers, who, writing in an educational journal, classifies school misbehavior into seventeen types and proceeds to give the suitable punishments for each type.   An example or two from his interesting article will make plain one all-too-common viewpoint regarding the treatment functions of the school.   After classifying all the varieties of school misconduct, he suggests the following, among other remedies.   Impertinence, if it shows its head in the classroom, is to be treated by means of these techniques:

a. Oral reproof.
b. Put offender in his place by a remark that will enlist pupils on your side.
c. Corporal punishment.
d. Dismissal from class.

The child who has a "show-off" attitude is to be dealt with as follows:

a. Put offender in his place by a remark that will enlist pupils on your side.
b. Removal of privileges.
c. Public acknowledgment of fault.[1]

[1] James, H. W.   "Punishments Recommended for School Offenses," *Elementary School Journal*, vol. 29 (October, 1928), pp. 129–131.

The viewpoint of one individual with such a punitive theory of discipline would be unimportant did we not have overwhelming proof that this type of thinking still dominates teachers' treatment of behavior problems.   Miss Nellie Campbell made a study of the way in which more than a thousand incidents of classroom misbehavior were dealt with by the teachers in 83 elementary schoolrooms.[2]   The problems were of the type made familiar by Mr. Wickman's valuable and much-quoted study.   Activities which disturbed classroom order constituted 40 per cent of the total, while withdrawn or recessive behavior constituted only 0.2 per cent of the series of problems.   Difficulties with school work, difficulties with authority, aggressive behavior, and immoralities (largely stealing and lying) constituted the remaining groups.   Miss Campbell discovered that 46 per cent of these incidents were met by the teacher with a verbal attack upon the child. Scolding was the most-used type of treatment.   Sharp commands, threats, sarcasm were other much-used methods of meeting the situation.   Aside from these verbal attacks other methods of punishment such as deprivations, keeping in after school, and in some cases corporal punishment, make up an additional 29 per cent, so that punitive methods are the only ones used in 75 per cent of the incidents.   Such methods as appealing to the child, or explaining the situation, or rewarding for good conduct, are adopted in but one-fourth of the situations, in spite of the fact that in the judgment of the teachers and student observers, as well as of educational experts, these latter modes of handling the situations were more successful.

If all of these methods seem astonishingly superficial in the light of what we know about individual children, we will do well to consider one of Miss Campbell's concluding statements.

The data of this study indicate that present practices fail to take into account adequately the significance of the disorder in relation to the personal development of the child.   Classroom

[2] Campbell, Nellie M.   *The Elementary School Teacher's Treatment of Classroom Problems.*   New York: Bureau of Publications, Teachers College, Columbia University, 1935.

teachers need more assistance to enable them to exercise skill in diagnosing individual cases, to ascertain the real causes of the difficulties in the classrooms, and to adjust the treatments to meet the individual needs of the pupils. Little evidence exists in their comments to indicate that in dealing with problem situations they had any other objective in mind than removing the annoyance or the disorder.[3]

The teacher, in short, uses superficial methods because her own view of the problem is superficial. She is still thinking for the most part of proper punitive measures to apply, rather than thinking of treatment, in any genuine sense of the word.

These findings of Miss Campbell's are in large measure the results which we might have expected, judging from the attitudes of teachers as Wickman found them. In his study it was found that teachers tend to regard as distressing the behavior which most upsets them, rather than behavior which is intrinsically more serious from the point of view of the child's welfare. Consequently it is not surprising that, in dealing with the misbehavior, teachers regard their own comfort and the quiet of the classroom as the goal, rather than the welfare of the individual child.

If these facts seem somewhat depressing, it should be added that it is not only the teachers but school administrators also who fail to think in terms of the individual. Dr. Roy Street reports on a group of children referred from "an average public school" to the psychological clinic of which he was the director.[4] The school has special classes for the retarded, and adequate medical and psychological help available. Yet of 107 school failures referred to the clinic for study, 67 were doing as well as their ability would permit. Their achievement in school subjects was up to the level of their mental ability. They were doing, for their mentality, average work or better, and yet were being regarded as failures. The effects on the child of being thus wrongly regarded as a failure have been adequately and amply described and will not be repeated

[3] Campbell, *op. cit.*, pp. 55–56.

[4] Street, Roy F. "Factors Related to Maladjustment in School," *Elementary School Journal*, vol. 34 (May, 1934), pp. 676–680.

here. The appalling fact that in this school two-thirds of the pupils branded as failures were pupils who were doing their "level best" speaks for itself. Obviously, even in this school which was as well or perhaps better equipped than the average for making suitable pupil placements, the practice falls woefully short of theory.

While every one familiar with schools knows teachers who are expert in the effective treatment of problem children, yet there can be little doubt that the average teacher still has a largely punitive viewpoint. And while school principals and superintendents in many instances are keenly aware of the needs of the individual and are trying to organize and administer their schools so as to make for better methods of dealing with each problem child, yet there are many who would fall outside this category. Most teachers have had little or no opportunity to learn the more individualized modes of dealing with children. The field of education is a large one, and while it is changing, new concepts permeate the total group but slowly. No criticism is therefore implied in our endeavor to take a realistic view of what educators are doing, and from that starting point to discuss what they might do, for the child who presents conduct disorders.

THE SCHOOL'S EFFICACY IN TREATMENT

It is not easy to determine with any accuracy the degree to which the school may be influential in changing the child's behavior. A study which bears on this point is the one reported by Miss Martens of the U.S. Office of Education, in regard to the clinical treatment program carried on in the public schools of Berkeley, California.[5] In this study 68 problem individuals, referred to the school's behavior clinic, were compared over a two-year period with 68 non-problem children, matched for age, sex, intelligence, and school place-

[5] Martens, Elise H., and Russ, Helen. *Adjustment of Behavior Problems of School Children*. U.S Department of Interior, Office of Education, Bulletin no. 18, of 1932. Washington, D.C.: Government Printing Office, 1932.

ment. Both groups were also compared with a problem group of 50 children, similar in age and type of difficulty to the problem group, but not treated by the clinic. The usual school aids to adjustment were available to this third group. The difference lay in the lack of intensive clinical help. When these three groups were compared, by means of a carefully scored and weighted behavior record, several of the findings were of interest. They may be briefly stated as follows:

1. The 68 problem children showed over a two-year period a very significant improvement in their behavior. The average behavior scores dropped from 247 to 185.
2. The 68 non-problem children, measured in the same way, showed a significant increase in conduct problems during the two years. The average behavior score increased from 81 to 107.
3. The 50 problem children not treated by the clinic, showed neither improvement nor deterioration, over a year period. The initial average score was 213, and at the end of the year 205.

This study, carefully made and evaluated, is rather clear-cut evidence that the planned treatment by the school clinic is effective in significantly improving conduct problems. Since the clinic made use, however, of home visits and adjustments, recreational resources, medical treatment and the like, it may be argued that it was these other types of treatment, rather than the changes which were made within the school routine and program, which were effective.

A partial answer to this argument is contained in the study made by Miss Beard of 500 boys and girls being carried as probation cases in Boston. The Judge Baker Foundation clinic made specific recommendations in regard to educational treatment in 30 per cent of these cases. Of the 148 recommendations 57 had to do with the change of school or class, 24 involved some adjustment to the curriculum in the present school situation, 27 more suggested adjustments involving the personal relationships between the child and the teacher, 31 suggested supplementary education, and 9 were recommendations that the child stop school. Not all of these recommendations were carried out but in those instances where educational treatment was fully carried out the result was distinctly measurable. Miss Beard concludes, "Of the 92 probationers whose school problems were solved, 57 per cent were successes while only 35 per cent were successes when their educational needs were not met." [6]

On a smaller scale, and with a group of children exhibiting less extreme problems, Dr. H. W. Newell finds similar results. He reports a study which he made of problem children referred by the schools to the child guidance clinic connected with the Board of Education in Cleveland. In dealing with these children particular emphasis was put on the aspects of treatment which fell within the school. Conferences were held with teachers and principals, specific objectives and specific types of discipline were suggested for each case. Great stress was placed on the notion of rewarding the child for even slight improvement, so that the child received attention for social behavior rather than for anti-social behavior. The teachers were urged to give the problem child special responsibilities, often special privileges. Dr. Newell's figures regarding the outcome of these cases show that where the school was co-operative and used its resources for personal treatment, the results were much better than in those schools where co-operation with the clinic was poor and treatment halfheartedly carried on or not at all. The following table gives the results.

OUTCOME OF CASES TREATED BY SCHOOL AND CLINIC [7]

	Total	Marked Improvement	Slight Improvement	No Improvement
Six most co-operative schools.......	20	13	5	2
Six least co-operative schools.......	12	2	6	4
Total clinic cases.................	72	26	31	15

While these numbers are very small they are in accord with the previous study and with the opinions of most clinical

[6] Beard, Belle. *Juvenile Probation*, p. 145. New York: American Book Company, 1934.

[7] Newell, H. W. "The Methods of Child Guidance Adapted to a Public School Program," *Mental Hygiene*, vol. 18 (July, 1934), p. 371.

workers that the part which the school and the teachers play
in treating behavior disorders is a very significant one.   The
school cannot by itself overcome serious home conditions, nor
can it entirely counterbalance harmful neighborhood conditions, but the weight of its influences, especially if school
treatment is a part of a well-considered plan of total treatment,
is often crucial.

THE SCHOOL'S RESOURCES FOR HELP

In dealing with any difficult child from the age of six to
sixteen, whether our concern with him is because of stealing
and delinquency, or enuresis and shyness, or disobedience and
a tendency to stay away from home at night, or truancy and
school failures, any thorough consideration of treatment must
involve the question, "What can the school do to help?" Here
is an agency exerting an important influence on the child's life.
It is a part of the child's environment which is under social
control, and hence capable of manipulation, whereas parental
attitudes, or financial considerations, or broad social conditions
over which we have no control, may block other avenues of
therapy.   In this school environment teachers and staff are
less involved emotionally with the child's problems than his
parents, hence more capable of altering their attitudes and
methods in dealing with him.   How then can the best and
widest use be made of this valuable treatment tool?

In trying to suggest some of the answers to this question,
the present discussion will deal with the practical everyday
measures which are feasible in almost any school which has
real interest in its individual pupils.   We shall be primarily
concerned with what can be done here and now, under present
conditions.   We shall not discuss those changes in educational
philosophy, method, and administration which, though they
might prevent problems from developing, are not immediately
practicable.

The Satisfaction of Achievement.   No matter what the core
of the child's difficulties, whether they center around the

home or the child's social adjustment, or whether they are inner problems of mental conflict, one essential feature of treatment is to make sure that the individual has a challenging but satisfying task. Of all the positive principles of mental hygiene this necessity of providing work that is meaningful, that is within the capacity of the child to achieve, that provides some sense of accomplishment, is one of the most important. There is no individual to whom this does not apply. And with those problem children who are suffering some handicap, physical, mental, or social, real or imaginary, this need of a satisfying task becomes doubly essential and doubly therapeutic.

For the child, the school experience represents the greatest single potential resource for this type of satisfaction. Here are the possibilities, for every child, of a task suited to his abilities, in line with his interests, and with a healthy, meaningful purpose. Consequently it is for this type of treatment help that we most often turn to the school in devising a therapeutic program for the individual child. It is probably the outstanding way in which the school can and does contribute to the more healthy and normal adjustment of the problem youngster. It may be worth while to consider some of the ways in which this may be accomplished.

1. *Placement in a suitable group.* In spite of all the study of children's abilities which has been made, every clinic could produce cases of the type of Donald. Twelve years old, having spent one year in first grade, three futile failing years in second grade and two years in third grade, he was referred to our clinic as a possible mental defective by the principal of the school. He proved to have an I.Q. of 98, and did better than average work on performance tests. For five years he had been increasing his feeling of inadequacy and "dumbness" because of a specific reading disability. He was, except for the reading class, totally misplaced in third grade, and found nothing challenging or satisfying about his work. For every boy of this sort, dozens of cases could be produced of the type mentioned in Mr. Street's study, where dull indi-

viduals, doing the best work of which they are capable, are pushed over their depths into higher grades where they are learning little but a feeling of failure.

Thus the first and obvious step in any school therapy is to make certain that the child is in the proper group for the type of ability which he possesses. The dull child who needs a special class, the boy or girl who needs to be in a slow-moving section, the lad who needs shop training, the very gifted child who needs the competition of an accelerated group, are all familiar examples. There is food for thought in the fact that problem children, by and large, seem to show better ability than the average in manual tests, along with a below average showing in tests of abstract intelligence. The children with abilities for which they can find no normal expression in school life tend, it would seem, to develop problems. In addition to grouping according to mental level there must also be suitable placement, occasionally in a special group, for the child who is suffering from deformities and crippled limbs and for the youngster who has a serious deficiency of sight or hearing.

Nor is it enough, of course, to provide merely a suitable group. The curriculum which is chosen must be one adapted to the child. Alice is a 16 year old girl who illustrates that aspect of the problem. Her problems are many. She is saucy and bold, both in school and at home. She is self-conscious about her poor physical appearance. She is bitter and upset about the second marriage which her father is contemplating. Her attention-getting ways in school have been so annoying that the school authorities are thinking of transferring her to another school (a measure which may be constructive but which is often used merely as a means of "passing the buck"). The high school was aware that she was a dull normal child, yet had allowed her for more than a year to follow a straight academic course, failing her algebra and science, becoming more and more of an educational as well as a behavior problem. Yet this same school offered various other courses, simpler than the college preparatory type, which were of interest to

Alice. The first move in dealing with this situation is to adjust her curriculum to her abilities and interests. The only reason why it had not been done long before is that no one of the teachers in contact with the girl, nor the girl's advisor, had thought in terms of treating the girl. They had thought only in terms of treating her misbehavior, and had sent her from class, scolded her, and made her sit for hours in the advisor's office. As in many similar cases, it was not lack of information which blocked a simple diagnosis and treatment of at least this sector of Alice's difficulties. It was a failure in point of view, a failure to think in terms of the needs of the individual.

2. *The utilization of special abilities.* In giving the difficult child some sense of accomplishment, the alert teacher will make particular use of any special talent or interest or hobby of the child. Often this is a particularly necessary part of the treatment when poor placement, or special disabilities have created a sense of failure in the child which is very difficult to overcome in the academic studies of the whole group. Sometimes such special talents may be drawn out in class activities such as deal with the arts and crafts. The child who displays an innate artistic ability, in spite of his D's in arithmetic, history and spelling; the girl whose singing voice is attractive, even though she is repeating the grade; the lad who excels in the simple craft activities of the class-room, in spite of his reading disability; these are the children who need to be encouraged and praised and given status in the eyes of the class for their achievement. The gymnasium, the school orchestra, the shop classes, the class trips and outings afford other activities in which special talents of skill or leadership or organizational ability may be observed and rewarded. Frequently a change in school placement may be justified in order to give the child an opportunity to display some talent. Thus it may be wise to transfer a boy from a parochial or public school without shop activities, to a school where such work is available, in order to give the child some sense of satisfying accomplishment.

those with poor posture or physical handicaps, are also resources to be utilized.

4. *Therapeutic attitudes on the part of the teacher.* In planning special treatment for the child, of the sorts outlined above, the attitude of the child's teachers is so important that it must be given special attention. Proper school placement, recognition of talents, even specific tutoring may all fail to give the child any adequate degree of satisfaction in himself, if the teacher's attitude is not constructive. The teacher must genuinely feel that each child has a need to succeed, just as she herself has a need to succeed. If she has this attitude, she will be quick to look for opportunities to give each child some deserved recognition for accomplishment, whether it be a report card mark, a few words of sincere praise, or approval by the group. Most of all she will make sure that such avenues of recognition are found for the child who presents serious behavior difficulties, knowing that no matter what the fundamental causes of these problems there is less likelihood of their occurrence if the child is feeling satisfaction in a job well done. Very frequently it is difficult for teachers or principals to accept this notion. It smacks too much of rewarding bad behavior, or offends in some way their moral sense by suggesting that the "bad" child should be allowed a thrill of pride in his own achievement. Dr. Newell, in the article referred to, states that the teachers and principal of one school agreed, quite reluctantly, to try such a scheme in dealing with three difficult children with whom the clinic was working. They endeavored faithfully to praise each modest improvement and to find ways of rewarding achievement. They were so delighted with the very favorable results that they immediately decided to select all the outstanding behavior problems in the school and try the same tactics.

One important element in the teacher's attitude is the use of the child himself as a standard of comparison. School marks are often vicious in their effect, causing the bright child to be careless and easygoing because he can always get good marks, and the dull child to be discouraged because no matter how hard he tries he can never get good marks.   Even with such a marking system the understanding teacher can do much to negate its ill effects.   She can stress the progress which the individual is making in comparison with his own past achievement, and can thus spur both the able and the less intelligent child on to constructive effort without making either feel discouraged.   If a more modern system of report card has been adopted this whole process is still simpler.

It will be obvious from what has been said that the teacher who is most successful in helping a child to feel that his accomplishments are worthy of his own self-respect will be an individual with considerable resourcefulness of her own.   A constructive point of view and a fertile imagination are both important.   Children cannot all get their sense of satisfaction in the same way.   Some will develop pride in their work in different subjects.   Others will be pleased because they have been praised for their athletic skill, or the neatness of their desks, or the hobby which they have developed.   Still others will be satisfied to have managed the school bank or to have helped organize a program for the school assembly.   The resourceful teacher can utilize these significant opportunities without appreciably adding to her own burden.

Affectional Security.   Although the various measures for creating in the child a sense of achievement constitute perhaps the school's major contribution to therapy, it is by no means the only contribution.   We shall mention more briefly some of the other ways in which the school and the teacher may be utilized to meet other treatment needs.

Many problems in the child are created or intensified by the unsatisfactory emotional situation in the home.   The child who feels rejected or unwanted at home frequently compensates by trying to get attention and affection elsewhere.   He is often the "show-off" or aggressive behavior problem in the schoolroom.   Treatment of such a situation is usually aimed at the home.   A change in the parent's approach to the child or even, if necessary, the choice of substitute parents may help to bring about the emotional security which is needed. Frequently, however, in addition to such measures the school may itself strike at the causes of insecurity by its methods of dealing with the child in the schoolroom situation.

One of the ways in which the teacher may be of constructive help with the insecure, attention-getting child is by increasing the legitimate opportunities for attention. Such a youngster should be given ample opportunities to recite, to stand up before the class, to answer questions, with generous praise for those occasions when his remarks are worth while and to the point. There will also be occasions when such a child may be given small responsibilities which give him harmless and satisfying ways of gaining attention. A position as monitor, passing out school supplies, an opportunity to put up posters or drawings on the wall, the glory of being the secretary or sergeant-at-arms of the class organization, are all legitimate chances of winning the attention of the group and the teacher. Still another range of possibilities lies within the realm of class programs, dramatics, school assemblies. Here the child who is pathetically or aggressively eager for some "show-off" experience can find a constructive way to meet his needs. The therapeutic possibilities of school dramatics we have only begun to explore. For some it provides opportunities for self-expression, for release of their own deep-seated attitudes. For the group we are discussing at the moment, it provides literally the "center of the stage" which is so often a substitute for the affection which is the underlying need.

Mortimer is an interesting lad whose behavior from the age of six has been a source of increasing difficulty to many community agencies. At the present time, aged 17, he is an inmate of a reformatory because of persistent automobile stealing. His last capture by the police was made after an exciting high-speed chase with police bullets whizzing about his ears. His future looks dark indeed. Intelligent efforts to treat his difficulties were blocked all the way through childhood by neurotic and rejecting parents, who resisted all attempted therapy. His turbulent and unsatisfying home environment was without doubt one of the major causes of his problem and delinquent behavior, and it seemed impossible to reach these parents. Yet when one looks back over Mortimer's behavior record, bristling with truancies, school expulsions, non-promotions, runaway trips, delinquencies and the like, there is one year which is singularly free from trouble. While he was in the seventh grade there were no complaints to school authorities, the visiting teacher, or to social agencies. And if we inquire further as to the reason for the temporary cessation of problems, we find it in the school. A gifted teacher, observing the boy's aggressive drive for notice and attention, gave some thought to the matter of satisfying this need. She interested Mortimer in drama. The interest "took," and she encouraged him to write a play, with the understanding that if it was of good quality it could be acted by the class. For months, along with the normal amount of regular school work, Mortimer worked on the writing of the play, then on the selection and direction of the cast, for by that time he had earned by his labors the right to direct the production. It was successfully staged for the school. Mortimer was much in the public eye, he received approbation from his own class group, and problems were practically non-existent. Whether similar educational therapy, carried on through successive years, would have been sufficient to overcome the vicious influences of the home, it is difficult to say. The fact that it was even temporarily successful is noteworthy evidence of the influence of treatment within the school.

It is often difficult to persuade the teacher to adopt this type of therapy with the attention-seeking child. Since he is already taking too much of her time by unnecessary questions, by disturbing the class with his grimaces and loud talk, or by other varieties of "show-off" behavior, she sees no reason for allowing him still further opportunity to exhibit himself or to draw the attention of the group to his activities. Unfortunately she is too prone to use the sort of punishments suggested by Mr. James for "show-off" tendencies. She endeavors to "put the offender in his place by a remark that will enlist pupils on her side." The net result of this is to remove her own and the group approval from the child. The motives which impel him to seek attention then must be satisfied by seeking disapproving-attention. The behavior symptoms are intensified. If the teacher then falls back on "removal of privileges" there is still less opportunity for normal attention, and again the tendency toward getting some notice in anti-social ways is strengthened. Finally the teacher, if she follows Mr. James's suggestion, makes a bad matter still worse by giving him attention for his bad behavior. He is to make "public acknowledgement of his fault." Here is the very opportunity he has been seeking, that is, to have all eyes fastened on him, to have some emotional recognition of himself as a person. He has now learned how to achieve his goal. If he is sufficiently anti-social, both teacher and class will pay attention to him.

If, on the other hand, the teacher follows the type of approach we have been outlining, each opportunity for legitimate self-display and legitimate recognition lessens the need for "pestiferous" and annoying ways of getting recognition. A number of the pupils with whom Dr. Newell felt the school had outstanding success were youngsters who were rejected at home and who consequently responded much better at school when their need for recognition was satisfied rather than attacked.

Such techniques are open to every teacher who is dealing with emotionally insecure children. They do not attempt to deal directly with the child's need for secure parental love, but tend to satisfy this need indirectly by providing social recognition and attention as a helpful substitute. Less frequently, in special cases, the teacher may by her own personal interest in the child become to some extent a satisfying parent-person and thus materially aid the child's general adjustment.

Such a personal relationship between pupil and teacher cannot be entirely or satisfactorily built up in class, or it becomes merely favoritism. It must depend primarily on contacts outside of class hours. It is much more likely to be successful with the younger child than with the older. Its success depends in large measure upon the degree of insight and understanding which the teacher possesses. The rejected or insecure child is often eager to stay after school and help the teacher with odd jobs, talk with her, and confide in her. If the teacher can accept this relationship without becoming too involved emotionally, if she can encourage the child to take responsibilities for her, to run errands, clean blackboards, take care of classroom property and the like, she has a genuine opportunity for treatment.   This will need to be more than the impersonal classroom relationship.   It will need to be more personal and more confidential.   Many teachers are afraid to lay aside their professional mask before any pupil. They would hesitate to be themselves while in a pupil's presence.   Such teachers could not make the relationship a very satisfying one to the pupil.

It is not enough that the teacher become, through this relationship, a relatively secure source of emotional satisfaction to the child.   She should also be aware of her responsibility for freeing the child from this relationship.   As the youngster feels sure of her genuine personal interest in him, she must gradually help him to feel that she is also interested in other children, that his interest in her must be shared by other pupils.   While it is undoubtedly the rare teacher who can successfully make use of this type of treatment relationship, it has real potentialities for the child.   To learn to feel some secure emotional bond to a parent person, and then to learn through this relationship that the child must share the parent person with others, and must more and more become independent of the relationship, is a most wholesome growth experience.   It is, on a smaller scale, the constructive emotional development which should come from the normal family life which the child has been denied.

Aids in Social Adjustment.   One of the normal functions of the school is to socialize the child, to teach him through the various contacts of group life the methods of reacting which will enable him to live comfortably with his fellowmen.   Often, for the child who is a problem, special attention must be given to this aspect of school experience, either because the child's problems are those of social maladjustment, or because a better group adjustment will provide satisfactions which make problem behavior less necessary in other areas.

The school has a particularly outstanding opportunity for dealing with the solitary, friendless child who for various reasons may be too shy or too fearful to become a part of the group. The organized recreational group, as we shall see in the next chapter, is likely to fail with this type of child because it is unable to lead him gradually into social contacts. The school is in a much more favorable position to develop in the child the beginnings of social techniques. The very solitary and quiet child is likely to concentrate on his academic work. To attempt to socialize such a child by putting him into a baseball game is usually as futile as it is distressing to the child. Rather the teacher would be advised to draw him into socialized activity first as a part of his work. The child who shrinks from group play can often be rather readily drawn into group association as a part of a class project, or can be encouraged to work in partnership with some other child. It is astonishing that under our present system of education children may sit for years in the same group without developing one close friendship or even a minimal degree of the techniques of group co-operation, partly because they have never learned to work with others, much less to play with them.

The clue to this field of therapy is that it is best to begin on the child's present level of social adjustment, no matter how poor that may be, and work gradually toward more social skills, wider circles of social activity, and more diverse types of social co-operation. The child may at first need encouragement even to co-operate with another youngster in a building project, or in a spelling contest, or in the designing of a bit of stage scenery. The next step may be simple social games in the classroom or the necessary co-operation in the work of a hobby club. Later there may be a willingness to learn the social and competitive skills required in the gymnasium classes, and gradually the child finds himself able to participate, without too much unhappiness, in the club activities, parties, and organized athletic teams of the school.

For children of the socially maladjusted sort, each social skill thus developed may be a painful and difficult process.

The girl who dreads to take part in the simple ring games of the classroom, and the boy who steps up, bat in hand, and faces the pitcher with a fear as abject as if he were going to his doom, are familiar enough to any teacher who has seen her pupils with sympathetic eyes. Again there is need, in this type of treatment, for the teacher to show confidence in the child and to point out and stress each bit of improvement in social skill, each new achievement in group co-operation.

Toward Reality. Another way in which the school is called upon to assist in therapy is in the treatment of the daydreaming child who is finding, in vivid and persistent phantasies, an escape from a world of difficult problems. In dealing with this type of boy or girl, the school is sometimes called upon to adjust the demands of the school program to the child's interest and abilities, in the ways which we have already discussed. This may be sufficient to reduce the phantasy to a normal degree, since the child is often driven into a daydreaming tendency by a program that is hopelessly difficult or ridiculously easy. In either case, work of suitable type to challenge but not discourage the child is the sort required.

There will be instances, however, particularly if the daydreaming is more deeply determined by causes outside of the school, where these measures will not suffice. In such circumstances the teacher may be able to draw the phantasy life closer to reality in a variety of ways. Compositions and themes offer an excellent way of getting older children to give some body and expression to their phantasies. Such topics as "Things I Dream of Doing," "What I Should Like to Be," "My Three Wishes," will often draw out from the daydreaming pupil some of the content which goes into his daydreams. For both the younger and older child, encouragement in the telling of imaginative stories will also be likely to reveal at least the direction of his phantasy life. Once the teacher has some notion of the type of phantasy which has meaning to the child, the whole purpose should be to follow this interest and give expression to it in every possible way. This is relatively easy in those instances where the child is daydreaming of himself as a great person. A great aviator, a general, a cowboy, or a musician are favorites among the boys, while the girls may be imagining themselves as movie actresses, debutantes, singers, or artists. The child may be encouraged to talk and write about these visions of "myself, grown very great" as one child put it. It is also healthy to let the boy or girl find out what requirements and training are necessary to become the creature of his dreams. This should not be done with the purpose of discouraging the child, but rather of helping him to see his phantasied life as a real possibility, with interesting vocational steps leading to it. The fact that his goal may be impractical is not especially important for the moment. Time, changing interests, and satisfactions in a real rather than a phantasy world usually correct these exaggerated goals. Mary finds that she does not have to become Cinderella if she has a moderately enjoyable time at the school party.

The purpose of treatment is the same when the phantasies deal with family life, or with sexual matters, but in such instances treatment within the classroom is less likely to be fruitful. It is probable that the process of bringing the child's daydreams into conscious expression and the discussion of family problems or sexual facts which relates them to reality will be better carried on by the skilled therapist rather than by the teacher. The discussion of such treatment is reserved for a later chapter.

Toward Independence. Not infrequently the school can be of great therapeutic help in dealing with the young child whose home experience has been such as to make him very dependent on adults for help, direction, and approval. As in some of the previous situations we have discussed, the primary goal of treatment will be to develop a healthier attitude on the part of the parents. The teacher may at the same time be supporting this therapy by the encouragement of independence in the child at school. For the most part this will probably be effected by wise use of group pressures and group ideals. It is the atmosphere of the schoolroom which has treatment value in such instances. The child who enters nursery school and finds that "we all take off our own overshoes here" is gaining help of this sort. And on up through the grades and high school the teacher can do much to make the classroom standard one of independent thinking and action. Where premiums are set upon self-reliance, initiative, and the ability to make choices, independence grows apace, and the dependent child is profoundly affected by the attitudes of both teacher and classmates. Since this is so much a function of the normal group experience and so little an aspect of individual treatment utilized for special cases, we shall not dwell on it longer here.

The Acceptance of Authority. Miss Elizabeth Dexter, writing from her experience in dealing with problem children in a public-school setting, points out that "upon entering school every child has a three-fold adjustment to make: he must learn to accept authority, to accept the competition of the classroom, and to find satisfaction in doing things for himself." [9] This first adjustment, to the authority of the teacher, may be a natural and painless process of adjustment to social control, but there are also instances where planned treatment effort on the part of the teacher is necessary to bring about this adjustment in the case of a problem child.

The school's help is particularly required with the child who through overindulgence or neglect, or through other factors, has never learned social restraint, and also with the child whose rebellion toward unwise authority at home carries over into rebellion against all authority at school. Miss Dexter describes a kindergarten child of the first type whose violent reactions to school authority results from the fact that his parents yielded to him on every point, humored him, dressed him, and indulged him in every way. In such a situation, without drastic coercion, the child must be made to feel the

[9] Dexter, Elizabeth H. "Treatment of the Child Through the School Environment," *Mental Hygiene*, vol. 12 (April, 1928), p. 360.

weight of group opinion. If he is to develop a normal and useful life, he must respond to group control. The teacher will do well to avoid disputes except on issues in which the group has laid down a rule. There it is quite reasonable to insist that the child abide by it.

In dealing with the child who is already rebellious and bitter against authority because of the repressive measures used at home, the techniques will of necessity be somewhat different. With such a child the teacher will be well advised first of all to use as few commands as possible, so that issues in regard to authority are not needlessly raised. When there is defiance, it is most unwise to meet it with an attacking punitive approach since this merely recreates the problem situation which exists in the home. Whenever feasible, defiance should be ignored and a reasonable explanation made to the child, giving him if possible some choice of action. It is only through such means that the child can gradually learn new adjustments to reasonable authority, so that he does not have to respond with the emotional reactions which he is accustomed to make to repressive authority.

Personal Counseling. In addition to the treatment procedures involving only the classroom situation there will occasionally be situations in which the teacher with an understanding of children's problems will be the one most capable of carrying on rather intensive counseling of the child. This will also apply more frequently to the school advisor. The techniques to be used by teachers in such a relationship are no different in kind than those used by psychiatrists, psychologists, or social workers counseling in similar situations. Consequently our consideration of these methods will be found in a later chapter on treatment interviews.

THE USE OF SPECIAL RESOURCES

A final and most important method which the teacher may use in the treatment of individual problems is to call upon the visiting teacher, the school psychologist, or the psychiatric clinic within the school system. This is mentioned last rather than first, because many school systems have no such resources, and it would be unfortunate if the teacher felt that she were helpless without them. Furthermore it is important to recognize that certain aspects of individual treatment belong primarily within the realm of the classroom teacher, whether such treatment is carried on co-operatively with the psychologist or visiting teacher, or whether the teacher is doing what she can without such skilled outside help.

The clinical specialists mentioned will of course have available broader resources for treatment than the teacher commands. They may, in dealing with the child's total situation, make use of foster-home placement or recreational groups, and may find necessary a deeper therapeutic approach to parent or child than the teacher would be justified in undertaking. They have open to them all the avenues of treatment described in this book, while the teacher properly limits her treatment function to those approaches which can be satisfactorily combined with her teaching responsibilities.

Some time must probably elapse before teachers learn to be comfortable about the use of such special clinical resources. A teacher who would pride herself upon discovering a child with defective vision and referring him to a physician, will on the other hand be reluctant to refer a serious family problem to the visiting teacher, or a deep-seated personality problem to the school psychologist or psychiatrist. Only as the teacher fully realizes that such a call for assistance is a credit to her professional alertness, rather than a reflection upon her teaching ability, will such resources be satisfactorily utilized.

TEACHERS' OBJECTIONS TO INDIVIDUAL TREATMENT

Occasionally, when it is suggested to a teacher that she use with a problem child some of the methods suggested in this chapter, she reacts with the thought that she cannot treat one child differently from another without being unfair or causing trouble. This is an interesting straw man which not infrequently blocks effective treatment of problem children in school. It is true that children resent emotional favoritism being shown toward one child. It is not at all true, however, that they react against differential treatment which has any sort of rational basis. The bogey exists largely in the teacher's mind. The children are well aware of the difficult individuals in their own group. Their crude diagnoses are sometimes more accurate than those of the teacher. They respond very readily to the notion that each individual is treated according to his own capacities, whether this be in the realm of behavior or of school achievement. They recognize that this is much more just and fair than when they are all "treated alike," without any regard to the differing standards to which they should be held, based on the differing factors which have developed them. The teacher or principal who deals with her pupils on a basis of understanding and insight will most assuredly treat them in ways suited to each individual child. And if this attitude prevails the possibility of effective treatment of the difficult child through the school environment is greatly enhanced.

BIBLIOGRAPHY

Allen, Elizabeth. "A Mental Hygiene Program in Grade Schools," *Mental Hygiene*, vol. 13 (July, 1929), pp. 289–297.

Anderson, V. V. *Psychiatry in Education*, chaps. 4 and 5. New York: Harper & Bros., 1932. 430 p.

Bassett, Clara. *Mental Hygiene in the Community*, chap. 8. New York: Macmillan Company, 1934. 394 p.

Beard, Belle. *Juvenile Probation*, chap. 8. New York: American Book Company, 1934. 219 p.

Campbell, Nellie M. *The Elementary School Teacher's Treatment of Classroom Problems*. New York: Bureau of Publications, Teachers College, Columbia University, 1935. 71 p.

Character Education. Tenth Yearbook, Department of Superintendence, National Education Association, chaps. 7, 9, 11. Washington, D.C.: National Education Association, 1932. 535 p.

Dexter, Elizabeth H. "Treatment of the Child Through the School Environment," *Mental Hygiene*, vol. 12 (April, 1928), pp. 358–365.

Groves, Ernest R., and Blanchard, Phyllis. *Introduction to Mental Hygiene*, chap. 8. New York: Henry Holt and Company, 1930. 467 p.

Louttit, C. M. *Clinical Psychology*, chaps. 6 and 7. New York: Harper & Bros., 1936. 695 p.

Martens, Elise H., and Russ, Helen. *Adjustment of Behavior Problems of School Children*. U.S. Department of Interior, Office of Education, Bulletin no. 18, of 1932. Washington, D.C.: Government Printing Office, 1932. 78 p.

Morgan, John J. B. *The Psychology of the Unadjusted School Child*. Revised Edition. New York: Macmillan Company, 1936. 339 p.

Newell, H. W. "The Methods of Child Guidance Adapted to a Public School Program," *Mental Hygiene*, vol. 18 (July, 1934), pp. 362–72.

Rivlin, Harry N. *Educating for Adjustment*. New York: D. Appleton-Century Company, 1936. 419 p.

Sherman, Mandel. *Mental Hygiene and Education*. New York: Longmans, Green and Company, 1934. 295 p.

Symonds, Percival M. *Mental Hygiene of the School Child*. New York: Macmillan Company, 1934. 321 p.

Thomas, W. I., and Thomas, D. S. *The Child in America*, chap. 5. New York: Alfred A. Knopf, 1928. 583 p.

Truitt, Ralph. "Mental Hygiene and the Public Schools," *Mental Hygiene*, vol. 13 (July, 1929), pp. 261–271.

Washburne, Carleton. *Adjusting the School to the Child*, chap. 10. Yonkers, New York: World Book Company, 1932. 189 p.

Wickman, E. K. *Children's Behavior and Teacher's Attitudes*. New York: Commonwealth Fund, 1928. 247 p.

Zachry, Caroline B. *Personality Adjustment of School Children*. New York: Charles Scribner's Sons, 1929. 306 p.

CHAPTER IX

The Intelligent Use of Clubs, Groups, and Camps

THOSE who have been most interested in working with the individual child and his problems have been somewhat slow to recognize the therapeutic possibilities inherent in group relationships. Partly because psychiatrists, psychologists, and social workers each pursue a professional training which emphasizes the individual, they are apt to lose sight of the significance and strength of social and group forces. In recent years, however, there has been an increased appreciation of the social methods which may be useful in treatment of the individual. As new research studies make plain the fact that the child's behavior and ideals are influenced more by his companionship group than by any other force except the family, use is beginning to be made of this information in a constructive way. If gangs and groups are potent influences in creating delinquency and problem behavior, may they not also be equally potent in developing normal behavior? We shall consider in this chapter the planned use of all such companionship influences as are likely to be utilized in altering a child's behavior. Organized clubs, groups interested in promoting special interest activities, and camps of all varieties are often used for such purposes. Likewise the encouragement or discouragement of companionship with particular friends may well be included.

The use of therapy of this sort will naturally depend upon the diagnosis which has been made of the child's problems. Not infrequently the child may be maladjusted because he has never achieved a normal relationship to others of his own age.

In other instances stealing or sex misconduct may be directly due to gang or group associations of an undesirable sort. In either type of case any wisely directed treatment must aim to develop a healthy group adjustment as a means of eliminating the causes of misbehavior. In still other cases in which the causes of maladjustment lie outside the realm of social relationships, group activity may still be useful as palliative therapy. The child whose adjustments at school and at home are very unhappy ones may profit greatly from normal and satisfying experiences as part of a group. This may be especially necessary as a means of treatment where efforts to remove the definitely causative factors are blocked in one way or another.

THE EXTENT TO WHICH GROUP MEMBERSHIP IS USED AS TREATMENT

There is limited information as to how widely the influence of group associations is brought to bear upon the difficult child. Our most complete data comes from the delinquency field and seems to indicate a definite trend in the use of such resources. Studies which have been made of the treatment of three large groups of delinquent children, quite comparable as to age, mentality, and degree of delinquent behavior, may be contrasted in this respect. The first is the study made by the Gluecks, of the treatment of 1000 juvenile delinquents examined by the Judge Baker Foundation clinic during the years 1917–22.[1] The second is the study made by Miss Beard, of 500 delinquents on probation, examined by the same clinic in the years 1924–27.[2] The third is a group of 143 delinquents who were intensively treated by Dr. Healy in Boston and by his associates in New Haven and Detroit, during the period 1929–33.[3] Each study contains information as to the degree

[1] Glueck, Sheldon and Eleanor. *One Thousand Juvenile Delinquents*, pp. 116–117. Cambridge: Harvard University Press, 1934.

[2] Beard, Belle. *Juvenile Probation*, pp. 106–114. New York: American Book Company, 1934.

[3] Healy, William, and Bronner, A. F. *New Light on Delinquency and its Treatment*, p. 154. New Haven: Yale University Press, 1936.

to which group and companionship recommendations were made and carried out as a part of treatment. The following statements summarize briefly the facts from each of these studies.

In the Glueck study it was found that in 112 instances recommendations were made for better recreational outlets or supervised recreational facilities. In 84 additional cases it was suggested that specific agencies be utilized to stimulate the boys' constructive interests. These recommendations would presumably not apply to the 301 boys who, it was suggested, were to be sent to institutions, the army, navy, or farm jobs. They should probably be considered in relationship to the 699 boys remaining in their own homes, in a foster home, or with relatives. Even so, the number of recommendations for treatment through social groups seems very small, being suggested in less than 30 per cent of the cases. Furthermore, approximately two-thirds of these recommendations were not carried out.

The showing is somewhat better with the probation cases studied by Miss Beard. Recommendations regarding recreational groups were made for 41 per cent of the boys and 34 per cent of the girls, and were carried out in approximately half of the cases.

The contrast is very sharp if these two groups are compared with the third. Dr. Healy states that of these delinquents 50 per cent of the New Haven groups, 60 per cent of the Boston groups and 80 per cent of the Detroit group became active members of a recreational group during the course of treatment.

While we cannot be sure that definitions in all three studies are strictly equivalent, the greatly increased use of social groups as therapy seems clearly demonstrated. It is probable that this represents at least the direction in which most clinics and agencies for dealing with the individual child have been moving. It should be realized that clinics dealing with delinquents only would make the greatest use of this type of treatment. This is partly due to the fact that delinquency often has its roots in a group situation, and also to the fact that delinquent children are usually 12 to 18 years of age, the age group to whom clubs and organized activities make the greatest appeal. In the Child Study Department, Rochester

S.P.C.C., which handles a group of problem children extending down into the lower age ranges and involving many types of problems beside delinquency, we find that recommendations for the use of social resources are made in approximately 40 per cent of the cases of children remaining in their own homes, but much less frequently for children going to foster homes. These recommendations involve membership in groups in 13 per cent of the cases and other suggestions in regard to companionship in 27 per cent of the cases.

RESULTS OF GROUP EXPERIENCE FOR PROBLEM CHILDREN

It is of course difficult to evaluate the worth of any particular aspect of treatment apart from evaluating the whole program of therapy. It is unfortunate that we do not have more reliable data on which to base a judgment as to the efficacy of this social therapy, since exaggerated claims have been made in regard to it. Not many years ago wide circulation was given to statements of the sort ascribed to a judge who is reputed to have said that no Boy Scout had ever been brought before him as a delinquent. This thoughtless generalization is amply answered by the following statement of W. I. Thomas in regard to Scouting. "The most serious limitation of the program is that it is not adapted to the underprivileged boy, does not appeal to or receive the boy who is a behavior problem, and practically does not touch the great mass of gang life... from which delinquents and criminals are largely recruited.[4] This statement which was made in 1928 would have to be modified at the present time, since the Scouting movement has made very definite efforts to adapt itself to the underprivileged and the problem boy, and has gone into institutions for delinquents to establish troops there. Nevertheless it does explain why generalized statements which point out that members of organized groups are not delinquent need to be regarded with great scepticism. Ordinarily the organ-

[4] Thomas, W. I., and Thomas, D. S. *The Child in America*, p. 174. New York: Alfred A. Knopf, 1928.

ized group has not interested itself in the section of the population from which delinquents come, nor has it regarded the problem child with much favor.

The newer trend in group organization on a therapeutic basis is indicated by the "Area Projects" in Chicago which utilize neighborhood and group methods in striving to correct the basic faults in the delinquency areas of the city. This work grew out of the research studies made by Clifford Shaw and his associates.

There is no doubt that group experiences, suitably planned as treatment, exercise a very significant influence on the child who is a problem. The best indication of clinical judgment on this point is the increased use of such resources. Some evidence of the influence of such treatment is contained in Miss Beard's study, previously mentioned. She points out that in the 96 cases where the probationers became active members of clubs or groups all of the 15 girls and 70 per cent of the 81 boys were ultimately successfully adjusted, a much better showing than for the group as a whole. She concludes "The proportion of success was twice as great where the recreational recommendations were carried out as where unsuccessful attempts were made." [5] Experience would indicate that perhaps the group with less serious problems would be easier to adjust in clubs, and this fact might modify Miss Beard's findings to some extent. We may safely conclude, however, that, like educational treatment, therapy through companionship groups seems closely related to the successful adjustment of problem children.

THE CHOICE OF THE GROUP

Many mistakes are made by well-meaning clinicians in suggesting the use of recreational resources. The psychiatrist who would be shocked at the thought of prescribing "some kind of sedative" for a child will advise "some sort of recreational outlet" and feel no twinge of conscience. The psychol-

5 Beard, *op. cit.*, p. 168.

ogist who makes specific and well-planned recommendations in regard to school treatment will advise that "this boy should be linked up to some group." Until we learn to use social therapy in the same planful way in which we use medical or educational therapy, results are bound to be poor. There are various ways in which we can improve our treatment techniques along this line.

The problem in the first place is one of knowing the community resources. The person working with the individual child must have some awareness of what is available in the way of groups. There are loosely organized clubs and classes in the churches and in the schools. There are more closely knit organizations such as the Boy or Girl Scouts, or similar continuing groups in the Y.M. and Y.W.C.A. or the J.Y.M.A. There are various groups in which some single activity is the organizing core, as in orchestras, harmonica bands, and handicraft groups. There are groups which link up closely with the home and directly involve the parents, such as the Cub Scout Program for boys ten to twelve. Without some knowledge of the various groups which operate in a particular community, we are no more prepared to treat the problem child than if we were unaware of the school or foster-home facilities.

Furthermore, if we are to deal effectively with the child before us, we must have some knowledge of the program differences of these various groups and must keep in touch with recreational leaders who can supplement our knowledge when necessary. We should know that the problem lad of fifteen is very rarely a good candidate for a scout troop. He is apt to be too sophisticated for such an organization, the bulk of whose membership is made up of boys of twelve, thirteen, and fourteen. We should recognize that one boy will respond best to the free program of a "Y" club which develops its program largely out of the interests and initiative of its boy members. Another lad would be lost in such freedom and would find himself much more effectively in the organized program of the Scouts, where each step is planned for the boy with specific rewards for achievement. We must know whether the settlement house does its work with closely knit natural gangs, in which an outsider would be resented, or whether the settlement groups are more artificial and activity-centered. Every group must be recognized as having differing methods of educational approach which will be more or less suitable to the child we have in mind.

Various factors, personal to the child himself, must also be considered in making the choice of a suitable group. The element of distance is very important. Even among the older boys served by the clubs of the Boys' Club Federation, it has been found that membership is almost entirely limited to one neighborhood area. In New York City 60 per cent of the boys who attend a club come from within a half-mile radius, and 85–90 per cent from within a three-quarter mile radius.[6] It is only in rare instances that lasting and successful group contacts are maintained where a considerable distance intervenes. If an experiment of this sort is to be made, ways of getting to and from the group meetings are a necessary item to be taken into account.

Factors which might tend to set the child apart from the group are also important. Is he the right age? Is he of somewhat the same level of social maturity? Here age may be used as a compensating factor, and the socially immature older boy or girl could fit into a younger group, when they might be lost in a group their own age. Are his interests reasonably congenial to those of the group? The solitary, superior child who is interested in astronomy is not going to fit readily into a rowdy athletic team. Is the child of a comparable cultural level with the rest of the group? Too great differences can cause havoc, as will be brought out in our discussion of camp placements. Will there be financial demands which the child cannot meet? Will nationality or race be a barrier? In one instance it was only after several years intervened that the author learned why one placement in a Scout troop, which seemed auspicious, had failed to develop. "I was the only Italian and some of the kids called me 'Wop.'"

[6] Figures from the Boys' Club Federation quoted by Thomas, *op. cit.*, p. 192.

That's why I didn't hang around them any more." Such factors merit careful consideration.

If to some it seems that we are elaborating unduly a very simple matter, it may be pointed out that our own clinical experience and that of others indicates that carefully chosen group placements, specifically planned, are much more effective than vague suggestions or ill-advised endeavors to enroll every boy in the Scouts or Y.M.C.A. or in a church group. A quotation from Miss Beard's study emphasizes this point. Speaking of the recommendations of the clinic in regard to recreation, she states, "only about one-third of the recommendations were specific as 'Try to interest Mrs. C. of —— Settlement House in Anna and give her an opportunity to develop new interests.' In every instance among the girls and in 90 per cent of the cases among the boys these specific suggestions were followed. The advantage of understanding neighborhood facilities and persons connected with them cannot be overemphasized." [7] It should be recalled that recreational suggestions in general were only 48 per cent carried out, clearly showing the importance of specific planning.

The types of groups mentioned in the preceding paragraphs include only those which are found in most cities. A new development in group organization, aimed directly at helping the child with behavior problems, is the "therapeutic group" described by Slavson.[8] Here the group is made up of problem youngsters, not necessarily of the same age. The aim of the leader is not centered upon the program, as in most clubs, but upon the gradual growth of healthy relationships. It is expected that the group will go through aggressive and destructive phases, but the children are helped to create a normally co-operative group spirit. Slavson stresses the point that such a relationship may be a substitute for the normal family relationships of which the children, in so many instances, have been deprived. Needless to say, the leadership of such a problem group is only for the trained and skilled group worker with

[7] Beard, *op. cit.*, p. 106.

[8] Slavson, S. R. *Creative Group Education*, pp. 22–23, and Appendix B, "Records of Therapy Groups." New York: Association Press, 1937.

unusual understanding and imagination. It holds many possibilities for treatment, and it is to be hoped that the plan will be tried in many communities.

Initiating the Child into the Group. If our diagnosis indicates that the child will profit from group experience, and we have gone to some effort to select a group which will meet the child's social needs, then the remaining steps need also to be carefully taken in order that the treatment may really be given a trial. One of these remaining steps is the interpretation of the child to the group leader. The more difficult the child's problems, the more important it is that the leader of the group have some understanding of the problems which may crop out, of the background from which these problems arise, and of the constructive interests and motives to which he may appeal in adjusting the child to the group. The degree of confidential information to be given to such a leader will depend upon his own degree of understanding and professional viewpoint. With any leader, however, it is only fair that he be given some knowledge of the child and that he be helped to regard the new member as a challenge rather than a bothersome nuisance in his orderly group proceedings.

It is of almost equal importance to prepare the child for what group membership will mean. Too often, if the child displays some eagerness for the class at the Art Gallery or the club at the Y, we are satisfied that nothing more needs to be done. Actually the child with little or no experience in organized social groups (and this is usually the child for whom such treatment is planned) often has grossly mistaken notions of what may be involved. He may wish heartily to be a Scout because to him scouting means overnight hikes. The fact that there are meetings, group organization, rules, and requirements, may be totally foreign to his thinking. A boy who adjusted very badly in camp had been wildly enthusiastic to go, because, as we later learned to our sorrow, camp meant to him a chance to go on solitary expeditions in the country. The thought of adjustment to group requirements never seriously crossed his mind either before nor, indeed, after he arrived at camp. Consequently a matter of fact discussion with the child, before he joins any group, of the activities it will involve, the companions he will meet, the requirements and rules of the group, and of the rewards both in achievement and in friendships which he is likely to find, will go far in improving the initial adjustment. Occasionally the parent, as well as the child, needs to be prepared for what is involved in group membership, if the venture is to be successful.

In this matter of social therapy, the first contacts with the group often determine the outcome. A leader who is slightly hostile to an odd newcomer, or blunders made by the boy or girl during the first association with the group, may be sufficient to spoil any possibility of satisfying and helpful relationships. Hence these careful preparatory measures are amply justified.

Following the Child's Adjustment. Workers who conscientiously follow up their therapeutic endeavors in the home or ask for reports from the school frequently fail to follow through on efforts in the field of social treatment. "Arrangements made for Joe to attend the Wildcats group at the A—— Branch of the Y.M.C.A." is often the last entry on the record regarding the results. This is unfortunate since further modifications or assistance are frequently needed.

Irene, 14, was abnormally shy and self-conscious, but attractive personally. Her major problems revolved about her conflict over her earlier incestuous relations with her father. While attempts were being made in interviews to resolve this conflict, the social worker made arrangements for Irene to enter a club at the Y.W. The group seemed well chosen, the leader was interested, Irene was willing to attend but fearful. Her first two contacts were very unhappy, because the group turned out to be very much of a clique, and in subtle ways gave her "the cold shoulder." The worker, learning this, immediately got in touch with the group leader. Arrangements were made for another girl, an acquaintance of Irene's, to join the group, and the leader brought in a third new member. This expansion of the club, and the fact that the leader's attention had been called to the existing clique, was sufficient to bring about a reorientation of the group, and Irene was able, for the first time in her life, to be a happily functioning unit in a social organization.

Such instances point clearly to the need of following, as well as of initiating, group memberships.

THE EXPERIMENTAL USE OF THE SUMMER CAMP AS TREATMENT

In the consideration of altering children's behavior through planned social relationships, the organized summer camp deserves an important place.   It has not only, in recent years, become a more frequently used technique, but it has also been the source of valuable lessons for clinicians which apply to the use of all types of groups.

There have been a few camps developed solely for the treatment of problem children.   Some of these have been expensive private camps for the problem children of the wealthy.   Three at least have been conducted for problem children coming to the behavior clinic or the court.   Camp Wawokiye, near Cleveland, for several years dealt with difficult children selected by the Cleveland Child Guidance Clinic.   Camp Onawama, near Flint, Michigan, cares for a group of problem and delinquent boys selected by the Detroit Department of Special Education.   A camp at Delaware, Ohio, has been maintained by the court of Domestic Relations of Franklin County.   All three of these camps have been described in different articles.[9] In addition to such specialized camps many others have given special attention to the needs of the individual problem child and have become adept in dealing with him.   Among such camps we might mention Camp Ahmek, Ontario, The Pioneer Youth Camp, Rifton, New York, The Scy Camp, Blue Ridge, Tennessee, and Camp Cory, Penn Yan, New York.[10]

[9] Camp Wawokiye is described in an article in *Mental Hygiene* by Dr. Rademacher, Camp Onawama in the same journal by Robert Amsden.   The camp at Delaware is described by Irving Wagner.   All three references are contained in the bibliography.

[10] Information in regard to the individual treatment of problem boys and girls in these camps are contained in the following references, all listed more fully in the bibliography.

Ahmek, *Camping and Character.*

Pioneer Youth (Coeducational Camp), *Creative Camping.*

Camp Scy, *Organized Camping and Progressive Education.*

Camp Cory, Reports of the 1931 and 1932 seasons, mimeographed by the Rochester (N.Y.) Y.M.C.A.

The full significance of the summer camp as a treatment procedure may be realized if we think in terms suggested in Chapter III as to the factors which determine behavior. When camp is prescribed as a treatment procedure for the seriously maladjusted boy or girl, there are left unchanged only the most basic and unalterable factors, the hereditary physical and mental endowment, and acquired physical defects and conditions. Every other influence which is causative undergoes significant change. The child is away from any parental attitudes which have been destructive. The companionship influences are completely altered, usually for the better. Any harmful cultural or neighborhood forces are replaced by the constructive and vital force of cultural standards set by a wholesome group of the child's own age level. Educational training, which may have been crippling and thwarting, becomes a fascinating array of interesting projects. Small wonder then that few problem children behave in camp as they have been accustomed to behave at home and at school. Changing such a weight of causative influences is bound to bring change in behavior. As Mr. Dimock suggests, camp has the added advantage of providing

> a unified, controlled, and complete life experience. The total life of the boy is lived in the camp. There is no conflict of conduct patterns and pressures of home, school, gang, or other group. Not only is there this thorough integration of the boy's experience, but the patterns and stimuli for his behavior are virtually under complete control. No other situation lends itself more readily to complete environmental control and unity, at the same time affording the fullest opportunity for the boy to satisfy all of his basic wishes, emotions, and interests.[11]

One further element which adds to the potency of the camp influence is that the boy or girl nearly always enters the experience with enthusiasm and has a mental "set" toward accepting the camp regime. Consequently the camp begins its work with the problem child in a more favorable position

[11] Dimock, H. E., and Hendry, C. E. *Camping and Character*, p. 146. New York: Association Press, 1929.

for treatment than the foster home, the institution, or any other treatment resource we have described.

Matching the Child and the Camp. In spite of this possibly glowing account of the potentialities which the camp has for treatment, it would be a serious mistake to suppose that every camp would succeed with every problem child. Since available camps are usually rather few, we must think in terms of choosing the child who will be helped by the camp, rather than of being able, ordinarily, to choose outright the camp which will fit the child. In considering camp placement we must take into account the intelligence level of the child and the camp group, the difficulties which may arise because of differences in cultural status, and the social skills which the child possesses. Other items are probably of less significance.

The intelligence factor is one which may easily be overlooked in planning camp placement. Camps vary enormously in the general mental level. Private camps, even those like Camp Cory, which supposedly serve a middle-class group, compare with the best private schools in their mentality rating. A survey of 208 boys at Cory by means of group tests indicated an average I.Q. of 114.[12] Less than 10 per cent of these boys rated as "low average" or below, while 40 per cent were "superior" or "very superior" in intelligence. Another study of intelligence in Camp Ahmek, which is a similar camp, gave an average I.Q. of approximately 112–114 (I.B. 131), in a group of 113 boys.[13] Such facts have vital significance when we are thinking of placing a bullying oversize lad of 13, with an I.Q. of 85, in such a group.

On the other hand camps with very different intelligence levels exist. The author from his experience with Camp Wawokiye would judge that the average intelligence quotient was between 90 and 100. Camp Onawama, according to Mr. Amsden, reports that the majority of its boys fall in the I.Q.

[12] Carson, Charles W., and Rogers, Carl R. "Intelligence as a Factor in a Camp Program," *The Camping Magazine*, vol. 3 (December, 1930), pp. 8–11.

[13] Dimock and Hendry, *op. cit.*, p. 160.

range from 70 to 85. It is perhaps significant that for an example of a boy who found it extremely difficult to adjust to the group, Mr. Amsden selects the brightest youngster in camp, with an I.Q. of 139. It is obvious that part of his difficulties come from trying to adjust to a much duller group. It is even more difficult for the very dull lad to adjust to a bright group. Experience at Camp Cory led to the conclusion that a boy with an I.Q. 25 points below the camp average would have difficulty in fitting into camp, unless other factors were decidedly favorable.

Unless consideration is given to this intelligence factor, camp placement may create rather than solve problems. An example may be cited of such a result at Camp Cory.

Henry is a lean, gangling, 15 year old boy, dull and unattractive in appearance. He is the son of a very intelligent professional man, and has been reared in a cultured home. Both his father and mother are much interested in church work and religious influences have been strong. In school Henry had been recognized as a slow boy, and placed in a special class. It so happened that he was one of the brightest of the special class, and received considerable praise from his teacher for his work. He was not regarded as a serious behavior problem.

When Henry came to camp, however, it was only a few days before he was one of the best known boys on the grounds. His name became a byword for describing any stupidity. His counselor at the end of a week rated him as markedly deficient in courtesy, self-control, helpfulness and consideration for others, as well as in ability to mix with other boys, modesty, tidiness, and leadership ability. He was one of the outstanding misfits in camp. The other boys continually made him the butt of their jokes, in spite of the efforts of the staff. At one time they had persuaded him that he was to be the pitcher on the camp team, and it was necessary to disillusion Henry when he wanted to call his family on long distance telephone to have them attend the game. As he became somewhat accustomed to this form of teasing Henry frequently responded by seeming even more gullible than he really was. He seemed to enjoy the attention which he obtained by being "the goat." To the end, however, he was infuriated when the boys called him names. Such epithets as "pig face," "pig eye," and "dish rag," never failed to arouse uncontrollable anger. Frequently, he would attempt to turn the tables by viciously teasing his tormentors.

Although he remained eight weeks in camp, Henry undertook few projects. He attempted mostly the handicraft types of work such as archery, leather-work, and making a model airplane. He did not excel in any of these but did sufficiently good work to obtain some satisfaction.

A psychological examination given at camp (in this case an individual Stanford Binet) showed Henry to have a mental age of eleven years, an I.Q. of 74. He was a rather verbalistic type of borderline boy, and impressed the examiner as being docile and suggestible. He admitted that he was unhappy because of the teasing of the other boys, but liked the camp activities. He showed very little insight into the whole situation. His ambition to be a missionary to Africa indicates how badly he misjudged his own abilities. Henry is an excellent picture of a docile low-grade boy who gets along splendidly when he is competing with boys of his own mental level. The camp environment, however, was so superior that he was goaded into "problem" tendencies by his own lack of ability to compete on a normal basis.[14]

In connection with the item of mentality the child's social skills must be considered, since one may compensate for the other. The child who is already a good swimmer or an able athlete may be able to adjust to the group even though below the mentality range which is acceptable. On the other hand the child who is mentally dull in comparison with the group, and also compares unfavorably in regard to social and athletic skills, is likely to have a very difficult time indeed. Incidentally the boy who has attended camp for one season is almost automatically acceptable to the group the next year. Frequently the phenomenon was observed at Camp Cory that a boy who had failed miserably to be accepted by the group his first season returned and was immediately accepted the following year. In large measure this is due to the fact that he has acquired some, at least, of the specific social skills which make adjustment possible. He "knows the ropes." He knows more of these skills than the newcomers. Consequently his status, no matter how serious his behavior problems may be, is much more assured. Even Henry, the boy described

[14] Carson and Rogers, *op. cit.*, p. 10.

above, made a moderately acceptable adjustment during his second season at camp.

The matter of social status needs also to be considered. The boy who brings his belongings to camp in a paper bundle, when blanket rolls and suitcases are the acceptable forms of luggage, is likely to be set apart at once. Similarly in matters of costume. It may be that the leading campers wear nothing at all save a disreputable pair of shorts and old sneaks. If so, it is highly important that the newcomer wear shorts also, and not trousers which are likely to cause him to be ostracized. Likewise, in private camps, spending money is an essential to social acceptance. The amount is much less important than the fact of having something to spend. While the examples cited have been from boys' camps, much the same factors are found among camps for girls. Fortunately such indications of cultural level are all highly superficial and hence easily provided for in the case of the problem child. In spite of their superficiality they are very significant for the adjustment of the child.

An experience which illustrates some of these considerations is the placement of a group of boys from foster homes at Camp Cory. Some of these boys were problems of behavior, others were not. Neither our own agency nor others had had very good success in placing "agency children" in camp, because they were so often unacceptable to the group, due to differences in mentality, social status, or social skills. Consequently the experiment was tried of having one complete tentful (nine boys) made up of youngsters from foster homes. They were not, of course, known as boys from any social agency. This scheme worked very satisfactorily for two seasons, and boys succeeded in camp who would almost certainly have failed of acceptance if placed in a regular tent group.

Interestingly enough physical handicaps have not, in the author's experience, been a serious bar to camp adjustment. Children will make allowances for sensory defects, deformities, or crippled conditions, whereas the child who is so unfortunate as to be mentally dull or unstable is much more likely to incur the "razzing" or displeasure of the group. A study by the author of the type of boys who could be accepted at Camp Cory includes this paragraph.

> Physical disabilities (except those which would make activity impossible) do not seem to prevent successful camp experience. The variety of physical abnormalities which were well assimilated into camp life was surprising. Boys who were lame, epileptic, and excessively overweight, profited a great deal. A boy who had been a semi-invalid most of his life until a few months before camp, made excellent progress. In no case was any physical disability a real cause for failure in camp.[15]

The summary of the study just quoted indicates some of the sorts of children who, during one summer at Cory, found camp a therapeutic experience.

> Given a very few essential conditions:
> *a*, adequate mentality;
> *b*, sufficient financial backing to provide clothes and spending money;
> *c*, assurance that parents will not interfere or take the boy home, there seems to be almost no limit to the types of problem children who can be helped in camp. This summer there were in camp: delinquents who had been in court for stealing, boys who had been expelled from school, boys who had been school problems, boys who were regarded as ungovernable by their parents, boys who were much spoiled, boys with temper tantrums, enuresis problems, etc. In practically all of these cases it was felt that camp had brought about definite improvement. In no case did camp have to admit failure when conditions *a*, *b*, and *c*, were met.

Most of the above considerations in regard to matching the child and the camp boil down to an application of the principle that "birds of a feather flock together." This principle, as it relates to age, mentality, and interests, has been well established by various studies,[16] and the suggestions which have

---

[15] This and the following excerpt are taken from the "*Report of the 1931 Season, Camp Lawrence Cory*," a mimeographed report from the Rochester Y.M.C.A.

[16] For a brief summary of such research see Partridge, E. A., *Leadership Among Adolescent Boys* (New York: Bureau of Publications, Teachers College, Columbia, 1934), pp. 14–17.

been made are merely specific applications of it to the camp situation.

A somewhat different type of approach to the problem of camp acceptability is made by Dr. Chassel. Speaking from experience with camp groups of younger children below the age of eight, Dr. Chassell classifies behavior problems into four major groups and comments upon the possibility of their treatment in camp.[17]

> First is the group of children whose problems largely arise from the home situation and are most evident there, but whose social adjustment is already acceptable. Such children respond excellently to camp.
>
> A second group he terms the "willing eccentrics" — children with a variety of problems, who have a desire and determination to be accepted by the camp group. Success with this group frequently depends upon whether they have some ability which can be developed, with adult help, into a technique of social acceptability. This may be some athletic ability such as swimming, or merely a gift for clowning, or an abundance of courage and daring.
>
> The third group, which he labels the "defensive eccentrics" are those who are so sensitive that they meet the camp situation by withdrawing into themselves, or by a counter attack upon the group. For these he suggests that success in a small or limited daytime group is essential, rather than being "thrown helpless into a strenuous twenty-four hour maelstrom."
>
> The fourth group, the very "aggressive eccentrics" with compulsive or sadistic tendencies he feels are doubtful camp risks because they may prove a definite hazard to the other children.

While these suggestions are thought-provoking, it is probable that they apply more strictly to the young child than to the group above ten. Certainly a number of individuals belonging to the third and some of those belonging to the fourth group are able to fit into the older camp, providing the camp and the child have been reasonably well "matched."

Organizing the Camp for Individual Treatment. When, in the light of the criteria suggested, camp placement has been

[17] Chassell, Joseph O. "Indications for Camp Prescription," *American Journal of Orthopsychiatry*, vol. 7 (January, 1937), pp. 82–95.

chosen as a means of dealing with the behavior difficulties of a particular boy or girl, what may we expect to happen? In what ways does the camp operate to alter behavior? Such questions can perhaps be answered in more concrete fashion by describing the camp procedure for dealing with problem boys at Camp Cory. This is cited only because of personal experience with the camp, similar methods having been used even earlier at certain other camps.

A unique feature of the program of this camp was that the various social agencies and the visiting teachers co-operated by sending to the psychologist brief reports concerning any boy with serious behavior problems who was coming to camp. In some instances the agency had initiated the plans for camp treatment and in others the parents had taken the initiative. In addition to these agency reports the parents filled out for every boy quite extensive blanks, which gave some of the facts regarding family, school, and behavior. A summarized account of this material was given to the counselor usually the day before the boy's arrival. In this way the counselors, who were for the most part mature college men with an interest in individuals, were prepared for each youngster, and, in the case of problem boys, knew the type of situation which was likely to arise and the special interests which the boy might like to follow. At the end of the first week of the boy's stay, the counselor made a behavior report, describing his social adjustment, his activities, any behavior problems which had arisen, and his own plan for dealing with the boy. This report was discussed with the psychologist, and further suggestions made for handling difficulties and encouraging healthy trends. During the last week of the boy's stay a final report was made covering behavior, camp activities, and the outstanding successes and failures in the boy's camp experience. The value of these reports was two-fold. Besides their value as a rather complete record of the boy's initial adjustment and of his final achievement, they served the purpose of making the counselor constantly aware of his therapeutic function. It is much less easy to dismiss a boy from consideration as being merely a "dope" (the favorite camp term for the misfit) when a report is to be written of the treatment attempted. The counselors did patient and excellent work in helping their young charges to gain healthy training from the camp experience. One wonders if a similar program might be adopted in schools.

Treatment Techniques in Camp.   As to the treatment methods used, the most vital and important was of course the camp regime itself.   Away from home, in an interesting and stimulating environment, the challenge of group activity was in itself enough in many instances to bring about normal behavior.   There were other treatment techniques available. To some extent tent placement was a useful tool, and a boy who found it impossible to adjust in a socially sophisticated tent-group might fit satisfactorily in a quieter, younger, or more immature group.   One very dull lad, sent by an agency, was very unhappy in a group of seasoned campers and had twice packed his things to go home within the first three days.   He was transferred to the tent of boys from foster homes, a somewhat less intelligent group and socially less mature, and here he adjusted with some comfort for the remainder of his stay.

The flexible use of the activity program was another major aid in treatment.   One of the most difficult boys in camp was a bright lad of eleven, an only child in a home where inconsistent severity on the part of the father and inconsistent indulgence by the mother had started the boy on definitely delinquent paths.   At camp it seemed almost impossible to cope with his revengeful stealing, his defiance of camp regulations, and his uncontrolled behavior, until the counselor, seizing upon a modest interest in nature study, urged the boy to start and organize a nature club, with a special hut of its own.   From this point on progress, though slow, was gratifying.   Here, as in the school room, the satisfying task is one of the major tools of therapy.

Group pressure as a treatment technique was largely used to fortify tendencies toward independent behavior.   Thus the infantile boy is urged to look after his own belongings and manage his own affairs, because everyone else in camp is doing so. Thus used to set up goals and ideals of behavior, group pressure was very effective. It was never used in dealing with problems of stealing, enuresis, or other definite aberrations from normal conduct. It is all too easy to use group opinion in such instances as a means of crushing rather than of helping the individual.

An example of group pressure used in a more direct fashion to enforce more socialized and less egocentric behavior is given in the following excerpt from the records of Camp Wawokiye. Jim was a fourteen-year-old boy of low average ability, some of whose problems are amply evident from the counselor's report of this incident.

> Jim and George had made life miserable for Walt and Bill, the two enuresis problems in the tent, until finally at a strenuous tent meeting it was decided that any member of the tent who referred to the enuresis in public would lose his next dessert. Jim agreed to this in pretty fair spirit. Later in a tiff with Walt he called him several names which revealed Walt's weakness. Though Jim was warned that it would mean the loss of his dessert, he persisted. The next meal was lunch, and when dessert time came, Jim waited until the bowl was nearly empty, and then grabbed it away from the boy who was serving. I warned him that if he ate that dessert he would lose the evening dessert, ice-cream. Fully confident that he could "get away with it" at night as well as at noon, he ate the noon dessert. After lunch I had a talk with him about the whole situation. He admitted that he had broken the group rule, but simply dared me to try and make him take his punishment. It was rather pathetic, the sublime confidence he had that he would be able to do here as he had done all his life, get around consequences. At night I told the group that no one would get their dessert until Jim had left the table. This brought a very strong group pressure against him, for no one really sympathized with him, and they all wanted their ice-cream. Jim became very violent. I told him we would wait all night if necessary, but that as long as he was going to try and grab his portion, no one would get any. At last the combination of group pressure and counselor pressure got too strong, and he said that he would not try to take any. So he sat and watched

the group eat, boiling more and more furiously inside. As soon as all were dismissed, he tried to take out his spleen on Bill and Walt, simply because he had to beat up someone. After a few minutes he began chasing Bill with a club, and I caught and held him. He was in a perfect rage, foaming at the mouth, and out-doing himself in swearing. Mr. S. and I held him for some time, cheering him up and cooling him off with a running fire of humor-ous talk. When he became more tractable Mr. S. took him off and had a long talk with him about his temper, and the trouble it might get him into. Jim grudgingly admitted after a long time that he had made a fool of himself. He even came back and joined the ball game in a fairly good humor.

Personal counseling of the boys is also a means which is very readily adapted to the informal and intimate associations of camp life. Again we postpone the discussion of particular techniques to the chapter on treatment interviews.

Camp Experience and the Home. In any short-time environ-mental treatment such as camp, the final effectiveness is meas-ured not by the genuine miracles which it is possible to achieve in a new setting, but by the extent to which improved behavior carries over into the old setting. In an attempt to increase this transfer, camps have experimented with reports to parents. Ward [18] tells of a camp report which is similar to the older forms of school report cards and in which the child is rated from Excellent to Very Poor in various camp activities and attitudes. He tells of some of the good and bad results of such a system. Parents occasionally complained in regard to the reports, and in at least one instance the author concludes that a boy who had been helped by camp was definitely hurt and harmed by the report to the parents. Its greatest draw-back is that it does not rate the child in accordance with his own effort and potentialities, but in comparison with the group average. At Camp Cory, descriptive reports were sent to the parents, commenting on the boys' adjustment and often making suggestions as to ways in which the home could carry forward the camp experience.

[18] Ward, C. E. *Organized Camping and Progressive Education*, pp. 92 ff. Nashville, Tenn.: Cullom and Ghertner, 1936.

A sample of the report sent to the parents is given below. In this case Fred was an eleven-year-old boy who was becoming a seriously disrupting influence in the schoolroom, largely because of extreme attention-getting behavior. The parents' attitudes toward the boy had probably done much to create the problem, though with limited information in regard to the home it is difficult to be certain. The Visiting Teacher had encouraged camp placement for the boy. In Fred's case the camp environment itself was enough to solve most of his problems, and the added advantage of a close personal relationship with an understanding counselor made his reactions almost completely normal. The parents were intelligent, and it was felt that the final hint in the report in regard to his need for affection would be understood, and might be helpful, yet would probably not create resentment or antagonism.

REPORT TO PARENTS
FRED LAWRENCE

Participation in Camp Program.

Fred's outstanding activity was swimming. He was extremely persistent in improving himself along this line. His counselor remarks, "While passing swimming tests he has shown an unusual blind sort of courage. Once he went down three times while attempting to pass a test before he would allow me to hold his head above water." He was very proud of his diving.

He entered into many of the other activities and games as well. Also thoroughly enjoyed "fooling around" with other boys, wrestling, etc. A couple of times he showed a real interest in the beauties of nature, which is unusual in a boy of his age.

Behavior Observation.

During his first four weeks Fred was ideally situated in camp. He took a strong liking to his counselor and the boys accepted him at once. There was some eccentric and show-off behavior at first, but the boys accepted it as real humor, and liked Fred very much. He was extremely anxious to be popular and his attempts to give gifts to friends or possible friends, was interesting. It probably represents a past method of action, because he had no need of purchasing friendships at camp. He was also very anxious to be of help and service. This too was probably a means of gaining friends, but a much more wholesome means.

Fred showed himself to be somewhat childish in his inability to take responsibility. He always was careless about his belongings and often needed help with things which other boys took care of themselves. He was slow, and often one lap behind in camp routine. It was noticed that very often in the middle of an activity Fred might stop for a few moments to rest. Whether this was a part of his general slowness or a real fatigue, is hard to tell.

During the second four weeks of his stay Fred was in another tent and again showed himself able to measure up to the requirements of group life. However, during his stay in this tent he was a bit more inclined to show-off. This may have been because the personal attachment to the counselor was less strong.

Further Comment.

It was felt by the staff that Fred was one of the most lovable boys in Junior Camp. It seemed that he made more progress and development than most of the boys. Our feeling is that when Fred is sure that he is liked he is at his best. When he has any doubt of this, extravagant behavior develops.

Not only was such a report sent to the parents, but a copy or sometimes a more extensive report was made to the interested agency. In this way it was frequently possible for the school, the agency, and the parents, to capitalize on interests which the boy had shown in camp, and to encourage these same or similar projects. Also it gave case workers added material to discuss with parents in order to improve their insight and understanding.

Results of Camp Treatment. If used in a thorough-going fashion, with placement thoughtfully made so that the child has a chance of fitting into the camp, with a camp chosen because of its treatment possibilities, and with measures adopted for carrying over into the home setting the advances made in camp, results are certain to be striking. There is as yet no real study of the outcomes, merely citations of individual cases which have been helped. Yet it is probably significant that psychiatrists and psychologists who have used camp as a part of a total treatment program are unanimous in their statements that it has been highly effective in most cases. There seems no question but that if intelligently utilized it is a valuable resource to the therapist.

THE REARRANGEMENT OF COMPANIONSHIPS

There is one other type of social treatment which often is used with a view to altering behavior. This is the effort, frequently made, to have the child break off certain companionships which have an undesirable effect and substitute new friendships presumably more constructive in their influence. A fourteen-year-old girl is going with three other girls, somewhat older, probably sexually delinquent, much more sophisticated than she. Efforts are made to break up this grouping. Two boys, 15 and 16, both have rather upsetting and abnormal home situations, and present problems at school. Yet neither boy seems to become involved in delinquency except in the company of the other, and each seems to exercise a very bad influence on the other. Together they truant and steal, and go for joy rides in automobiles. Separate, their problems are much less serious. Consequently efforts are made to break up the association. Such suggestions crop up rather frequently in records of treatment, perhaps most frequently in the field of delinquency.

Such methods of treatment are of necessity so individual and so related to a particular situation, that it is only possible to make a few general comments in regard to them. In the first place it may be stated rather dogmatically that efforts to change a child's companions merely by prohibitions are almost certain of failure, whether those prohibitions are laid down by the parent, the social worker, or even by the judge or probation officer. We must recognize that if the child is associating with a friend or a group of friends, and this association is sufficiently close to have a harmful effect on the child's behavior, it is quite evident that these friendships are in some way satisfying to the child. The boy or girl may be looking up to their more sophisticated or delinquent companions because they admire certain qualities lacking in themselves. The child may associate with less well-trained, less cultured friends, because he is seeking to find his own mental level. He may be finding compensatory satisfactions in being a hanger-on in a "tough" group and thus acquiring a reputation and status himself. Whatever the motives, these should be determined so far as possible and substitute friendships encouraged which will have similar, but constructive, values. Often, of course, some organized group may provide the satisfactions which have heretofore been obtained through undesirable friendships.

INDIRECT VERSUS DIRECT TREATMENT

With this discussion we bring to a close the consideration of the many ways in which behavior may be altered by manipulating the environment of the child. The changing of parental attitudes, the manipulation of the school and social environment, the use, in serious situations, of a completely new and therapeutic environment outside of the home, have all been suggested as means of attacking the causes of problem behavior. There has been, in some quarters, a tendency to look down upon such methods of treatment as being in some way inferior to direct methods of psychotherapy, which deal with the child himself. This viewpoint is both unrealistic and unfortunate. We shall not be inclined to look down upon treatment involving the manipulation of the environment, if we recall the fundamental axiom upon which it is based, namely, that most children, if given a reasonably normal environment which meets their own emotional, intellectual, and social needs, have within themselves sufficient drive toward health to respond and make a comfortable adjustment to life. Manipulative and environmental therapy makes use of many commonplace experiences and influences to alter behavior, but its wise use involves skill and judgment quite equal to that of the psychotherapist, operating in a more restricted but more intensive field. A clinician is scarcely competent to deal with children's behavior problems unless he has some mastery of the wide resources of indirect therapy, as well as of the more specialized resources of direct treatment which we shall consider in the following section.

BIBLIOGRAPHY

General References Regarding Group Treatment

Beard, Belle. *Juvenile Probation*, chaps. 5, 6. New York: American Book Company, 1934. 219 pp.

Busch, Henry M. *Leadership in Group Work*, chaps. 7, 9. New York: Association Press, 1934. 305 pp.

Partridge, Ernest De A. *Leadership Among Adolescent Boys.* New York: Bureau of Publications, Teachers College, Columbia, 1934. 109 pp.

Preventing Crime — A Symposium, ed. by Sheldon and Eleanor Glueck, part VI, "Boys Clubs and Recreation Programs." New York: McGraw-Hill Book Company, 1936. 509 pp.

Slavson, S. R. *Creative Group Education.* New York: Association Press, 1937. 254 p.

References Dealing Especially with Camp Treatment (Applicable also to Other Groups)

Amsden, Robert L. "The Summer Camp as a Behavior Clinic," *Mental Hygiene*, vol. 20 (April, 1936), pp. 262–268.

Chassell, Joseph O. "Indications for Camp Prescription," *American Journal of Orthopsychiatry*, vol. 7 (January, 1937), pp. 82–95.

Dimock, H. E., and Hendry, C. E. *Camping and Character*, chaps. 8, 9. New York: Association Press, 1929. 364 pp.

Institute on Character Education in the Summer Camp. Reports for 1935, 1936. New York: Association Press.

Lieberman, Joshua. *Creative Camping*, chaps. 18–20. New York: Association Press, 1931. 251 pp.

Osborne, E. G. *Camping and Guidance.* New York: Association Press, 1937. 192 pp.

Rademacher, E. S. "Treatment of Problem Children by Means of a Long Time Camp," *Mental Hygiene*, vol. 12 (April, 1928), pp. 385–394.

Wagner, I. A. "Summer Camp for Delinquent Boys at Greenwood Lake, Delaware, Ohio," in *Preventing Crime*, ed. by Sheldon and Eleanor Glueck, pp. 331–353. New York: McGraw-Hill Book Company, 1936.

Ward, C. E. *Organized Camping and Progressive Education.* Nashville, Tenn.: Cullom and Ghertner, 1936. 180 pp.

PART IV

Dealing with the Individual

Treatment Interview Techniques: Education, Persuasion, Release

THUS far our discussion of treatment methods has included the many ways of modifying or removing the causes of the child's problems through manipulation of the environment. We come now to a discussion of all those means whereby behavior may be altered through a face-to-face contact. Our interest will be largely directed toward the processes involved in the treatment interview, though certain other allied techniques will also be considered. Attempting to change attitudes and behavior through a personal contact is one of the oldest, but one of the least investigated, means of treatment. In this realm where so much depends on the personal interactions and responses of worker and child we find more the skills of an art than the technique of a science. Nevertheless there is reason to hope that even these subtle relationships may be helpfully studied by scientific means and more accurately known and guided. As a preliminary to such a study we shall endeavor to describe and classify some of the methods used with children.

Because so little is known with certainty about psychotherapeutic methods and results, there is a strong temptation to build elaborate hypotheses with little factual foundation. We could easily become lost in the maze of theories about psychotherapy which are developed by various schools of thought. We shall endeavor, however, to confine our discussion to the methods used, rather than to the theories propounded, by clinical workers. Even this goal is not easy of attainment, since case records almost invariably contain meager accounts of psychotherapeutic processes. The information on which diagnosis is based is recorded in full, and even the more specific and concrete steps in treatment are described, but the account of the treatment interview all too often omits the part which the worker played and records only the child's responses. A verbatim record of intensive psychotherapy with one child, giving in full all the conversation of both child and therapist, would be a new and valuable contribution to our thinking. Even that would fail to record the inflections and facial expressions which are no doubt a significant element. Although one clinic is considering the installation of a dictograph, and another is experimenting with one way screens in the interviewer's office, there is still no significant investigation of this sort in progress. We shall therefore be handicapped by lack of thoroughly accurate data.

THE QUALIFICATIONS OF THE THERAPIST

In evaluating the results of other treatment methods it has been pointed out that the personal qualifications of the worker are a factor in determining the outcome. The success of foster-home placement and of therapeutic procedures in the school and club can be shown to depend to some extent upon the training and the attitudes of the worker, teacher, or counselor involved. This is much more true in the interviewing process where, in many instances of deeper therapy, it is the personal relationship itself which is of outstanding importance. There are some who maintain that the success and quality of all direct therapy depends entirely on the emotional relationship between therapist and child. Though this statement may be extreme, we will do well to focus our attention first on the qualifications of the therapist, as a factor of fundamental importance in this type of treatment.

It is unfortunate that in studies such as those made by the Gluecks, where it was demonstrated that one probation officer was often much more successful than another though working with comparable boys, no scientific study was made of the personality differences which might account for this variation.   Such studies, when they are made, will make possible a clearer definition of the personality traits which promote therapy.   We shall then be in a position to know why some individuals, in their relationships to problem children, are more helpful and more able to induce independent growth in the child.   Until that time, it is necessary to fall back on the judgments expressed by clinicians.   While descriptive terms are vague, there would seem to be considerable agreement among these judgments.

Objectivity.   It is generally conceded that to be helpful as a therapist the clinical worker needs to have an objective attitude.   This has been variously described as "controlled identification," as "constructive composure," and as "an emotionally detached attitude."   The term as used in clinical practice is defined somewhat differently than in the strictly scientific field.   There is included in the concept a capacity for sympathy which will not be overdone, a genuinely receptive and interested attitude, a deep understanding which will find it impossible to pass moral judgments or be shocked and horrified.   A person with this attitude differs on the one hand from the cold and impersonal detachment of the individual with Jovian tendencies, and differs quite as sharply from the deeply sympathetic and sentimental individual who becomes so wrapped up in the child's problems as to be quite incapable of helping.   It is, to come back to the first description of it, a degree of sympathetic "identification" with the child sufficient to bring about an understanding of the feelings and problems which are disturbing the youngster, but an identification which is "controlled," because understood, by the therapist. It is a quality which is perhaps more easily defined in negative than positive terms.   The individual who takes the child's problems unto himself, until his sympathies and hopes and fears are bound up with the child's behavior and attitudes, is not objective.   Frequently this is evident in the inability of such a person to face facts about the child, or in a tendency either to be defensive or hypercritical of the child. It is rare for parents to achieve any large degree of objectivity in regard to their children. It is probable that, in so-called "deep" therapy, the therapist loses some of his objectivity as the emotional relationship deepens. Certainly instances of this could easily be cited from clinical experience. It may be that less complete objectivity is required for intensive psychotherapy over a long period. However that may be, a fundamental degree of this quality is essential for the child to be able to unburden himself without fear; fear on the one hand of being rejected and condemned, fear on the other hand of finding only sympathy, without the strength which comes from a detached view.

Respect for the Individual. A second qualification of the effective therapist is a deep-seated respect for the child's integrity. If the child is to gain real help to grow in his own way toward goals of his own choice, the therapist must create a relationship where such growth can take place. The worker who is filled with a reforming zeal, or who is unconsciously eager to make the child over into his own image, cannot do this. There must be a willingness to accept the child as he is, on his own level of adjustment, and to give him some freedom to work out his own solutions to his problems.

We should be forced to admit that there is not as great a degree of agreement upon this qualification as upon the first. Some clinicians, if judged by their actual methods, definitely select the goal to be reached and influence the child in that direction. Still others would maintain that the child must be completely free, in the therapeutic relationship, to make any choices and decisions, even though his choice should be clearly anti-social rather than social in its direction. Perhaps a compromise viewpoint is possible if we are aware that frequently in environmental therapy the worker does select the treatment goal and arranges circumstances so as to develop the child in that direction. In psychotherapy the aim is to leave the major responsibilities in the hands of the child as an individual growing toward independence.   The more this is and can be done, the more lasting and effective the treatment. It cannot be accomplished at all unless the therapist has the capacity to see the child as a separate individual, who has both a right and obligation to maintain his separateness.

An Understanding of the Self.   Another essential element in the personality make-up of the therapist is a sound understanding of himself, of his outstanding emotional patterns, and of his own limitations and shortcomings.   Unless there is this considerable degree of insight, he will not be able to recognize the situations in which he is likely to be warped and biased by his own prejudices and emotions.   He will not be able to understand why there are certain types of children or types of problems, which he is unable to treat satisfactorily.   Thoroughly to understand and be objective in regard to the child's problems the therapist must have some insight into his own personality.

It has been said, and used to be said with great vehemence, that such insight was possible only through psychoanalysis and hence that every therapist should be psychoanalyzed. This opinion, for various reasons, seems to be growing less prominent.   In the first place, it is not borne out by common observation.   Of the individuals in this country who might be considered as outstanding in the results of their therapeutic effort with children, it is probable that less than half have been psychoanalyzed.   In view of this somewhat doubtful value of analysis, its prohibitive cost becomes a barrier to most clinical workers.   Finally there is good reason to suspect that a well-adjusted, emotionally mature individual with some knowledge of psychological mechanisms has as helpful a degree of self-insight as the more maladjusted individual who has been psychoanalyzed.   Certainly the individual whose own life is reasonably well adjusted, and whose own emotional needs are in large measure satisfied, is capable of becoming a helpful counselor.   Perhaps the outstanding quality of some of the lay and professional people who, without much expert knowledge, have acquired reputations as trusted advisers is the fact that they are "comfortable" people, with an acceptance of themselves and an adjustment to others which gives them freedom to be objective and helpful in regard to those in trouble. Thus while there is agreement as to the necessity of self-insight there is still dispute as to whether there is more than one way of obtaining it.

Psychological Knowledge. Finally, the therapist can scarcely expect to do satisfactory work without a thorough basis of knowledge of human behavior and of its physical, social, and psychological determinants. It might seem more logical to put this qualification first, but the experience of every clinic would bear out the viewpoint that a full knowledge of psychiatric and psychological information, with a brilliant intellect capable of applying this knowledge, is of itself no guarantee of therapeutic skill. The essential qualifications of the psychotherapist lie primarily, as we have pointed out, in the realm of attitudes, emotions, and insight, rather than in the realm of intellectual equipment.

THE BASIS OF RESULTS

It is especially important in the field of psychotherapy that the clinician have clearly in mind the basis of any results. Psychotherapy does not in some mysterious way add to the individual, nor does it change his capacities or abilities. It brings about changes in the child in two ways. It is in the truest sense a process of release, a process of freeing the individual from obstacles, conflicts, and emotional blockings which inhibit normal development toward maturity. The reliance of the therapist is not entirely upon his own skill, but in the drive of the individual toward a comfortable social adjustment. Every child or adolescent wants to achieve, wants to be loved, wants to be grown up. It is the work of psychotherapy to release these normal desires and allow them to function. A part of any improvement comes about as a result of freeing these elemental urges toward growth and adjustment.

In addition to such a releasing process, psychotherapy brings results because learning takes place. The processes of education and re-education are present in large measure in every type of psychotherapy. Indeed a consideration of the positive and rebuilding aspects of the different psychotherapeutic approaches is essentially a consideration of different ways of encouraging the learning of new insight and new ways of adjustment. An understanding of these basic mechanisms is necessary if we are to approach the discussion of direct treatment in a realistic and critical fashion.

CHILDREN WHO ARE SUITABLE FOR INTERVIEW THERAPY

We cannot, in any more than the most general fashion, delimit the group for whom psychotherapy is a feasible or possible technique. Certainly it is not for all problem children, although some of the earlier child-guidance clinics made a pretext of carrying out such a policy. Ordinarily it is not for children of pre-school age, though modifications of the interview technique are being used experimentally, as we shall point out, with very young children. Neither is it for the dullest children, those of borderline mentality or below. It is of interest that of the fifty-five "bad boys" described by Dr. Hartwell as for the most part subjects of psychotherapy, two-thirds are specifically described as being average or above in mentality. In general it has been felt that below the average range children do not respond particularly well to psychotherapy. In our own clinic, however, a study revealed that, of the children for whom some type of treatment interviewing was planned, a considerable proportion was in the dull normal group.

It is usually to be observed that treatment through planned interviews is most likely to be used with the adolescent. Manipulation of the environment is no longer so easy in this age range and changes, if there are to be any, must be within the child.   It might also be added that psychotherapy is especially useful to the child who fundamentally desires help. The definition of this attitude is not easy, but it may be suggested by pointing out that the child with real mental conflict or the child with anxieties and guilt feelings is usually open to such a technique, where the overindulged, thoroughly egocentric child is difficult to reach by such means because he is apt to be much more satisfied with his present adjustment.

The proportion of problem children customarily dealt with by direct treatment procedures would vary greatly from one clinic to another depending on a variety of factors.   In our own clinic such treatment is planned in 21 per cent of the cases, but actually carried out in less than this proportion, according to a study of 292 cases.   On the other hand, Dr. Healy reports for the group of 143 delinquents handled by three clinics under his supervision that 31 per cent received intensive psychotherapy (10 interviews or more), 49 per cent received some, and only 20 per cent received no psychotherapeutic help.[1]   Some of the discrepancy between these clinical groups would be explained by the fact that our clinic deals with all age levels, while Dr. Healy's group was primarily adolescent; our clinic is a community service clinic, Dr. Healy's study was an experimental one, in which cases were treated as intensively as possible, to see what might be the maximum of favorable results.   Obviously in any clinic the proportions will be determined by factors such as these.

The Setting of the Treatment Interview.   We shall not here go into an extended discussion of the means of developing a contact or of establishing some basis of rapport with the child. This has been discussed in various books dealing with diagnosis and need not be repeated here.   Nor will we discuss the diagnostic and exploratory function of the interview for similar reasons.   It is the therapeutic aspect of interviewing which concerns us, and, recognizing that treatment may be

[1] Healy, William, and Bronner, A. F.   *New Light on Delinquency and Its Treatment,* p. 154.   New Haven: Yale University Press, 1936.

mingled with diagnosis even in the first interview, there is reason for considering the therapeutic functions separately.

There is first of all the question of whether treatment contacts should be formal or casual, that is, planned for a definite time and place, or undetermined, casual, and spontaneous. Clinical experience seems to be increasingly unanimous that if help is to be obtained the contacts should be on a planned basis. Even the counselor in the school or institution where casual contacts are easy and frequent is not likely to get very far below the surface without arranged contacts. One reason for this is that the spontaneous and casual contact does not make for an explicit acknowledgment of the fact that the child wants help and is coming for help. This acknowledgment is valuable in making the child feel that he may unburden himself freely.

The actual physical setting of the interview is less important. There should be privacy, freedom from distraction, and adequate physical comfort. Whether or not toys, play material, and children's books will be in evidence depends somewhat on the therapist and the philosophy of treatment which he holds. Certainly some material of this sort is generally advisable. Of more importance is the setting which is provided by the attitude of the counselor, previously described. It is well in initiating the contact for the counselor or therapist clearly to imagine and feel the probable reactions of the child. To the child this is a new type of experience, hence one about which he is both curious and afraid. It is quite probable that he has been threatened with being "sent to a doctor," or "sent to the school advisor" by parents, teachers, or others. It is highly probable that he has found adults more ready to criticize and pass judgment than to be understanding and non-critical. Hence the therapist will do well to allow the relationship to develop somewhat slowly, and to recognize frankly and verbally the child's skeptical reactions to the situation.

EDUCATIVE TECHNIQUES

We come then to a discussion of the ways in which the interviewer, whether he be psychiatrist, psychologist, social worker, or counselor, can make his contacts effective in changing attitudes and freeing the child for normal growth. Because of the pre-scientific character of this field of effort, we find various ways of classifying and categorizing the methods utilized. Nearly all who have endeavored to analyze the processes, however, agree that informational or educative procedures are important. In general these terms include those treatment processes in which a change of the child's intellectual content, either in the reception of new ideas or in the reorganization of old ones, is expected to bring about a change in emotional attitudes and behavior. An acquaintance with case records, participation in case conferences, or direct experience in treatment relationships will indicate that this simplest type of psychotherapy plays a very considerable rôle. We find it used in a variety of ways and shall attempt to illustrate some of these approaches.

Informational Methods. A boy of low average ability has, through a combination of unfortunate environmental pressures, become imbued with the notion of becoming a lawyer. His mental ability does not warrant such a choice, and the tensions and strivings set up by this false goal are producing in him some tendency to daydream of himself as superior and successful. In dealing with this situation the clinical worker does not attempt to persuade, but gives the boy full information about legal training, information which he has lacked. The number of years of formal education ahead, the type of study required, the approximate cost, the period of legal apprenticeship following law school are all described, as fairly and impartially as possible. Likewise training for other occupations is discussed, including some of the simpler mechanical trades for which the boy is fitted. The boy is interested, asks further questions, being obviously much impressed by the long period of training required for the legal profession. He expresses his second choice of vocation as being that of an auto mechanic. A few weeks later it is learned that he has decided he no longer wishes to be a lawyer, but would rather finish his training in a high-school trade course and become a mechanic.

It is by such a process that children and adults frequently change their course of action. Supplied with adequate factual information for making a choice, the decision is left in their own hands. It goes without saying that the result makes much more for growth and development than in those instances where the child is persuaded or argued out of an unfortunate course of action.

The clinician's best function, in many instances, particularly when dealing with the older child, is to serve in this purely informational fashion, giving the child the pertinent data out of which he can construct his own goals, which then serve to influence his reactions. The data may be of any sort. Frequently, as in the illustration cited, it may be information in regard to vocations, or school curricula. It may have to do with health, giving the child accurate information about his own physical condition so that he may decide the degree to which he will co-operate in a medical program. Such a course is more effective in the long run than an attempt to persuade a child to wear glasses, follow a diet, or accept medication.

The information may have to do with the child's mental ability.

> Harold is a stocky, attractive boy of 11, functioning at a mediocre level in the sixth grade. His father is serving a jail sentence for public intoxication. The psychological examination shows the boy to have an I.Q. of 160, with most exceptional all-round ability. The clinician, in talking with him, gives him practical but accurate information as to his mental ability. Harold is told that if 100 or 1000 boys of this age were tested, he would rate in the top 2 per cent. (Actually this is an understatement.) Some information is given as to the need of minimum intellectual capacity for college achievement, and the fact that his rating is decidedly above this minimum. He is also told of various scholar-

ships which are available for assisting boys with limited financial backing to go through college, providing their school record is outstanding. He responds decidedly to this information, and makes much more satisfactory effort in his school work.

Informational Methods and Children's Goals. The examples cited illustrate one of the major aims of this simple fact-giving type of therapy, namely, to be effective in changing some of the individual's motivating goal ideas. The child's goals are determined to some extent by his emotional needs, yet they are to some extent influenced by the information available to him. Often crucial information, given to the child by the therapist, may enable him to select a new goal, with similar emotional satisfactions, but more constructive in its direction. Dr. Sadler calls this education as to goals a "positive image-making," which helps the individual to visualize himself in a new light, carrying on new activities not characteristic of his present self. He would go further than the process suggested here and encourage his patients (mostly adults) to daydream of themselves as being victorious and successful in their new rôles.

Informational Methods and Mental Conflict. Factual education may also serve quite another purpose, namely, to assist the child to assimilate mental conflicts which have been disturbing him. Such treatment was used in the case of Philip, referred to our clinic by Children's Court.

Philip was an overgrown Polish boy of 14 when he came to the clinic on a serious delinquency charge. He had broken into the house of his next door neighbor in the middle of the night, had made his way to the room of the 18-year-old daughter, and had attempted to strike her over the head with a crude lead pipe blackjack. Fortunately the blackjack struck the head of the bed, the girl awoke and screamed, and Philip was captured. The situation as it revealed itself was plainly an acute personality problem. Philip was an inarticulate, shy boy of better than average mentality. He was much the youngest of four children and associated little with his older siblings. His father was dead, and his relationship with his mother was one of obedience rather than trust and confidence. He was not at all social, but did have two good friends, both of them very respectable boys. He was gifted along mechanical lines. Everyone knew him as a very quiet, very colorless, well-behaved boy. He had literally no sex information, and no sources of such information. As he became adolescent, he mulled over his perplexities about sex. The girl next door, whose bedroom window was visible from his own, became the object of his daydreams, and time after time he concocted imaginary means of disrobing her in order to answer his fundamental questions regarding female anatomy. Finally he acted out one of these daydreams.

In treatment of Philip the whole aim was educational. Throughout a number of contacts with the boy very complete sex education was given, in as matter-of-fact a manner as possible. Male and female anatomy, intercourse, reproduction, the birth process, masturbation, boy and girl relationships were discussed with more than usual thoroughness. Because he was so inarticulate himself, this was a somewhat one-sided process. Later after a period of a few months, these topics were brought up again to make sure he had assimilated the information. This was practically the only type of treatment used, with the exception of some reassurance to the mother that her boy was not abnormal. It was not felt safe to interpret to the mother the full significance of her boy's actions, since she was herself too repressed.[2]

There can be no question but that ignorance of normal sexual facts was a determining factor in creating the conflict in this boy's mind which eventually led to delinquent behavior. No deeper type of approach, but a simple mode of personalized education was used to attack the cause of that problem. It was hoped that adequate information would sufficiently reduce the conflict and tension and confusion which led to his phantasy life and in turn to his attack on the girl. Because Philip found it difficult to verbalize his conflicts, this treatment was used without too precise a knowledge of the content of his phantasies or his perplexities, save that they were sexual. It may well be that there were aspects of his problem which we did not know and which remained untreated. Three years

[2] This case is also quoted in the article by the author in "The Clinical Psychologist's Approach to Personality Problems," *The Family*, vol. 18 (November, 1937), p. 238.

have elapsed, however, and there has been reasonably satisfactory personal adjustment without further delinquent behavior.

The question may well be raised whether in such instances it is the factual information which has been of help or the personal relationship to the therapist. Could the same results have been obtained, for example, by supplying the boy with written material containing the sex information which he needed? At the present time this must remain an unanswered question. In the writer's judgment the essential part played by the personal contact is that the child develops enough confidence in the person of the therapist to accept the information. The therapist must have sufficient status in the eyes of the child, and must have developed a sufficient state of rapport so that the facts are considered to be reliable and worthy of acceptance. It may also be said that the child learns from the therapist certain attitudes toward sex, as well as facts about sex. However, these attitudes might also be learned from a printed page, so that they do not depend entirely on a direct personal relationship. It is evident that at the present time the influence of the therapist in this type of treatment is a matter for speculation rather than a topic upon which we have exact knowledge.

Conflicts which may be dealt with in this fashion probably lie more frequently in the sexual realm than in any other, because it is in this area that our taboos make it most likely that information will be lacking. Conflicts arising over fear of the consequences of masturbation may often be solved by giving adequate information as to the harmlessness of the act as usually practiced. Here the function of the therapist is clearer since it is important that he have sufficient status and rapport to allow the child to accept the information given, even though it conflicts with previous information from other sources. An example may be cited from the psychiatrist's interview with a 15-year-old boy in our clinic. Although living in an orphanage, he was influenced to a considerable degree by his unstable mother, who visited him frequently and had helped to increase his concern over masturbation, one of his many problems. The psychiatrist had assured him that masturbation would not give him a disease or make him go crazy. The following excerpt is taken from one of the treatment interviews.

> About his sex habits he says that his mother has frequently talked to him about them. She has asked him questions about it and warned him and threatened him as to what would happen if he did such things. He says that she has such funny ideas. He was told that perhaps women do not understand boys' problems of that kind as well as men and he says that it was easy for him to talk with the interviewer.

Here the psychiatrist definitely gives himself more status than the mother in regard to this particular question. Such a procedure could only be wisely used where it was advisable to reduce the parent's hold over the child.

Occasionally conflicts in other areas may be handled in this same informational fashion. The adolescent who is full of a confused fear about going insane because of insanity in the family is an example. Accurate and reliable information may assist the child to assimilate and reduce his conflict. If the psychoses in the family were of organic origin, then it may be possible completely to reassure the child. If there is a background including functional psychoses, facts in regard to the likelihood of inheritance help to reduce the fear to a definite chance, which can be faced, such as the chance of injury when crossing the street, so that it is no longer a vague, ill-defined, and absorbing fear.

Clarification of Issues. Another type of educational therapy involves not the giving of new information but the explanation and clarification of conflicting demands which the child is facing. Here the interviewer's purpose is not to persuade the child or weight the factors toward a certain conclusion, but to help bring some organization out of the confusion which exists, so that the child is more able to make a valid decision. The instances where such clarification has been of help usually involve a perplexing issue which the child is unable to face realistically because of strong emotional components. An adolescent girl, unhappy in her foster home, fearful of making new contacts, and with no relatives but a stepmother whom she dislikes, is upset by the friction with her foster mother and vacillates in her desire to leave the home. Helping her to think through clearly the possible choices ahead of her, the possibility of transferring to a new foster home or to a wage home, or of remaining in the present situation, and helping her to see the positive and negative implications of each choice, will bring about sufficient clarification so that she can more comfortably make a fairly clear-cut decision. She decides to remain in the foster home and make new efforts to reach an adjustment there. Not infrequently the young unmarried mother must similarly be helped to think through in clear-cut fashion all the issues involved in the decision to keep her baby, to give it for adoption, or to make some other plan. Such a process is truly therapeutic in the fullest sense, if the worker refrains entirely from imposing any decision, but leaves that fully up to the child.

Occasionally a modification of this approach which can only be described as a process of "going one better" is of help in the initial treatment of rebellious, delinquent children who do not outwardly want help, and who react to any restriction by defiance. A boy, for example, shows no particular regret over his stealing episodes and seems to have only negative goals of defying law or parental authority. He is expecting the clinician to do as others have done, either condemn him or persuade him to some ideal code of behavior. The clinician instead inquires about his stealing, which has included petty thefts from home and stores and the rifling of parked cars. Would he break into a house to steal things? Would he steal valuable things or only those of minor value? Would he hold up a person to steal? No, he would do none of these things. The clinician wants to know why not. For perhaps the first time the boy is in need of formulating his positive and more social goals, as opposed to those which he feels are unsocial and unacceptable to him. If the clinician genuinely accepts the possibly feeble verbalization of these goals, a basis is laid for rapport and for constructive treatment. The same sort of approach has been tried in our clinic with the sex-delinquent girl who is defensive and defiant in regard to her behavior. The clinician sets out to find the behavior she will not condone, the degree of delinquency or promiscuity which goes beyond her own social code. This is helpful to the child in formulating positive goals and allows the therapist to meet the girl on a genuine even though relatively low level of socialization.

Facing Consequences. In counseling with children, particularly those whose behavior difficulties have social implications, it is sometimes useful to acquaint the child with the consequences of his actions, consequences both to himself and to others. This is very different from the threats which have usually been made to the child as to the dire consequences of his behavior. It is definitely educational and objective, presented by the interviewer as simply another bit of data upon which the child may act. The child who has been involved in sex practices with other children should feel fully accepted by the clinician and should feel no attitude of blame or criticism. Yet in addition to therapy which strikes at the root of the problem, the child should also understand that the community is apt to be harsh in its treatment of sex offenders and that this is a part of the reality which he must face. Likewise with the delinquent child it is well to face frankly with him, as a friendly person, not a critic, the possible outcome of court action or the possible consequence of a repeated offense. Most frequently this type of treatment should be a part of a more general process of assisting the child to face his whole situation. Sometimes, in more critical instances, this objective painting of consequences may serve as a temporary deterrent to anti-social behavior, while deeper and more fundamental forces are being set in operation.

The Usefulness of the Educative Techniques. To what extent can the problem child be altered in his behavior by methods such as have been described of an educational and informational character? We have, to be sure, no evidence of their effectiveness, save that they are widely used by counselors, social workers, and clinicians. We can define only in the most tentative fashion the probable areas where they may prove effective.

It would seem that where ignorance of facts is a source of mental conflict or emotional tension such educational therapies may prove valuable no matter how deep-seated the problem may seem. A condition of the use of such treatment should be sufficient rapport between therapist and child to make it possible for the child to accept this selected and personalized data. In other types of behavior and personality problems these educative techniques would seem to be most usable when the problem itself is relatively superficial rather than deeply emotional. It may prove effective with a child who is puzzled and confused and misbehaving because he is in the wrong course in school, but it is of doubtful value in dealing with a long-standing pattern of tantrum behavior. It is more likely to be effective in dealing with a child whose general adjustment in various life areas is reasonably satisfying than with a child who is poorly adjusted in many ways.

The major mechanism of effectiveness of this sort of treatment would seem to be in the little understood realm of goals. Whether we term it a super-ego, or a collection of cultural traditions and controls, or a goal-idea, it would seem clear that behavior is to some extent modified by the individual's picture of himself as he would like to be. This picture may be modified by new information or it may be defined more clearly by the child so that it has more influence on his behavior. It is by accomplishing these modifications and clarifications that educational therapy usually becomes effective.

Its effectiveness in situations of mental conflict arising from ignorance seems to be due to a somewhat different mechanism. Here the conflict is a false one because based on ignorance and the new information dissolves one side of the emotional equation. The child has a strong desire to indulge in sex practices, but a strong fear of going insane. There is first of all some help to the child in expressing these repressed desires, and when the new information reveals the dilemma to be a false one he can face his situation realistically and is able to inhibit his behavior to some extent, without conflict, in conformity with his own ideal of himself.

THE USE OF PERSONAL INFLUENCE

Oftentimes, in the interview relationship, what starts out as an educative type of treatment ends by the injection of personal influence. The therapist does not merely talk to the child of possible vocational choices, but endeavors to influence him to choose a particular one. Similarly in deeper forms of therapy the worker may persuade the child to adopt a certain course of action, or may suggest concepts and beliefs to the child. Such methods may be illustrated by the following phrases, all common enough in treatment interviews.

"You are not going to wet the bed any more..."

"I want you to do this for me next week..."

"Let me tell you some of the reasons why you should attend school..."

The one element which these statements have in common, whether we define them as suggestion, persuasion, or in some other terms, is that they place the motive for change in the therapist rather than in the child. Treatment is not based on the child's wish or desire but on the therapist's influence. The situation is not that the child decides "I want to..." but that the therapist influences him by telling him, "I want you to do, or to believe, thus and so." In even the most objective relationship there is no doubt a subtle element of this sort. The therapist does not have to put his wishes into words for the child to realize them. Yet in a great many instances this use of personal influence is a conscious and definite attempt to remake the actions or attitudes of the child. It is, in fact, probably the commonest method used by lay advisors or counselors without professional training. What usefulness does it have as a therapeutic tool?

To Use or Not to Use?   Nowhere do we find more genuine
confusion, both in theory and in practice, than in this matter.
While all of the older treatises on psychotherapy lay great
stress on suggestion and persuasion, those topics play less
and less part in more recent discussions.   The conflict and
confusion which exist are well exemplified by these contra-
dictory quotations from Dr. William Sadler's recent book on
psychiatry, based on a long clinical experience.   Mentioning
the rather widespread use of suggestion as therapy he comments: "But suggestion is only of temporary value in dealing
with mental and nervous disorders; the real cure consists in
finding out the truth and facing it and then in re-educating
and retraining, putting desirable and wholesome methods of
viewing life and reacting to one's environment in the place of
undesirable and unreliable reactions."   At other points he
mentions the risks of suggestion and persuasion, the danger of
suppressing problems rather than solving them.   Yet in speaking of re-educating the individual, once a true analysis of the
condition is made, he upholds the use of such therapy in the
most vigorous terms.   He mentions that it may be necessary
to persuade the individual, "to employ argument after argument" to show him his mistakes.   "It is necessary literally to
hammer the new ideas into the mind during the earlier stages
of treatment."   A few pages further on he states the same
viewpoint in more moderate terms: "When the patient once
has confidence in his physician, we are able to make our greatest and most rapid strides in educational therapeutics by
means of discreet and sincere persuasion."   If we but turn
the page we find that the author drops back to his first opinion
in these words: "Persuasion then is a useful, even though superficial technique of psychotherapy.   It is in reality a form of
suggestion and is wholly unsuited to the cure of the more
complicated and long-standing neuroses." [3]   In spite of this
last statement one gains the impression that Dr. Sadler favors
the use of these strong personal influences during the re-

---

[3] These quotations are from Sadler, William S., *Theory and Practice of Psychiatry*
(St. Louis: C. B. Mosby, 1936), pp. 951, 982, 987, and 988 respectively.

educative period, once the causative factors are clearly recognized by the patient. His opposition to it seems to be directed toward the use of such methods as a total means of therapy, in which the causes are not analyzed.

Dr. Samuel Hartwell is perhaps the most direct exponent of such techniques in working with children. He has stressed the viewpoint that the deeper the rapport between therapist and child the more suggestible the child becomes. In these deeper states of rapport the therapist can develop and encourage desirable reaction patterns, and can attack undesirable patterns by means of direct suggestion and influence. Dr. Hartwell states that in superficial rapport the child is not particularly suggestible. "If he is told anything that he is to accept, he must at the same time be given what he considers valid reasons for accepting it. At this stage he has no special interest in the psychiatrist's personality, and what is said to him or done for him he considers in terms of himself." In the second degree of rapport "he is slightly more suggestible now and is willing to accept opinions and ideas when they are based on my viewpoint." In the deepest state of rapport "he is suggestible to the greatest possible degree. He considers things in the light of my emotional response to them rather than in the light of his own." A child in this state of attachment "wants his psychiatrist to be his best friend. He wishes to please him more than he wishes to do anything else. Out of loyalty to his friend he is perfectly willing to alter his emotional life as far as it is possible for him." [4]

While these quotations indicate the degree of reliance placed in personal influence by some experienced psychiatrists and psychologists, it should also be pointed out that changes wrought solely by persuasion or suggestion, or accomplished purely through the weight of personal influence, are very likely to be temporary. Such methods place emphasis upon the notion of remaking the individual rather than of releasing

[4] These quotations are from Hartwell, Samuel W., *Fifty-five Bad Boys* (New York: Alfred A. Knopf, 1931), pp. 14, 15, 19, and 21 respectively.

his own strengths. They rely upon decisions made for the child rather than upon the more basic process of decisions made by the child.

The Limitations of Personal Influence. The limitations of this type of therapy are shown most clearly in the attempts to treat personality and behavior disorders by means of hypnosis. A case from our own clinic is in point. A boy of eleven, of superior intelligence, and with a background of frequent home changes and rejections which rendered him most insecure, was a persistent enuretic. Various methods had been tried and failed. After he was placed in a foster home which seemed to meet some of his deeper emotional needs, it was decided to attack his symptomatic behavior directly by means of hypnosis. The treatment was carried on by Dr. Griffith Williams, now of Rutgers University, in collaboration with Mr. Gordon Riley, psychologist on the clinic staff. The boy was trained until he was able to go into a fairly deep trance and carry out post-hypnotic suggestions of a neutral sort. Then such suggestions were made as that he would ask the foster mother for a chamber to keep under his bed so that he could use it just before he retired. These suggestions were carried out post-hypnotically, but the enuresis continued in spite of more frequent use of toilet facilities brought about through suggestion. In later trances, as specific suggestions were made attacking the symptom more directly, such as suggesting that he would wake at intervals during the night, it became more difficult to gain the boy's co-operation, and finally it was impossible to induce a trance state at all. This represents a clear picture of the limitations of hypnotic suggestion, and the limitations of conscious suggestion and persuasion seem very similar. When suggestion or persuasion cuts definitely across the deeper emotional purposes and needs, it can hardly be effective. It is probable that the clinician who uses it effectively has a shrewd intuitive judgment as to when his influence can support a feeble but genuine desire within the child.

Such an explanation would also probably account for the type of episode reported by Dr. George Mohr.   In a first contact with an enuretic child he made some remark to the effect that he hoped the child could give him a good report of a dry bed the next time they met.   When the child returned for another appointment, he reported that there had been no enuresis in the interval.   Dr. Mohr became interested in this sudden disappearance of the difficulty and asked the child what he thought was the reason. "Don't you remember?" the child replied.   "You asked me to stop."

Its Usefulness.   Clinical experience would seem to indicate that the conscious desire of the therapist to influence the child can be helpful in certain situations, in spite of its risk and limitations.   In the first place it is sometimes useful as a definitely temporary measure, either to inhibit harmful reactions or stimulate desired reactions on the part of the child, in order that more basic therapy may take effect.   The author has occasionally persuaded children not to run away from home or foster home, confident that merely a delay of this behavior would allow more time for constructive effort.   (On the other hand, of course, there are times when sound therapy allows the child to run away and learn from the experience.) Dr. Hartwell in reporting a case to the American Orthopsychiatric Association told how he definitely used personal influence in the early period of treatment of a seriously maladjusted boy, in order to prevent him from committing suicide.   At a later time when the boy was showing healthy tendencies, but was afraid of joining group activities, Dr. Hartwell let him know that he liked sports and athletics and that he wished the boy to enter such activities.   "I want you to do it because you're my kid."   The only justification for this last powerful persuasion is that if it served to tide the boy over the initial difficulties of group adjustment, he would then find social contacts satisfying in themselves.   In such instances personal influence may be likened to a hypodermic given as a temporary measure, either to inhibit or stimulate behavior of a certain type until the more lasting therapeutic influences can take effect.

It is also possible, as both Dr. Sadler and Dr. Hartwell seem to imply, that, in cases of mental conflict, once the true issues are understood by the child and the problem is one of re-educating and reconditioning attitudes, suggestion and persuasion have their place in hastening the process.

Certainly anyone working with children should recognize the essential superficiality of this type of treatment. It is probably never wise or efficacious to use it as a sole method of treatment, though it may have its use as a supplementary technique. We cannot expect profound and lasting alterations of behavior or attitude to be based either on the therapist's assurance that "you are becoming better and better," or on the therapist's plea to change "because I would like you to."

EXPRESSIVE THERAPIES

Of quite a different character are the methods of treatment which rely almost entirely upon the expression of feelings by the child, with the therapist taking a minimum part in the process. Some of the most original experimentation in treatment methods has taken place in this field, and we shall consider several ways of dealing with children which look to the curative powers of expression.

Catharsis. The value to the individual of "talking himself out," of unburdening to a passive listener his problems and perplexities, anxieties and fears, has been amply dwelt upon in earlier treatises on psychotherapy. It is a question whether the desire for this sort of release of tension is more common in adults than in children. Certainly in clinical practice there are more adults than children who spontaneously wish for someone to whom they can talk freely. Children rather rarely pour out their feelings spontaneously, such a response coming only after rapport is well established. The difference may be due to selective factors. Parents primarily bring children to clinics because of disturbing behavior. Adults come of their own volition when they feel the need of help. In any event, the spontaneous need for an outlet for repressed feelings is not frequently met in working with children. It does occur, however, especially in older children. Such a boy was George, sensitive, somewhat neurotic, bitterly unhappy about his home situation. This 17-year-old lad made use of his first interview with the psychologist to pour out for two hours all his feelings of resentment toward his father and his conflicting sense of duty and filial loyalty. It was quite apparent that anyone who would listen sympathetically would have received the same flow of pent-up attitudes. Such a catharsis, even where the therapist is a listener only, has a constructive effect, since the child clarifies his feelings by verbalizing them, and gains a release from tension which makes it possible to face the real situation more constructively. There is no type of psychotherapy so safe or so consistently helpful in a small way.

Ventilation of Conflicts. There are certain types of mental conflicts in which this "talking out" process is all that is needed in the way of therapy. This is particularly true where the conflict centers around some doubt or confusion as to the past, rather than has to do with present forces. Such conflicts are not infrequent. One child suspects he is adopted, spends much time puzzling over this and develops a phantasy in regard to his true parents. Another boy who has lived until adolescence in foster homes has heard remarks and rumors regarding his own illegitimacy, and broods over these confused possibilities. There are various situations of this sort, usually relating to some past aspect of the family life which to the child is mysterious and unsolved. Here the type of therapy which is needed is aptly termed "ventilation." It differs from catharsis primarily in that the material is not revealed so spontaneously.

Dorothy had been removed from her own home at the age of nine because her father, an abnormally sexed, possibly homosexual individual, of whom Dorothy was very fond, had been having incestuous relations with her while her stepmother was pregnant. Dorothy had revealed the situation to a neighbor child by talking of the "treatments" which her father had been giving to her and evidently understood little of their significance. The father was sentenced to jail and later disappeared. The stepmother had never cared for Dorothy and the child was placed in a foster home, where she spent the next five years. She was a girl of superior intelligence, and school adjustment was not a problem. She was shy and socially reticent, abnormally sensitive about living in a foster family, but resentful toward the stepmother. As time went on there was more and more evidence of conflict in regard to her father. She confided to the foster mother at times that "I worship my father. I don't know where he is." At other times she would cry and make such remarks as, "I don't know why I was taken from home. I don't know yet what happened to me." As this confusion became more marked, her school work also slumped. When she was fourteen, the social worker felt she must have help with the girl.

Therapy in this case took the form of first establishing a good rapport with the psychologist — a man, since her whole pattern of adjustment to men was more favorable than to women — and then encouraging her to talk freely about her father. She showed very clearly a desire to know more about the reasons for her removal from home, saying "It's all muddled." The psychologist led her to talk through this episode of five years before, explaining sex relations, explaining the strong social taboo which had sent her father to jail. She recalled that she had not liked the experience, and the fact that enjoyment of intercourse would come only with maturity, was interpreted to her. She also seemed to have some questions as to whether she had been "damaged," and this was discussed frankly with her. The whole approach was objective, some of the reasons for the father's actions being mentioned, but no attempt made to gloss over the unpleasant aspects of the situation.

These interviews were sufficient to deal with the type of confusion and conflict she had expressed. The problem of her better social adjustment continued to need attention, and during the following year her adolescent desires for independence caused considerable friction between Dorothy and her foster mother. Her relationship to her own father or to the foster father was not a problem however.

In such situations as Dorothy's, treatment is frequently impeded because there is a hesitation to acquaint the child with possibly unpleasant facts — the explanation of illegitimacy, or adoption, or immoral parents, or, as in this case, serious sexual irregularities. This is unfortunate since it is nearly always true that the conflict caused by doubt is much more serious than any unhappiness over unpleasant but known facts. Where permission can be gained to talk freely with the child on such topics, they can almost invariably be cleared up. Usually the reaction of the child is relief at such an airing of his perplexities. This type of therapy is of course very similar to such informational treatment of conflicts as was dealt with earlier in this chapter. It differs only in the emphasis put upon the child's expression and clarification of his conflict, and in the lesser amount of genuinely new information which is given. It is a useful type of treatment wherever there is anxiety and perplexity growing out of past situations. Often nothing needs to be done about these conflicts except to bring them to light. In such a process of "ventilation" of mental conflicts the child's feelings are not expressed as spontaneously as in catharsis, but much the same gains are observed. The expression of inhibited feelings and attitudes, encouraged on the basis of good rapport between therapist and child, seems to have constructive value. Some ingenious ways of encouraging this expression of feeling through various media other than words invite our further attention.

Expression through Play Techniques. Dr. David Levy has been a leader in the experimentation with dolls as a means of therapy with children. He has suggested the use of the amputation doll, a metal doll which can be completely dismembered and restored, as a means of giving the child freedom of expression. The doll may be identified by the therapist as the child's mother, father, or rival sibling, and the youngster allowed to play with it as freely and destructively as he wishes. It is particularly in the realm of sibling rivalry, however, that Dr. Levy has perfected this technique, and has endeavored to put it on a more controlled and scientific basis. He has used it with children of ages three to thirteen, though it is obviously more suited to the younger group.

The method, in brief,[5] is to present to the child a group of three figures: a mother doll, which is a metal amputation doll with clay breasts added; a baby doll, which is celluloid and is held in the mother's arms, nursing at her breast; and a brother or sister doll (the sex is made the same as that of the patient) modeled from clay. The situation is first described in neutral fashion, and the child is asked in regard to the brother or sister doll, "What does he (she) do?" Free activity of any sort is permitted with the dolls, and with other play material in the room. Later, hostility is definitely activated or encouraged by adding such a statement as: "When the brother (sister) saw the baby she thought, 'That nasty, nasty baby at my mother's breast.'" In most of the cases the material was presented to the child several different times, usually in different interviews, though sometimes several times in the same interview.

As Dr. Levy analyzes the children's reactions to this situation, several elements seem to stand out. There is first likely to be a "prevention of hostility" on the part of the child, consisting of escapes from the situation, inhibited movements, and the like. Gradually, and with encouragement that anything is permitted, the child shows more and more hostility, the hostility seeming to show rather definite relationships to the particular emotional and behavior patterns of the child. Very repressed children tend to punish the brother or sister doll for each act of aggression against the baby and the mother. Children who were themselves in a strong rivalry situation seemed to have more difficulty expressing their hostility and show more tendencies toward "prevention of hostility." Children who were feeding problems tended to center their attack on the mother's breasts, though the baby was generally the center of attack. The hostility as it is given more and more expression by the child may involve the crushing, biting, and destruction of the baby doll, in a variety of ways,

---

[5] For a full account of the procedure the reader is referred to Dr. Levy's monograph on his experiment, "Hostility Patterns in Sibling Rivalry Experiments," *American Journal of Orthopsychiatry*, vol. 6 (April, 1936), pp. 193–257.

such as crushing the baby in a toilet, or hitting it with a hammer. It may involve the dismemberment of the mother doll, removal of the breasts, crushing them, or breaking them in pieces. The brother or sister doll may be slapped, punished, crushed, or smeared with clay. Often, once this full degree of feeling is expressed, it extends to other objects in the room, or must be repeated many times, as in crushing many baby dolls, for example.

Following this aggression or in connection with it the child may attempt to defend his actions by blaming the therapist and putting the responsibility on him, or justifying the aggression in various ways, as "The baby was bad," or "She (the mother) is dumb." Not only is the child defensive but frequently he endeavors to make restitution by putting the doll together, putting the baby back at the breast, and the like.

A portion of one of the records cited by Dr. Levy may serve to illustrate the process and its ramifications more clearly. The boy whose responses are given was four years old, with a sister one year old. He was having night terrors and was timid with other children though formerly aggressive. He was friendly to his baby sister if they were alone, but when either parent played with the baby would become hostile and jealous, fighting for attention. For several weeks after the birth of this baby sister he denied that he had seen her, when asked by an outsider, though this was contrary to fact. During the first interview with Dr. Levy there was random play. The sibling rivalry material was presented at the second interview, and the five presentations of it during the second and third interviews with the child's reactions are recorded below.

Experiment: Trial I: He says, "The brother watches."
Trial II: Waits. Asks, "What does he (brother) want to do?" Removes the baby gently and says, "Now we'll have to take these away." Removes breasts, places mother doll in lying position and gently amputates a leg and reinserts it. (I ask, "What will the baby do?") He replies, "She'll cry." Then he searches drawers for other toys, shoots a gun, plays with pliers, roams about office looking for toys, and plays with trains.

Trial III: Continues to play with trains and says, "I did it before."

Trial IV: (Usual stimulus) Listens attentively, says, "He gets mad." Then he quickly pushes a train. Then roams around, finds pliers and cuts a wire. Gets interested and cuts a number of times. (I bring him back to the play material.) He says, "The brother hit the baby hard," and shows how by hitting the brother doll against the floor. (I said, "Let him hit the baby.") Patient says, "I don't want to." Then he removes the breasts, makes a "ball" out of them and puts little breasts of clay back on the mother doll. (I asked why the brother hit the baby.) He replied, "He wanted to," and hits the couch with his hand. Then he picked up baby doll, hit it against the floor, then did the same to the mother doll. (I asked why he hit the brother doll.) He replied, "Because he hit the baby and he's going to do it every day." He then makes a big ball of clay, and says he made a big one last summer, and "Look how big it is now." Sticks pliers into the clay and pulls out pieces of it. Then puts some with pincers on the brother's buttocks and squeezes them. (I ask why he did that.) He said, "To make him pretty," and smears the entire back with clay. He says, "It's paint," and then takes it off with a stick.

Trial V: (3rd interview). Enters rapidly and immediately opens drawers and picks out trains. (I set up the sibling rivalry material.) He asks, "Do I have to play with that?" (I say, "Not unless you want to.") He says, "I don't." (I say, "I'll put it down anyway, you might want to play with it later.") He asks, "Why do we need a brother?" Plays with trains. Gets interested in rubber dagger and belt and wants to wear it. Wears it through hour, then puts clay in a wagon. (I asked why he put clay on the brother's back.) He said, "To fill up a hole." (The rubber doll has a hole for whistle in the upper dorsal region.) Then he said, "The brother stamped on the baby like this," and he stamped his foot on the ground. (I said, "Let him do it to the baby if he wants.") He then stamped on the baby many times and then said, "Can I pull it apart?" Pulled baby apart, and said, "I put clay on the brother because he crashed the baby." (I said, "Why clay?") He said, "Because he doesn't like clay." Then he rummaged through the drawer, found a male amputation doll and asked if he could pull it apart. (I said yes.) Then he pulled it apart. (I asked who he was pulling apart.) He said, "A man." (I asked who the brother wanted to pull apart.) He said, "The baby and the lady but he doesn't want to." After pulling the man apart he said, "Is there any-

thing else to pull apart?" and answered his own question —
"The lady." He then put the man together, asking meanwhile
if he has to come tomorrow again, "'cause maybe there's a
party." (I said I'd like to see him again and would he come?)
He said yes.

After pulling the man apart he picked up the mother doll,
removed the breasts, and said, "I'm not going to play with her
any more." Took her apart quickly then put her together.
Asked a lot of questions about when I got the dolls, when did I
buy the mamma, what day, and when I answered he replied,
"My, how old." (I asked when the baby was born.) He said
the 31st of May, and he was born the 29th of May. "Was I
before her?" (I asked on what day.) He said Saturday.
(These are true dates of his and sister's births.) Then played
with trains. Stopped, asked what time it was and playfully
stuck himself with a dagger. (I asked why he did it.) He said,
"Because that's to stick people with." Then plays with a rubber stamp and spends about ten minutes stamping. Is surprised
that each time it stamps the same thing. Then spends rest of
time with cars, shooting, and then makes cars race.[6]

There were two more interviews with this boy in which
further and more generalized hostility was expressed. Also
during the fifth and last contact the therapist encouraged
him to end the interview by restoring the family group to
the original form. This brought out more resentment against
the mother and only a grudging co-operation with the therapist. (Ordinarily Dr. Levy did not attempt this rather
artificial reconstruction of the family scene.)

Reports of the behavior of this boy showed a marked change
during the period of therapy. He became a "protective
brother" showing little or no jealousy of his sister and no
fighting for attention. He is regarded as one of the most
successful cases in the series, possibly because the release of
hostility was gradual, leading from the inhibited and tentative
aggressions to fully expressed and gratifying attacks.

Such material is suggestive and helpful in our thinking in
regard to therapy. The attempt toward analyzing it on a
scientific basis also indicates a positive trend. It is unfor-

[6] Levy, *op. cit.*, pp. 248–249.

tunate for his analysis of the child's responses that Dr. Levy used dolls made of differing material, since each material undoubtedly affects to some extent the type of response made. There is also no analysis of the fact that some children who were the youngest of a pair centered their hostility on the baby doll, where one might have expected destruction of the brother (sister) doll. Though the method has only been used on a small number of cases, and of these but twelve are reported in the study, it is nevertheless a type of therapy which offers much opportunity for experimentation, particularly with the younger child.

Informal Use of Play Techniques. Ordinarily when such play materials as dolls, modeling clay, and drawing materials are utilized in therapy, it is not done on such a formal or controlled basis as that described by Dr. Levy. Free play with such material may be just as valuable in permitting the child's expression of emotion, though with free play any strict comparison between cases is out of the question. Two examples from our own clinic records may illustrate the less formal use of play technique.

Freddie, a hyperactive eight-year-old, was regarded as a serious school problem. He had been poorly handled by the school, having been severely punished and whipped by the principal who complained of his whispering, his annoying behavior, his insolent manner when punished and other "delinquent" behavior. While therapy was primarily aimed toward the alteration of the school situation, a series of interview contacts on a play basis assisted Freddie in dramatizing and acting out his feelings which he did not express with much freedom in words. To quote one such incident from the record, "Examiner gave Freddie modeling clay. He made a figure.

"Who is it? Guess."

Examiner: "Your father? Me?"

"No, it's the principal. He's got flat feet." He made a fist on the figure. "Gee he's mad." Vindictively he knocked off the head and the fist, jumped the figure around the table singing, "Poor Mr. W—— (the principal)," and gradually annihilated it.

A somewhat more complex illustration in which the child uses her play to express some of the conflict within herself, is given below.

Marie is an illegitimate child of poor heredity, who has from earliest infancy had a history of extreme neglect and rejection. She was placed with relatives in homes where drunkenness, neglect, and immoral conduct were the rule. During the eight years of her life there have been more than a dozen placements, the last four being foster homes selected by the agency. In these homes Marie's attention-getting behavior was so extreme that she was given up by one home after another. She has been deceitful, jealous of other children, over-affectionate and over-dependent, very desirous of attention, and curious about sex matters. Her school placement is suited to her dull normal mentality, but her behavior in school is full of attention-getting devices. Although her need for affection and security has been recognized, it has been very difficult to break the vicious circle of insecurity and extreme behavior. A new placement was made in a carefully selected home where there was an older girl but no children of competing age. An account of one contact with the psychologist shows how Marie used the play situation to express some of her problems.

Marie began the interview very formally. She immediately said that she was getting along very well in the foster home, that she was doing very well in school, that she had a great many friends, that she got along with everybody, that she and Margaret got along very well. Feeling she had reported all about herself, she said, "now I want to play puzzles and do tests." Examiner suggested that perhaps she would like to play with clay. She said she wanted to make a house with clay. At first she just fiddled with the clay, making long rolls of it. She then began to put these rolls together to look like the front of a house. She asked examiner to make a little girl who lived in this house. Examiner made a figure which Marie named Barbara. Barbara came to call on examiner and then went back home to the house because she had to dust, and then she had to play at home. Then Marie brought the little girl back to call on examiner. She said Barbara was a very good little girl and always did what her mother told her — "but Shirley doesn't." "Who is Shirley?" "Shirley is another little girl, she belongs to Mrs. —— what shall I call her?" Examiner suggested maybe her name was Brown. In the character of Barbara, Marie then told examiner that Mrs. Brown's little girl Shirley was a very naughty little girl. Examiner invited Barbara in to tea. Barbara then said, "Thank you." When examiner offered Barbara milk and bread and butter, Barbara again said, "Thank you; yes, I like bread and butter." Marie in her own character explained that Barbara was a very polite little girl and always did the right thing.

Then she took the doll back very quickly, and walked her to examiner's desk again and pounded on the table. "This is Shirley. Shirley swears and slaps people." When examiner said, "Hello Shirley," Shirley said, "Let me in! Give me some bread and butter." When examiner pretended to talk to Barbara, Shirley said, "Shut up. I don't want you to talk to Barbara. I want more bread and butter and jam." When examiner gave Shirley more food, Shirley threw the food at Barbara and said, "Shut up, I'm going home. No, I'm going to stay because you don't want me." Then Shirley went home.

Now the doll was brought back in the character of Mrs. Brown. Mrs. Brown told what a nice little girl Barbara was and what a bad girl Shirley was. Then Marie pounded on the desk and said, "This is Shirley. Give me some tea. I want some bread and butter" and then Marie said, "Now Shirley is swearing. She says awful things, I can't say them." Then Mrs. Brown said, "Shirley go on home." Shirley said, "No, I won't. I will swear at you." Mrs. Brown said, "Shirley is not a good little girl, she swears, she is not polite. She did something very bad." Then Marie said, "I can't say it, what Shirley did."

She immediately put Mrs. Brown in the house and began to make another long roll of clay. Then she brought Mrs. Brown back to examiner. "I am sorry Shirley did such a bad thing." Examiner asked, "What did Shirley do?" Marie said, "You say to Mrs. Brown, 'Shirley broke my window, she threw a stone!'" Examiner said, "I didn't know Shirley threw a stone." Then Marie said, "This is not Mrs. Brown, this is Barbara." Barbara said, "Shirley broke a dish. I am a good little girl. I never play with Shirley. I am a good little girl. I don't swear. I tell Shirley not to do those things, that God sees them. Shirley stole some gum, she wanted me to take some but I wouldn't. Shirley is an awful bad little girl. Her mother should give her a licking and make her stay in the house and not let her play with her toys." Barbara was then removed very quickly to the other side of the table. A few seconds later she came back in the character of Mrs. Brown. "Shirley thinks it's funny when she swears and contradicts. She thinks I won't do anything because I haven't done anything. I guess I am a wrong kind of mother." Examiner said, "Does Shirley think she is not your little girl?" Mrs.

Brown said, "I have to go right away" and the doll was quickly taken home.

Marie said to examiner, "You telephone to Mrs. Brown," so examiner telephoned to Mrs. Brown. Mrs. Brown then talked for a long time about what a bad girl Shirley was and how Shirley had thrown a stone and broken a window. "When her father gets home he will paddle her and then she will cry." Mrs. Brown left the telephone and Marie made a noise of crying. Examiner then telephoned to Mrs. Brown again. Mrs. Brown said, "Shirley got a licking. She broke two windows. She threw stones. She broke two of our windows and broke your windows, too. She doesn't like you, that's the reason she broke your windows." Examiner said, "Doesn't she like you, Mrs. Brown? Is that the reason she broke your windows?" Very quickly Mrs. Brown said, "I made a mistake. No, she didn't break our windows, she just broke yours." Examiner said, "Would Shirley come over to see me?"

Immediately the doll was brought over to examiner's desk. She knocked on the desk. "This is Shirley, I am sorry I broke your window. I didn't mean it. Another little girl put a rock in my hand and I threw it." Examiner said, "Why did you throw a rock?" Shirley said, "I was mad; you like Barbara better than me and I was mad. I want to come often to a tea party at your house. You could have Barbara if I came. Oh no, she can't come. She is going away to her grandmother's." Examiner then asked if Barbara were going to say good-bye before she went away. Then Marie said, "This is Barbara." Barbara said, "I am going away to my grandmother's to visit. I will be gone a long time, but when I come back may I come to see you?"

It was then time for examiner to meet another appointment. Marie objected very much to having to go, she wanted to stay and wanted to come back again. Examiner assured her she might come back another time and play. Then Marie said, "Do we have to put away the clay?" When examiner picked up the pieces of clay, Marie took the doll and said, "Oh, save Barbara. Put her away so that she will be safe." She watched examiner put the lid on the box to be sure Barbara was not destroyed. She went very unwillingly from the office.

In this complex and imaginative play situation Barbara and Shirley seem to definitely represent the socially approved and socially disapproved aspects of Marie's own personality. Shirley has ample opportunity to express her hatred for the world, her jealousy of other children, and toward the end, her desire to be approved and liked. Yet in Barbara the child also shows her recognition of society's demands for conforming behavior. Marie is too defensive and protective to express her feelings plainly in an ordinary interview. Yet in this play situation she achieves some direct expression of her feelings, and some clarification of her own conflicting attitudes. We shall discuss shortly some of the therapeutic results of such an experience.

There are many other forms of activity which may be used in the same therapeutic fashion as those above. Drawings may give a child the opportunity to caricature and destroy unloved members of the family, or by their warlike content to give some expression to his destructive moods. (The new "finger painting" encouraged in progressive schools has real possibilities in this connection.) Imaginative literary compositions may give a child an avenue for his emotional expression. Poetry, dancing, soap-carving, and even mechanical construction may and probably do offer similar outlets. The reasons for the selection of modeling clay and dolls as the material most used, are practical ones. In the older child, expression through verbalization can usually be encouraged, and is more easily interpreted and less roundabout. The other avenues of expression which have been mentioned do give emotional satisfaction and become therapeutic in a broad sense, but are not necessarily a part of the interview process. With the small child verbalization is difficult, and materials which relate directly to his problems and upon which he can vent his feelings freely are helpful therapeutic agents.

A recently published series of articles [7] tells of the way in which all of the activities mentioned above are used as means of diagnosis and therapy at the Psychiatric Institute, New York City. Under the guidance of Dr. Howard Potter and Dr. Louise Despert stories, drawings, and play with toys have

---

[7] This series goes under the general heading "Technical Approaches Used in the Study and Treatment of Emotional Problems in Children" and is published in the *Psychiatric Quarterly*. See the bibliography following Chapter XI for complete reference.

all been utilized with the seriously maladjusted children under the care of the Institute. The methods are original and suggestive, and merit brief description.

In the use of stories several approaches are used. Children are asked to retell folk tales which have been told to them, and changes from the original presentation are carefully noted. The children are also asked to write imaginative stories of their own, which of course are studied for significant emotional patterns. Likewise a story written by the psychiatrist is told to the children and they later write it or retell it to the psychiatrist. This story is built around the common emotional stresses of growing up: parental attitudes to children, sibling jealousy, leaving home, finding a mate. The authors feel that in the expression of these stories children find expression and release for their own emotional difficulties, and this is often indicated by a continually recurring "theme" of aggression or anxiety which runs through the child's productions. From the point of view of therapy, the stories are used as a means of promoting insight, by gradually helping the child to see the meanings and identifications which are implicit in the stories.

Drawings are used in similar fashion, and in this, as in the use of other techniques, emphasis is placed on the necessity of quantity. Frequently several hundred drawings are made by a child patient, and it is upon the basis of these large numbers that the child's trends are diagnosed.

A new technique of interest is also proposed. The child is put in a room by himself and allowed to use a knife to scrape cardboard, after suitable explanation of the use and dangers of a knife. Ostensibly the purpose is to get a large quantity of cardboard scrapings which can be made, by the addition of glue and water, into plastic material for modeling. The major purpose however is to encourage free expression of the child's aggressive feelings and wishes. It is reported that the result is usually a temporary increase of symptomatic behavior, many aggressive fantasies reported in the interviews with the therapist which follow immediately each period of scraping, and the clearer development of the child's main concern or "theme." These changes persist until the child has worked out some type of solution to his conflicts, when his behavior improves and his aggression decreases. It is the belief of the experimenters that no child improved without first finding release through aggressive expression and thus gradually gaining some insight.

Description is also given of the use of the playroom for diagnostic and therapeutic purposes with very young patients. The attempt to use free imaginative group play, or "collective fantasy," is also described. Its success seems much less clear than that of the other approaches. On the whole the series is the most thorough and thoughtful presentation of the uses of play techniques, both for diagnosis and therapy, which has yet appeared. It is significant that the authors feel that the child will make use of any reasonably appropriate channel to express his feelings, particularly his aggressions, and thus to find some release from tension. It is also of interest that in many cases they definitely use the child's drawings, stories, or other products of play, to interpret his behavior to him. They would thus make use of more than the expressive, releasing effects of play and would use it as a basis for interpretive therapy.

Expression through Drama. Alert teachers and students of progressive education have recognized some of the personal values inherent in dramatic expression. Recently there have been two interesting experiments in the specific use of the drama for therapeutic purposes. The first of these is the use of puppet shows, as developed at Bellevue Hospital, New York City, in the treatment of children who are serious personality and behavior problems. This experiment is well described in an article by Dr. Loretta Bender, and is briefly summarized here.[8]

Puppet plays, some of them traditional folk-lore dramas,

---

[8] Bender, L., and Woltmann, A. G. "The Use of Puppet Shows as a Psychotherapeutic Method for Behavior Problems of Children," *American Journal of Orthopsychiatry*, vol. 6 (July, 1936), pp. 341-354.

some of them constructed dramas which illustrate basic family problems, are presented to the children in the observation ward of the psychiatric division. The hero of the dramas is Caspar, a puppet character with considerable strength and resourcefulness, yet with very human weaknesses. He is always active and curious, "he can do what he likes without being bad." A monkey, with instincts more primitive and less restrained, is another favorite character. The alligator and the witch, or a pair of cannibals, are the "villains" of the various dramas, and are frequently identified with parents by the child audience.

One of the essential features of these puppet shows is the free expression encouraged in the children. At every crucial point the children are asked what Caspar should do next. They are encouraged to shout imprecations at the forces hostile to Caspar, to warn him, to express all their own hostile feelings through this symbolic medium. In one play Caspar is greatly annoyed by the way in which his newborn sister takes parental attention and affection away from him. He is left alone to care for the baby, and the children are asked what he shall do. "Caspar gets a good deal of hearty advice from the audience to throw the baby out the window, to kill it, to throw it in the furnace, etc." Caspar, on the witch's advice, gives the baby sour milk, which sickens the baby, who is taken to the hospital. Eventually, however, the parents pay attention to both Caspar and the baby, Caspar decides to protect rather than harm the baby, and the family dance together happily.

The insistence on a constructive dramatic solution of the problem is very marked in this clinical experiment, which in this respect differs from the general use of expressive techniques. Dr. Bender in writing of the puppet shows states her position strongly. "The symbolic characters can give a free expression of aggression without causing anxiety or fear in the child, and also can give a free expression of love. The latter should by no means be overlooked. There seems to be some tendency on the part of students of child psychology to emphasize the aggressive and destructive tendencies in the child and to neglect the equally strong love and constructive tendencies. There should always be a happy solution to every problem." [9] Whether these happy endings accomplish the re-education which the author desires it is difficult to determine. It is possible that the same results would obtain merely from the release of pent-up feelings of guilt and aggression, leaving the child free to work out his own solution to his problems in whatever may be a realistic way for him. Study of this point, even in a subjective way, would be of real value.

There is no question that the children tend to identify the puppet characters with personalities and forces in their own situation. This is amply clear from their own verbal expressions. It is probably not necessary further to identify, as Dr. Bender does, each of these characters with some aspect of Freudian ideology. Thus the unrepressed monkey is the id, the alligator represents oral aggression, Caspar's stick is a phallic symbol, etc. The validity of the experiment's results does not, however, hinge on the validity of these theoretical identifications.

One feature which is emphasized in this puppet experiment is the group expression of feeling. To find that others hate the baby, that others wish to kill the old witch parent, is a peculiarly releasing experience, since any feeling of guilt is reoriented and nullified by the group expression and acceptance of such attitudes. This is one type of psychological mechanism which has no doubt been too little used in psychotherapy. It is obviously much more potent in its effect than for a therapist to reassure the child that others have harbored hostile feelings toward siblings or parents. Dr. Bender and her associates have come to feel that this type of group therapy is more effective than individual treatment with children of the sort they receive.

Another experiment in the more direct use of the drama as psychotherapy is being conducted by Dr. Moreno.[10]   He

---

[9] Bender and Woltmann, *op. cit.*, p. 342.

[10] For a brief account of this experiment see Murphy, Gardner, "The Mind is a Stage," *Forum*, vol. 97 (May, 1937), pp. 277–280.

has, in a private sanitarium, a rather elaborate stage, built in three ascending concentric circles.   On this stage, which so easily offers various levels of participation, the child or patient is encouraged to take part in a drama.   The skeleton of the drama is planned by the psychiatrist, but the players act their parts spontaneously, responding to the life problems presented in ways which are natural to them.   The use of such a scheme involves considerable ability in group leadership which is by no means included in the equipment of every clinician.   It seems to have two values, first, the spontaneous liberation of emotion, hostile feelings and the like; and next, the possibility of finding through the drama a constructive solution to the individual's problems.   The child who is antagonistic toward his parents may freely, in the dramas, express that hostility.   The repetitions of variations of the drama, however, offer a neutral type of re-education in more comfortable and acceptable modes of parent-child relationship.   The experiment is a very new one, worth further observation.

The Values of Expressive Therapy.   Unlike as are the activities which take place in the therapies described in this section, there is a strong fundamental likeness between them.   Whether the child is savagely smashing a celluloid doll, or loudly vocalizing his hatred of the old witch of the puppet show, or merely talking frankly of his fears, anxieties, and guilt feelings, he is gaining a free and definite and concrete expression of his deeper attitudes which is largely denied to him in ordinary life situations.   There is value in such expression which would seem to be twofold.   There is the value of release, of freeing the child from the tension of pent-up feelings, and of thus making him mentally, and no doubt physiologically, more fit to meet the real situation.   The child who has harbored puzzled and confused feelings of guilt because of his illegitimacy, or because of some other circumstance which has affected him can be released from his confusion to face the actual difficulties of his reality.   The child who hates his parents can express that hatred and find less need of being antagonistic at home.   As Dr. Levy's cases would indicate, the expression of strong hostility against a sibling in the interview situation makes for less emotional tension and discharge in the real situation.   The child who has been extremely hostile to his sibling is less aggressive after such treatment. The child who has strongly inhibited all jealous reactions begins to display them to a normal degree, evidently feeling less need for the inhibitions.   This frank release of fundamental wishes, desires, and attitudes in the treatment situation is doubtless one of the major gains from such therapy.

In addition, however, there is a reduction in the feeling of guilt.   Hatred, jealousy, and a desire to destroy are not attitudes receiving social approval, and even the very small child has had ample opportunity to feel the weight of this cultural fact.   Hence the tentative and fearful way in which the child shows aggression toward the toy symbols of parent and sibling. Hence the need for excusing and rationalizing their destructive action.   But through the process of play therapy, and especially perhaps in the puppet dramas, the child comes to realize that there is no guilt in having such feelings.   Actions toward the parent or sibling may still need to be inhibited to gain social approval, but there is great gain to the child in knowing that these "wicked" thoughts and feelings are common to others as well as to himself, and that he may recognize such feelings in himself and still retain his self-respect.   It is this opportunity to recognize and admit the primitive and hostile emotions within oneself that constitutes the second outstanding value in such therapy.

A more debatable point is the value of working out symbolically through the play or dramatic situation a socially constructive solution of the child's problem.   This is attempted by Dr. Levy in the case cited, where he endeavors to have the boy, after full expression of his hatreds, restore the family situation.   It is even more strongly shown in the puppet shows, where the children are encouraged to develop some socially suitable ending of the drama.   In large measure such attempts are of the same nature as other efforts at personal influence. Their results may no doubt be gauged by similar criteria. If the so-called solution is something entirely suggested by the therapist, then its long-time value is presumably very small.   If it tends simply to reinforce motives and choices which the child is already making for himself, it may serve to hasten and strengthen the re-educative process.

As will be very evident from the cases cited and the uses made of expressive therapy, it is most valuable when there are strong guilt feelings on the part of the child, particularly when such guilt feelings arise because of hostile feelings toward another. Since resentments and hatreds toward family members or toward others are a very common element in situations of problem behavior, this type of treatment is likely to be of frequent use.   Although several of the forms described are more adapted to the preschool than to the older child, the principles of therapy through free expression of feeling are applicable to any age group.

BIBLIOGRAPHY

See Bibliography following Chapter XI, page 357.

Treatment Interviews: Deeper Therapies

WHAT IS MEANT BY DEEP THERAPY?

IN CLINICAL practice one hears frequent reference to the "depth" of a treatment process. The term may have reference to the degree of insight or self-understanding which is achieved. Thus Dr. Lippman states, "Perhaps we may be able to say that the more insight the child can receive during the process of treatment, the less superficial that treatment is. The time element need not be the determining factor. He may be seen several times a week for many months and still remain at a superficial level with respect to his conflicting problems." [1] In addition to insight, however, there is probably another element which is also implicit in the description of a process as "deep" therapy. This is the state of rapport between the child and the therapist, which may extend to the most complete dependence. It is with those therapeutic methods which aim toward giving the child self-insight, or in which the emotional relationship between child and worker is a very strong one, that we are concerned in this chapter. The methods of psychotherapy which we have been considering do not involve either of these elements to a marked degree. They are more superficial, and may be more widely used without risk than the approaches we shall now describe.

INTERPRETIVE THERAPY

We have already discussed (Chapter VII) the method of interpretive treatment as it is used in dealing with adults.

[1] Lippman, H. S. "Direct Treatment Work with Children," *American Journal of Orthopsychiatry*, vol. 4 (July, 1934), p. 376.

The process as it is used with children is fundamentally the same. The aim of the therapist is to have the child understand and emotionally accept a consistent and rational explanation of the patterns of his behavior. Once the child understands his own emotional and behavior history, as it were, he is to that degree more capable of coping with it. Several authors have stressed the fact that such treatment may be effective even if the interpretation itself is incorrect, as long as it provides a consistent and systematic basis on which the child can work towards more integrated behavior.[2] Certainly the fact must be faced that different clinicians may interpret differently similar phenomena of personality development, and yet each may achieve some measure of success in therapy. A consideration of this would lead us to make interpretation as simple and factual as possible in order that we do not confuse or overelaborate our treatment procedures.

The Case of John. Some examples of the use of interpretive therapy with children may illustrate something of its variety and the basis of its effectiveness. The treatment of John S. is an example of a simple and fragmentary, but effective, type of interpretation.

John's mother came to the clinic to ask for help with her 15-year-old son. She was an intelligent, somewhat erratic individual, reluctant to ask outside assistance. Two recent temper storms, however, had brought her to the conclusion that something must be done. On one occasion the family had been preparing to drive to John's grandmother's home, a trip which he anticipated. John became annoyed at several small delays, and when his mother finally told him he could not take his bicycle as he had planned, he burst into a rage, smashed a window, and stormed about the house. On another occasion a reprimand from his father sent John into a screaming, kicking tantrum which ended in a pitched battle with his father. The mother admitted

[2] See Rosensweig, Saul, "Some Implicit Common Factors in Diverse Methods of Psychotherapy," *American Journal of Orthopsychiatry*, vol. 4 (January, 1934), p. 413, and Shaffer, L. S., *The Psychology of Adjustment* (New York: Houghton Mifflin Company, 1936), pp. 478–479.

some parental differences over discipline, and also told of John's intense dislike of Betty, his ten-year-old sister.

Interviews with John showed him to be a very childish and dependent boy. He would not go home from the first interview on the street car, but insisted his mother call for him. Although he had lived in the city all his life, he professed an inability to find his way about. His antagonisms toward his sister were all on a ten-year level: the proper difference in bed-time hours, whether he should have to eat all the food on his plate when she did not, and the like.

Treatment took the form of getting John to go over the events of his early history until he understood their influence on him: his first five years living with his grandmother, who favored and spoiled him, moving to the separate home which his parents then established and the coming of his baby sister, the competition with his sister, his repeated patterns of tantrum behavior to gain his own way, which he could remember clearly as far back as the age of eight. As he went over this material during several interviews he was able to laugh at himself and to see how his childish patterns originated. The psychologist also interpreted this material to him in clearer terms. Another means used to help John attain insight was to describe in concrete terms the dependency and egocentric tendencies of the child, and the ways in which those characteristics were changed in the mature adult, who is able to take responsibility for himself, whose interests are socialized, who is able to face reality. He was encouraged to analyze the ways in which he was mature, his reading interests, for example, and the many ways in which he was immature. From the time that treatment contacts began, the tantrums diminished greatly in number and severity until they were no longer a problem. John sometimes became upset by the dictatorial and unreasonable requests of his father, but in these instances his behavior represented a fairly normal reaction.

He was soon talking about ways in which he would like to change. He wished he might be responsible for his bedtime hour. He wished he might become a boy like Fred, one of his chums. (Fred was a social playboy, sophisticated but hardly mature. He represented to John, however, a step upward in his goal ideas.) Later John wished he could manage the money for his own clothing, and entirely on his own initiative wrote a note to his father itemizing the past year's clothing expenditures, and asking that the same amount be paid to him on a monthly basis so that he could buy his own. This the father refused to do.

John's school work was a failure at the time he was brought to the clinic, in spite of his adequate intelligence.   Although there was some improvement in his effort he failed two of his high-school subjects but faced the situation quite realistically and made his own plans as to what to do.   This was in marked contrast to his earlier very irresponsible attitude toward school.   At this point treatment contacts ceased because he seemed reasonably able to cope with his own problems.   There had been only eight interviews in a three-month period.

An interesting postscript is added by a casual contact nearly three years later.   John has made good progress in school, and is almost ready to graduate.   He talks in mature fashion about his father's financial poor judgment, which has kept the family pinched economically.   John tells of securing a paper route which he held for a time, and gave up in order to take an after-school job in an office, where he is earning $5 per week.   He is sorry that he obtained this job partly through the influence of a relative. He wishes he might have obtained it entirely by his own efforts.

In John's situation we see the full effect which insight can bring about.   There were, to be sure, other reasons why the process was so successful.   John was adolescent and would have been forced to modify his pattern somewhat by increased contact with others.   Once he had chosen a more mature goal, his father's inadequacies had the effect of challenging the best in the boy.   Yet the immediate change in the tantrum behavior and in the competition with his younger sister are some indication of the influence which is to be attributed to the achievement of insight through interpretation.

The Use of Dreams.   Ordinarily it is the child's past and present behavior and attitudes, as related by him to the therapist, which are interpreted and become the basis of insight.   Some therapists would also use the child's dream material in this way.   Dr. Lippman, who cites the case given below, stresses the fact that dreams cannot be used as material for interpretation unless there is a very good relationship between therapist and child.   This is necessary, since dream material is not so obvious in its significance as John's tantrums, and if the child is to accept the interpretation he must have first accepted the therapist.   The case of James illustrates the interpretation of recurring dreams.

James is an 11-year-old boy who has suffered for years from terrifying dreams in which he is constantly being chased by a man with a knife or gun.   He has had this recurring dream of being attacked when he is unable to run or scream to his father for help. He came willingly to the clinic, because of the suffering resulting from these dreams.   A series of interviews disclosed an intense father hostility.   This was intensified by a marked fondness for his mother who quite completely rejected the father.   Several times James made statements which indicated a past fondness for his father and a wish to regain his father's affection.   During one of the interviews James said, "What's the use of trying to get well this way?   It won't do any good just to talk, I still dream just as bad as I always did," and he proceeded to relate another dream in which he was being attacked by a terrifying man. At this point his recurring dream was interpreted to him.   It was explained that the attacking man was his father, who was punishing him for the feelings of hostility which he bore him.   He was told that in the dream he is constantly being attacked, because he feels the need of being punished for his evil wishes against his father.   The reason that he cannot call for help, or run from danger, is because, deeply, he feels that he deserves the threatened punishment.   Besides, he would be calling for help from the one whom he actually wishes to attack.   Following this interpretation which he accepted, it was pointed out that he was actually deeply fond of his father and would like very much to love him, but he was unable to do so, because his mind was continually occupied with the wrongs that the father had committed against him.   He was impressed again and again in the succeeding interviews with the importance of replacing his feeling of hatred with a feeling of love, and that only in this way could his guilt be decreased, with a resulting lessening of his terrifying dreams.   It is interesting in this case that in the interview following the interpretation of the dreams, James stated that though his dreams upset him as much as ever he could recall none of them clearly, but he was certain that the attacking man was no longer present in his dreams.   Unfortunately the treatment had to be discontinued at a stage when he was anxious for further assistance.[3]

In dealing with James the psychiatrist first established a good basis of rapport, then interpreted to the boy his own emo-

[3] Lippman, *op. cit.*, p. 377.

tional patterns, and then suggested new reaction patterns. One might question to some extent the advisability of impressing "again and again" the need for developing a feeling of love. Had the psychiatrist's efforts been directed toward giving the boy a clearer understanding of the father-son relationship this therapy of the personal-influence variety might well have become unnecessary. The immediate cessation of the initial dream-symptom, the attacking man, is familiar to anyone who has used this type of interpretive therapy. While the disappearance of the symptom does not mean the completion of treatment, it does indicate the potency of the method employed.

A Failure of Interpretive Therapy. Since failures in therapy often reveal more than a recounting of successes, the following case, in which a type of interpretive therapy seemed for a time successful, but eventually proved to be a failure, is given in fragmentary form to illustrate some of the conditions which seem essential to the success of such treatment.

The judge of the Children's Court asked the Child Study Department for help with Robert, a tall, sandy-haired boy of 17, who had been arrested for molesting a 7-year-old girl and handling her genitals. A brief investigation had revealed that this was not a first offense, but had occurred on a number of occasions within the past few years, twice within the past three months. His parents also reported that they were concerned about his practice of masturbation.

Robert's father had held a steady and respected position in the community until seven years previously, when he had a stroke. Since that time he has been partially incapacitated, and unable to work, being quite irritable, showing poor emotional control, weeping under any emotional strain. The mother has been a hard-working person of more stable temperament, carrying much of the economic burden of the family. Robert is the only living child, there having been two miscarriages in the seven years prior to his birth.

Robert proved to be of dull normal mentality, suitably placed in the 10th grade in a shop course. He was frank and friendly, and seemed eager for help. He told of several friends, and his vocational and recreational interests were normal. He showed occasionally in his conversation an abnormal sensitivity to stimuli, typical of the neurotic. He had to leave class because his teacher had an offensive odor, he sometimes skipped school because he felt he must get out and have freedom, he over-reacted to pain, and in other ways showed symptoms of instability. He spoke of having had two girl friends, and these friendships seemed those of the ordinary adolescent. There had been mild petting, but none of the sex behavior which he had exhibited toward small girls.

In going back over his sexual history Robert recounted one incident which he had never told anyone before. At about the age of eleven or twelve, when he had little sex interest, very little sex information, and no knowledge of female anatomy, a boy named Alexander invited him to his room, and there taught him to masturbate. Following this Alexander went to take care of his small sister, four or five years old, who was awakening from her nap. He showed Robert her genitalia and also showed him how to handle her genital parts. On several later occasions Alexander and Robert engaged in mutual masturbation. Less than a year after this Robert enticed a little girl into his house and endeavored to handle her improperly. The later episodes all followed a similar pattern.

It seemed obvious that the profound conditioning experience which Robert reported was at the root of his behavior. For a boy just coming into adolescence to have his sex interest awakened and specifically directed toward small girls, under circumstances certain to produce profound guilt feelings, seemed sufficient to explain his delinquencies. Consequently the treatment plan, while it included an adequate and healthy recreational program and some work with the parents to relieve them of their concern about masturbation, was centered largely on the effort to give Robert some insight into his own behavior.

During the treatment contacts, various aspects of Robert's adjustment were discussed, but his sex behavior was an important topic of these interviews. During one of the early interviews there was occasion for the psychologist to question him as to his sex information. On the whole his intellectual knowledge seemed fairly complete. Some misconceptions were cleared up, and he was given the Dennett pamphlet, "The Sex Side of Life" to read for himself. He was also encouraged to tell again of his experience with Alexander. An excerpt from the fifth interview relates the attempt at interpretive treatment.

"There was quite a long discussion about his interest in small girls. It seemed peculiar to the examiner that in spite of the information which Robert has given about his early experiences

with Alexander he does not seem to have any clear understanding of why small girls excite him sexually. He said that
although he tries to fight it down yet there are occasions when he
sees a small girl and the feeling surges over him very strongly.

"Examiner decided to try the experiment of teaching him on
an intellectual level the pattern that has caused his difficulty with
the hope that emotional acceptance of this would gradually
follow. Went over with him a number of times in different ways
the sequence of his sex experiences. Tried to show him how the
strong arousal of his sex feelings at the age of eleven or twelve
and the direction of those feelings toward small girls would naturally influence his later feelings. Also pointed out his normal
interest in girls of his own age which has developed along with
this first interest.

"Suggested to him that instead of trying to fight his feelings
about small girls that he should rather laugh at himself for this
evidence of his eleven-year-old attitude still coming to the top at
the age of seventeen. Stressed the normality of his interest in
older girls and in the normal course of sex relationship. It was
difficult of course to estimate how much of an effect this type of
treatment had. Examiner expects to return to the subject later
on and see if it has helped Robert to gain any lasting insight."

This modified process of interpretation in which the boy played
much less than the ordinary part, seemed to make headway.
Robert felt that his masturbatory activities decreased. He began to go out with girls his own age, and to take a more active
interest in them. A portion of the eleventh interview, three
months later, illustrates this.

"There was some conversation in regard to Bob's association
with various girls. He seems to be attending a number of dances
and going on quite a few dates with girls his own age. This
seemed to be a good time to check up on some of his sex attitudes.
It was interesting that when examiner asked him about the wave
of sex feeling which he had commented on in earlier interviews, he
said that he still had these same feelings but in his discussion of
them it became evident that they are now nearly always directed
toward girls of his own age rather than toward small girls. On
the other hand only a couple of nights ago while driving he saw a
small girl standing on the corner. He evidently felt a very strong
compulsion to follow out some of his previous tendencies, 'but I
just stepped on the gas.'

"In order to see whether the rather didactic approach used in
the earlier interview had had any effect examiner asked him to
explain what was the cause of his strong sex interest in little girls.

In talking about this he seemed at first to show no insight at all.

"He thinks that this interest has died down because he has more to think of, because he goes around more with girls, etc. Gradually as he thought it over he began to stress the point of view that he had passed through a certain stage and that now he does find his interest centering more in girls of his own age. He has some realization of the fact that when he has strong sex feelings at the present time they are mostly quite normal ones and the sort which will come to any boys his age. He talked quite freely of the petting he had done and of how some aggressive girls had tried very hard to arouse him. Generally he thinks this has a rather negative effect.

"It seemed to the examiner that Bob has relatively little insight into his original problem and the reasons why his attitude has slowly changed. Nevertheless his whole sex attitude and interest is at the present time a much more normal and healthy thing than when he was first seen."

There was only one further interview with the psychologist at this time, though the probation officer continued a diminishing supervision for a time. Fifteen months later Robert was again arrested for molesting two little girls. He was now over nineteen and beyond the care of the children's agencies. The protection of the community made institutional care a necessity. The psychologist had one interview with Robert at this time. His story indicated that for ten months there had been no sex episodes but that in the past five or six months there had been several incidents, molesting small girls on three occasions and teaching two smaller boys to masturbate. Robert was much disturbed about himself, and showed more guilt feelings than ever before. He was quite willing to have the judge send him to an institution.

The Causes of Failure. What are some of the reasons for the failure of this case, which from many points of view seemed hopeful? There were many constructive elements in the picture, and Robert, though of a mildly neurotic disposition, showed many normal drives. Why did the treatment fail?

To the writer it would seem that one basis of the failure was the inadequate type of interpretation. Robert needed to go over his past experience sufficiently to realize and feel the explanation of his behavior. A slower, but more intensive, process would have been well repaid. If a certain amount of didactic method seemed advisable this too should have been repeated until it became a part of Robert's mental organization. Much the same comment might be made as to the re-education of Robert's sexual attitudes.   This was probably too superficial to be lasting and needed repetition and a degree of "overlearning."   It would seem likely that another reason for the failure was the inadequate use of expressive therapy.   His willingness to go to an institution would indicate that his feelings of guilt had been more extreme than had been appreciated and probably never adequately reduced through full release of his feelings.   Again this would probably have been accomplished through more frequent contacts, more encouragement to "talk out" every aspect of his sex conduct and feelings.

It is interesting to note that Dr. Sadler in dealing with adult patients asks the patient as part of his treatment to write a composition on his own situation, describing his problems, how he "got that way," and what he proposes to do about it.[4] This he feels tends to reinforce the interpretation which has been developed in the interviews with the psychiatrist.   The composition is discussed with the psychiatrist, and if the patient fails to show an adequate understanding of his own situation he must rewrite it until it shows sufficient insight.   Such a process has not been generally tried with children, though occasional use of it has been helpful with superior adolescents of good verbal abilities.   Such a treatment technique emphasizes the fact that the attainment of insight is a slow, learned process, not something which comes to the child in a flash.

The Effectiveness of Insight.   These presentations of cases whose treatment centers about the development of insight on the part of the child also suggest the situations in which such treatment may be most effective.   In general it may be said that interpretive therapy has its greatest usefulness with children whose problem behavior follows a definite and repeated pattern, presumably caused by emotional factors.   Thus we

---

[4] Sadler, William S.   *Theory and Practice of Psychiatry*, p. 1133.   St. Louis: C. V. Mosby, 1936.

might well choose this type of treatment with a girl who continually steals useless small articles, particularly from women,
and hides them away, without making constructive use of them.
First would come the determination of the emotional pattern
responsible for such stealing, and then the self-interpretation
of the girl, guided by the clinician, in order to produce understanding and insight. Similarly it might prove to be one
effective aspect of treatment in dealing with a small boy who
persistently steals in order to treat his acquaintances and thus
"buy" friends. It would almost certainly be an ineffective
method in dealing with the boy who steals in company with
others, in a variety of ways, where the behavior seems conditioned primarily by cultural factors.

Like the use of suggestion and persuasion, insight therapy
may produce definite damage if unwisely done. It is not a
casual type of therapy, and should not be undertaken unless a
careful diagnosis has made the patterns of behavior clear, and
the time is available for intensive contacts with the child. A
wrong interpretation or one which is prematurely forced on the
child may definitely set him back in his personality development. It is also probable that, as in Robert's case, interpretive
therapy which has been inadequately carried through, leaving
the child with the same behavior symptoms, is worse than no
treatment at all. It leaves the child more discouraged and
more hopeless in regard to himself. Hence this type of therapy
will only be utilized by those with considerable psychological
training and counseling experience, or under the supervision of
such a person.

PSYCHOANALYSIS OF CHILDREN

Judged from a quantitative viewpoint, the treatment of
children's problems through psychoanalysis is negligible. Of
the thousands of children who are dealt with each year in the
child guidance and behavior clinics in this country, only a mere
handful are treated by psychoanalysis. In Europe the proportion might be somewhat larger. Because we are concerned
with the practical methods usable in the treatment of chil-

dren's problems, we shall touch rather briefly on this treatment technique, leaving to others a discussion of the important effect which psychoanalysis has had upon our understanding of children's problems, and of the ways in which its therapeutic methods have been absorbed into other techniques.

Fundamentally, child analysis makes use of both of the elements which characterize deep therapy, the development of insight through interpretation, and the reliance for much of the treatment on the emotional relationship or transference, which takes place between the child and the analyst. The process through which these goals are to be reached is based on a regular series of contacts, one, two, three or more per week, with the analyst. Judging from the case accounts, there is usually little or no attempt to change or alter any of the environmental circumstances. There may be some contacts between the parents and the analyst, generally for purposes of obtaining further diagnostic material rather than for purposes of treatment. The analytic interviews themselves are much less formal than when an adult is being analyzed. The child is usually permitted much freedom, and play techniques are utilized to draw out further expressions of his feelings and attitudes. The length of an analysis is of course its prohibitive feature. One hundred analytic hours would be regarded by most Freudians as a minimum amount of time in which to complete the analysis of the child, the termination of the process being determined by the progress which is being made.

The Interpretive Methods of Analysis. There are certain differences between the technique of interpretation as we have described it and its use in an analysis. In the first place the child analyst of the classical school aims toward giving the child complete insight into his behavior. We might think of this as being broader in scope than the type of interpretive therapy we have discussed, and also deeper. The analyst may go through several layers of interpretation, discovering and explaining deeper and deeper subconscious motives and patterns. It is because of this goal of completeness of interpretation that the analyst rarely regards the process as finished. Even in the cases which are selected for publication, a majority of those which the author has examined are regarded by the analyst as incomplete. For example, an analysis of an 8-year-old boy with a stealing compulsion extended over an eight-month period, with frequent interviews. The symptoms disappeared and the boy seemed to be making a normal family and social adjustment. Nevertheless the therapist concludes, "It can by no means be regarded as an analysis since only a fraction of the psychic material had been thoroughly worked through." [5]

A second difference in the interpretive process is that the interpretation is not usually made on the simplest basis which will explain the facts but is made in terms of a preconceived ideology, frequently unverified, sometimes fantastic. In any interpretive therapy there is a risk that the individual bias and the preconceived notions of the therapist will influence the interpretation which is made. Ordinarily the worker will try to keep this tendency at a minimum. Psychoanalysis, however, makes the belief of a particular school of thought the *sine qua non* of interpretation, thus emphasizing rather than minimizing this tendency. Likewise in interpretive therapy there is a risk of going beyond the facts and getting into realms of speculation. In the cases of John or Robert, previously cited, their behavior goes back to conditioning experiences rather clearly and closely associated with present behavior. With John his early experiences of being overindulged are adequate explanations of his tantrums. With Robert the traumatic sex experience at eleven sets the pattern of his later behavior. Such interpretations remain close to known facts. When children's problems are interpreted, however, in terms of fears of castration or desires to kill the father and possess the mother, such interpretations would need to be backed by careful links of objective evidence in order to have any scientific standing whatsoever. Where child analysis traces a behavior difficulty back to a definitely conditioning experience, it appears to be

[5] Levy, Estelle. "Psychoanalytic Treatment of a Child with a Stealing Compulsion," *American Journal of Orthopsychiatry*, vol. 4 (January, 1934), p. 22.

on more valid ground. Too often, however, experiences are interpreted in terms of unverified ideology rather than as simple facts. An example may make this plain.

In the account of the analysis of 8-year-old Peter, a lad with a stealing compulsion, there are occasions when the boy produces boastful fantasies about overcoming his parents, hitting his father, and the like. Throughout an extended presentation of the analysis there is no clear indication that the boy knew of the fact of sexual intercourse. There is not the slightest indication that threats of genital injury had ever been made to him by anyone. Yet in interpreting the case the author thus proceeds from the factual to the speculative. "The cause of Peter's asocial conduct was by now fairly well defined. The analysis of his fantasies disclosed two determining elements: the first was the wish to be great and powerful like his father, and the second was the wish to take his father's place with his mother. At first, we could see nothing but the wish to reverse the position of father and son, but as the fantasies grew bolder and revealed more of their content, we could see that he also wished to gain the relationship with his mother that his father enjoyed.

"It was natural that this wish to depose his father should awaken in him the fear of his father's wrath, the castration fear. To cover this, he stressed the opposite reactions by resorting to boasting and exaggerating. His stealing, and his fantasies of revolt and vengeance against all persons in authority, also sprung from the same source." Later in summarizing the case the analyst states, "Peter's analysis showed very clearly the rôle the castration wish and the penis envy played with him. . . . There is no doubt that his stealing had its basis in his castration complex." [6] This type of interpretation based not on the revealed data, but on a preconceived theoretical psychology, is typical of child analysis.

Some Distortions. Because of the fact that the analyst approaches the child with fixed general notions of the probable

[6] Levy, Estelle, *op. cit.*, pp. 17–18, 21–22.

causation of his behavior, he tends very definitely to influence the type of information given by the child. To some extent this too is a risk involved in all therapy. The child tends to talk in ways which he thinks are appropriate with this person. Such a tendency must be guarded against rather than emphasized, as is often the case in analysis.

This trend is clearly indicated several times in an account of a child analysis given by Steff Bornstein. The presentation of the case is of especial interest because it gives in more than usual detail the analyst's part in the process. The subject was a 3-year-old boy who had developed the practice of retaining his stool for two or three days before permitting defecation to take place, and then showing great terror during the experience. In the initial interviews the child gives an indication that his fears have some connection with a bedpan, and eventually it was found that a traumatic experience had occurred in connection with the bedpan. The analyst, no doubt wisely, does not immediately try to find out the reason for the fear of this object. He does, however, definitely determine the trend of the conversation in various ways, such as getting the boy to draw naked figures. "It must be admitted that I seduced the child to speak of sexual things by giving him the idea that one can draw a boy naked.... Such small provocations may be undertaken by an experienced child-analyst; they speed up the work in the beginning." During the third interview the child remarks that he would like to have "a tummy as big as a tree," that "bad men cut the trees down," and later, drawing a boy, states, "He has a peepee as big as a tree." On the basis of this real interpretation begins, and again it is the therapist who takes the lead, rather than basing his interpretation on observed or expressed attitudes. "Then I gave him the first purely analytical interpretation. I drew conclusions from the connection of associations in this hour about something in him that was pressing to become conscious but to which he could not give clear expression. I said, 'You want to have a peepee as long as a tree. But you say that the park keeper who looks out for the trees is cross and that bad men cut trees down.

Perhaps you think that a peepee can be cut down like a tree?'
I avoided intentionally saying more clearly that there might be
a causal relationship between his fear of the guard and his desire
for a large penis." [7]

This type of process in which the direction of the interviews
is determined by the therapist's suggestion, and in which the
interpretation of the material so produced is based on the therapist's convictions rather than the child's statements, is not to
be condoned.   Such procedures would utterly destroy any hope
of making therapy more scientific.   With such methods, all the
subjective elements of the process are magnified, and those elements which might produce objective information are dis-
torted.   Its end result is to give us a very clear picture of what
is in the therapist's mind, but it only confuses the question as
to what attitudes and ideas the child really holds.

Transference.   The use which the analyst makes of the transference, or the emotional bond between the analyst and child,
seems to be somewhat less stressed in child analysis than in
working with adults.   Essentially, however, the analyst expects
the child during the earlier stages of the analysis to use him symbolically as an object of emotion, reacting toward the analyst
as he has reacted in the past to parents, siblings, or others.   The
child may become very dependent, or may show violent resentment and hostility toward the therapist.   The aim of treatment
is to free the child from this very close emotional bond, leaving
him capable of selecting other love objects.   It is not surprising
that this deep bond, extending over a long period, should make
child analysis difficult.   It generally constitutes a threat to
the parents, who feel their own place being usurped, and many
analyses are broken because parents will no longer co-operate.
This may be true even when the probable situation has been
carefully explained to them in advance.   Lippman discusses
several of these technical difficulties which stand in the way of
a satisfactory child analysis, and warns of the careful preparation of child and family which must first be made.

[7] Bornstein, Steff.   "A Child Analysis," *Psychoanalytic Quarterly*, vol. 4 (January,
1935), pp. 202, 205.

The Results of Psychoanalytic Treatment.   Unfortunately psychoanalysts have not favored the investigation of their methods by evaluative research.   Consequently there is no study of any kind in regard to the results of such treatment in children's cases.   One such study of the results of the analyses of 33 adults has been published by Kessel and Hyman.[8]   Of this small group of cases 5 had been specifically "cured" by the treatment, 6 were "cured" by a combination of environmental changes and analysis, 8 were modified to some extent, and 14 were left the same or worse, the last category including 1 suicide and 6 who developed serious mental disorders.   Since this was a group of patients referred to analysts by physicians, they presented serious problems at the outset, and the 43 per cent of failures may be due to this fact.   Nevertheless the small proportion of cases in which a satisfactory adjustment was reached is not such as to induce great confidence in a method which has the disadvantages of being exceedingly costly and time-consuming.   Whether the results would be any better in children's cases we have no means of ascertaining.

One possible reason for the generally disappointing proportion of successes in analytic treatment deserves attention.   Analysts have conceived their notion of treatment so narrowly that they have neglected every type of therapy except that which develops insight.   While they are often successful in this primary goal, the individual fails to make any satisfactory general adjustment, because of the therapist's failure to recognize any reality outside of the patient's emotional life.   Intellectual retardation, unsatisfactory family conditions, unwholesome social factors are often overlooked entirely.   The need of more than this narrow viewpoint is affirmed by two eminent psychiatrists, Dr. Healy and Dr. Alexander, who have endeavored to treat delinquents by means of psychoanalysis.   These experiments have been much more successful in revealing interesting and probably causative traumatic experiences and mental con-

---

[8] Kessel, Leo, and Hyman, Harold T.   "The Value of Psychoanalysis as a Therapeutic Procedure," *Journal of the American Medical Association*, vol. 101 (1933), pp. 1612–1615.

flicts than they have been in effecting normal adjustment.   Dr. Healy comments as follows:

> One might say that it is all very well to help an offender work through his inner conflicts, but such an individual needs also new environmental associations to help him stabilize.   One cannot expect good results, even after analysis, by placing a man in jeopardy.   The released offender is not only handicapped economically but also by reason of his reputation.   Nor would I leave out of account the simple psychology of habit-formation. In such cases as these we are considering, habit-formation can be thought of sometimes in terms of acquired criminalistic skills. The individual is prone to receive suggestions from many contacts which offer him renewed opportunities to use these skills.   Under such stress these are matters that have to be considered whether the individual has been psychoanalyzed or not.   I must admit that we see little hope for treatment even by psychoanalysis unless we have better social and economic adjuvants.[9]

It is probably safe to conclude that as a means of therapy in children's problems a complete psychoanalysis is primarily an experimental procedure.   If it is objectively conducted it will add much to our stock of information about the inner life of the child.   If used in connection with other types of therapy it may be very significant and successful, giving the child inner freedom and insight, while external opportunities are provided for normal adjustment.   The type of child most suited to analysis might be difficult to define.   Primarily, however, it is a process which should only be considered for the child of normal intelligence, with serious patterns of stereotyped or compulsive behavior which seem to have their basis in mental conflict. Because it is expensive in time and money it cannot be widely used.   It goes without saying that analysis should not be attempted save by those with thorough psychological training and acquaintance with analytical procedures, the latter being gained preferably through having been analyzed.

[9] Healy, William.   "Psychoanalysis of Older Offenders," *American Journal of Ortho-psychiatry*, vol. 5 (January, 1935), pp. 27-28.

See also, Alexander, Franz, and Healy, William.   *Roots of Crime: Psychoanalytic Studies*.   New York: Alfred A. Knopf, 1935.   305 pp.

THERAPY THROUGH A CONTROLLED RELATIONSHIP

In a previous chapter (VII) some attempt was made at defining the treatment approach which is known as relationship therapy. This process is similar in a number of ways to psychoanalysis, or more exactly to Freudian psychoanalysis, but differs significantly from it in one respect especially. It places its major emphasis on the curative power of the emotional relationship itself rather than on any insight gained by the individual through the interpretation of his past experiences. Of the two elements which have been mentioned as characteristic of deeper therapy, Freudian analysis may be said to stress insight and interpretation, relationship therapy the emotional situation which grows up between therapist and child. What this emotional situation is we shall try to define more closely. Before attempting this, it may be well to picture the process which goes on in such therapy.

Besides the two cases given quite fully in Dr. Taft's book, case records have been published by Dr. Allen and others illustrating this type of treatment.[10] These records will repay careful reading. A much briefer presentation of a case is made by Catherine Gould, and is here cited.[11] One of the outstanding elements of this, as of other cases coming under this category, is the undirected flow of the child's interest, and the attention which is paid to emotional reactions between child and therapist, rather than to the content of the youngster's verbal productions.

The Case of Edward. Edward, the child whose treatment Mrs. Gould describes, had been a problem to the school from the time he entered kindergarten. Hyperactive to an extreme

---

[10] See the following references: Taft, Jessie. *The Dynamics of Therapy.* New York: The Macmillan Company, 1933.

"1934 Symposium." *American Journal of Orthopsychiatry*, vol. 4 (January, 1934), pp. 323–358. Case presented by Dr. Frederick Allen.

Blanchard, Phyllis. "1937 Case for Symposium," *American Journal of Orthopsychiatry*, vol. 7 (July, 1937), pp. 383–422.

[11] Gould, Catherine A. "Case Illustrating the Use of Direct Personal or Psychological Treatment," *Visiting Teacher Bulletin*, vol. 12 (April, 1937), pp. 11–16.

degree, he was very difficult to control. He was working far below his mental ability in school. If he was punished for misbehavior he would defiantly repeat it. If the teacher praised his work or tried to show him affection, Edward would tear up the work or attack the teacher. By the age of ten he had a far-reaching reputation.

At home he was the middle one of three children, with an older sister who was "good" and a baby brother whom Edward had bitterly resented. The parents each had their own emotional problems, and showed Edward relatively little affection, though it was the social worker's judgment that they would accept him much more if he conformed. Yet five years of treatment directed toward modifying Edward's home and school environment had failed to achieve conformity, and for a time he was excluded from school. When he returned to the fourth grade in the fall, the worker initiated treatment which has many of the elements of relationship therapy. The account continues in Mrs. Gould's words.

> The visiting teacher arranged interviews with E. twice a week for half-hour periods. He was encouraged to express his real feelings and was limited in his activity only by the time limit of the interviews and by the necessity of refraining from damage to property in the room and to the person of the visiting teacher. No matter how hostile and aggressive were his feelings, they were accepted as well as his positive ones, and interpreted to him. He was not led to feel that the visiting teacher wished him to modify his school behavior.
>
> During the first interviews he was sullen, suspicious, and uncommunicative. Then followed a period when he was apparently testing the new relationship with the visiting teacher, to find how secure he might be with her. During this period his behavior in school became modified, although he was still unable to put forth any effort academically. His contacts with the visiting teacher were rather superficially friendly but little material of analytic value was brought out. As he became more secure in the visiting-teacher relationship, he began to express more and more open and violent aggression. The situation was intensified because of the visiting teacher's carrying on treatment simultaneously with another child in his room, Daniel Allen, who happened to have the same name as his younger brother. The climax of his expres-

sion of hostility toward the visiting teacher came in the third month of treatment:

> ... E. began making faces and guttural noises. "You're the dumbest cluck I ever saw," he said. V. T. said it must make him mad for other children to come to her office. He began a train of rapid talk — something about locking Daniel Allen in the gym at the "Y"; then he went into pantomime, pretending to draw a gun, saying, "Stick 'em up," ... There were many noises and then, "I don't care if I yell — I'll get you fired, and then you can't bring other kids down." V. T. said, "It does make you mad for other kids to come down, doesn't it?" The play grew wilder, he picked up a box, saying, "I'll bump this over your head." There were many noises, twisting of his face, and then aiming at the wall, "Bing-bing, now you're dead." V. T. interpreted that she could see that he had pretended to kill her but that sometimes he liked her too. ...

In this excerpt from the interview we of course see E. expressing his inability to share the visiting teacher with other children just as in the home situation he was unable to share the mother with his siblings. In an interview a few days later he was physically ill on discovering that the visiting teacher was married and was helped to express his rivalry and resentment that he had to share her interest with a father-person, just as he had to share his mother with his father. This interview occurred the day before the Christmas holidays. In the next interview after expressing these feelings he was able to work through to an expression of his positive feelings also:

> ... V. T. talked with him about the times before the vacation, saying that he must have been very mad with her and that she knew how he felt. E. began fussing with the file and said, "The only one I like is only you; they've had a lot of sissies around here." V. T. accepted this. ...

During the interviews that followed E.'s expressions of hostility did recur but were never so violent. He many times gave evidence of trying to extend the limits set in the beginning of the treatment situation by coming down when he had not been given an appointment or by trying to change his appointment to a time which he knew had been given to Daniel; he often showed extreme resistance to leaving. He threatened to "rant and rant" when V. T. refused to let him play with the telephone, but left it alone after V. T. told him to go ahead and "rant."

Following this there were further interviews in which he expressed more openly his hostility toward his small brother, and toward a new principal.

During the last two months of treatment E. showed increasing interest in his school work and increasingly less antisocial behavior. He showed greater ability to share the visiting teacher with other children and once or twice forgot an appointment because of interest in some work in his classroom. He worked up a flourishing magazine route and developed many recreational interests outside of school. He got much satisfaction from his "Y" membership and undertook several carpentering projects with his father and also independently at home. He began to speak of several children as his "friends." By the spring holidays he was able to accept the termination of treatment and regular interviews were discontinued, seven months after they had been started. In May he dropped in to tell the visiting teacher that he had gotten satisfactory marks on his report card. This year he is not considered a school problem in any way and evidence of adjustment outside of school continues good. His parents now express a great deal of pride in him. Although he drops in occasionally to sell a magazine to the visiting teacher, he expresses no need nor desire to come back for regular interviews.

The Basis of Effective Relationship Therapy. A careful reading of this case will reveal some of the ways in which relationship therapy differs most significantly from psychoanalysis. In the first place it deals entirely with present situations, and makes no attempt to interpret or explain past reactions. Furthermore, it is not only present feelings and reactions, but primarily those feelings which center on the worker, which are the core of the process. The child's suspicion of the visiting teacher, his ambivalent responses of hatred and love, his desire to be the sole object of her interest, his gradual acceptance of the fact that he may get satisfaction from the relationship, but must share the worker with others, these are the changing attitudes which spell progress. In no other type of treatment effort does the emotional situation between therapist and child occupy such a place of central prominence. We see new reason for its being called "relationship" therapy.

We have spoken before of the quality of this interaction of personalities. It is briefly described by Dr. Allen in these terms:

I am providing an opportunity for this child to experience himself in a new and present relation, and in terms of the present and not in the past. I am in a position to deal with the feeling the child expresses toward me. I can understand his struggle to control without giving in. I can understand his need to dislike me without threatening him with my own dislike. He can be friendly without being engulfed by my friendliness. I can help him to experience these feelings as his own with less anxiety, and enable him to resume growth with less anxiety and denial. In this experience I do not protect him from his own feelings, nor do I provide an opportunity for him to gratify them. He can dislike me but he can't attack me; he can love me but he can't fondle me. The feeling has to be accepted as arising from his own internal environment, and not as a result of the things I say or do to him.[12]

It is the faith of those who have used this process that the changes in the child's acceptance of himself and of reality, which take place in this relationship, are effective in other situations. The fact that Edward learns to share the visiting teacher with other children is presumed to make it easier for him to share his parents with his younger brother. The fact that he learns to experience freely both the satisfying elements and the limitations of the relationship with the worker makes it easier for him to accept in similar fashion his relationships with his teacher and with other children. He has learned, for the present, how to live deeply with another person, and to accept his positive and negative feelings toward that individual. Hence, proponents of such therapy would say, he has learned to live more constructively with any individual.

Such is the basis on which relationship therapy rests. Although not specifically stated by those who have written of it, its effectiveness depends primarily on the psychological phenomenon known as "transfer of training." Because the child has learned to live successfully in one segment of his experience, the treatment relationship, it is expected that he can adapt himself more successfully in other segments of his life. The fact that this has worked out well in some cases such as Edward's makes it imperative to investigate further the basis of such

[12] Allen, Frederick H. "Therapeutic Work with Children." *American Journal of Orthopsychiatry*, vol. 4 (April, 1934), p. 197.

therapy. In the intellectual realm "transfer of training" has been found to be rather disappointing. The development of accuracy in mathematics has not been found to make the individual an accurate thinker. The discipline of Latin grammar has failed to produce a logical mind. Yet possibly in this realm of emotional experience, the findings may take a different trend. Transfer of training is facilitated when there are many common elements between the two situations. Thus training in Latin does facilitate the learning of French. Hence in the emotional realm, it may be that because there is much that is common to our relationship with mother and teacher, father and employer, sibling and colleague, a satisfactory acceptance of one human relationship may be effective in others as well. More exploration is sorely needed.

Some Other Characteristics. Whatever the final answer as to the broader effects of the therapeutic relationship, there are other aspects of this way of dealing with children which claim our attention. One is the healthy sense of the limitations of treatment which seems to be implied. There is no notion that the child is completely reorganized through such a process. He has accepted the help which he needed at this point, and has become, if therapy has been successful, more able to face and solve his present problems. He has been helped on the road to maturity. It is a recognized possibility, however, that he may at a later date require more help if overwhelmed by new problems. There is none of the theoretical assumption, so frequent in psychoanalytical literature, that an individual may gain complete insight, be permanently integrated, and solve all his problems. The viewpoint of relationship therapy seems more realistic and has the more comfortable goal of restoring the individual to normal functioning, setting him one step forward on the road of growth, and leaving him capable, for the present, of handling his own problems.

A fresh and stimulating emphasis on the integrity of the child as a significant entity is characteristic of this approach. The aim is to encourage the child's separateness, his realization of himself as an individual, and the acceptance of responsibility for himself. The process by which this is brought about is well described by Dr. Taft in a statement which would apply to Edward, although it is made with reference to another child. "Because I do not fight Helen back, do not try to conquer her but see and admit the nature even of the negative feelings which naturally arise when her efforts to conquer me come to naught, she is forced for lack of anything to oppose, to fall back upon other aspects of herself, and slowly, with many denials, withdrawals, and negative interludes, she begins to project the positive will, the possessive attitudes." [13] It is at this point that therapy definitely makes for the growth of a more responsible individual.

A point which is evident even in the brief case of Edward, and which is a necessary concomitant of this type of relationship, is the therapist's determination not to impose himself on the child. There is no attempt to get the child to conform, to give up his behavior symptoms, nor to recreate the child according to the therapist's ideal. He is left free to choose his own goal, and the purpose of therapy is to allow him to select it in a more genuine, less anxious, inhibited, or aggressive fashion. The child is to make use of the relationship to the extent that he is able, but the therapist has a strong sense of his own limitations and will not try to "make over" the child in any mold.

A Comparison with Psychoanalysis. Looking at the case of Edward from the point of view of method, it will have been noted that there is nothing in the way of interpretive therapy as we have previously described it. No attempt is made to have the child understand his past reactions. There is, to be sure, some clarification of his present feelings for the therapist, but this is a different sort of interpretation. The therapist is anxious for the child to realize, feel, and accept all his hostile and friendly attitudes as they come, and to aid in this he clarifies and points these attitudes out to him. As Dr. Taft says, "In fact there really is no intellectualized interpretation at all

[13] Taft, Jessie, *op. cit.*, p. 100. By permission of The Macmillan Company, publishers.

(nor would there be with an adult from my point of view) beyond my constant effort to comprehend and respond overtly to the salient feelings and impulses of the hour as present living realities, which a child, like an adult, usually seeks to deny consciously." [14] This of course represents a viewpoint very different from that of the orthodox child-analyst.

Another point at which relationship therapy differs sharply from psychoanalysis is the degree to which theoretical ideology is kept in the background. The whole attempt is to sense accurately the feelings of the child in real, not preconceived, terms. Consequently, although relationship therapy has its theoretical basis in the thinking of Otto Rank, it has in large measure become a process rather than a system of thought, and its use is not dependent upon agreement with Rank's formulation of psychology. A therapist may quite successfully deal with children on this basis without any clear understanding of Rank's basic views regarding the birth trauma or the positive will. Indeed it may be said that the only Rankian notions which are implicit in relationship therapy are principles of the therapeutic process, rather than any theories of psychology. Hence, the obtrusion of doubtfully validated theory into the treatment situation is in large measure eliminated.

The Usefulness of Relationship Therapy. To a greater degree than almost any other treatment means we have discussed, the use of relationship therapy depends upon a certain viewpoint and philosophy in regard to others. It cannot therefore be picked up or laid down as a mechanical tool of treatment. To some workers and clinicians it could never be a congenial approach. To others it represents a mode of treatment which holds real possibilities. Even to this latter group, however, it is not an approach which may be used in every case. Like psychoanalysis, it is a relatively slow process, and not to be entered lightly. Hence we may regard it as of most probable usefulness in cases where environmental therapy has already proved futile, and where the child's problems seem to arise from inner

[14] Taft, Jessie, *op. cit.*, p. 94. By permission of The Macmillan Company, publishers.

tension rather than from any external factors. In an exact sense, relationship therapy is not now used with any large proportion of children's cases, nor is it ever likely to be. Although its underlying principles may influence much of the clinician's work, its use as a specific, intensive, therapeutic approach will be limited to serious personality problems. At the present time it seems impossible to lay down any principles even as to the choice of parent or child as the subject for such treatment. The degree to which a need is felt for help and the degree of the child's independence from his parent will probably influence the choice.

It may be remarked that while a therapeutic relationship is not to be lightly entered into, yet it is a process with fewer risks of damage to the child than psychoanalysis or other types of interpretive therapy. That it can be badly misused, however, is evident from the fact that some social workers have endeavored to "do nothing" in the process because of their misunderstanding of the term "passive," and that others, under the same misconception, have permitted children to do them bodily harm in the "therapeutic" relationship! Consequently the need for thorough understanding of the principles of such therapy, and the need for adequate supervision by an experienced counselor, must be stressed.

OTHER FORMS OF DEEP THERAPY

To some extent treatment, especially of the more intensive variety, is an individual thing, based on the abilities and idiosyncrasies of the therapist. It is not to be assumed therefore that the classification of deep therapy which has been used would be acceptable to all, nor that it includes all the variations of intensive treatment.[15] There is indeed one other mode of

[15] Some readers may be puzzled by the fact that while there is a discussion of Freudian analysis and Rankian therapy, there is no mention of the contributions of Alfred Adler to our treatment techniques. Adler has had a very important influence on clinical work with children, particularly in the realm of diagnosis, but also in therapy. Because he has had very wide acceptance, his thinking has been absorbed in such a variety of ways that it is quite impossible to draw any line to delimit the area in which he has affected clinical work. He has not set up any separate school of thought in regard to treatment, which only means, as someone has remarked, that the imperfections in his theories and techniques tend to be eliminated rather than perpetuated.

therapy which, although it has no specific name nor theoretical background, is encountered with sufficient frequency, and is so often successful that it deserves comment.

Some psychiatrists and psychologists begin a process of intensive treatment by consciously building up the closest sort of personal attachment between the child and themselves. It is a less objective relationship than we observe in either psychoanalysis or relationship therapy. It savors much more of a parent-child relationship. The therapist may have the child visit his home frequently, or even, in some cases, take the child to live with him temporarily. A usual result is that the therapist definitely becomes the parent-person and may become rather biased and defensive where the child is concerned, exhibiting a profound faith in the child's good qualities and in the degree of his improvement. He endeavors to alter the child's behavior through suggestions and personal influence, much as a parent might do.

Perhaps the only significant way in which this type of treatment differs from a genuine parent-child relationship, or from the naïve attempts of lay counselors, is that the therapist's belief and trust in the child is not allowed to fail because of lapses on the part of the youngster. Recurrence of behavior and personality difficulties is expected, and the child is made to feel that, in spite of anything he may do, he will still be trusted and will still occupy his place in the affection of the therapist.

It goes without saying that many individuals would be personally incapable of carrying on this sort of treatment. It is obvious too that very few children can be thus "adopted," even temporarily, by the therapist. Yet there is also no question that this substitute parent relationship can effect the most profound changes in the life of a child. He is given the satisfaction of a very understanding parent relationship in place of the usually turbulent and unsatisfactory past experience with parents. He is guided and helped, influenced and educated into more normal ways of reacting to life. The author has observed children, with a very dubious prognosis, enormously altered by such association. Such experiences are an additional commentary on the forces inherent in human relationships.

If we were to endeavor to fit this highly individual form of treatment into the scheme which we have adopted, we would recognize that, to some extent like relationship therapy, it rests primarily on the deepest sort of rapport. Unlike relationship therapy however, the clinician assumes in the most complete fashion the responsibility for, and the direction of, the child's life. It is consequently a mode of therapy full of risks for all concerned, and it assumes an omnipotence on the part of the therapist which can only be justified by the most extreme need on the part of the child.

It may be mentioned in passing that inexperienced counselors, club leaders, teachers, and untrained social workers frequently try to help individuals in very similar fashion, but with very different results. With the best intentions of helping, but with no realization of the emotional situation which will develop, they set about to tie the boy or girl to them with bonds of closest personal friendship. As the child becomes more attached and more dependent, they tend to fear this relationship in which they have entangled themselves. If the child fails to live up to their expectations, they not infrequently turn on him with a savageness of rejection which is only equaled by their former affection for him. Thus a boy's worker took into his home a very difficult adolescent boy, with whom various agencies had failed. By a very close relationship with the boy, and the most extreme use of personal influence, he brought about surprising alterations in the lad's behavior. But when, due to several unfortunate circumstances, the boy temporarily lapsed into his previous delinquencies, stealing a car and driving to another city, the worker turned on him because he had broken his promises, and vowed he would have the boy arrested and given as severe a sentence as possible. It will be seen that this experience might have been a genuinely therapeutic one if the worker had understood his own rôle and had been able to be reasonably objective. It also illustrates the thin dividing line which separates this highly personalized form of treatment from harmful bungling in human lives.

TERMINATING A TREATMENT RELATIONSHIP

Any clinical worker is well aware of the fact that failures in treatment occur as frequently from inability to bring the process to a constructive conclusion, as from any inadequacy of knowledge or skill in initiating treatment. Consequently some attention needs to be given to the termination both of the emotional bonds which grow up in treatment and of the intellectual processes. This applies to all of the forms of deeper therapy which we have described, and to the many intermediate forms which tend to defy classification.

It is in the breaking off of deep rapport with the child that blunders are perhaps most apt to occur. It has been said that any surgeon can open an incision, but to close it leaving the organs functioning properly is a real test of skill. In a very true sense this applies to the therapist's relation to the child.

Ideally, as in the case of Edward, the treatment process should aid the child's adjustment sufficiently so that he may obtain his love satisfactions from his parents, his associates, and other individuals in his normal environment, rather than from the therapist. If this occurs there will be, as there was with Edward, a decreasing need for the therapist's help and a gradual breaking off of the contact, with friendly interest still maintained, but no deep rapport. In such a situation the termination of treatment is decided as much by the child as by the clinician. It is his lessening need which indicates the conclusion of therapy.

Where this ideal process does not or cannot occur in simple fashion, the therapist must plan, in concluding treatment, to transfer the affect which the child has bestowed upon him to others in the child's environment. If the burden of intensive psychotherapy has been carried by the psychiatrist or psychologist, a point may be reached at which the child has sufficient insight to no longer need such intensive help, yet a need for affectional support still persists. The social worker, or a foster mother, or a school adviser or visiting teacher, may then be brought more strongly into the treatment picture and may gradually take over the rôle which has been carried by the clinician. Like other aspects of treatment, this should not be left to chance but should be carefully planned in advance. Often joint interviews in which the child talks with the therapist and with the worker who is to assume this rôle are helpful in effecting the shift. The aim should always be to have the child eventually obtain his emotional satisfactions from persons in his own natural environment, from parents, relatives, foster parents, teachers, or friends, and to make unnecessary his bond to the therapist. If the contact with the therapist is broken abruptly without a gradual substitution of other sources of satisfaction, it may result in real harm to the child.

It is possible that the handling of this relationship may be easier if it has been acknowledged explicitly during the treatment period. Dr. Burling, for example, feels that it is important that the child's attitude of devotion and affection for the therapist should be brought out into the open. He feels that this makes it easier for the child to recognize and accept his own feelings. On the other hand the social worker or other therapist will then be more likely to think of rapport "not as a bond to compel the client to behave as she thinks best, but as a dependency which it is her privilege to help him outgrow." [16]

Insight and Re-education. In discussing the methods of interpretive therapy the need was stressed of repetition, of thorough learning, as a prerequisite to insight. Even this full achievement of self-understanding is not, however, the end of the process. The child needs not only to understand himself, but to be re-educated so that he can develop new patterns of meeting life situations. John, the boy whose experiences opened this chapter, needs not only to see his tantrums and his behavior as childish, but needs to learn ways of being grown up. James, who dreams of his father as a bogeyman, needs not only to recognize and understand his ambivalent fear, but also to learn what qualities his father has that he can respect

---

[16] Burling, Temple., "The Value of Explicit Acknowledgement of the Transference," *American Journal of Orthopsychiatry*, vol. 4 (October, 1934), p. 522.

and love. Robert, with his guilt-ridden compulsion to molest little girls, needs to see himself as sexually infantile, conditioned by an early experience, but he also needs to learn what normal adolescent heterosexual companionships are, and how to promote and enjoy them. In short, insight is only a partial fulfillment of the therapeutic task, and slow re-education is a function for which we must assume equal responsibility. It is not always necessary that the re-education be carried on through interviews with the therapist, since often some other means may be found by which the environment can bring the needed lessons. Again, however, it needs to be carefully included in the treatment plans, and as conscientiously carried out as were the first steps for establishing rapport.

To what extent teaching devices of a more or less mechanical sort may be a help in re-education remains to be investigated. Dr. Sadler urges patients to imagine themselves clearly in new and more mature rôles, daydreaming their actions and plans in these new rôles. He also requests his patients, as has been mentioned, to write a composition telling, among other things, what they plan to do about their problems, thus summarizing for themselves, as it were, their own re-educative process. In this same category would fall the constructive solutions of the puppet dramas described in the previous chapter, in which the solution to the child's emotional problems is dramatized for him. The acting out by the patient, on Dr. Moreno's stage, of the new rôle he is to play is another adaptation of this same notion. It is probable that we shall see new developments in this field of treatment as the full importance of re-education is recognized. Intensive therapy will hold greater promise of success when we have given as much consideration to its conclusion as to its commencement.

THE GOALS OF THERAPY

The more philosophical reader must before now have puzzled over these questions: "Where does treatment lead? What is the purpose of therapy? What is our goal for the child?"

Such interrogation marks belong properly to every chapter in this book, but they seem especially insistent in our consideration of direct therapies. Frequently there seems to be confusion, since some of the treatment procedures described aim toward one goal, others toward another. This confusion is real, and is evident in practice as well as in the literature regarding treatment. Whether fortunately or not, the goals of treatment effort are not decided by the study of techniques, but by the philosophy of the person using them. This is not a dilemma peculiar to work with children's problems. The physician has the same problem. His knowledge of obstetrical techniques is of no help to him in those baffling situations where either the mother or child may be saved but not both. He must settle that question on other grounds than medical skill. The problem of goals is more continually in the foreground, however, in work which deals with the behavior of human beings because of the fact that behavior has so many social implications. What do we wish to accomplish in dealing with the child?

Since we are concerned primarily in this volume with practical methods rather than with theories or philosophies, we shall not endeavor to answer, but merely to raise this question, and point out the two types of answers discernible in clinical work. On the one hand are those who are striving to bring the child and his behavior into conformity with generally accepted standards of conduct. On the whole, much of our work with individuals is primarily motivated by such a goal. We wish to bring about normal behavior in the delinquent, in the social deviate, in the child who is troublesome in school. Until one considers the matter closely or comes in contact with the individual delinquents and deviates, this seems to be a clear-cut and understandable goal. But in regard to the particular child, what is "normal behavior"? Do we expect from the mental defective average behavior, or behavior average for his mentality? Do we expect from the Italian delinquent boy behavior which is average for the city, or behavior which is normal in privileged neighborhoods, or behavior which is average in his own under-privileged cultural and social group? Do we expect of the sixteen-year-old girl sex conduct and attitudes which were "normal" twenty years ago, or conduct which is normal in her own group? And what is, or was, normal in either situation?

Not only from the point of view of the individual is this viewpoint questioned. If we are, in general, endeavoring to adjust children to the social group, must we plead guilty to being defenders of the status quo? Are we accepting society and social norms as being fixed, and insisting that the individual conform to them? There is no doubt that in some instances social work and even clinical work has been used as a means of blocking social progress. Unless the worker with individuals is alive to the significant movements and trends in our present-day culture, he may easily be seduced into upholding some fixed notion of the socio-economic situation. Thus we find that we are under the complex necessity of assisting the continually changing individual to make his adjustment, not to a fixed social norm, but to a society which is also continually changing in its organization, its beliefs, its codes of behavior, and its customs and ideals.

If we turn from these perplexities to find some other goal of treatment which might be more clear-cut, we find a second school of clinical thought which maintains that the goals of therapy are within the individual. The aim to be achieved is the comfort of the child, or the child's happiness, or the child's inner growth, rather than any social goal. Usually it is assumed that the growing or satisfied child is also social, but occasionally someone flatly maintains that the goal is the child's inner growth, whether or not it leads to social adjustment.[17] In general those who expound the deeper forms of therapy are apt to describe their goals in such fashion. Unfortunately this answer solves our problems no more than the other. We live

[17] Such for example is the view of Dr. Taft, who states that "as I see it therapy in the sense of socially desirable behavior can never be the goal of this type of analytic relationship. It is a purely individual affair and can be measured only in terms of its meaning to the person, child or adult; of its value, not for happiness, not for virtue, not for social adjustment, but for growth and development in terms of a purely individual norm." (*Dynamics of Therapy*, p. 109). By permission of The Macmillan Company, publishers.

in a social world, and inner growth and contentment and satisfaction cannot be maintained without a modicum of accommo-
dation to the views of our social group.

All this, however, is a problem for the philosophers and for
each individual to solve.   If one were to judge from observation
of clinical work, it would seem that most of those who work
with children have both of these goals in view.   They wish
both to develop so far as possible the psychological growth of
the individual and his own inner satisfactions, and wish also to
have him show a reasonable conformity to social demands.
It is where these goals conflict, as they occasionally do, that
difficulty arises.   What about the experienced young homosexual, where therapy looking toward normal sex attitudes has
a very dubious outlook?   Shall we decide that his own satisfactions will be best achieved by relieving his feelings of guilt
and allowing him to adjust on a frankly homosexual basis, or
shall we look upon him as a serious social deviate and aim for
conformity?

On one point clinical experience is clear.   Our work cannot
be measured or evaluated save in the degree to which it aids
the individual to fit normally into the group.   It will have been
noted that every study of results, whether of environmental
treatment or interview therapy, is a research in social outcomes.
There is no measure available for possible improvement in the
inner growth or contentment of the individual.   Hence by and
large our work with problem children tends to be judged by its
success in producing socially effective citizens.

This discussion, strictly speaking, is a digression from our
major concern with therapeutic techniques.   Yet it is well to
recognize that each worker with problem children has in mind
some goal of treatment effort.   This is perhaps particularly
true in the deeper forms of therapy.   The more clearly the
therapist has defined that goal, and the more consistently he
holds to it, the more effective will his treatment efforts be.

BIBLIOGRAPHY

Treatment Interviews and Counseling

Allen, Frederick H. "Therapeutic Work with Children," *American Journal of Orthopsychiatry*, vol. 4 (April, 1934), pp. 193–202.

Burling, Temple. "The Value of Explicit Acknowledgement of the Transference," *American Journal of Orthopsychiatry*, vol. 4 (October, 1934), pp. 518–523.

Blanchard, Phyllis. "The Child with Difficulties of Adjustment," chap. 22 in *Handbook of Child Psychology*, ed. by C. Murchison. Worcester, Mass.: Clark University Press, second edition, 1933.

Elliott, H. S., and Elliott, G. L. *Solving Personal Problems*, chaps. 11–14 incl. New York: Henry Holt and Company, 1936.

Hart, Bernard. *Psychopathology*, pp. 125–153. Cambridge University Press, 1927.

Hartwell, Samuel W. *Fifty-five Bad Boys*. New York: Alfred A. Knopf, 1931. 359 p.

Lippman, H. S. "Direct Treatment Work with Children," *American Journal of Orthopsychiatry*, vol. 4 (July, 1934), pp. 374–381.

Lowrey, Lawson G. "Treatment of Behavior Problems: Some Illustrations of Variations in Treatment Approach," *American Journal of Orthopsychiatry*, vol. 4 (January, 1934), pp. 120–137.

Potter, Howard W. "Psychotherapy in Children," *Psychiatric Quarterly*, vol. 9 (July, 1935), pp. 335–348.

Rosensweig, Saul. "Some Implicit Common Factors in Diverse Methods of Psychotherapy," *American Journal of Orthopsychiatry*, vol. 6 (July, 1936), pp. 412–415.

Sadler, William S. *Theory and Practice of Psychiatry*, Part V. Psychotherapeutics. St. Louis: C. V. Mosby, 1936. 1231 p.

Shaffer, L. S. *The Psychology of Adjustment*, chap. 16. New York: Houghton Mifflin Company, 1936.

Young, Pauline V. *Interviewing in Social Work*, chaps. 15–17 incl. New York: McGraw-Hill Book Company, 1935.

References Dealing Specifically with Relationship Therapy

Blanchard, Phyllis. "1937 case for Symposium," *American Journal of Orthopsychiatry*, vol. 7 (July, 1937), pp. 383–422.

Gould, Catherine A. "Case Illustrating the Use of Direct Personal or Psychological Treatment," *Visiting Teacher Bulletin*, vol. 12 (April, 1937), pp. 11–16.

Rank, Otto. *Will Therapy*. New York: Alfred A. Knopf, 1936. 291 p.

Robinson, Virginia. "Psychoanalytic Contributions to Social Casework Treatment," *Mental Hygiene*, vol. 15 (July, 1931).

Taft, Jessie. *The Dynamics of Therapy*. New York: The Macmillan Company, 1933.

Taft, Jessie. Review of the third volume of Rank's "Tecknik der Psychoanalysis," *Mental Hygiene*, vol. 15 (October, 1931), pp. 845–854.

"1934 Symposium." *American Journal of Orthopsychiatry*, vol. 4 (July, 1934), pp. 323–358. (Presentation of treatment of a case by Dr. Frederick Allen. Discussion by various others.)

Recent References Dealing Specifically with Psychoanalysis of Children

Healy, William. "Psychoanalysis of Older Offenders," *American Journal of Orthopsychiatry*, vol. 4 (January, 1934), pp. 24–30.

Levy, Estelle. "Psychoanalytic Treatment of a Child with a Stealing Compulsion," *American Journal of Orthopsychiatry*, vol. 4 (January, 1934), pp. 1–23.

Lippman, H. S. "Technical Difficulties Encountered in Child Analysis," *American Journal of Orthopsychiatry*, vol. 5 (January, 1935), pp. 27–31.

Psychoanalytic Quarterly, vol. 4 (January, 1935), Child Analysis Number, contains the following articles among others:

Bernfeld, Siegfried. "Psychoanalytic Psychology for the Young Child."

Freud, Anna. "Psychoanalysis and the Training of the Young Child."

Portl, Anni. "Profound Disturbances in the Nutritional and Excretory Habits of a Four and One Half Year Old Boy: Their Analytic Treatment in a School Setting."

Angel, Anny. "From the Analysis of a Bed Wetter."

Bornstein, Steff. "A Child Analysis."

Other Types of Direct Therapy

Bender, L., and Woltmann, A. G. "The Use of Plastic Material as a Psychiatric Approach to Emotional Problems in Children," *American Journal of Orthopsychiatry*, vol. 7 (July, 1937), pp. 283–300.

Bender, L., and Woltmann, A. G. "The Use of Puppet Shows as a Psychotherapeutic Method for Behavior Problems of Children," *American Journal of Orthopsychiatry*, vol. 6 (July, 1936), pp. 341–354.

Despert, J. Louise. "Technical Approaches Used in the Study and Treatment of Emotional Problems in Children," *Psychiatric Quarterly*, vols. 10–12 (October, 1936, to January, 1938). Part references as follows:

Part One. "The Story, a Form of Directed Phantasy" (Howard W. Potter, co-author) vol. 10 (October, 1936), pp. 619–638.

Part Two. "Using a Knife Under Certain Definite Conditions," vol. 11 (January, 1937), pp. 111–130.

Part Three. "Drawing," vol. 11 (April, 1937), pp. 267–294.

Part Four. "Collective Phantasy," vol. 11 (July, 1937), pp. 491–506.

Part Five. "The Playroom," vol. 11 (October, 1937), pp. 677–696.

Part Six. "Correlation of Facts — Evaluation of Methods," vol. 12 (January, 1938), pp. 176–194.

Levy, David M. "Hostility Patterns in Sibling Rivalry Experiments," *American Journal of Orthopsychiatry*, vol. 6 (April, 1936), pp. 183–257.

Levy, David M. "The Use of Play Technic as Experimental Procedure," *American Journal of Orthopsychiatry*, vol. 3 (July, 1933).

Liss, Edward. "Play Techniques in Child Analysis," *American Journal of Orthopsychiatry*, vol. 6 (January, 1936), pp. 17–22.

Murphy, Gardner. "The Mind is a Stage," *Forum*, vol. 97 (May, 1937), pp. 277–280.

CHAPTER XII

Making Treatment Effective

THROUGHOUT the preceding chapters, our consideration has ranged, with but one exception, over all the major forms of effort which are carried on in order to restore unhappy, problem, and delinquent children to a normal place in the community picture. The one exception is the field of medical treatment, which is significant in many cases, of basic importance in some. Since, however, it is the one aspect of treatment which is always carried out by physicians, and since it has been very adequately discussed elsewhere,[1] we have not included it in this volume. In general, however, it may be said of the approaches and techniques which have been described that these are the ways in which clinics, social workers, and counselors are endeavoring at the present time to help children. Some of them are highly subjective, personal modes of help. Others are beginning to assume the status of experimentally validated means of assistance. No apology is needed for their variety and confusion in a field which is professionally so young and in which the need is so much greater than our scientific resources for meeting it.

VARIETY AND SELECTION OF TREATMENT MEASURES

If there is one emphasis which stands out in this presentation it is that treatment, as it is actually carried on, is a tremendously inclusive front, in which one resource or another is marshaled

[1] See, for example, *Child Psychiatry*, by Leo Kanner, chaps. 19–30. Springfield, Ill.: Charles Thomas. 1935. We have found in our own clinic that specific medical suggestions are a part of treatment in 24 per cent of the cases. This figure would vary according to definition of terms, but it suggests the important part such treatment plays.

into service depending on the needs of the particular child-situation. The program of a Scout troop, techniques of increasing parental insight, the guidance of a teacher, the skilled effort of foster parents, the constructive regime of a modern children's institution, the aid of glandular therapy, the resources inherent in long-continued contacts with a sympathetic therapist, all of these, and many more of which they are representative, are the elements which we fit together into the most helpful plan for the individual child. Not only are these elements many and varied, but fair consideration of each grouping finds certain situations in which they are definitely and genuinely helpful. The number and variety of resources upon which it is possible to call is growing rather than decreasing as our understanding of children deepens and becomes more thorough.

It is a necessary corollary of this variety that treatment of a difficult child becomes, whether consciously or not, a selective process, in which we choose those skills, resources, or methods of approach which are most likely to be of help in each case. It is the thesis of this book that as we make that selection more deliberately, more intelligently, with a greater degree of scientific accuracy, the quality and therapeutic results of our work will increase. Our selection must of course be based upon a thorough consideration of the child himself, a consideration of his constitutional make-up, his abilities, the type of behavior he has developed, the attitudes he shows, and the degree of inner tension which he feels. It must also be based upon an intelligent consideration of the child's situation, the attitudes and flexibility of his parents, the community and social situation in which he is living, and the educational demands to which he is subjected.

What Type of Organization? A practical problem growing out of this survey of treatment methods is the question of organization. How shall work for the individual child be organized in such a way as to promote best the intelligent selection and the skilled application of the most appropriate forms of treatment in each case? This is a question which cannot be given any complete answer save in terms of a specific local situation, with adequate consideration of local resources, tradition, and potentialities. There are, however, some general issues which may be raised.

In the first place it might be the aim to set up organizations which within themselves would be prepared to offer the wide variety of help needed by the problem child. This, because of the enormous range of resources involved, is a practical impossibility, although some organizations definitely endeavor to approach this goal. Such an organization is the Alfred Willson Children's Center of Columbus, Ohio, in which a great variety of functions is centered. The child who comes to this agency for help finds the following treatment resources within the Center: medical service, family case-work service, foster-home placement service, recreational groups, a summer camp, and a psychologist who carries on intensive psychotherapy.[2] Only in matters of school adjustment or institutional care do they need to go beyond their own limits. This is indeed an unusual set-up and for the smaller community may offer excellent possibilities, since it has the advantage of close co-ordination of a variety of treatment services without the unwieldy size which would be found if similar services were combined in larger cities.

For the most part, however, the organization of treatment services has not followed, and probably should not follow, such a direction. Ordinarily a special clinical unit is formed, whether in connection with the schools, social agencies, or some other institution, to act as the core or center of treatment work. It is of course also true that such clinical units ordinarily have other important functions. In many instances they are called upon for strategic educational services in the education of parents, teachers, physicians, social workers, or other community groups. They may also have in some instances a group of cases in which their function is purely diagnostic. Such functions also raise pertinent questions of organization, but we shall deal

[2] See chapter 19 of *Preventing Crime*, ed. by Sheldon and Eleanor Glueck, McGraw-Hill Book Company, 1936.

here only with those problems connected with sound organization for the facilitation of effective treatment.

THE SPECIALIZED CLINIC

Since in general the size of the community and the size of the task makes it impossible to concentrate all the treatment functions in one agency, we find that clinical units tend to develop in one of two ways. The first is that the clinic may take on a specialized function, offering only certain forms of treatment service. Thus we find clinical units, under various names and titles, developing in this way when connected with school systems. Only those children are accepted for treatment where the solution of the problem seems to lie largely in the educational realm. All the services of the school are called upon to assist the child, not only such resources as proper placement and curriculum, but also special tutoring, psychotherapy, and recreational resources within the school. If the problem involves largely family or community situations, however, the clinic sends the child elsewhere for help. Its own services are limited to treatment within the school.

Other clinics, among them some of the child-guidance clinics organized independently of other agencies, have specialized in a different manner. Only those cases are accepted in which it seems that the clinic itself, with a minimum of outside aid, can be successful. This means ordinarily that the child and the parents must be of good intelligence, the parents very willing to co-operate with the clinic, and the problem such that there is a strong likelihood that it can be worked out in the family situation. An initial interview is used to determine whether the case is likely to be one which the clinic should accept. If foster care or some other type of treatment outside the scope of the clinic is needed, the case is referred elsewhere.

Another type of specialization is that adopted by the Philadelphia Child Guidance Clinic in which cases, to be accepted for treatment, must be suitable subjects for relationship therapy. This means, primarily, that either the parent or child, or both, must feel a sufficient need for help to make such treatment a possibility. In addition there would doubtless be required certain constructive aspects of the situation sufficient to justify this rather intensive type of therapy. Obviously only a small proportion of those coming to the clinic would fall within this narrow category. Hence many fail to return after an initial contact, and many others are guided to other agencies and organizations for help.[3]

The Results of Specialization. In the instances cited above, those interested in dealing with the individual child have endeavored to meet the problem created by the breadth of treatment resources by offering only a narrowed or specialized type of treatment in any one organization. One result of this is a high degree of proficiency. The school clinic, specializing primarily in educational treatment, develops outstanding skill in this field. The fact that the Philadelphia clinic has especially followed and developed one type of intensive therapy has enabled it to make very significant contributions to our knowledge of treatment. Indeed, one of the main justifications for this type of organization is that it permits of more refined and specialized experimentation in a particular field of therapy.

From the point of view of the children served, this approach has a number of disadvantages. There is first of all the confusion and often disappointment of the client who is turned away. The medical specialist can be reasonably sure of referring a patient who falls outside his specialty to another competent physician. Our resources in the field of behavior problems are not so great, and refusal by one clinic may mean much less satisfactory assistance or no assistance at all.

More important, perhaps, is the inevitable human tendency to overuse the tools with which we are familiar. In spite of the attempt of these clinics to select their cases, we find school treatment as the only field of effort in cases where the parents should

[3] For a more extended discussion of the various criteria which clinics have in the selection of their cases, see Stevenson, George, *Child Guidance Clinics* (Commonwealth Fund, 1933), chap. 7.

be the focus of therapy. We find intensive clinical service being given to the family where foster-home placement would be more wisely utilized. We find psychoanalysis or relationship therapy being used in situations where a simpler form of treatment would be equally or more successful. This situation grows up partly because we tend to apply the techniques with which we are familiar to any situation which arises. It also grows out of the fact that no initial interview, no matter how skillful, can ever foresee the various circumstances or situations which may arise during the course of treatment. Family crises, serious delinquencies, unforeseen neighborhood factors, all have a way of altering in midstream the course which treatment should take, and it is not always considered feasible or wise to transfer the child to another agency in the midst of the treatment process.

It should perhaps be a matter of amusement that, in fields of treatment in which they do not so directly participate, clinicians have been quick to see the fallacies of specialization. From time to time, programs have been proposed or initiated in which juvenile delinquency and misbehavior is to be solved through increased recreational resources and the wider participation of children in group activities. Thoughtful leaders, both in the recreational and clinical field, have realized that such a program has tremendous value, but only if used intelligently as one of several resources. A close parallel exists in the independent child-placing agency. It has been recognized that it is poor community planning to allow such an agency to accept problem children for foster-home treatment on their own initiative. They are almost certain to overuse the foster home as a means of treating all problems. It is preferable that applications for help should be handled by a children's agency with various resources available, such as family case work, foster-home placement, and institution care. The treatment of the child and his family will then be based upon the situation itself, rather than upon the fact that the agency has a certain type of service to offer.

On the whole, then, there is a considerable burden of proof

placed upon the clinical unit which proposes to specialize in certain narrow types of treatment. If other agencies in the community offer other types of treatment, if experimentation and research are major objectives of the work, then such a plan may be justified. Otherwise it has grave weaknesses.

THE CLINIC AS A CENTER OF CO-OPERATION

A second answer or solution to this whole problem is exemplified by those clinics which put themselves in a position to arrange for any needed type of treatment by building up a close and co-operative arrangement with various agencies which offer a variety of services. Thus the clinic itself may be prepared to offer only psychotherapy and intensive case work or therapy with parents. Through co-operation, however, with the child-placing agencies, the schools, children's institutions, and the like, the widest range of treatment may be planned and carried out for a particular child. It is possible that this type of clinical unit is more likely to develop in the city of moderate size where it is obviously impractical to have a number of different clinics offering each a specialized type of treatment. The clinic with which the author is connected is very definitely a clinic of this sort, which may account for some bias in its favor.

In general, such a clinic has a better opportunity of adequately handling the problems of the child, because it feels some assurance at the outset that, whatever the treatment needs of the child, they can be met, the only limitation being the organizational resources of the community. Hence there is less likelihood of stressing one type of treatment rather than another. Every sort of therapeutic help is available, either directly or indirectly, and the clinic tends to act as an organizing center, bringing to a focus on the child and his situation all those elements of community service which can be of help. This is not only an effective method of treatment but serves the added purpose of being as well a stimulus to better community organization. If certain types of therapy are not possible because the community does not have an adequate child-

placing service, or a progressive children's institution, or proper
visiting-teacher service, the clinic can help as much as any other
agency to make these needs felt.

The growth of this co-operative concept has tended to alter
the function and the organization of many clinics which origi-
nally "took over" the child and his problems in order to effect
treatment.   Treatment is instead recognized as something too
broad to be entirely handled in one agency, and an effective
co-operative arrangement with many other agencies is regarded
as necessary.   There has been a gradual growth of child study
and guidance clinics which have their roots in co-operative inter-
agency functioning.

Difficulties in the Way.   The question is fairly raised as to
whether such a clinical unit, in which the possibility of many
sorts of treatment rests on co-operation, can be successful.
Shall the clinic direct all the treatment of cases which come
to its attention, or shall it merely request co-operative service
when it is needed?   Certainly if the co-operation is merely of a
superficial sort, treatment will not be carried out.   The cele-
brated study made by the Gluecks of 1000 juvenile delinquents
studied by the Judge Baker Clinic in Boston in the years 1917–
22 indicated that the mere laying down of a treatment plan is
not enough.   Only in one-fifth of the cases were the clinic
recommendations fully carried out by the court and the community agencies.[4]   Obviously this is a study of co-operation
which does not function.   There is no need of laboring the point
that such inadequate treatment effort is relatively futile.

The solution which the Gluecks propose is that the clinic
should direct the treatment.   This prospect sounds attractive
until we realize that essentially it takes us back to the concept
of a self-contained organization offering all types of treatment.
In the long run the clinic cannot direct the treatment of a case
unless it is willing to take the administrative responsibility for
that treatment, and the moment it does so it has assumed a

---

[4] Glueck, Sheldon, and Glueck, Eleanor. *One Thousand Juvenile Delinquents*, p. 129.
Cambridge: Harvard University Press, 1934.

management task of such proportions that it will entirely over-shadow the legitimate clinical work.

A consideration of all aspects of the problem of organization brings us back rather forcibly to the fact that a clinic which has developed a thoroughgoing co-operation with a variety of agencies offering placement, recreational, institutional, medi-cal, educational, and case-work services has perhaps the most satisfactory set-up, if service to the child is regarded as the criterion. How this co-operation may be made continuously effective is a matter we shall next consider.

The Case Conference as a Means of Promoting Co-operation. In our own experience we have found that the case-conference discussion of the individual child has been an invaluable means of creating and promoting necessary inter-agency co-operation. Unlike the procedure in some clinics, these case conferences are not composed primarily of clinic staff, nor are they dominated by the clinic point of view.   Ideally the conference includes representatives of those organizations, schools, visiting-teacher department, court, or protective agency, which have dealt with the child and know his past experience, and also of those agen-cies which are likely to be dealing with the child in the future. This latter group may be the probation officer, a child-placing agency, a family agency, or a children's institution, depending on the nature of the case. Often it is impossible to foresee even the general direction which the treatment plan may take and hence impossible to include the agencies which will be helping in treatment. In the discussion the clinic staff member acts as a catalytic agent, as it were, to bring out the pertinent experi-ence of each conference member, and also contributes the find-ings of the clinic in regard to the child's abilities and attitudes and the significant patterns evident in his behavior. The major elements which have been shown to be causative in the child's behavior are briefly summarized, in the light of information given. On the basis of this discussion it is usually possible to develop a plan of treatment which will have as its goal the alter-ation of the more crucial causes of difficulty. Whatever type of treatment resource is needed, the group can give or obtain it, and the responsibility for the various aspects of treatment can be allocated.   If the situation is not sufficiently clear to allow such a treatment plan to be made, further diagnostic steps may be planned which will clarify the child's needs, and a later conference, after these steps have been taken, can proceed to plan treatment.

A word might be said as to the atmosphere of these conferences.   At their best they are true discussions, with a give and take, a sharing of various professional viewpoints, which takes the edge off of any individual bias or prejudice.   When such conferences hang upon an authoritative viewpoint expressed by one group or one person, they have lost much of their value. Unfortunately many workers, in this as in any other field, would much prefer the comfortable status of following some authoritative leader, rather than of thinking independently and contributing to the discussion the viewpoint of the case which their own experience and training have given them.   Psychiatrists, because of the prestige of the medical profession, are particularly likely to be forced into this authoritative rôle, and may unwittingly change the conference group into an audience. Occasionally this possibility is intensified by psychiatric social workers whose training has given them rather more of dependence than of self-confidence.   Consequently in planning and conducting such conferences, it should be kept in mind that it is the aim to develop independence of thought and action, not only in the children whom we are trying to help, but in the workers who will be dealing with these and with other children. Rightly managed, such sharing conferences become the best and most practical means of using and strengthening the co-operative relationships, with a wide group of agencies offering a range of treatment services.

Some clinics feel that they have outgrown such conferences. They make the point that treatment begins, consciously or unconsciously, the moment the child or his parent enters the office, and diagnosis continues, if the worker is alert, until the time the case is closed.   Hence the preferred process is to be alive to the various elements in the situation, modifying both diagnosis and treatment as new facts or new responses come to light. From this point of view a conference to plan treatment at any one point seems artificial.

There is much that is valid in this notion, since the incompleteness of diagnosis at any given time and the need for modifying treatment as new circumstances arise are evident. Yet the value of making, at some point, a cross section of the case situation, and of looking at it with regard to its future potentialities, is great. It is of especial value in avoiding gross mistakes and in setting treatment in a direction which is fundamentally correct. All too often a worker who has been proceeding in the more gradual way works conscientiously with the child over a long period of time, when a careful group consideration of the case, viewed from all angles, would have plainly indicated that the father should have been the focus of treatment. Or after faithful months of effort in another case in working with parental attitudes the fact becomes evident, as it would have become earlier from a pooling of information and experience, that the work with the parents is futile, and placement outside of the home is indicated. It is in these major aspects of the general direction of treatment that the co-operative case conference is of special value.

THE RÔLE OF EACH PROFESSIONAL GROUP

Doubtless some readers have been puzzled throughout this book by the lack of rigidly defined lines between the professional groups which may participate in clinical service. Traditionally the guidance clinic for children has been made up of psychiatrist, psychologist, and social worker, with some differentiation between the functions each performs. Briefly stated, the traditional notion was that the social worker investigated the case and carried on the bulk of treatment work with the parents, the psychologist made the psychometric tests and carried on tutoring and a limited amount of psychotherapy with children, and the psychiatrist devoted himself primarily to diagnostic and treatment interviews with the child.

This too rigid differentiation seems to be gradually disappearing in actual work with problem children. In the first place other professional groups have rightly insisted upon their part in the process. The pediatrician, the sociologist, and the recreation worker have been taken on as staff members in some clinics. In the school clinics the counselor with a combination of educational and guidance training is filling an important place.

Furthermore, the old professional lines are becoming less clearly marked. It is still true that in cases involving serious neurotic or pre-psychotic symptoms, or where organic conditions are closely related to the behavior symptoms, the psychiatrist's training makes him the individual most capable of giving assistance. It is likewise true that in situations where the determination of mental abilities, or the diagnosis of educational difficulties, or the understanding of normal child development is important, the psychologist's training makes him the authority. In the field of material and environmental adjustments, in the ability to gather together the pertinent information regarding the individual child, the social worker has training which surpasses the others. Yet a frank examination of the treatment methods actually used with children reveals that few of the procedures fall strictly and definitely within one professional field rather than another. Most of the treatment methods we have discussed fall within a realm where there is much professional overlapping.

The truth of this statement is corroborated by the varying rôle given to the different professions in different clinical organizations. In one well-known clinic we find the traditional procedure with psychiatrist, psychologist, and social worker all limited by rule as to their function. The social worker may not interview the child but deals with the parents, the psychologist carries on largely a psychometric function, the psychiatrist interviews the child. In another clinic, equally well known, social workers, psychologists, and psychiatrists all carry on intensive psychotherapy with children or with parents, as the case may require. The psychiatrists in training are supervised by an experienced social worker. The whole staff is regarded as a group of therapists, with somewhat different emphases in their professional background. In still another clinic the diagnostic and therapeutic work is carried on by psychologists and social workers, with occasional psychiatric consultation on a few cases.

While this may seem confusing, it is also healthy. It indicates primarily that there is no one professional group adequately trained to do an all-round job of diagnosis and therapy with problem children. It indicates that we may be seeing the birth of a new professional group, skilled in dealing with human maladjustments, with training drawn from the fields of medicine, psychology, sociology, social work, and education. Certainly it is fortunate that, during this period of change and development in dealing with children's problems, several professional groups are making their contribution. It will be of interest to watch the further growth of clinical organizations, each developing experimentally in somewhat different directions. It would be a rash prophet who in the light of the present variety in procedure would venture to predict or define the part to be played by any single professional group. At the present time the function of each staff member in treatment will be determined to a considerable extent by his individual experience and aptitude, not solely by his professional label.

THE RESULTS OF PLANNED TREATMENT

At some later date it may be possible to solve some of the questions regarding the most effective organization for treatment by evaluating the results obtained under different policies. At the present time the available material does not allow of such refined analysis. It is possible however to give some general facts in regard to the proportion of successful outcomes in the present-day clinics dealing with difficult children.

The most competent studies of this sort have been made by students of the Smith College School of Social Work, under the direction of Miss Helen Witmer.[5] Thirteen such follow-up

[5] Witmer, Helen M., and students. "The Later Social Adjustment of Problem Children: A Report of Thirteen Follow-up Investigations," *Smith College Studies in Social Work*, vol. 6 (September, 1935), pp. 3–98.

studies, including a variety of clinics, show a rather astonishing similarity of results.   In all, nearly one thousand children were studied and their social adjustment rated after varying periods of one to five years following the clinic contact.   In general it may be said that with delinquent and problem children of varying ages the treatment failed in about twenty-five per cent of the cases, the children showing at the conclusion of the clinic contact the same or more serious problems.   Of the other seventy-five per cent somewhat over half were making a good community adjustment.   The others were in no immediate need of help, but still exhibited some problems and were handicapped to a degree in their adjustment.   When one considers that at the outset of treatment practically all these children were failures in community life, the showing is a very encouraging one.

While material of this type may be over-interpreted, since it is based on rating judgments of only partial validity, there is one comparison which is worth noting.   The three groups of children which seem most comparable in the studies are those referred to the Worcester Child Guidance Clinic, the Judge Baker Guidance Center, and the Boston Psychopathic Hospital.   In each case the children seem roughly comparable as to type of problem (mostly behavior disorders and delinquency), age, home, background, intelligence, and the like.   It is perhaps significant that the Psychopathic Hospital group showed over twice the proportion of failures found in the first two groups. The most likely explanation would seem to be that due to various circumstances the examination of the third group was more superficial, and the treatment less intensive.   Treatment consisted either of psychiatric interviews carried on at the hospital or recommendations which were given to the referring social agency, with no adequate co-operative basis for promoting the fulfillment of these recommendations.   In the first two clinics, which were more specifically organized for children's work, making use of a wider variety of treatment resources, and offering more intensive therapy, the results are very distinctly better.

The only extreme variations from the general picture of clinic results are in the treatment of psychotic or mentally defective children.   In these groups more than half failed to make a successful community adjustment.

An investigation of cases studied in our own clinic tends to corroborate some of the general findings of Miss Witmer's students and to bring out certain other elements.   A follow-up study of 58 consecutive cases, first accepted in January, 1934, was made one year later.   All but 9 of the group were rated as "poor" or "failures" in community adjustment at the time the case was accepted.   At the close of the year, 13 were in institutions where they had been placed as a part of treatment, and their community adjustment cannot be rated.   (It is not made clear in Miss Witmer's study as to what classifications were given in such instances.)   Of the remaining 45, the outcome was unknown in 2 instances, 3 of the group were rated "poor" or "failure," 16 were rated as "fair," and 24 were making an adjustment rated as satisfactory or better.   While not all of these categories are precisely comparable with Miss Witmer's, 40 of the 56 known outcomes are favorable, which is similar to her findings in other clinics.   This study also indicates that it is important to measure not only the final adjustment but also the initial adjustment of the child in order to get any accurate notion of the degree of improvement which has been brought about through treatment.

Another aspect of the situation which was investigated was the relationship between the degree of improvement and the extent to which the treatment plan was carried through.   The treatment plan in each case developed out of a planning conference of the sort described above.   The method of investigating this question and the findings are quoted from the study.

The cases were divided into three groups by a crude measure — those where recommendations were less than one-third carried out, where they were one-third to two-thirds carried out, and where they were better than two-thirds carried out.   The first group was found to have been better adjusted when referred, had made the least average progress, and ended the year with a rating of average adjustment. The second group was less well adjusted when referred, made slightly more progress but ended the year with a rating of below average adjustment. The third group, where recommendations were quite fully carried out, contained the greatest proportion of failures in adjustment, yet made much the greatest degree of progress, and at the end of the year were the best adjusted group. To check this finding further, consideration was given to the nine cases in which the treatment plan was fully carried through. This small group had made the greatest improvement of all, an average improvement of more than two steps on our five point rating scale.[6]

While this study, and most of those made by the Smith College group, involve only a small number of cases, they seem to indicate strongly that planned therapy, seriously undertaken on a co-operative basis with other agencies, is surprisingly effective.

A Fundamental Consideration. A conservative interpretation of the researches to which we have referred would permit the following generalization: The treatment of problem and delinquent children by means of the selective use of a wide variety of therapeutic procedures is effective with three children out of four in restoring them to a moderate community adjustment. There is not in this material any definite proof that one type of organization is more effective in therapy than any other. Such questions must wait for further data.

In planning any effective organization of clinical, counseling, or advisory services for children, this fact must, however, be borne in mind. Whether the clinical unit is located with a school or state hospital, with a university or social agency, as an independent unit or in connection with the juvenile court, the children who come or are brought for help will exhibit similar problems. The roots of these difficulties will show similar ramifications, whether the child is being brought to the court or is a habit problem taken to the university clinic. In order to have the necessary resources the clinic must have roads

---

[6] Rogers, Carl R. "Three Surveys of Treatment Measures Used with Children," *American Journal of Orthopsychiatry*, vol. 7 (January, 1937), p. 56.

open to every sort of therapeutic service, either service which they are ready to offer themselves or which can be obtained through some other source. Unless there is available to the child the whole range of treatment possibilities suggested throughout this book, the child cannot be helped, in the most effective way, to find a path to normal living.

BIBLIOGRAPHY

Glueck, Sheldon, and Glueck, Eleanor. *One Thousand Juvenile Delinquents*, chaps. 8 and 13. Cambridge: Harvard University Press. 1934.

Preventing Crime: A Symposium, ed. by Sheldon and Eleanor Glueck, chap. 18. New York: McGraw-Hill Book Company, 1936. 509 p. "The Worcester, Massachusetts, Child Guidance Clinic" by Samuel W. Hartwell, chap. 19. "The Alfred Willson Children's Center, Columbus, Ohio," by Bertha Fulton.

Stevenson, George S., and Smith, Geddes. *Child Guidance Clinics*. New York: Commonwealth Fund. 1934. 186 p.

Witmer, Helen M., and students. "The Later Social Adjustment of Problem Children: A Report of Thirteen Follow-up Investigations," *Smith College Studies in Social Work*, vol. 6 (September, 1935), pp. 3–98.

Component-Factor Method of Case Analysis

INSTRUCTIONS

The purpose of the blank which accompanies these instructions is to provide a means for objective analysis and diagnosis of the individual's situation, and in addition to assist in the development of a rational plan of treatment. To be of the greatest assistance, the blank should be carefully filled out from the available case history, with frequent reference to the illustrative ratings. Where adequate information is lacking, no more than a tentative rating should be made. It is well to file the completed sheet in the record for later comparison and evaluation.

The steps in the process may be briefly summarized thus:

1. Describe briefly the hereditary facts in the case, reading first the area to be considered under this heading. Enter this description in the appropriate space on the Record Sheet. Then, being guided by the sample ratings make an "x" in the appropriate square on the Summary Diagram at the top of the Record Sheet. Influences extremely destructive to the child's welfare and adjustment are rated −3. Influences ideal for the child's development are rated +3. The o rating indicates the average heredity. Having made the rating on heredity, describe and rate the physical factor, referring to the definition of this area and the illustrative ratings. Continue until all eight factors are briefly described and rated.

2. Going over each factor, consider those elements of it which might be altered, giving special consideration to those factors rating lowest. (Heredity is of course never alterable, mentality rarely so.)

3. Jot down under Treatment Plan the suggestions which seem feasible for altering the situation. These should be couched in realistic, specific terms, not merely as wishful thinking.

4. Considering the effect these treatment measures will have on the child's situation, re-rate each factor on the diagram, adding an

arrow to the x, thus, x——>, to indicate the amount of change to be reasonably expected within a year's time. The number of arrows and their length will give some notion of the extent to which it is possible to change the total situation, and the degree to which the behavior symptoms may be changed.

Rating on Hereditary Factor

Consider the child's strain of inheritance, as evidenced by parents, relatives, siblings; hereditary predispositions to disease; feeblemindedness, epilepsy, or psychoses in the ancestry; evidence of neuroses or physical or emotional instability in the ancestry; marked social inadequacy in the ancestry as shown by chronic alcoholism, repeated jail terms. On the constructive side consider freedom from disease and taints and marked social adequacy.

Illustrative Ratings — Heredity

−3   Both parents feebleminded.

−2   Mother of borderline mentality, father dull, three uncles have jail records. Maternal aunt in State Hospital, diagnosed dementia praecox.

−1   Mother has history of chorea, father alcoholic. Both parents average intelligence. Paternal uncles run a hardware store. One sibling regarded as hyperactive.

o   Parents normal intelligence, sibling dull, no State Hospital or institutional care for family or close relatives. Mother shows a few neurotic tendencies.

+1,⎫ *Both parents healthy, high-school graduates, three siblings
+2 ⎭ making average school progress, grandparents were long-lived farmers.

+3   Parents college graduates, good health. Grandfather a civic leader, uncles are physicians and business men.

Rating on Physical Factors

Consider the child's inherited physical and neurological constitution; his physical development, size and weight in relation to the norm; physical defects, inferiorities, or abnormalities; glandular dysfunction; physical instability, nervousness, hyperactivity; disease history, with special attention to long periods of illness, or diseases such as tuberculosis, epilepsy, encephalitis, venereal disease, chorea; defects of the special senses. On the constructive side consider freedom from illness or defects, superior physique.

* This illustration is rated as being between "+1" and "+2," with clinicians favoring a "+1" rating. Other illustrations with two ratings are to be similarly understood.

Illustrative Ratings — Physical

−3   Convulsions in infancy, petit mal seizures at present time. Frail and underweight. Eye defect requiring glasses.

−2,   Child has club foot which causes slight limp. Usual child-
−1   hood diseases, is restless and hyperactive.

−1,   Twenty pounds overweight but normal height, at age 12.
0   Has had mumps, chickenpox, measles, none seriously. Teeth are very irregular, and misplaced, require straightening.

+1   Infancy normal, usual childhood diseases, no serious sequelae, appendectomy at 10, size and weight normal for age.

+2,   Physical condition good. Above average height and weight
+3   for age. Few illnesses, and those always brief. Seems to resist infection. Physically stable. Athletic type of build.

Rating on Mentality Factor

Consider the child's mental capacities as shown by his development, intelligence-test ratings, school achievement, vocational achievement. Consider special abilities and disabilities which have a bearing on his mental functioning. Consider the quality of his intelligence, alertness, persistence, ability to concentrate.

Illustrative Ratings — Mentality

−3   Clear case of mental defect, low-grade moron.

−2   I.Q. 72; in slow-moving section, responses are slow and labored, attitude dull and apathetic.

0   I.Q. 96, making ordinary school progress, marks are B to D.

+1,   I.Q. 113, does better than average work in shop activities.
+2   Reads popular science magazines intelligently at age 12.

+2   I.Q. 125, doing fair work in academic course.

Rating on Family Influences

Consider the family circle within which the child has developed — the attitudes which have surrounded him. Consider the emotional atmosphere within the home — marital discord or harmony, sibling rivalries, attitudes of domination, over-solicitude, rejection, or normal parental love. Frictions or conflict in regard to illegitimacy or other family irregularity. The child's reaction to the home is also to be considered — reactions toward parents and siblings, toward family standards and discipline. Degree of community of interest with other members of the family.

Illustrative Ratings — Family

−3 Mother quite openly immoral, father a weak individual who plays little part at home except when drunk when there are terrific quarrels. Mother controls children by beatings. They are at least partially aware of her immorality.

−2 Parents not congenial; whole home dominated by father who is rigid, puritanical, and uses excessive discipline. He favors daughter and rejects this boy. Home atmosphere very tense. Mother furtively takes the boy's side.

−1 Father died when child in infancy. Mother centers all her attention and affection on this only child. Mother is extremely over-solicitous and over-indulgent, and has few outside interests.

o This boy is somewhat his father's favorite, and being the oldest child, tends to dominate his younger sibs. Parents are both interested in the home, seem happy together, and have a great deal of affection for their children.

3 Parents are very congenial. Family atmosphere harmonious and pleasant. Many special interests and activities fostered by parents. Children encouraged to develop independence. This child feels very secure in the parental affection.

RATING ON ECONOMIC AND CULTURAL INFLUENCES

Consider the family income, status of father's occupation, social standing in the community, degree of comfort and educative influences within the home; consider the community type — whether delinquency area, residential area, rural area; consider the community standards of behavior and culture; the school, libraries, and recreational resources available.

Illustrative Ratings — Economic and Cultural

−3 Father unemployed, family on relief, home barren, children sleep three in a room. Home is located near the tracks, in a semi-business neighborhood. No conveniences.

−3,⎫
−2 ⎬ Home is foreign — little English spoken. Father a laborer, unemployed, home meagerly supported by earnings of eldest son. Neighborhood is made up of similar homes.

−2,⎫
−1 ⎬ Child lives in isolated farm foster home, on dirt road, mile from district school, few neighbors. Family do not take daily paper, and but one farm magazine. Trips to town are infrequent.

o Father is a carpenter, employed part time. Home is a small bungalow, outskirts of city, on unimproved road. Many vacant lots. Good school.

1 Parents own their own farm, home is comfortable farm home. Family own radio and car. School is a consolidated school with fifty pupils, one-half mile from home.

3 Father a physician, home in good residential area, near playground. Scout troop meets in neighborhood church. Strong PTA group at the school.

RATING ON SOCIAL FACTOR

Consider range and extent of child's social experience; isolation or group contacts; the type of companions available; the social skills the child has achieved considered in relation to his age; experience in group membership and leadership; organizing ability and social initiative; status in the schoolroom group; friendships, with own and opposite sex, considered in relation to age; social relationships with adults; social adjustment to the neighborhood and community; general social maturity or lack of it.

Illustrative Ratings — Social
−3 This child is the sissy of the neighborhood — picked on by other boys, unhappy when with them. At school gets on satisfactorily, is well liked by the teacher, has trouble at recess. Has no real friends but spends most of his free time with sister three years younger.

−2 Child has always been kept from much contact with other children; in a group is shy, backward, cannot play games; has two friends younger than self; gets on easily with adults.

−1 This girl belongs to a YW club, attends irregularly; prefers to stay by herself and read; is a passively accepted individual in the schoolroom; has some companions in the neighborhood but no close friends.

0 Boy 13, belongs to no organized club or gang. He has one chum with whom he goes to movies, builds model planes, etc. Friendly with his school and neighborhood group. Plays on corner lot when urged by the group.

1 Boy 12, enthusiastic Scout, member of his grade team at school, lives in isolated home and has few neighborhood companions, goes to visit one of his Scout friends frequently. Is fair in baseball and swimming.

3 This girl is president of her high-school class, popular at parties, interested in boys, has a girl chum who has been her companion for years; has taken an active part in school athletics.

RATING ON EDUCATION — TRAINING — SUPERVISION

Consider the education, training, and supervision which the child has had outside the home. Ordinarily this will mean primarily his school experience. Consider such things as the type of school which the child has attended; the changes of school; the continuity and consistency of school experience; consistency of discipline, both in school and between home and school; the degree of healthy stimulation, the extent to which tasks have been adapted to ability; the insight shown by teachers and school authorities; the behavior ideals actually inculcated; the co-operation and similarity of viewpoint between home and school.

Illustrative Ratings — Training and Supervision

−3 Boy 14, has been in five schools, of very diverse types, two parochial, two public, one rural. Discipline has ranged from rigid to lenient, work has always been too difficult for him.

−2 Girl 12, kept in 5th grade because of two school changes, but capable of 6th to 7th grade work. Just "gets by" in her work. Parents have had a disagreement with teacher and openly discuss her failings with the child.

−1 Boy of 11, has always attended small country school, meagerly equipped, dominated by stern, browbeating teacher. He is satisfactorily placed in view of his mentality.

  o Girl 10, has always attended this school. Discipline and educational policy are both routine and unimaginative. Work is adapted to this girl's ability, but is presented in rather drab fashion.

  3 This child is in high school. Has always attended a school where teachers are high caliber, and discipline is maintained largely through child's self-discipline in working on challenging projects. High standards of workmanship are self-imposed. Parents are interested in school and take active part in supporting its policies.

Rating on Self-Insight

Consider in relation to the norm for his age, the degree to which the child has or lacks understanding of his own situation and problems; consider such things as defensiveness, inability to admit faults, or tendency to depreciate self and exaggerate faults. Consider not only intellectual understanding of problem, but emotional acceptance of the reality situation. Consider child's planfulness and willingness to take responsibility for self; ability to be objectively self-critical. Consider stability of attitudes — whether erratic and changeable or cautious and settled.

Illustrative Ratings — Insight

−3 This girl blames every one else for her troubles and readily excuses herself. She will not face the fact that her situation is serious, and has a breezy optimism entirely unrelated to reality.

−2, This boy's sex behavior indicates real mental conflict. He
−1 can give a fair verbal account of the cause of his behavior, but
his actions are little influenced.

o This boy has a rather inadequate knowledge of his own assets
and liabilities, he has thought only a little about his own
future; he realizes to some extent the fact that his parents
tend to keep him childish. He shows no serious behavior
problems.

2, Living in a most unhappy home situation, this boy makes
3 calm judgments as to the degree to which he and stepfather
are to blame, and helps make plans for his own future, away
from home, on a carefully reasoned basis.

COMPONENT-FACTOR ANALYSIS

SUMMARY DIAGRAM

Factor	-3	-2	-1	0	$+1$	$+2$	$+3$
Heredity.....							
Physical......							
Mentality....							
Family.......							
Econ-Cultural.							
Social........							
Educ-Training							
Self-Insight...							

x = present situation; $\longrightarrow$ shows expected change with treatment.

RECORD SHEET

Name.........................

Born............Age....Grade...

Behavior Problems...............

....

....

....

....

....

Brief Description (of facts upon which rating is based)

Hereditary	Economic and Cultural
Physical	Social
Mentality	Education-Training
Family	Self-Insight

Brief Descriptive Diagnosis — (stressing interrelationships of factors which may not be apparent in ratings)

Treatment Plan

....

....

....

....

....

....

....

Index

b. following page number indicates reference in bibliography.

Abnormal mentality and personality, and foster-home placement, 81–83
Accomplishment, need for, 11
Achievement
 satisfaction of, 229–230
 techniques of improving, 233–235
Adjustment
 measures of, 20–22
 of parent as factor in changing parental attitudes, 214–216
 aids in social, 240–242
Adolescents, psychotherapy with, 285–286
Affection
 attitude of, in foster homes, 74
 of child as factor in removal from home, 158–159
 parental, 8
Affectional security, in school, 236–240
After care, planned, 129–131
Age
 of child as factor in considering removal from home, 162
 of children in foster homes, 67–70
 of institutional children, 135
 relation of, to success of foster-home care, 86–88
Agency skill, relation of, to foster-home success, 93–95
Aggressive behavior in the school, treatment of, 238–239
Aichhorn, A., 125–127, 146 b.
Alexander, F., 127–128, 146 b., 338
Alfred Willson Children's Center, Columbus, O., 361
Allen, E., 247 b.
Allen, F., 198–199, 220 b., 340, 343–344, 357 b.
Allport, G. W., 18, 38 b.
Amsden, R. L., 275 b.
Anderson, V. V., 247 b.
Angel, A., 358 b.

Apathy, and nutrition, 7
Association tests, 22
Attitudes, family, as a focus of treatment, 179–221
 parental, 179–218
  importance of, 179–184
  means of changing, 184–210
  motives for change, 212–213
  parents' learning ability as factor in changing, 216–217
  parents' own adjustment as factor in, 214–216
  treatability of, 210–218
 parent-child, attempts to alter, 182–184
Attitude therapy, 210
Authority, acceptance of, 244–245

Baker, H. J., 34–37, 38 b., 39 b.
Barker, M. B., 78, 79, 85, 108 b., 150
Bassett, C., 247 b.
Beard, B., 220 b., 227–228, 247 b., 250–251, 253, 256, 275 b.
Beck, S. J., 38 b.
Behavior
 aggressive, in the school, 238–239
 factors that influence, 4–12
 influences of nutrition on, 7
 of child and removal from foster home, 154–156
 school's part in changing, 222–248
 school's resources in changing, 229–246
Behavior factors, Detroit Scale of, 33–35
Behavior patterns
 causes of, 12
 inheritance of, 6
Behavior problems, 5, 40
 institutional placement as treatment for, 109–144

Behavior problems
seriousness of as factor in removal from home, 172-173
Bell, H. M., 22, 38 b.
Bell Adjustment Inventory, 22
Bender, L., 316-318, 358 b.
Bernfield, S., 358 b.
Bernreuter, R. G., 18-19, 38 b.
Blanchard, P., 247 b., 357 b.
Bloodgood, R. S., 145 b.
Body types, 4-5
Bornstein, S., 336-337, 358 b.
Bowler, A. C., 145 b.
Broken home, 8
Bronner, A. F., 115, 146 b., 149
Bronner, E. B., 214-215, 220 b.
Burling, T., 357 b.
Busch, H. M., 275 b.

Campbell, N. M., 224-225, 247 b.
Camps, use of as treatment, 249-275
and the home, 270-272
individual treatment in, 266-268
placement in and intelligence, 261-263
placement in and social skills, 263
placement in and social status, 264
results of treatment in, 272-273
treatment techniques in, 268-270
Case conference, as means of promoting co-operation, 367-369
Case histories
evaluation of as diagnosis, 31-37
disadvantages of, 35-37
Catharsis in therapy, 302-303
Change, environmental, potentialities of, 63-65
Change of environment, extent of as treatment, 148-150
criteria for, 150-153
Changing behavior, school's part in, 222-248
Changing parental attitudes. See Attitudes, parental
Child
initiating, into the group, 257-258
institutional, characteristics of, 134-136
mentally retarded, institutional care for, 137-138
older and institutional placement, 140-141
ordinal position of, in family, 9
removal of, from home, 147-176
removal of, from foster home, 174-175
spoiled, and institutional placement, 138-139

Children
problem, results of group experience for, 252-253
psychoanalysis of, 332-339
suitable for interview therapy, 285-288
Children's Village, The, 139
Character education, 247 b.
Chassel, J. O., 266, 275 b.
Chorea, 7
Clinic
as center of co-operation, 365-369
Clubs, use of as treatment, 249-275
Community protection, and institutional placement, 171-172
Community situation, duplication of in institution, 128-129
Companionship group and behavior, 10, 46
Compensatory behavior, 7
Component-factor method of diagnosis, 40-60
basis of, 40-41
comments on, 56-60
description of, 41-50
example of, 52-56
Cooper, J. M., 145 b.
Co-operation of family, as related to removal of child from home, 161
Cory, Camp, 259, 261-272
Cottage plan in institutions, 128
Craig, E., 146 b.
Criteria, for placement from institution into community, 130
for removal of child from home, 165-168
Cultural influences and behavior, 9-10, 46
rating of, in component-factor method of diagnosis, 46-48

Daydreaming, treatment of in school, 242-243
Deeper therapies, 322-358
interpretive therapy, 322-332
meaning of, 322
other forms of, 348-350
psychoanalysis of children, 332-339
through controlled relationship, 340-348
Deformity, 7
Delinquency and social influence, 9-10
Delinquents
ratings of on performance tests, 136
results of institutional treatment of, 115-118
success of foster-home placement of, 79-81
Despert, J. L., 314, 358 b.

Detroit Scale of Behavior Factors, 33–35
Dexter, E. H., 244, 247 b.
Diagnosis
    descriptive, 50
    levels of, 16–17
    methods of, 16–60
        component-factor method, 40–60
        ego-libido method, 26–31
        personality tests, 24–26
        requirements of, 58–59
        method to use, 59–60
        reasons for using "method," 57–58
Dimock, H. E., 260, 275 b.
Direct education, as means of changing
    parental attitudes, 185–191
Disadvantages of institutional placement,
    131–132
Discipline
    consistency of, in foster homes, 73–74
    effect of, on behavior, 9
Dolls, use of in play therapy, 305–314
Downey Will Temperament Test, 18
Drama, use in therapy, 316–319
Dreams, use in therapy, 325–327
Dudley, V., 71, 73, 75, 105, 108 b.

Economic factor, in diagnosis, 46–48
Economic status and behavior, 10
Education
    direct, as means of changing parental
        attitudes, 185–191
    in diagnosis, 48
    in psychotherapy, 284–285
Educative techniques in psychotherapy,
    288–297
    clarification of issues, 293–295
    facing consequences, 295
    the goal idea, 296–297
    informational methods, 288–293
    usefulness of, 295–297
Ego-libido method of diagnosis, 26–31
    and treatment, 30
    weaknesses of, 30–31
Elliott, G. L., 357 b.
Elliott, H. S., 357 b.
Elliott, M. A., 146 b.
Emotional excitability, relation to body
    acidity, 7
Emotional needs, as factor in changing
    parental attitudes, 185–191, 214–216
Encephalitis, 7
Endocrine glands, 7
Environment, extent of change of, as
    treatment, 148–150

Environmental change, potentialities of,
    63–65
Environmental treatment, place of, 175–
    176
Epilepsy, 7
Epileptic traits and success of foster-home
    placement, 82
Expressive therapies, 302–321
    catharsis, 302–303
    drama, 316–319
    play techniques, 305–316
    values of, 319–321
    ventilation of conflicts, 303–305

Family, attachment to, as related to suc-
    cess of foster-home placement, 91–93
    attachment to, as related to institutional
        placement, 140
    attitudes as a focus of treatment, 179–221
    co-operation as factor in removal of
        child from home, 162
    influence of on behavior, 8–9
    loyalties as factor in removal of child
        from home, 161
    other aspects of treatment within, 218–
        219
    rating in diagnosis, 45–46
    situation as related to removal of child
        from home, 156–158, 160–162
Fenton, J. C., 145 b., 146 b.
Fenton, N., 119, 128, 130, 132, 133–134,
    135, 145 b., 146 b.
Folsom, J. K., 15 b., 220 b.
Foster home, characteristics of, 65–77
    discipline in, 73–74
    economic status of, 71
    intelligence of children in, 67–70, 83–86
    location of, 70
    number of children in, 65
    "own" children in, 105
    parentage of children in, 67–70
    selection of, 101–103
    special advantages of, 66
    type of children in, 67–70
    types of, available, 70–73
Foster-home placement, as treatment, 63–
    108
    abnormal mentality and personality
        and, 81–83
    age as a factor in, 67–70, 86–88
    individual treatment through, 101–105
    institutional placement compared with,
        66
    planning the termination of, 106–107

Foster-home placement
relation of heredity to success of, 88–91
relation to other children in, 104–105
results of, 77–97
seriousness of behavior as related to success of, 79–81
sex-delinquent girls and success of, 78–79
sex misconduct and, 68–70
social agency skill and success of, 93–95
success of, 93–95
stealing problems and, 68
when to use as treatment, 97–101
Foster home, removal of a child from, 174–175
Foster parents
age of, 71
essential qualities in, 73–77
selection of, 103
Freeman, F. N., 78, 83–84, 108 b.
Freud, A., 358 b.

Garrett, A., 210, 220 b.
Gartland, R., 189
Gesell, A., 6
Glands, endocrine, 7
Glandular imbalance, 7
inheritance of, 7
relation to behavior, 7
Glueck, S., and Glueck, E. T., 78, 95, 116, 125, 130, 141–142, 143, 146 b., 148, 250–251, 275 b., 280–281, 366–367, 375 b.
Goal idea, and therapy, 296–297
Goals of therapy, 353–356
Gould, C. A., 340, 343, 357 b.
Group
activities in institutions, 124
placement in suitable, 230–232
Group membership as treatment, 249–275
choice of group, 253–259
experimental use of summer camp as treatment, 259–273
extent used, 250–252
following the child's adjustment, 258–259
initiating the child into the group, 257–258
rearrangement of companionships, 273–274
results of, for problem children, 252–253
therapeutic group, 256–257
Group therapy, 318
Groves, E. R., 247 b.

Growth, limits of, 4
Guilt feelings, reduction of through therapy, 320
Gundlach, C., 85, 108 b.

Haines, A. R., 78, 85, 108 b., 148, 152–153, 168–169, 176 b.
Hart, B., 357 b.
Hartshorne, H., 9, 10, 15 b., 48
Hartwell, S. W., 148, 157, 285, 299, 301–302, 357 b.
Healy, W., 69, 73, 77, 81–83, 84–85, 95–96, 108 b., 115, 127–128, 146 b., 149, 183, 220 b., 250–251, 286, 338–339, 358 b.
Heath, E., 198–200, 220 b.
Hendry, C. E., 275 b.
Heredity
and behavior patterns, 6
and instability, 6
and intelligence, 5
as related to success of foster-home placement, 88–91
rating in diagnosis, 42–43
Hewins, K. P., 108 b.
Hill, A. S., 34, 39 b.
Hixenbaugh, E. R., 181, 220 b.
Home, advisability of removing a child from, 147–176. See Removing a child from home
Home background of institutional children, 134–135
Home, foster. See Foster home
Home situation, duplication of in institution, 128–129
Hopkins, C. D., 78, 85, 108 b., 148, 152, 168, 176 b.
Hudson State School, 119
Hyman, H. T., 338
Hypnosis, 300

Ideals, effect on behavior, 9
Illness, relation to behavior, 7
Independence, development of, 8
part school can play in development of, 243–244
Individualized treatment
in camp, 266–268
in institutions, 119–134
results of, 133–134
in the school, 223–226
teacher's objections to, 246–247
through foster-home care, 101–105
Inferiority, and physical defects, 7

Informational methods in psychotherapy, 288–293
  and children's goals, 290
  and mental conflict, 290–293
Insight
  and re-education, 352–353
  effectiveness of, in interpretive therapy, 331–332
  rating of in component-factor method of diagnosis, 48–50
Instability, and heredity, 6
Institute for Juvenile Research, 69, 78
Institution, placement in, as treatment, 109–146
  and community protection, 171–172
  and foster home, 66
  disadvantages of, 131–132
  duplication of home and community life in, 128–129
  group activities in, 124
  individual approach in, 120–122
  individual treatment in, 119–134
  intelligence of children in, 122
  planned after care of, 129–131
  providing the proper task in, 122–123
  psychotherapy in, 124–128
  regimented treatment in, 111–119
  results of individual treatment in, 133–134
  results of regimented treatment for delinquents in, 115–118
  types of, 111–133
  vocational work in, 122–123
  when to use as treatment, 136–144
Institutional care
  and sex differences, 141–142
  for the mentally retarded child, 137–138
  for the older child, 140–141
  for the spoiled child, 138–139
  when family ties are strong, 140
Institutional child, 134–136
  age of, 135
  home background of, 135
  intelligence of, 135–136
  manual skill of, 136
  physique of, 136
Intelligence
  and behavior, 5
  and camp placement, 261–263
  and heredity and training, 5
  and interview therapy, 285
  as related to success of foster-home placement, 83–86
  effect of foster home on, 83–86

of children in foster homes, 67–70, 78
of institutional children, 122, 135–136
Interaction of forces influencing behavior, 11–12
Interpretive methods of analysis, 333–335
Interpretive therapy, 322–332
  a case of failure of, 327–330
  causes of failure of, 330–331
  effectiveness of insight in, 331–332
  use of dreams in, 325–327
Interpretive treatment in changing parental attitudes, 191–197
  and individual's capacity for acceptance, 195–196
  terminology used, 194–195
Interview therapy. See Psychotherapy
Irgens, E. M., 220 b.
Irritability, relation of nutrition to, 7

Jensen, F., 221 b.
Jones, M. E., 108 b.

Kanner, L., 15 b.
Kenworthy, M., 26, 221 b.
Kessel, L., 338

Laird, D. A., 18, 38 b.
Learning ability of parents as factor in changing parental attitudes, 216–217
  age as factor in, 217
  emotional stability as factor in, 217
  intelligence as factor in, 217
Lee, P., 221 b.
Levine, R., 108 b.
Levy, D. M., 221 b., 305–314, 320, 358 b.
Levy, E., 358 b.
Levy, J., 10
Lieberman, J., 275 b.
Lippman, H. S., 322, 325, 337, 357 b., 358 b.
Liss, E., 358 b.
Lodgen, P., 215–216, 221 b.
Louttit, C. M., 15 b., 248 b.
Lowell, F., 22, 39 b.
Lowrey, L. G., 357 b.
Lowry, F., 211, 214, 220 b.

Making treatment effective, 359–375
Manual skill of delinquent and problem children, 136
Marital friction
  as a factor in removal of a child from home, 160–161

Marital friction
  attempts to alleviate, 181–182
  influence of, on behavior, 8
Markey, O. B., 72, 108 b.
Martens, E. H., 226–227, 248 b.
Mathews, E., 18, 38 b.
May, M. A., 9, 10, 15 b., 48
Mayo, L. W., 145 b.
Mead, M., 15 b.
Measures
  of adjustment, 20–22
  of traits and tendencies, 18–20
Mental conflict, and informational methods in psychotherapy, 290–293
Mental instability and heredity, 6
Mentality
  abnormal, and foster-home placement, 81–83
  rating in diagnosis, 44–45
Mentally retarded child, institutional care of, 137–138
Method of diagnosis, reasons for using, 57–58
Mohr, G., 301
Moore, K., 221 b.
Moore, M. V., 221 b.
Moral laxity in home, as factor in removal of child, 173
Morgan, J. J. B., 248 b.
Morlock, M., 158, 176 b.
Motives, as related to changing parental attitudes, 212–213
Motor behavior, 6
Mowrer, E. R., 181–182, 220 b.
Mowrer, H. R., 181, 182, 191–195, 213, 220b.
Murphy, G., 221 b., 358 b.
Murphy, J. P., 107 b.
Murray, M. E., 145 b., 146 b.
Myerson, A., 6

Need for affection, 11
Needs, of organism, 10–11
Neglect, as factor in removal of child from home, 173–174
Neurotic Inventory, Thurstone, 18
Newell, H. W., 228, 235, 239, 248 b.
Nimkoff, M. F., 220 b.
Noble, H., 72
Nutrition, influence of, on behavior, 7

Objectivity, as qualification of therapist, 281–282
Organic defects, and success of foster-home placement, 83

Organic influences on behavior, 7
Organism, needs of, 10–11
Organization of clinic, 360–371
  clinic as center of co-operation, 365–369
  rôle of professional groups in, 369–371
  the specialized clinic, 362–365
Orphanages, results of treatment in, 118–119
Osborne, E. G., 275 b.

Parents
  adjustment of, as factor in changing parental attitudes, 214–216
  foster, 73–77
  learning ability of, as factor in changing parental attitudes, 216–217
Parent-child attitudes, attempts to alter, 182–184
Parental attitudes. See Attitudes, parental
Parental rejection, 8, 183
Parole, criteria for, 130
Partridge, E. De A., 275 b.
Performance tests, ratings of delinquents on, 136
Personal Attitudes Test, Sweet, 20
Personal influence, use of in therapy, 297–302
  limitations of, 300–301
  usefulness of, 301–302
Personality
  abnormal, and success of foster-home placement, 81–83
  and body-chemistry, 7
  tests, 17
    limitations of, 25–26
    prognostic value of, 26
    use of in diagnosis, 17–26
Personality Inventory, Bernreuter, 18–19
Persuasion, in therapy, 297–302
Philadelphia Child Guidance Clinic, 362–363
Phillips, A., 85, 108 b.
Physical
  defects, 7
  factor, rating in diagnosis, 43–44
Physical care, lack of as factor in removal of child from home, 171, 173–174
Place of environmental treatment, 175–176
Placement in school group, 230–232
Planned treatment, results of, 371–375
Play techniques in therapy, 305–316
  informal use of, 310–316

Play techniques in therapy
  use of dolls, 305-314
  use of stories, 315
Portl, A., 358 b.
Post-encephalitics, success of foster-home
  placement of, 82
Potter, H. W., 314, 357 b.
Problem
  behavior, 5
    as factor in removal of child from
    home, 172-173
  Case, Record of, Detroit, 32-35
  children, results of group experience for,
    252-253
Professional groups, rôle of in clinic, 369-
  371
Prognostic scales, for post-institutional
  adjustment, 143
Psychoanalysis of children, 332-339
  comparison with relationship therapy,
    346-347
  interpretive methods of, 333-335
  results of, 338-339
  some distortions, 335-337
  transference, 337
Psychological knowledge, as qualification
  of therapist, 284
Psychoneurotic Inventory, Woodworth, 18
Psychotherapy, 279-358
  and education, 285
  and intelligence, 285
  and release, 284-285
  basis of results in field of, 284-285
  children suitable for, 285-287
  clarification of issues, 293-295
  deeper therapies, 322-358
  educative techniques in, 288-297
  expressive therapies, 302-321
  facing consequences, 295
  goals of, 353-356
  in institutions, 124-128
  informational methods, 288-293
  interpretive therapy, 322-332
  interview therapy, 279-358
  psychoanalysis of children, 332-339
  qualifications of therapist, 280-284
  therapy through a controlled relation-
    ship, 340-348
  use of personal influence in, 297-302
  with adolescents, 285-286
Psychotic
  tendencies, inheritance of, 6
  tendencies and success of foster-home
    placement, 82

Psychotic children, results of treatment
  of, 373
Punitive methods, used in the school, 223-
  226

Qualifications, of the therapist. See
  Therapist

Rademacher, E. S., 275 b.
Rank, O., 197, 220 b., 347, 357 b.
Rappaport, M., 78, 79, 85, 108 b., 150
Ratings, reliability of in component-factor
  method of diagnosis, 50
Rearrangement of companionships, 273-274
Reckless, W. C., 145 b.
Record of Problem Case, Des Moines
  School, 32-35
Re-education, importance of in relation to
  therapy, 352-353
Reeves, M., 145 b.
Regimented treatment in institutions,
  111-119
  results of for delinquents, 115-118
  results of in orphanages, 118-119
Rejected child in school, 236
Rejection, parental, 8, 183
Relationship therapy, 340-348
  an example of, 201-209
  as means of changing parental attitudes,
    197-209
Release, in psychotherapy, 284-285, 319-
  320
Reliability, rating in diagnosis, 50
Removing a child from home, 147-176
  as related to family situation, 156-158,
    160-162
  child's affection as factor in, 158-159
  child's behavior as factor in, 154-156
  child's security as factor in, 159-160
  criteria for, 165-168
  degree of moral laxity in home as factor
    in, 173
  elements requiring consideration, 153-
    165
  other justifications for, 170-173
  physical neglect as factor in, 173-174
  placement opportunity, 164-165
  research on criteria for, 168-170
  seriousness of behavior problem as
    factor in, 172-173
Removing a child from a foster home, 174-
  175
Requirements for a satisfactory method
  of diagnosis, 58-59

Resources of school in changing behavior, 229–246
  acceptance of authority, 244–245
  affectional security, 236–240
  aids in social adjustment, 240–242
  personal counseling, 245
  placement in a suitable group, 230–232
  satisfaction of achievement, 229–230
  techniques of improving achievement, 233–235
  therapeutic attitudes on part of teacher, 235–236
  use of special, 245–246
  utilization of special abilities, 232–233
Results
  of camp treatment, 272–273
  of foster-home placement, 77–97
  of group experience for problem children, 252–253
  of individual treatment in institutions, 133–134
  of planned treatment, 371–375
  of psychoanalytic treatment, 338–339
  of regimented treatment for delinquents, 115–118
Reynolds, B., 220 b.
Riley, G., 300
Rivalry, sibling, 8–9
Rivlin, H. N., 248 b.
Robinson, V., 220 b., 357 b.
Rogers, C. R., 20, 38 b., 108 b., 176 b.
Rorschach test, 23
Rosanoff, I. R., 22, 38 b.
Rosensweig, S., 357 b.
Russ, H., 248 b.

Sadler, W. S., 290, 298–299, 302, 331, 357 b.
Sayles, M. B., 107 b.
Scale of Behavior Factors, Detroit, 33–35
School's part in changing behavior, 222–248
  efficacy of in treatment, 226–229
  individual treatment in, 223–226
  resources in changing behavior, 229–246
  teacher's objections to individual treatment, 246–247
  use of punitive methods in school, 223–226
Schwartz, L. A., 23, 38 b.
Schwesinger, G. C., 15 b.
Security
  affectional, in school, 236–240
  of child as factor in removal from home, 159–160

Selection
  of foster home, 101–103
  of foster parents, 103
Self insight, rating of in component-factor method of diagnosis, 48–50
Sex
  delinquent girls and foster-home placement, 78–79
  and institutional treatment, 141–142
  problems and foster-home placement, 68
Shaffer, L. S., 357 b.
Shaw, C. R., 9–10, 15 b., 46, 145 b., 253
Sherman, M., 248 b.
Sibling rivalry, 8–9
Size, relation of to behavior, 5
Slavson, S. R., 256, 275 b.
Slawson, J., 118, 122, 135, 136, 145 b.
Smith, G., 375 b.
Smith, M., 145 b.
Smith, R. B., 21, 38 b.
Social
  adjustment, aids to in school, 240–242
  agency skill and success of foster-home placement, 93–95
  influences on behavior, 9, 10
    rating in diagnosis, 46–48
  skills and camp placement, 263
  status and camp placement, 264
Society for the Reformation of Juvenile Delinquents, 109
Solenberger, W. E., 145 b.
Special abilities, utilization of, 232–233
Specialized clinic, 362–365
  results of, 363–365
Spoiled child and institutional placement, 138–139
Standardized stimuli, 22–24
Stevenson, G. S., 375 b.
Stockard, C. R., 6
Success of foster-home placement, 77–95
Suggestion in psychotherapy, 297–302
Summer camp. See Camps
Sweet, L., 20, 39 b.
Symonds, P. M., 21, 39 b., 248 b.

Taft, J., 340, 346, 357 b.
Teacher, therapeutic attitudes on part of, 235–236
Techniques of improving school achievement, 233–235
Terminating a treatment relationship, 351–353

Tests
    performance, scores of delinquent boys
        on, 136
    personality, 17
    use of in diagnosis, 17–26
Theis, S. V., 73, 77, 87, 88, 95, 108 b., 118–119
Therapeutic attitudes on part of teacher, 235–236
Therapeutic group, 256
Therapist, qualifications of, 280–284
    objectivity, 281–282
    psychological knowledge, 284
    respect for the individual, 282–283
    understanding of the self, 283–284
Therapy
    attitude, 210
    relationship, as means of changing parental attitudes, 197–209
    through a controlled relationship, 340–348
        basis of effective relationship therapy, 343–345
        comparison with psychoanalysis, 346–347
        goal of, 345–346
        usefulness of, 347–348
Thomas, D. S., 107 b., 248 b.
Thomas, W. I., 107 b., 248 b., 252
Thurston, H., 107 b.
Thurstone, L. I., 18, 39 b.
Thurstone, T. G., 18, 39 b.
Training, rating of in component-factor method of diagnosis, 48
Traits, measures of, 18–20
Transfer of training in relationship therapy, 343–345
Transference in psychoanalysis of children, 337
Traxler, A. E., 38 b.
Treatability of parental attitudes, 210–218
    importance of therapist in, 217–218
Treatment
    deeper therapies in, 322–358
    definition of, 12–15
    extent of change of environment as, 148–150
    family attitudes as focus of, 179–221
    foster-home care as, 63–108
    group membership as, 249–275
    indirect vs. direct, 274–275
    individual
        in camp, 266–268

    in the school, 223–226
    in institutions, 119–134
    institutional placement as, 109–144
    interpretive, in changing parental attitudes, 191–197
    interview techniques in, 279–358
    planning for, 51–52
    result of planned, 371–375
    through physical change within the home, 219
    use of camps as, 259–273
Treatment relationship, termination of, 351–353
Truitt, R., 248 b.
Twins, 6
Tyson, D. K., 145 b., 146 b.

Understanding of the self, as qualification of therapist, 283–284
United States Children's Bureau, 108 b., 116

Van Waters, M., 145 b.
Vernon, P. E., 39 b.
Vitamins, and behavior, 7
Vocational work in institutions, 123

Wagner, I. A., 275 b.
Ward, C. E., 270, 275 b.
Warwick State School, 119
Washburne, C., 248 b.
Watson, G. B., 38 b.
Watson, M., 26–30, 39 b., 221 b.
Webster, L. J., 108 b.
White House Conference on Child Health and Protection, 107 b., 176 b.
Whittier State School, 119
Wickman, E. K., 224, 248 b.
Wile, I. S., 234
Will Temperament Test, Downey, 18
Williams, G. W., 300
Williams, R. R., 139, 145 b.
Williamson, M., 108 b.
Witmer, H. M., 73, 79, 179–181, 182–183, 213, 220 b., 371, 373, 375 b.
Woltman, A. G., 358 b.
Woodrow, H., 22, 39 b.
Woodworth Psychoneurotic Inventory, 18, 20
Word-association, 22

Young, P. V., 357 b.

Zachry, C. B., 248 b.